ARTfolio2022

A Curated Collection of the World's Most Exciting Artists

ARTfolio2022

A Curated Collection of the World's Most Exciting Artists

Edited by
Douglas King

Juror
Kristin Rivas

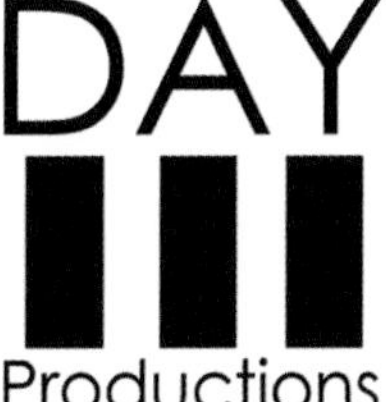

DAY
Productions

Art Folio 2022: A Curated Collection of the World's Most Exciting Artists
copyright © 2021 Day III Productions, Inc.

Edited and designed by Douglas King
Copy edited by Jessica Manley

First Printing, December 2021. Printed in South Korea.
ISBN: 978-1-7376256-1-2

Artists and galleries interested in receiving entry information for the next Art Folio competition can visit artfolioannual.com for details.

Cover artwork: by Susan Foley

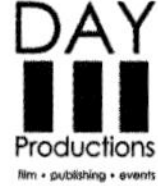

ArtFolioAnnual.com
DayIIIProd.com

CONTENTS

Introduction

The world has changed.

A short, four-word sentence that holds so much truth and power in it: The world has changed.

Many art galleries have permanently closed their doors due to the pandemic, providing even fewer opportunities for artists to exhibit their work and art lovers to experience it. International art shows have had to pivot to virtual exhibitions because of travel restrictions, lockdowns, and the fear of gatherings larger than ten people.

But art continues to be a powerful force in society. One only has to look at the murals dotting our cities that celebrate the lives of those lost to police violence—George Floyd, Breonna Taylor, Sean Bell, to name only three. The biggest tragedy is how many individual murals there are.

Art often helps us face and emotionally deal with terrible situations. Pablo Picasso painted *Guernica* (1937) in protest of the bombing of the Basque town of the same name by the Nazis at the bequest of Francisco Franco during the Spanish Civil War. It is considered one of his greatest works.

We need art. Always. It helps us cope with loss, helps us bring focus to unrighteousness, helps us when we are locked in our homes or studios, alone. It helps us deal with our emotions. Art is necessary for a healthy life. Art is necessary for happiness and joy.

If you think I'm being overly dramatic and imposing too great an importance on art, I turn your attention to art therapy. To quote from the American Art Therapy Association, "Art Therapy is an integrative mental health and human services profession that enriches the lives of individuals, families, and communities through active art-making, creative process, applied psychological theory, and human experience within a psychotherapeutic relationship."

So, despite the world-altering global pandemic and limited artist opportunities, I decided it was as important as ever to publish the third edition of *Art Folio*. It has not been easy. In the face of challenges, art has still been created on easels around the world, in studios in every country, sometimes on kitchen tables or outdoor picnic tables. Art is still being created, and we need that art now as much as ever.

When I started *Art Folio*, it was to provide a platform for artists to have their work published and thus be seen in a different context. My focus was on the artists—doing what small part I could to advance careers and provide exposure when before there may not have been any. With this third edition, the above mission is still our main motivation. We must publish art for the viewer so they have something beautiful to look at despite being sequestered in their home away from friends and family, so they can escape into the wonderful, colorful worlds that exist only on canvas and paper.

Art Folio is a celebration of art. It is a celebration of those who take the time to create it and for those who enjoy viewing and studying it. And art is a celebration of life. For many of us, art is life. It is our livelihood, and it is the one activity that brings a positive life force into our hearts, minds, and bodies.

I believe in the life-producing power of art, both as a creator and a viewer. I know for me, and I don't believe I am alone in this feeling, that when I have not created for an extended amount of time, I begin to feel anxious and depressed. Yet, when I sit down at my easel, when I gather my sketchbook and pens around me, in the moment of inspirational spark, it is like the Big Bang happening once again, this time producing art instead of life—but enhancing life.

Again, at the risk of sounding overly dramatic, I believe art is as important to life as the air we breathe. You may not die without art, but your life would be much paler, anemic, and dispirited.

We cannot control the world or stop it from changing, but, as artists, we can control how we perceive the world, then illustrate that perception through acrylic, oil, pastel, wood, metal, photography, digital tools, or any number of other mediums, ultimately producing a work that can change how others perceive life.

I hope you enjoy this year's edition of *Art Folio*. It is my desire that each life is filled with art, whether in its creation or appreciation. Let your world be changed by the art in these pages.

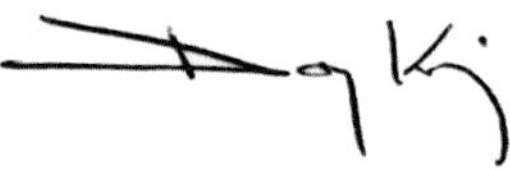

The Art Folio 2022 curation took place in August 2021. The first step in the weeks-long process was compiling all the artists' submissions and their hundreds of images into the categories. This edition's curator, Kristin Rivas, reviewed the work of all the artists, then selected who would be included, the individual category winners, and in most cases, the exact work that we would publish in this edition.

We greatly appreciate the time and effort that Rivas spent reviewing and selecting the work for the third annual *Art Folio*, and, to each of the artists selected, congratulations and thank you for creating the work that helped us cope in this year of change.

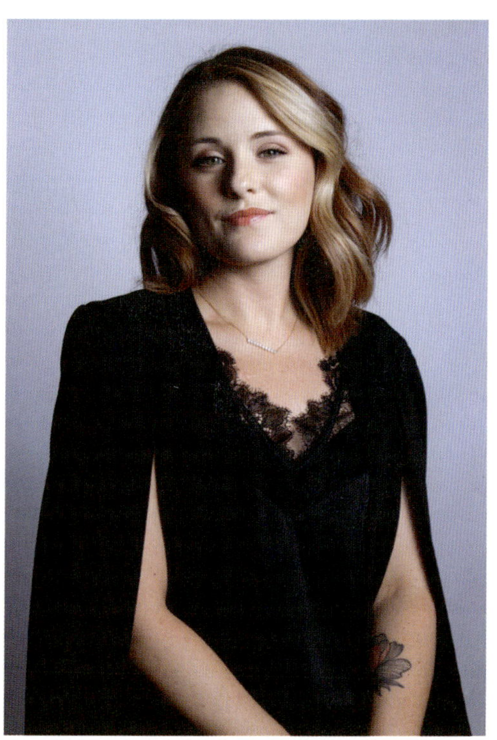

Kristin Rivas – Curator, 2022

"It is such an honor to be asked to be the juror for *Art Folio*! My great passion in life is art and being able to share it with others," says Kristin Rivas, the *Art Folio 2022* edition juror. "There are so many talented artists that applied this year. I applaud each artist for putting themselves out there and submitting work, as it takes courage."

Kristin Rivas was born and raised in North Texas. She had a passion for fine art from a very young age and has held diverse careers in both business and banking; however, her artistic tendencies ultimately led her to the art world. After graduating from Texas Woman's University with a bachelor's in art history, she continued her studies within The University of North Texas' graduate program, focusing on Abstract Expressionism. During her time at North Texas, Rivas published multiple papers on modern and contemporary art in India, including the impact of the Kiran Nadar Museum and the work of Bharti Kher.

"My best friend in college is the one who really ignited my passion for art. One day, she asked me to paint with her, which in turn prompted me to take an art history course. I had started a nursing degree but didn't feel like it was quite right for me," Rivas says. "After one art history class, I was hooked. With no regard for exactly what my future would hold or how I would make money, I decided to major in art history. People would always ask what I was going to do with my degree, and I would always instinctively say that I was going to own my own gallery. I had no idea how to actually do that. After seven years working at Samuel Lynne Galleries, I finally feel like I'm living my dream, and I could not be happier with my decision to pursue art. I am immersed in art every day and am so thankful that I get to live my dream!"

Rivas has been with Samuel Lynne Galleries since 2014 and was appointed director in 2016. Her passion for Dallas' art community has landed her several board positions and prominent affiliations in the community. From 2017–2020, Rivas was president of the Dallas Art Dealers Association (DADA), an affiliation of established, independent gallery owners and art organizations in the Dallas area. She also serves on the Curatorial Committee for Dallas Children's Advocacy Center (DCAC)—Art for Advocacy and volunteers with the Business Council for the Arts. Rivas has juried multiple art shows, including Texas & Neighbors Regional Art Exhibition, VAGF's Crème de la Crème Art Show, along with TVAA's annual art exhibition, to name a few.

samuellynne.com

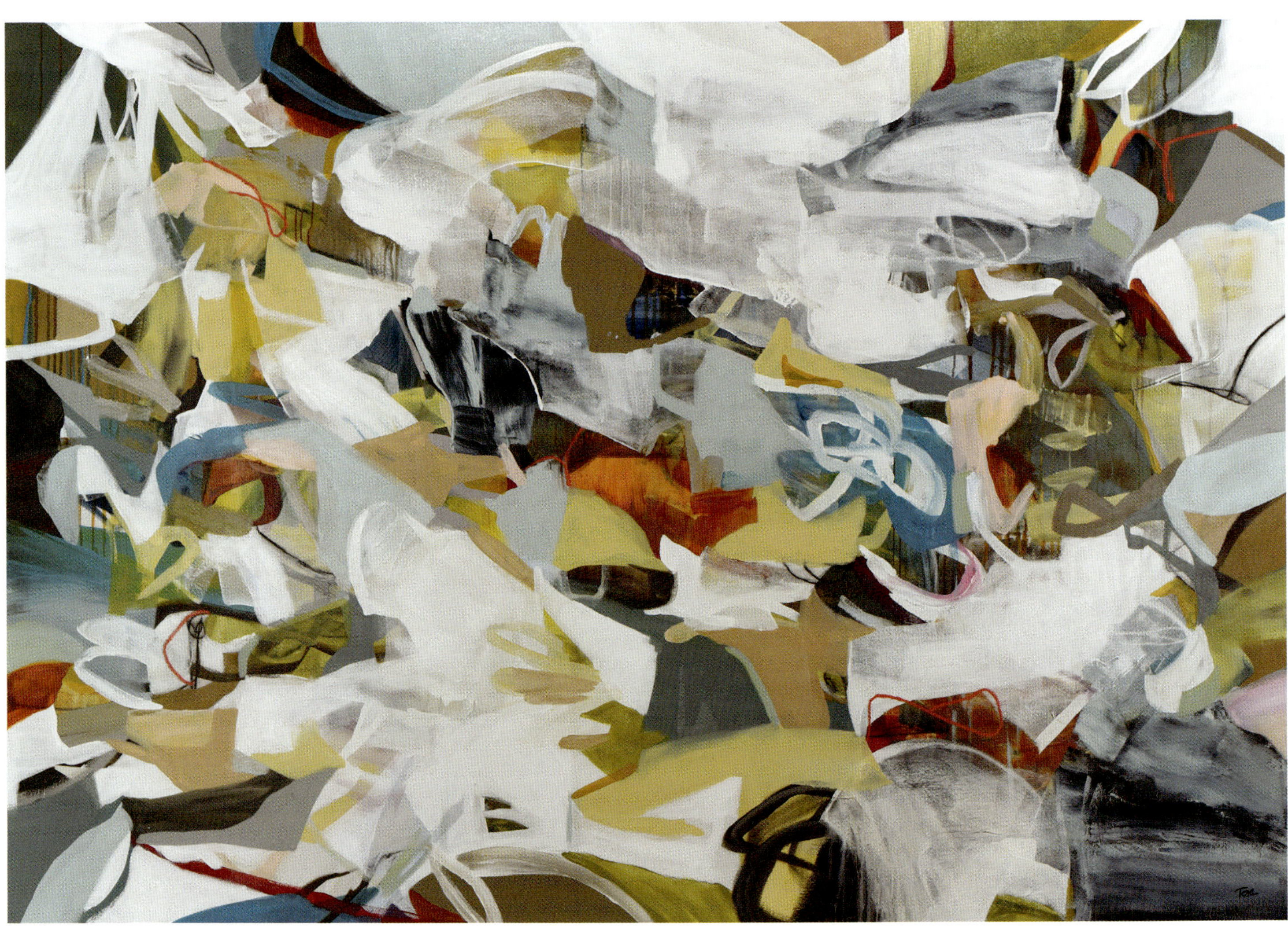

Cat Tesla

Internationally recognized artist Cat Tesla creates nature-inspired abstract paintings. Tesla loves building layers by painting and drawing, scraping back, then adding more, then pouring glossy, translucent glazes over the surface. Tesla's artwork provides the viewer with a bold, graphic element from a distance, but up close they're rewarded with rich organic details and texture.

Using nature as her muse, Tesla combines color, shape, and line, resulting in a gestural, free, and multilayered painting that uses acrylic, oil, inks, graphite, wax crayon, and oil pastel. Each of Tesla's paintings begins with a ritual—taking a hike or sitting outside, doing mindful meditation. Tesla explains: "Coming to the studio centered and without expectation allows me to have a conversation with the canvas. A mark is made, in response another, and another, and the dance begins."

Tesla's process is inspired by the work and teachings of Franz Kline and his concept of automatism. He essentially believed in first "pouring out," then editing. Tesla begins with an automatic drawing in graphite and wax crayon, then translucent layers are applied, followed by more mark-making (drawing) and more paint layers.

Grand Finale
Acrylic, oil, oil pastel
60 x 84 in.

OPPOSITE
Mochalicious
Acrylic, oil, oil pastel
66 x 44 in.

catteslaart@gmail.com
artbycat.com
@cattesla

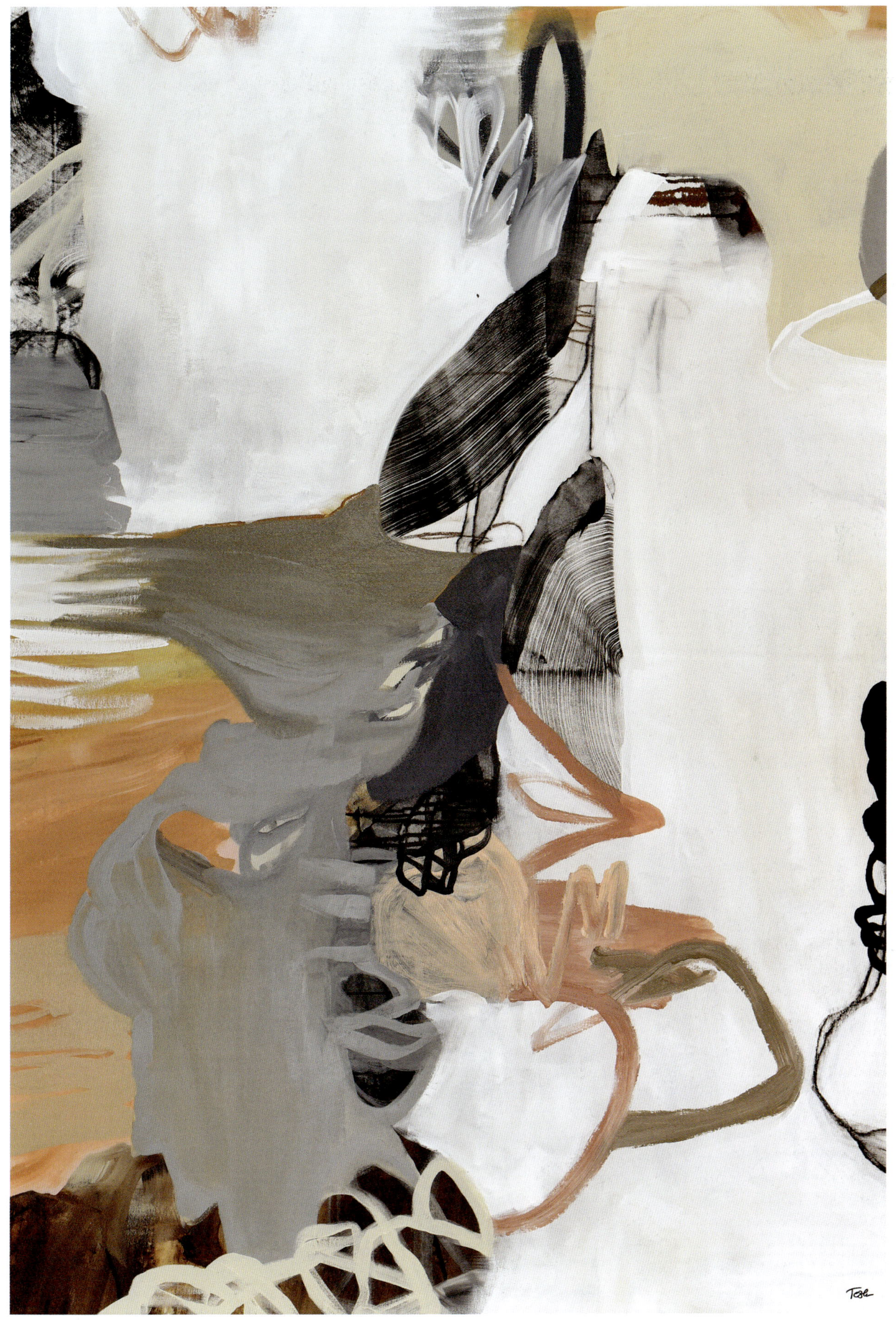

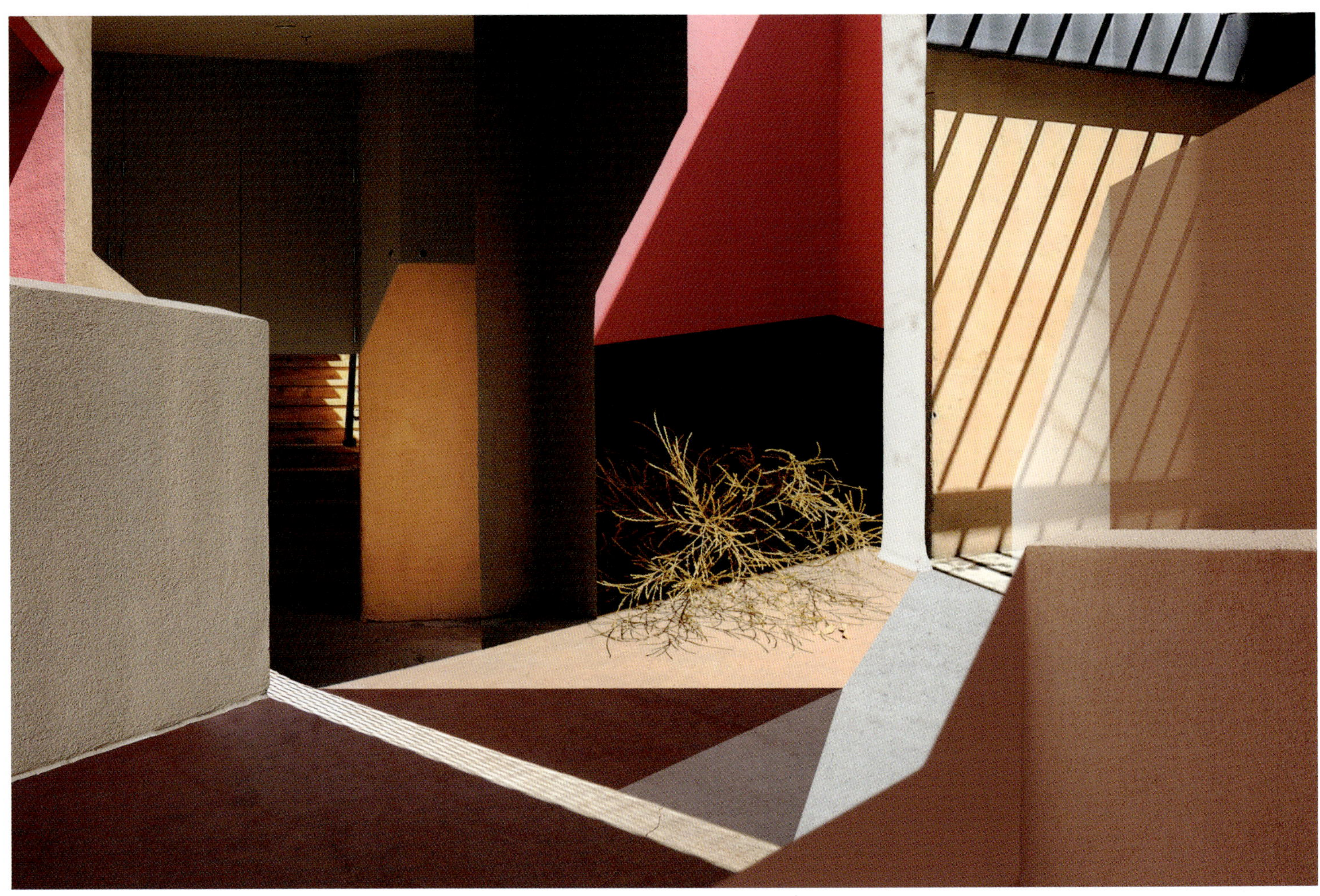

Natalie Christensen and Jim Eyre

Natalie Christensen's and Jim Eyre's composite images of surreal cityscapes embody the disquieting experience of how our lives have been transformed by the ravages of COVID-19.

"We have retreated from our daily routines and into our homes for an unprecedented period of time," Christensen says. "In response to this isolation, Jim and I created these hypnogogic landscapes to reflect upon the experience of roaming inside our smartphones in the time of coronavirus. For many of us, that has become the sole place to process the impact of so much change and loss. When the digital realm is all we have—rather than a supplement to 'real life'—for some, the hollowness is more apparent."

Expanding on their work from *ALTEREDSTATES/ ALTEREDSCAPES*, Christensen and Eyre are again combining photographs from their respective communities and responding to the experience of leaving behind their former lives and participating in a global effort to stop the spread of the virus. Architectural fragments and elements of the landscape are mingled to present diverse psychological experiences of this new world we are living in—such as shock, loneliness, yearning, fear. "Unable to go out into the streets, we are paradoxically creating intentional chaos as we seek some kind of order, healing, or catharsis in an increasingly unpredictable world," Christensen says.

Isolation
Archival natural pigment prints on Italian cotton rag
27.7 x 39.5 in.

OPPOSITE
Spike
Archival natural pigment prints on Italian cotton rag
39.5 x 27.7 in.

n.christensen@
artworkinternational
.com
nataliechristensenphoto
.com
@natalie_santafe

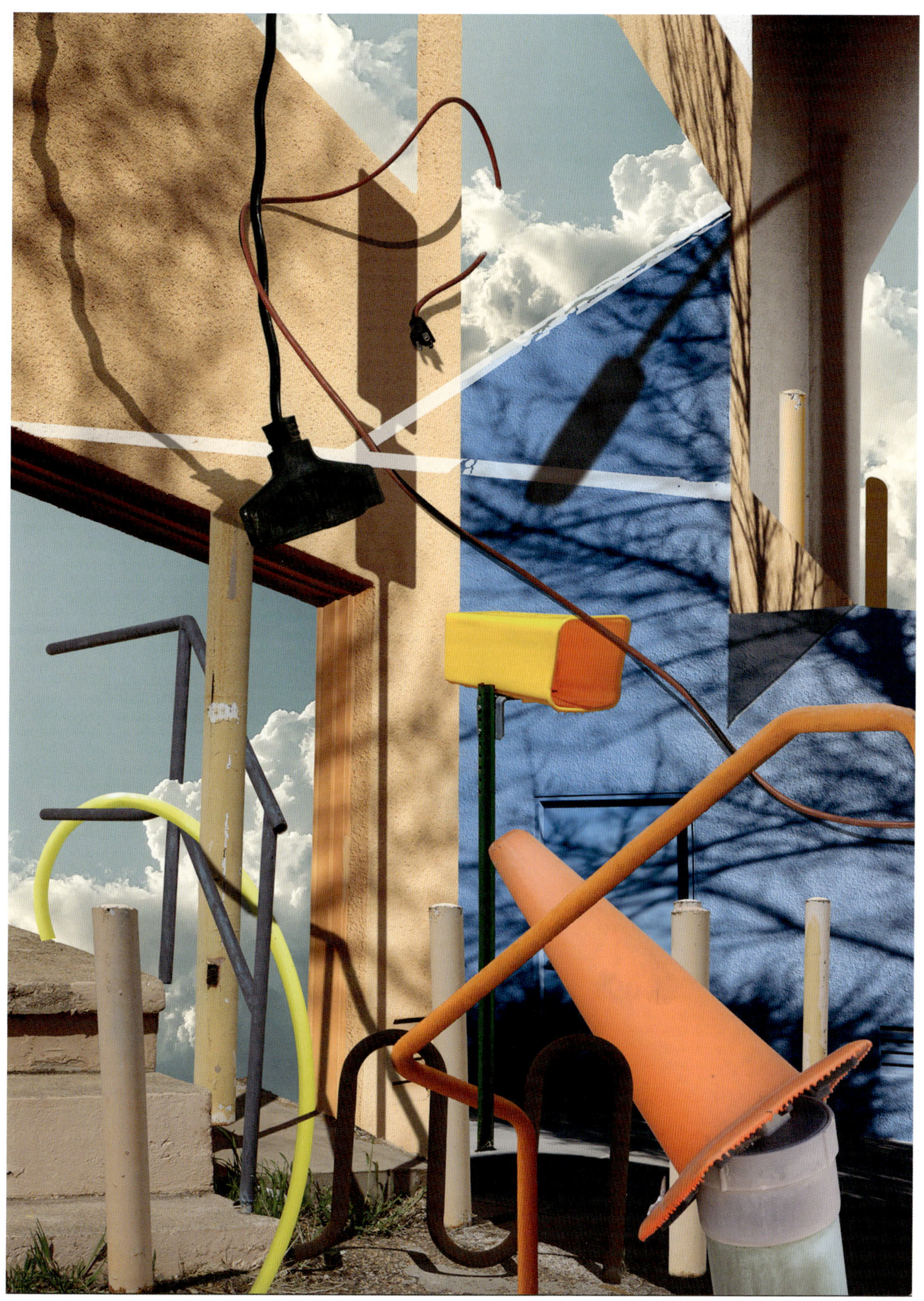

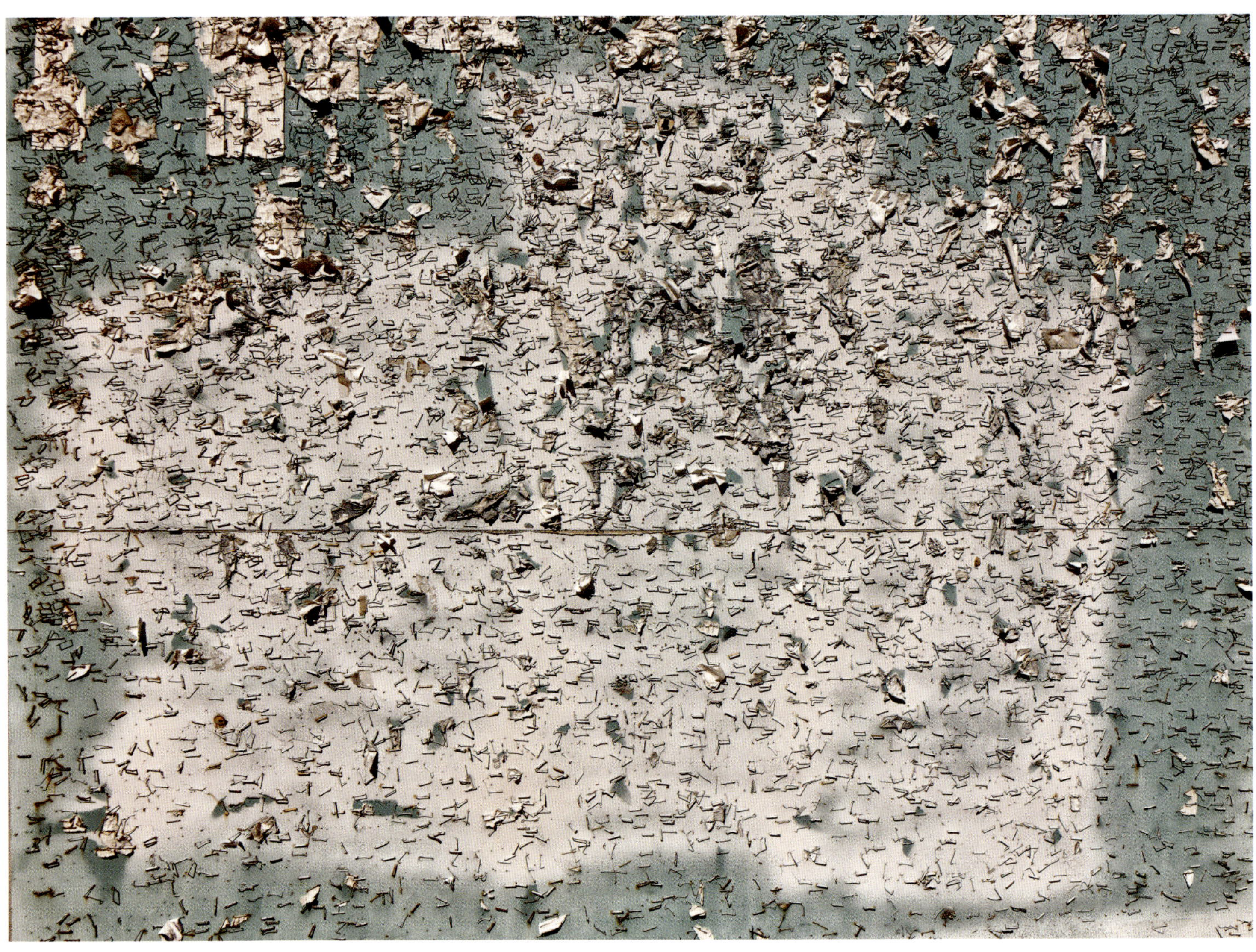

Jeff Corwin

Before Jeff Corwin devoted himself full time to his personal work, he spent forty years in the world of commercial photography. The majority of his clients were ad agencies and graphic design firms. Over the first few years, Corwin developed a style that, with the assistance of artificial lighting, helped him to see past the clutter and create photographs that were more design than immediately recognizable objects. "I worked with whatever was there, all the mundane things that most people walk by or do not notice. I saw great imagery in graphic shapes, shapes that repeat, like patterns in ceilings from ugly fluorescent lights or rows of desks or chairs," Corwin says.

While certainly not working with the same control he enjoyed in the advertising world, Corwin's latest work provides, in some ways, more. He has found that he can bring the same vision he used for his commercial work into his landscape work. The photographs Corwin produces now are one hundred percent informed by his experience shooting for clients. "I see how I see and, after forty-plus years of making photographs, it seems foolish to try and change now. I trust that what I have learned works. I have even brought artificial light into the landscapes!" Corwin says.

Staple Detail
Photography/
Ultrachrome print
30 x 40 in.

OPPOSITE
Puddle 11
Photography/
Ultrachrome print
20 x 20 in.

jeffcorwin@
artworkinternational
.com
jeffcorwinfineart.com
@jeffcorwin_mt

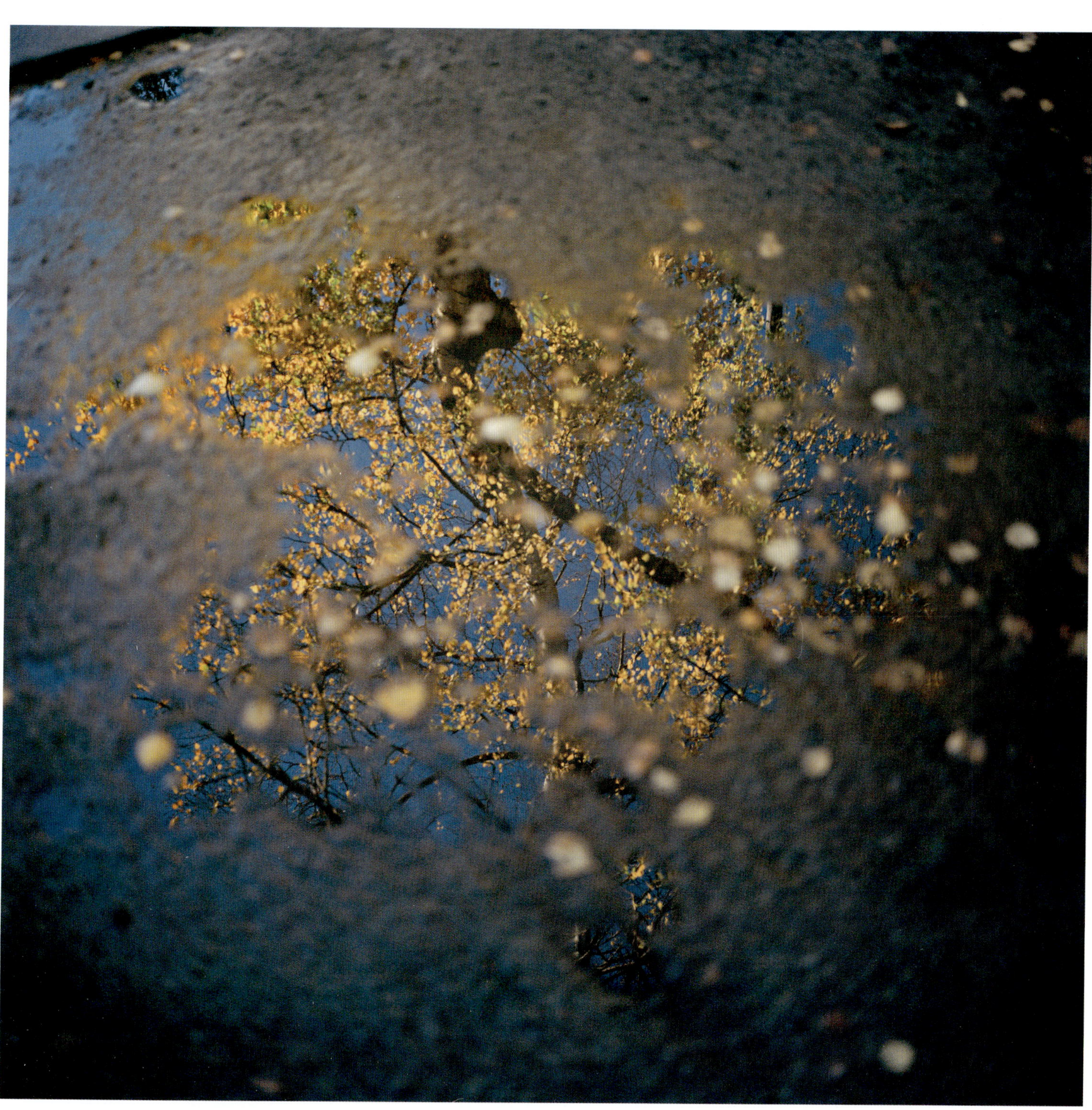

ABSTRACT PHOTOGRAPHY

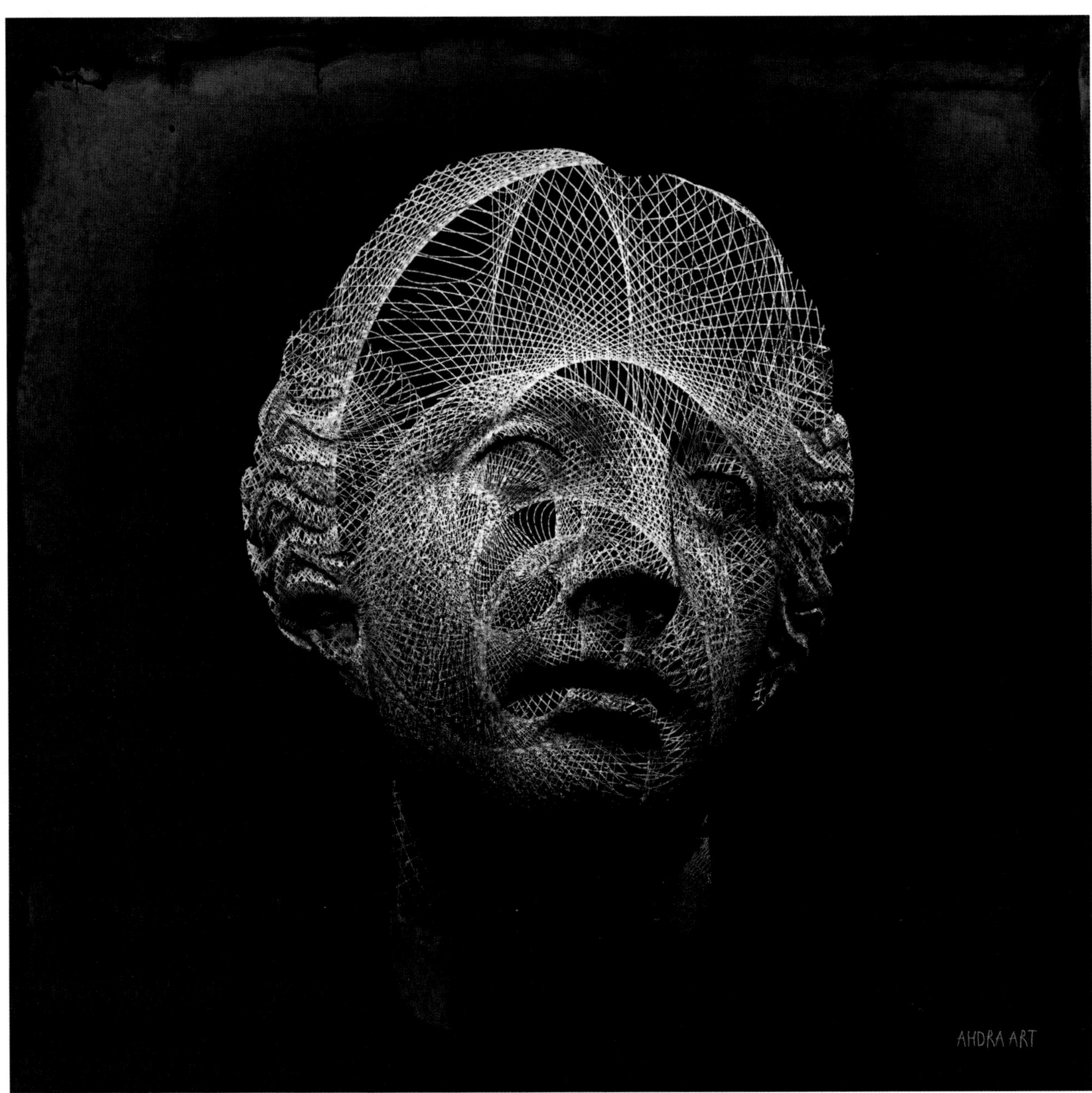

Deborah Anderson

Deborah Anderson's photographic creations are visual projections of moments in life based in subjective experience as well as objective fact. They have become a narrative reminder of where she has been, where she is, and where she is going.

Photography has taught Anderson how to "see" not just look at subject matter. It has become an entirely new way of looking at the world, which then becomes much more interesting and complex. Always drawn to the provocative, edgy, and controversial, and moved by the political environment and issues that impact our daily lives and the larger world, Anderson's photos are derivations from a place of unsettlement, with a constant yearning to put things right and desire to share these images with others.

Digital photography offers a medium in which Anderson is limited only by her imagination. It has opened her inner world of reality by allowing her to create images in weird and wonderful ways, and to convey a creative perspective on any subject, from mundane to fantastical.

Tattered
Digital Photography
12 x 12 in.

blanche6028@aol.com
ahdraart.com
@blanche6028

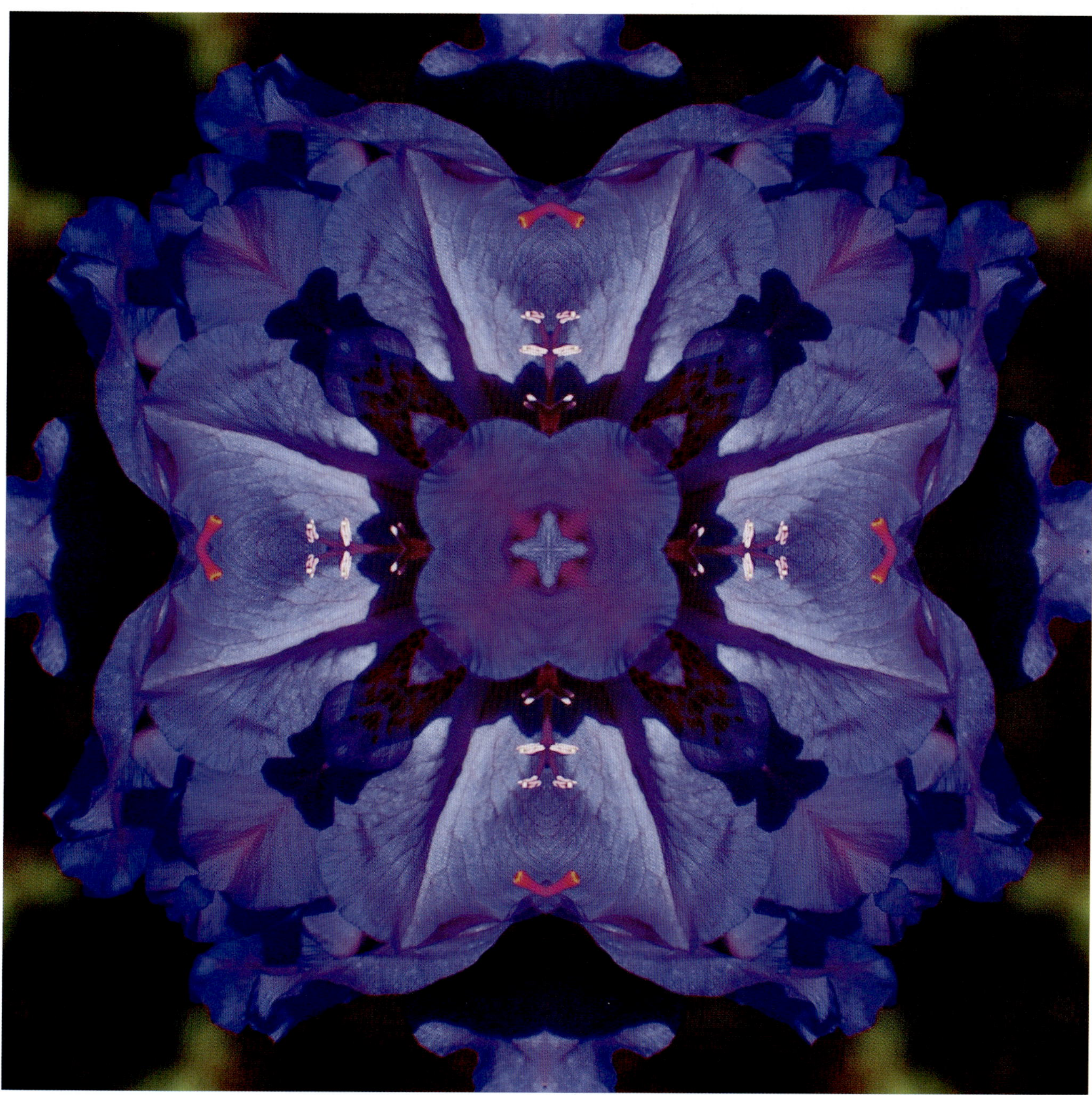

Petra Bernstein

Petra Bernstein's inspiration comes from the natural world. Her artwork ranges from close-up paintings and photographs of flora and fauna to abstract interpretations of nature's mystery. In her series *Nature with a Twist*, Bernstein takes magnified photos of botanicals that she manipulates into intriguing images. Her goal is to celebrate nature's beauty by capturing the inner details of flowers and transforming them into her own interpretation—creating a new variation without losing the essence of what already exists. In addition to her digital abstractions, she uses double exposure photography to incorporate her paintings into her photographs. This technique allows her to create a new space filled with mysterious and transparent layers that are intended to spark the viewer's curiosity.

"My art is free from boundaries. Reality and abstraction coexist and need no explanation. The unexplained is far more intriguing, as it resides beyond the picture plane," Bernstein says.

Spider Wart
Photo Print on Aluminum
30 x 30 in.

pmbernstein@comcast
.net
petrabernstein.com
@petra.bernstein

ABSTRACT PHOTOGRAPHY

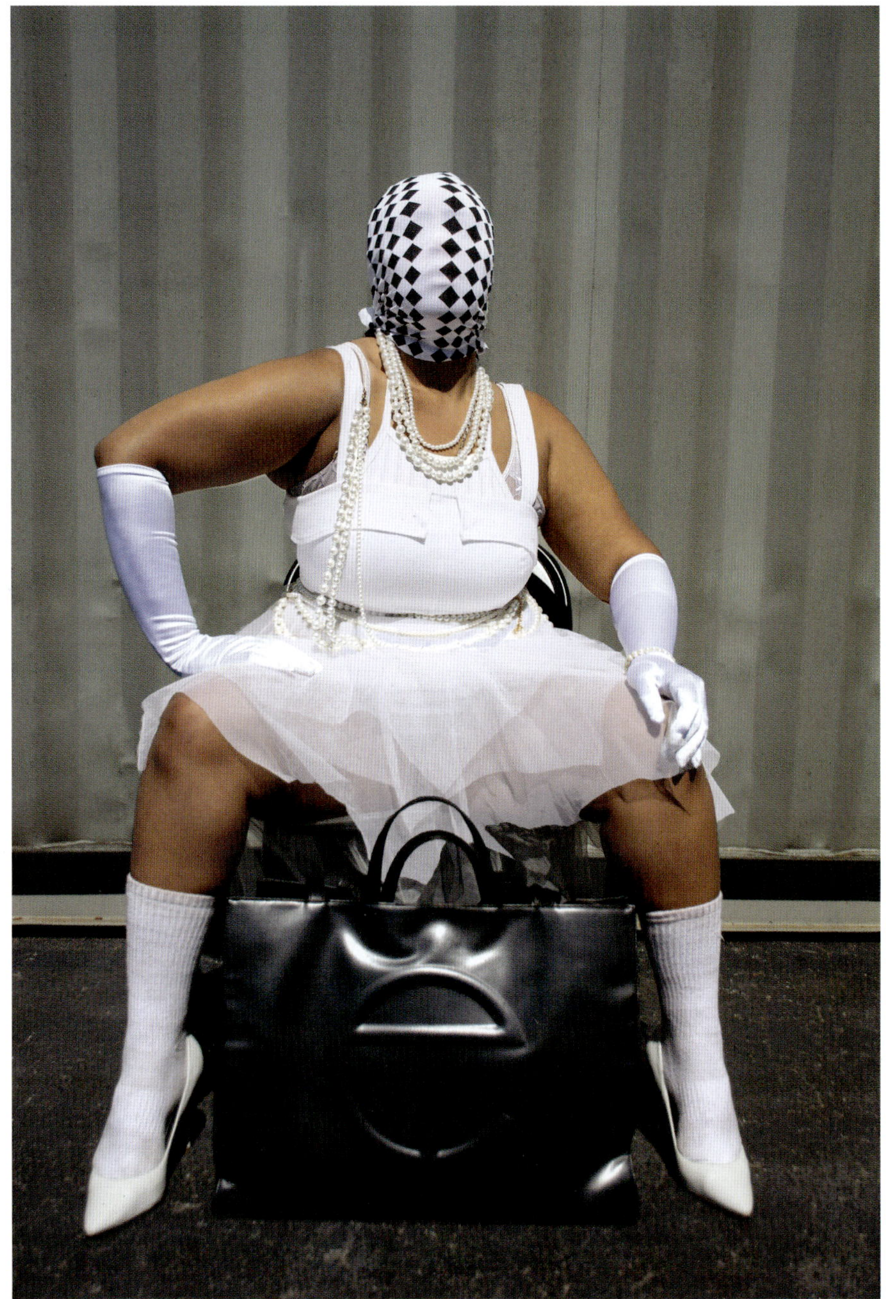

Ron Evans

Ron Evans is a color theorist. He uses color to express himself, his experiences, feelings, etc., all while exploring his creativity. With color theory, Evans' intent is also to prove that contrasting colors can effectively coexist in one space.

In his photo series *Stacking*, the work consists of characters that are disguised while portraying a narrative with gendered and nongendered roles. Each character in the series is attached to a color equation (e.g., white plus black equals gray; yellow plus blue equals green; pink plus blue equals purple; yellow plus red equals orange).

As an artist, Evans intends to show the world that color is more than something pulled from a crayon. He intends to show the world that color is an art and can be used in many different forms of life.

Bag Lady with the Pearls
Photography
30 x 20 in.

ronevansphotography@ymail.com
rontheartist.com
@rontheartist

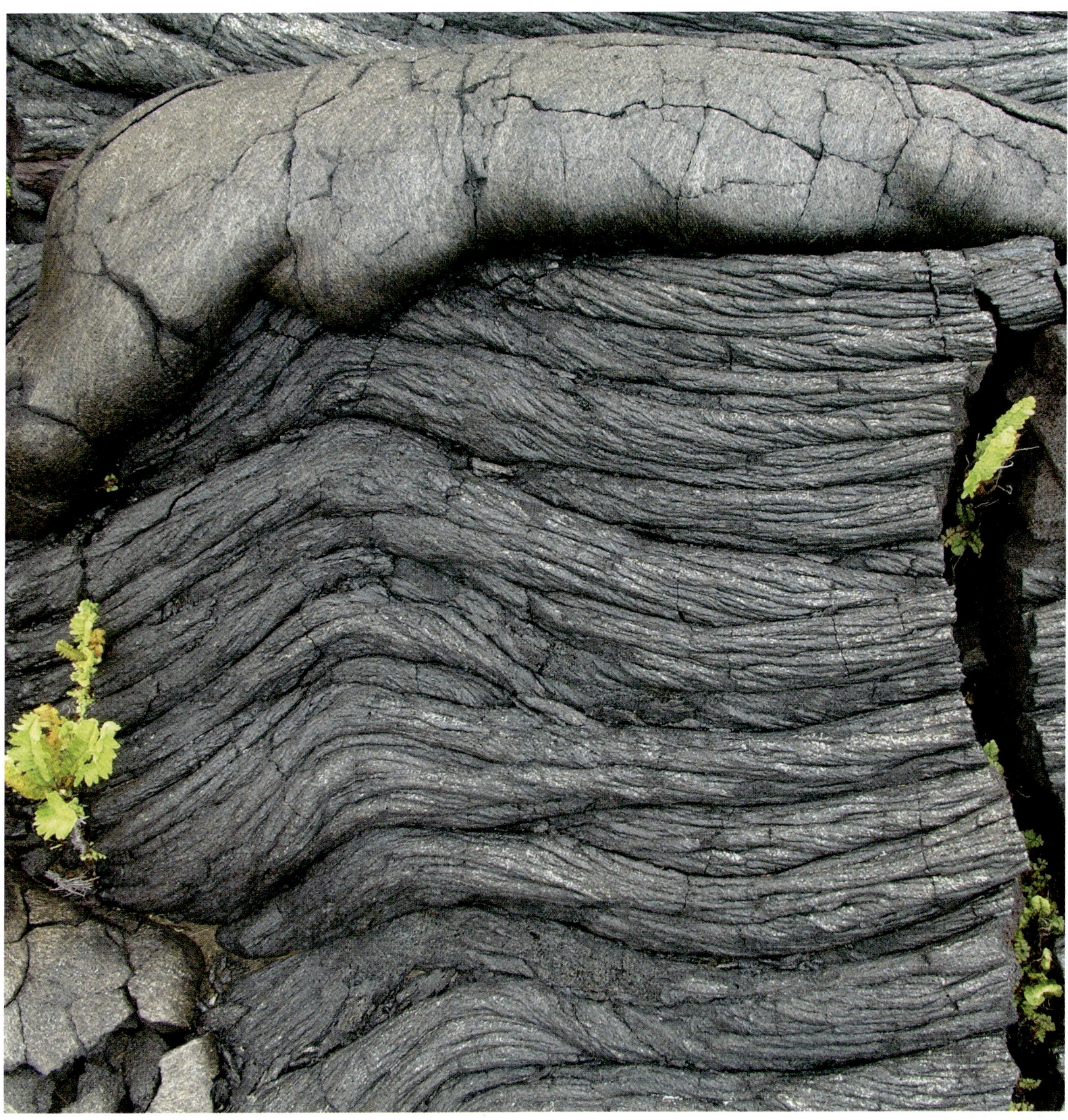

Bob Evermon

Bob Evermon's work has always been anchored in natural forms, line, color, and structure, exploring the depth, poetry, and beauty of the visual language. The artist feels his subject matter lands somewhere between Andy Warhol's and Andy Goldsworthy's in its nature. "Like Warhol, I am taking a common everyday subject that people walk on, in this case, the lava structures of the Kilauea Volcano or the blue lines of the Sunshine Coast, and presenting them as a visually complete work of art," Evermon says. Most of these natural paintings could not be improved by any artist and, like Warhol's *Campbell's Soup Cans*, they are visually complete. Evermon's paintbrush is the liquid magma from deep inside the earth and the glaze that comes from the minerals that take many years to create deep, rich colors. Goldsworthy works with nature and changes it to make it more visually interesting. Evermon composes and writes the stories of pieces that nature has already changed into works of art.

Pele on Top
Unaltered photo of
Kilauea Volcano
48 x 36 in.

bob-evermon@dccnet
.com
@evermon.4mg.com

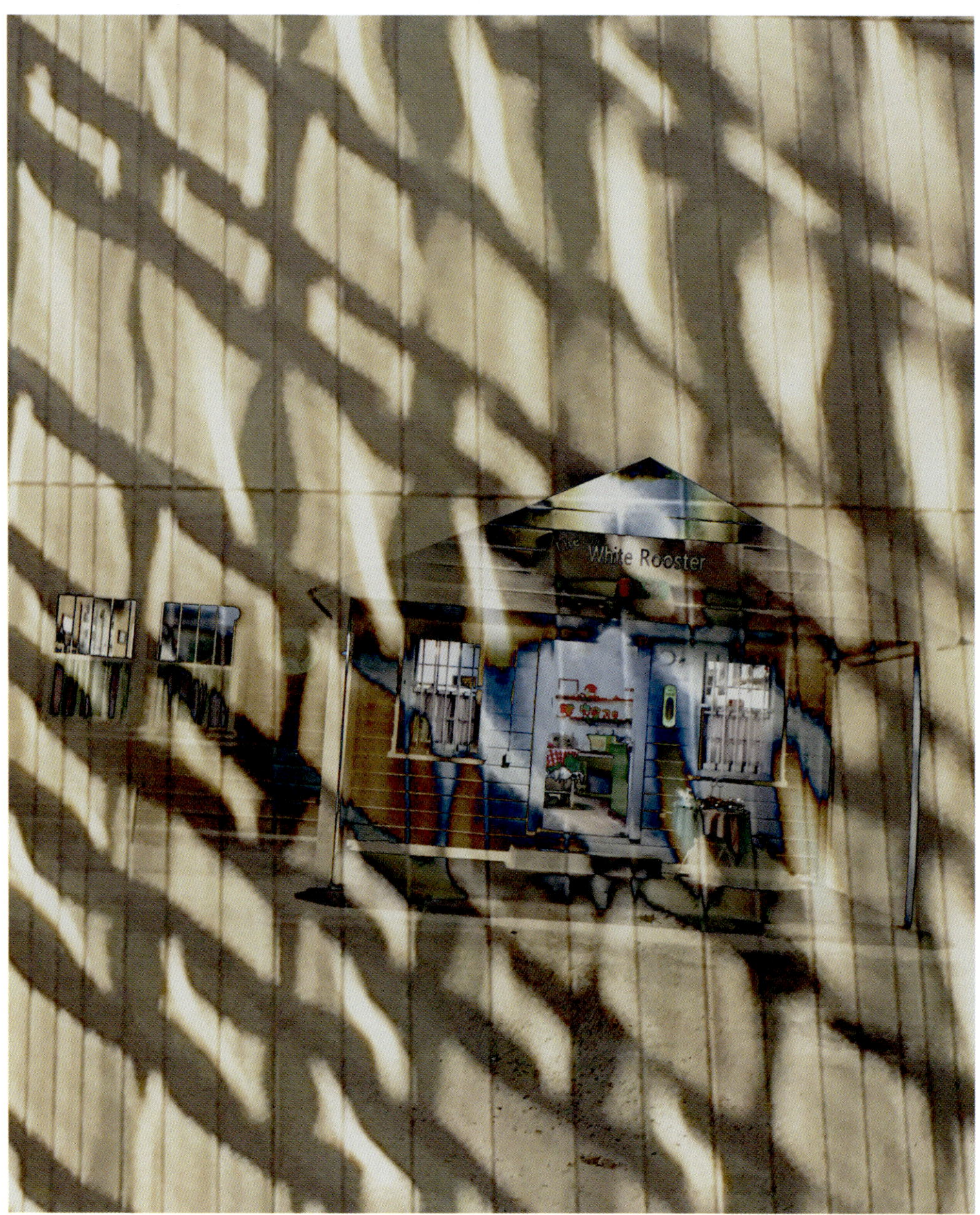

April Fretwell

April Fretwell's current artwork involves psychological and emotional themes, in particular her personal journey during the global pandemic and significant life changes. Heavy anxiety is her daily enemy in almost every area of her life, especially as she strives to be a good mother, accomplished artist, and overall successful woman. Fretwell's anxiety causes a real struggle with self-doubt and emotional exhaustion—very problematic when she approaches making art. Ironically, her soul needs artistic self-expression to thrive and move toward spiritual fulfillment.

Fretwell follows her emotional intuitions toward line, shape, value, and color to communicate feelings, deal with problems, and clear her head. "I enjoy drawing non-objectively with ballpoint pens and sometimes crayons or color pencils on a variety of surfaces as a way to release creative, anxious energy. I 'remix' these drawings by combining them with my digital photographs of places, objects, and people that I am drawn toward," Fretwell says. This technique helps the artist deal with and express her state of mind, and she hopes it evokes emotional release for the viewer.

Finding Home
Digital photography, digital layering/double exposure
10 x 8 in.

aprilfretwel@gmail.com
@aprilfretwellstudio

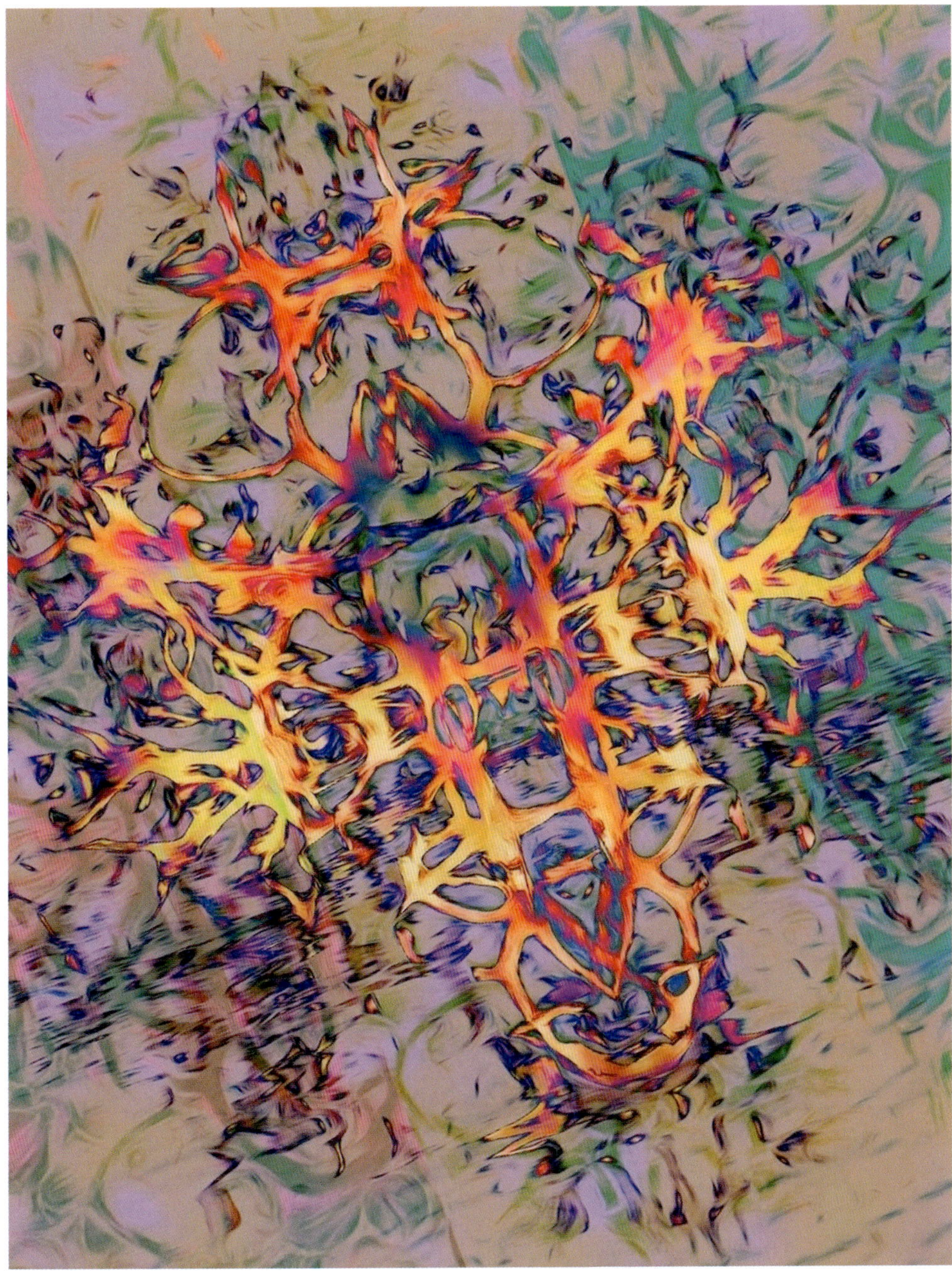

Rick Hurst

Rick Hurst's work is an ongoing exploration of universal components in the origin of cosmic life and its evolution. Each artwork is a unique window into that continuum, anywhere from the first spark of life energy to the sophisticated harmony and complexity of the human mind.

Hurst sees universal energies in the world around him—the life forces of nature, the vibrancy of color, the vitality and strength of architecture. All of his designs begin with original photography that captures the beauty and spirit of nature and the real world. He melds these photos into digital artworks, using multiple exposures, layers, color transformations, and art filters.

Nature and architecture are the foundations for many of the artist's abstract designs.

Hurst's purpose is to interpret and reveal those energies to all who view his art—to awaken curiosity and prompt introspection, to feed their inner being, to have his designs resonate with them.

VITAMIN E - Micro view of an essential building block of life
Digital transformation on metal panel
40 x 30 in.

rickhurstart@gmail.com
rickhurstart.com
@rickhurstart

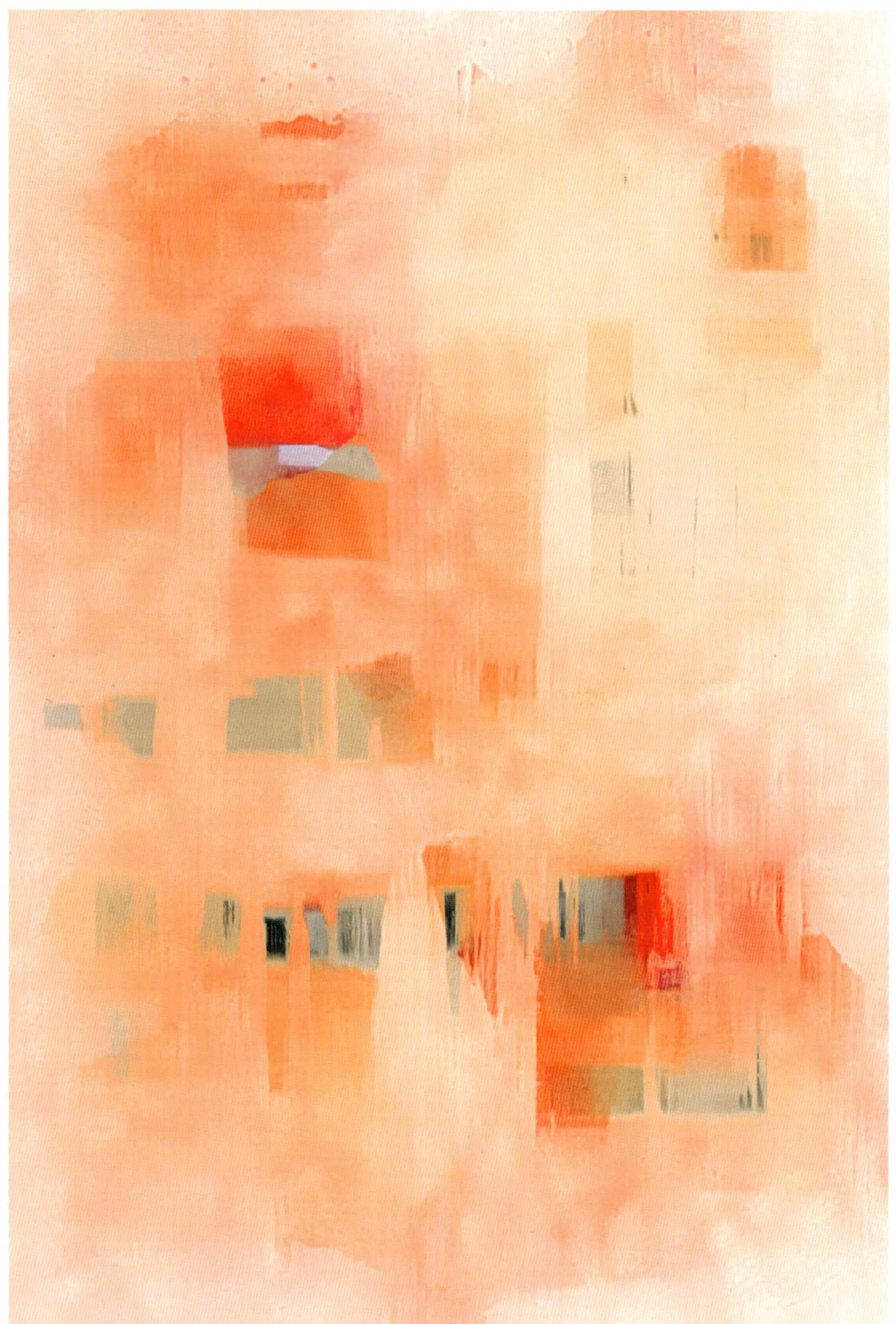

Barb Kreutter

Over many years as a professional weaver and glassblower, and now as an artist whose principal medium starts with the use of a camera, the interplay of color has been Barb Kreutter's primary creative motivator. She has always been drawn to capture the subtle, beautiful patterns and textures found in our everyday life.

Photography has allowed Kreutter to not only capture what she sees but to express how she feels when seeing it. Over the past few years, she has been exploring the technological components within her camera in conjunction with using more creative editing techniques to create her images.

She often will tell others: "It is my wish that you will enjoy how I see life as if you were standing next to me and are inspired to look more carefully at the world around you. I think you will discover beauty where you thought there was none."

Crying Glacier
Digital Photography
2000 x 1333 px

kreutter@telus.net
kreutter.zenfolio.com
@barbkreutter

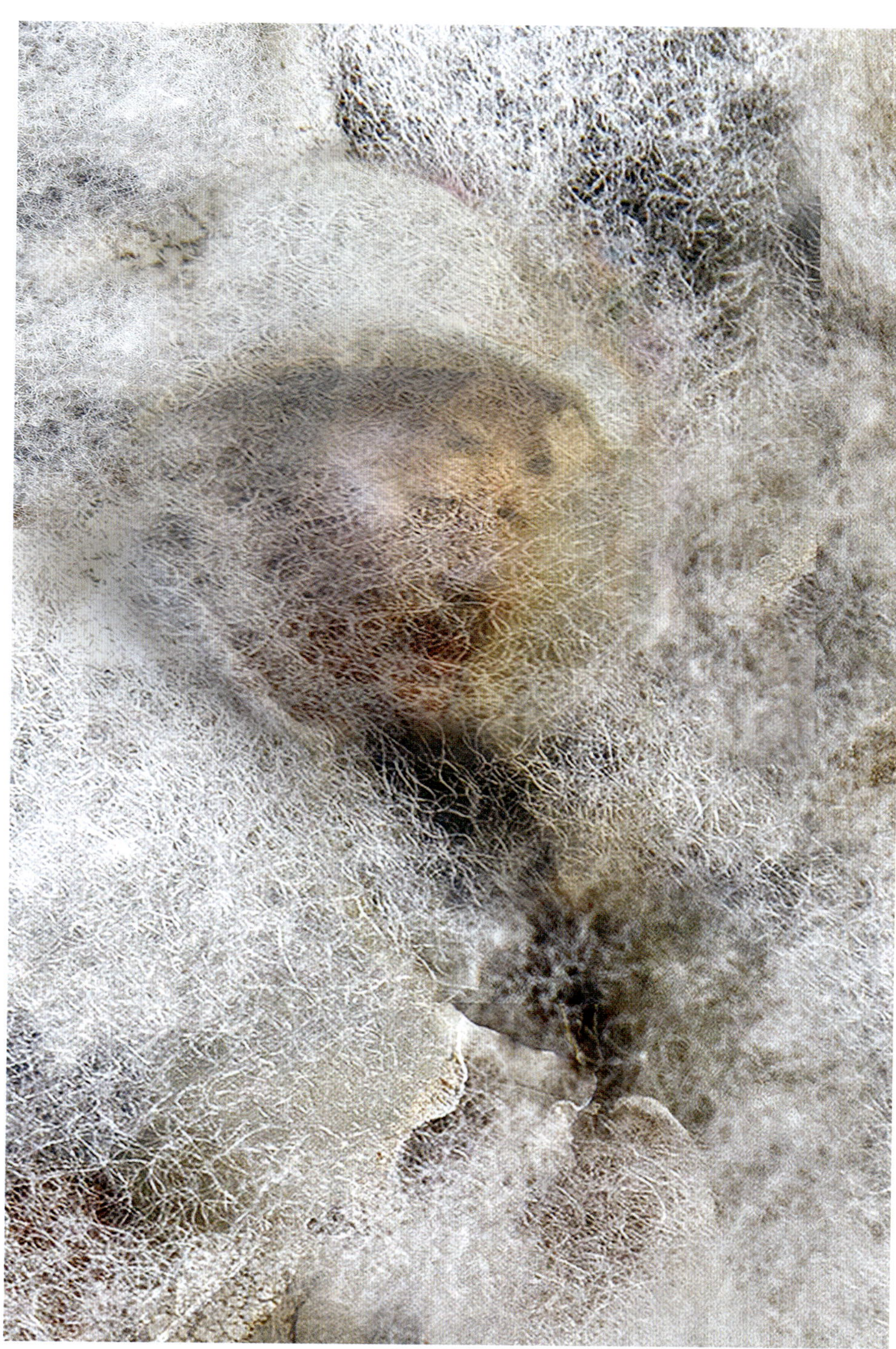

Peter Toth

Peter Toth is a photographer, painter, three-dimensional artist, poet, and "photo impressionist." The artist draws his inspiration from the unique cultures and landscapes he finds on his travels around the world.

"My photography is my starting point," Toth says. "I find places that touch me in a special way, and as I begin work on an idea, I gather photographic images from my computer library. My abstract photography comes to life in a process of manipulated layers on the computer screen." Some of these layers may be mixed-media paintings photographed and combined as another layer, adding greater dimension to the final image.

Ultimately, the process creates these imaginary places. Each element and texture complements or contrasts until they begin to convey the proper aesthetic and story of a place.

Mongolian Sheep Herder
Photography
34 x 22 in.

peter3031T@gmail.com
peterTcontemporary
.com
@peterTfineart

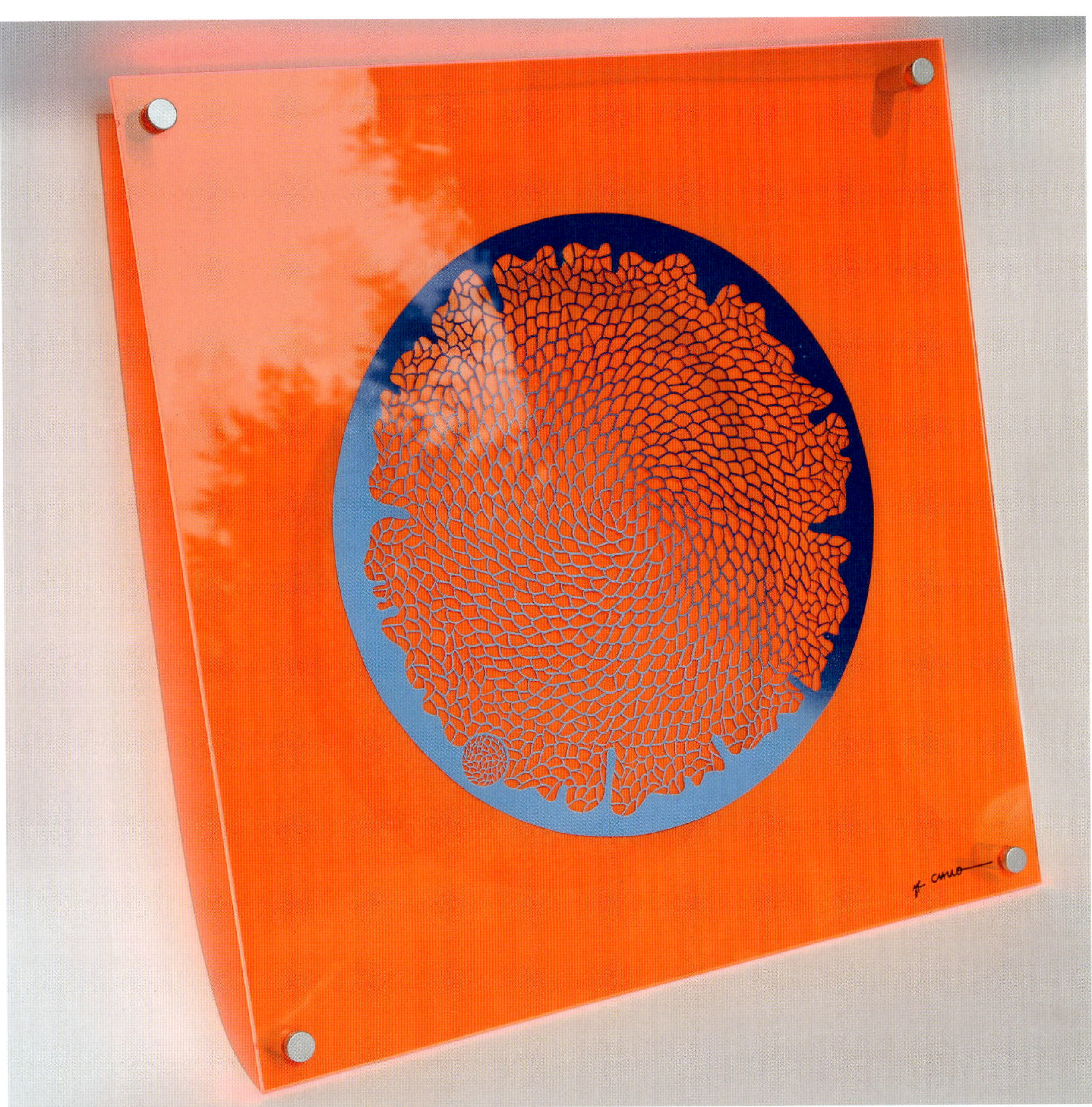

JR Chuo

JR Chuo is an artist working with cut paper and spray paint whose work explores the notion of facades in society that conceal harsh realities. His work is influenced by a wide range of styles, from the traditional Japanese art forms of kirie and ensō to street art and graffiti.

Before discovering the wide array of possibilities present in paper-cut art, Chuo used acrylic paint and pencil as his primary media. However, since 2015, his interest in paper developed and he now focuses solely on paper-cut art, cutting all of his designs by hand in a meditative and spiritual process, similar to that of painting ensō circles.

The *Fluoro Tokyo Collection* is inspired by the fluorescent colors and patterns of dying corals and the chaotic beauty found in urban transport and subway systems.

The detailed process of creating his work involves cutting paper by hand and using spray paint to produce vibrant paintings. Additionally, Chuo suspends his hand-cut paper pieces in fluorescent acrylic, drawing attention to the detail and precision of the artwork.

Midosuji
Paper cut, spray paint, acrylic
19.5 x 19.5 in.

OPPOSITE
Mini CHUO Reef 5
Paper cut, spray paint, canvas
8 x 8 in.

jrchuo15@gmail.com
jrchuo.com
@jrchuo

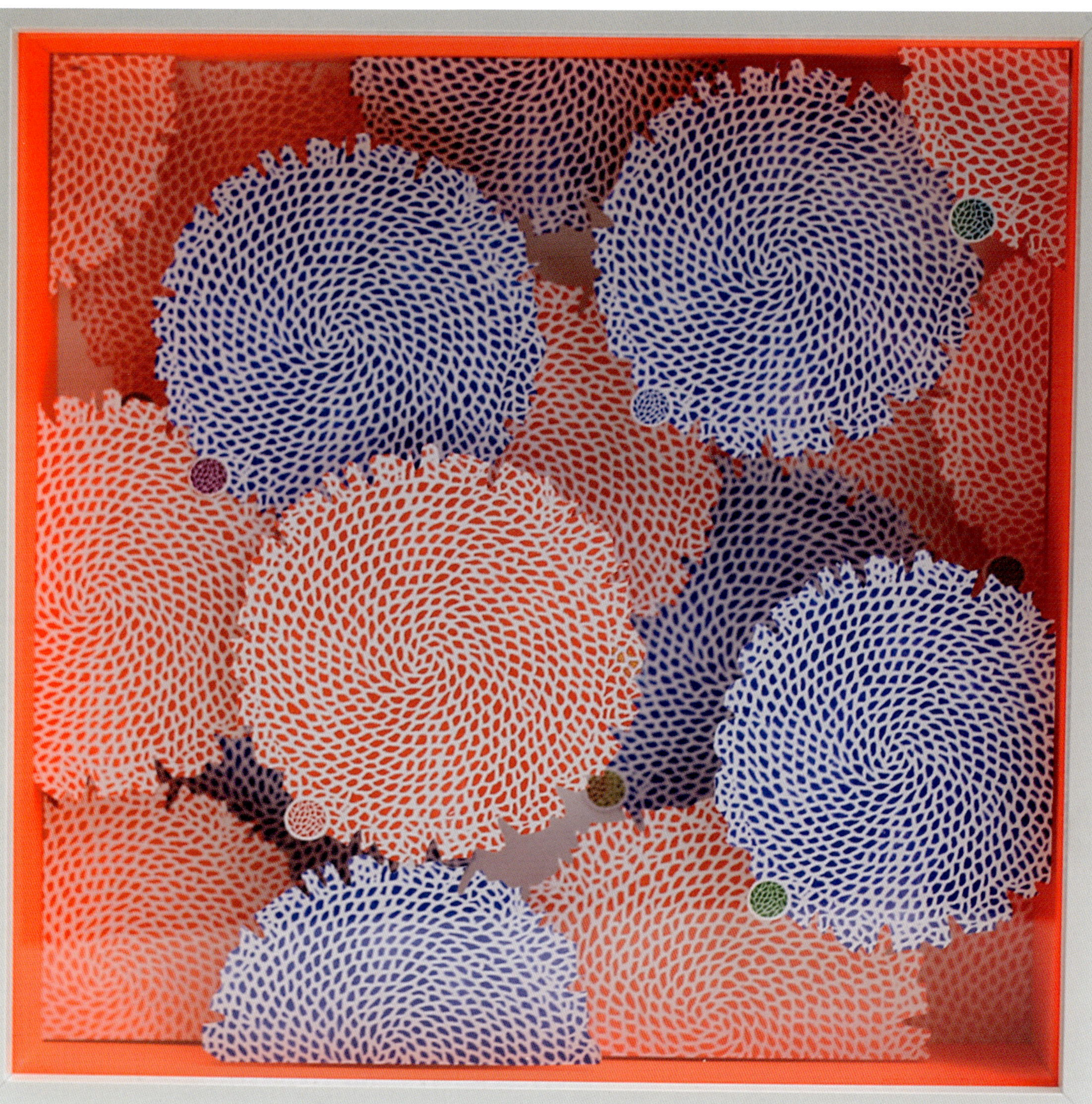

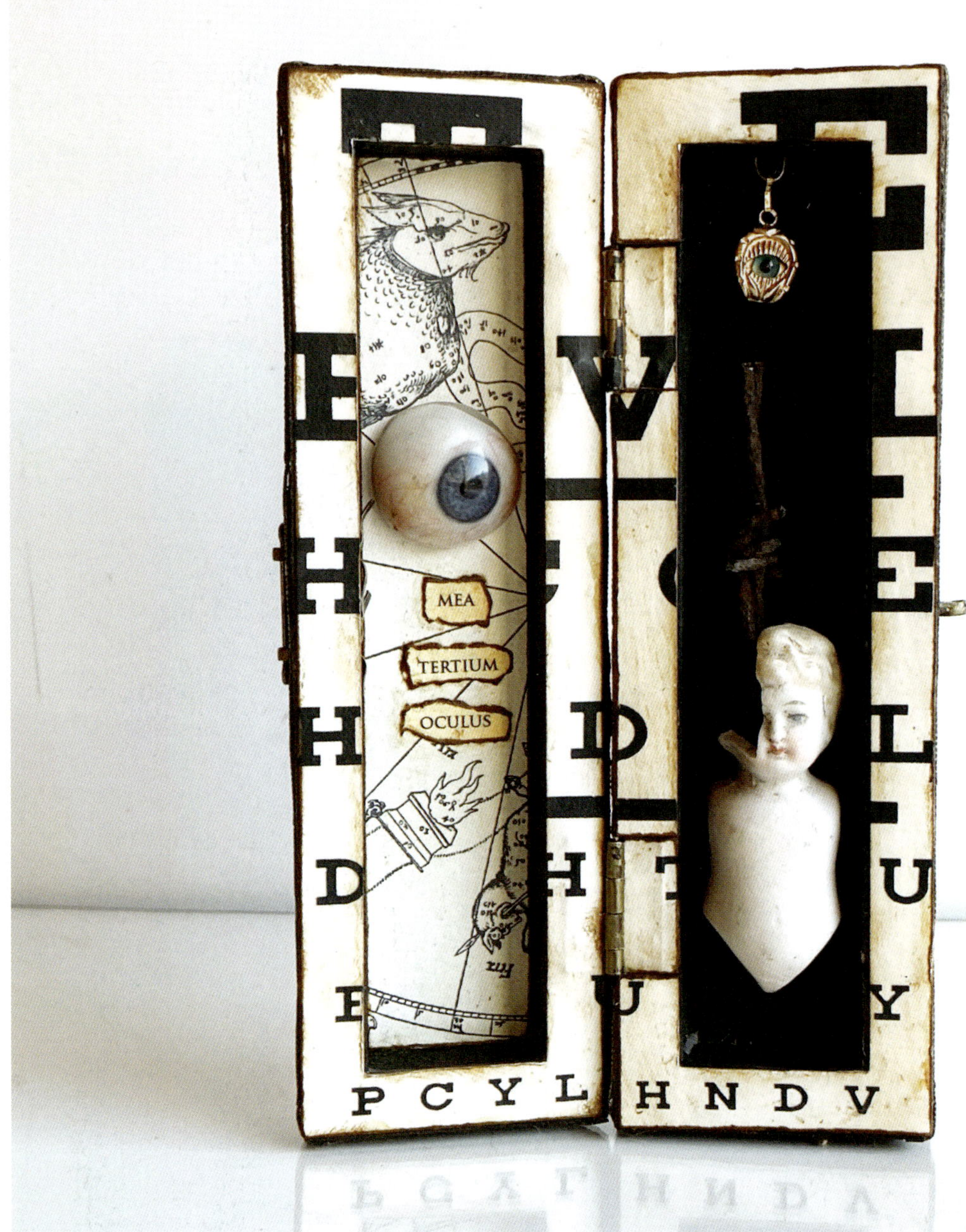

Jody West

"There is always inspiration to breathe new life into old found objects from the past," sculptor Jody West says. "Regardless of the age or value of the material, using it to create a piece of assemblage artwork gives the potential to ignite a new appreciation for that original object."

West's inspiration began from a treasure trove of photographs, ephemera, and antiques inherited from her family. Now, virtually anything that crosses her path during visits to antiques stores, strolls through the woods, or simply rummaging through an old box that holds the possibility of a forgotten piece of history can inspire a piece.

West brings a passion for design, collage, assemblage, antique ephemera, vintage photographs, and found objects to her work. Many pieces are inspired by one component, and the rest of the piece comes together as she adds additional objects. Some pieces have a more personal meaning and some are just whimsical and inspired by joining random salvaged items together in a new and interesting way.

Mea Tertium Oculus
Mixed Media Found Objects
7 x 4.25 x 1 in.

OPPOSITE
Space Cowboy
Mixed Media Found Objects
25 x 15 x 6 in.

jwest140@shentel.net
jwestfoundart.com
@jodywestfoundart

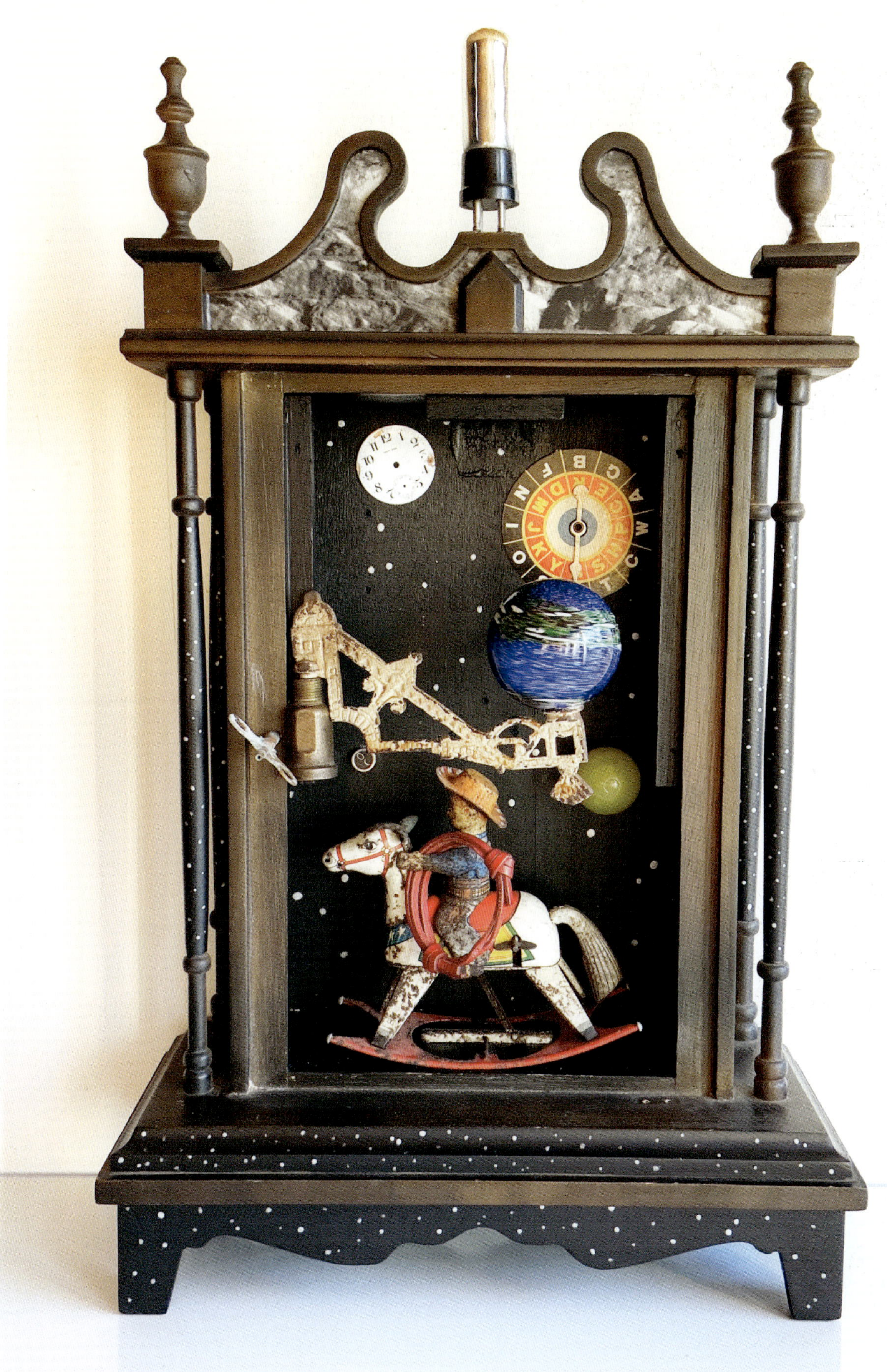

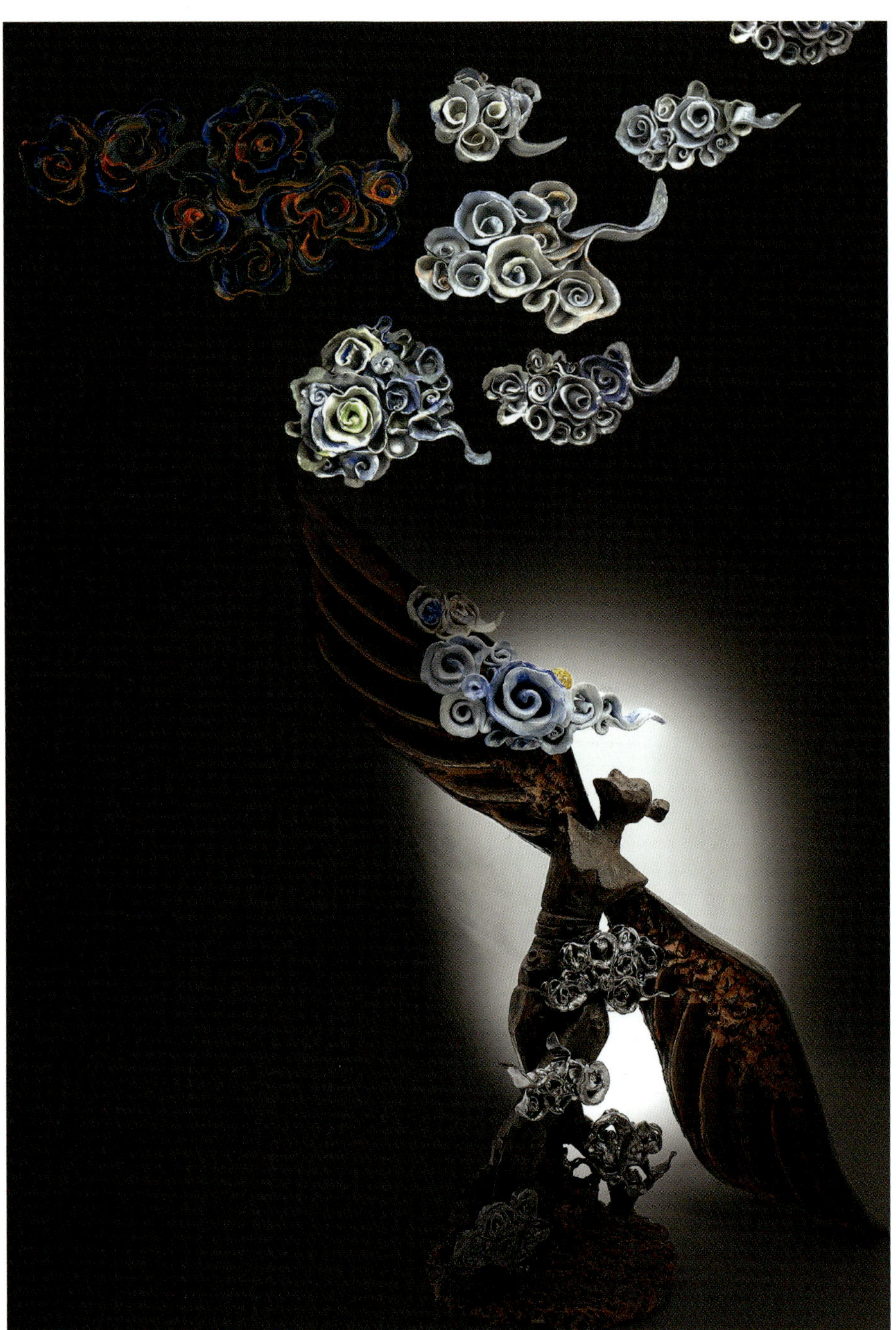

Christy Chor

Christy Chor is a nature lover, ceramic artist, and storyteller. Nature is her inspiration—the majesty of the landscape, the orchestra of wildlife, and life experiences are the natural flow of energy. She believes Mother Nature's charismatic beauty is found within poetic and chaotic moments. The eternal femininity of Mother Nature has inner beauty and resilience. She brings love and natural harmony to humankind yet responds with rage to human-made interruption and imbalance.

Inspired by poems about women's vision and fight for liberty, Chor reflects that many women are still receiving unequal treatment in different aspects of society. Some women may be uncertain about themselves and do not know how far they can reach by spreading their wings of faith.

Chor's latest body of works tells the tale of how courage and confidence can lead us toward change, a catalyst for achieving eternal goals.

Eternal Change
Cone 6 Stoneware with glazing (hand-building)
23.5 x 23 x 8 in.

christyymchor@gmail
.com
@christychor.com

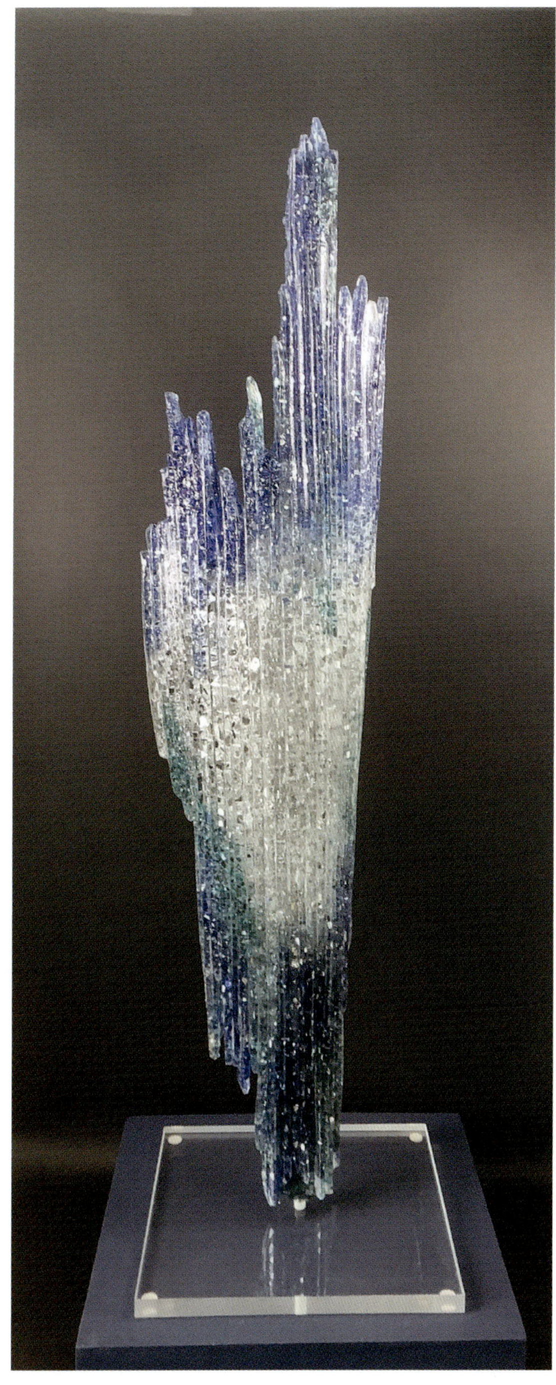

John Denis

Glass sculpture is not a common medium. The translucency of the material adds depth, light, and vitality to the work, opening the possibilities of the subject matter.

To begin a piece, John Denis sketches, drawing from a culmination of influences including nature, music, and sometimes modern architecture. He focuses on a particular form and how it changes its movement through time. With this in mind, he finds brilliant hidden snapshots in nature that can be pulled up and used as a point of reference for the composition.

Music has always played a role in Denis's process. He has an upright piano in his studio that acts as a collaborator when he needs a different perspective. "I have always thought that there is a strong correlation between sculpture and song," the artist says. "When a piece is finished, it should pose a few interesting questions without giving itself away."

Frequency
Glass and acrylic
75 x 21 x 21 in.

john@johnjosephdenis.com
johnjosephdenis.com
@johnjosephdenis

SCULPTURE/DIMENSIONAL

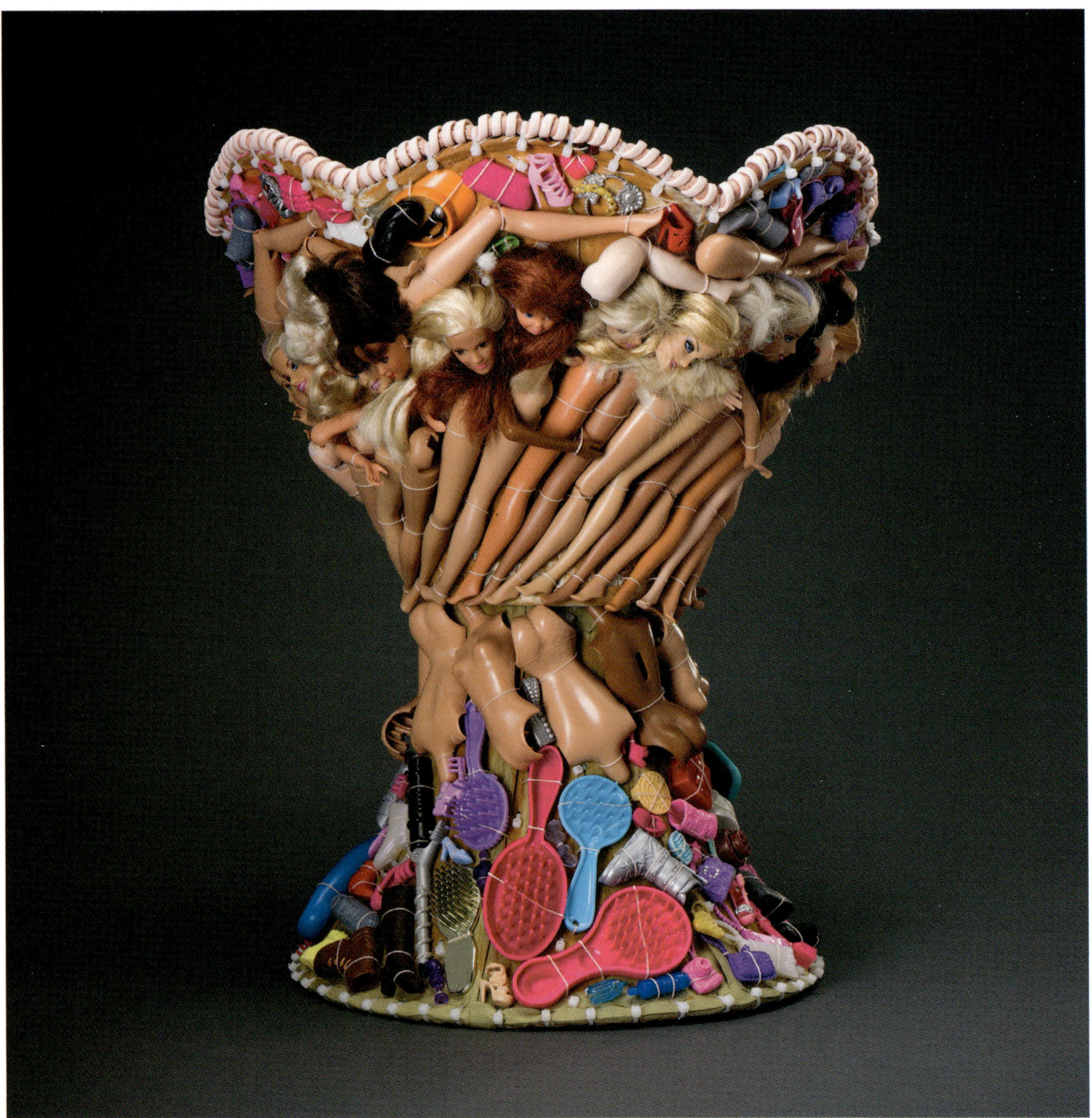

Emily Dvorin

Emily Dvorin is an award-winning sculptural basket maker, who exhibits, teaches, and speaks across the country. Her work focuses on repurposing and transforming common materials into innovative, "transordinary" vessels that reflect abstract ideas, including societal excess and throwaway consumerism. She manipulates, constructs, alters, coils, and weaves to develop pieces that marry modern aesthetic with whimsy.

Dvorin strives to change the definition of basketry by exploring contemporary interpretations of a traditional craft using nontraditional ingredients. She believes that anything can be basket material.

Thus, as unorthodox mediums are reinterpreted as fibers, she illustrates the concept that even unexpected objects that we take for granted can tell a visual story and become works of art.

Greater Than The Sum Of Its Parts
Assemblage using lampshades, Barbie parts and accessories, thread and cable ties
19 x 16 x 16 in.

emily@emilydvorin.com
emilydvorin.com
@emilydvorin

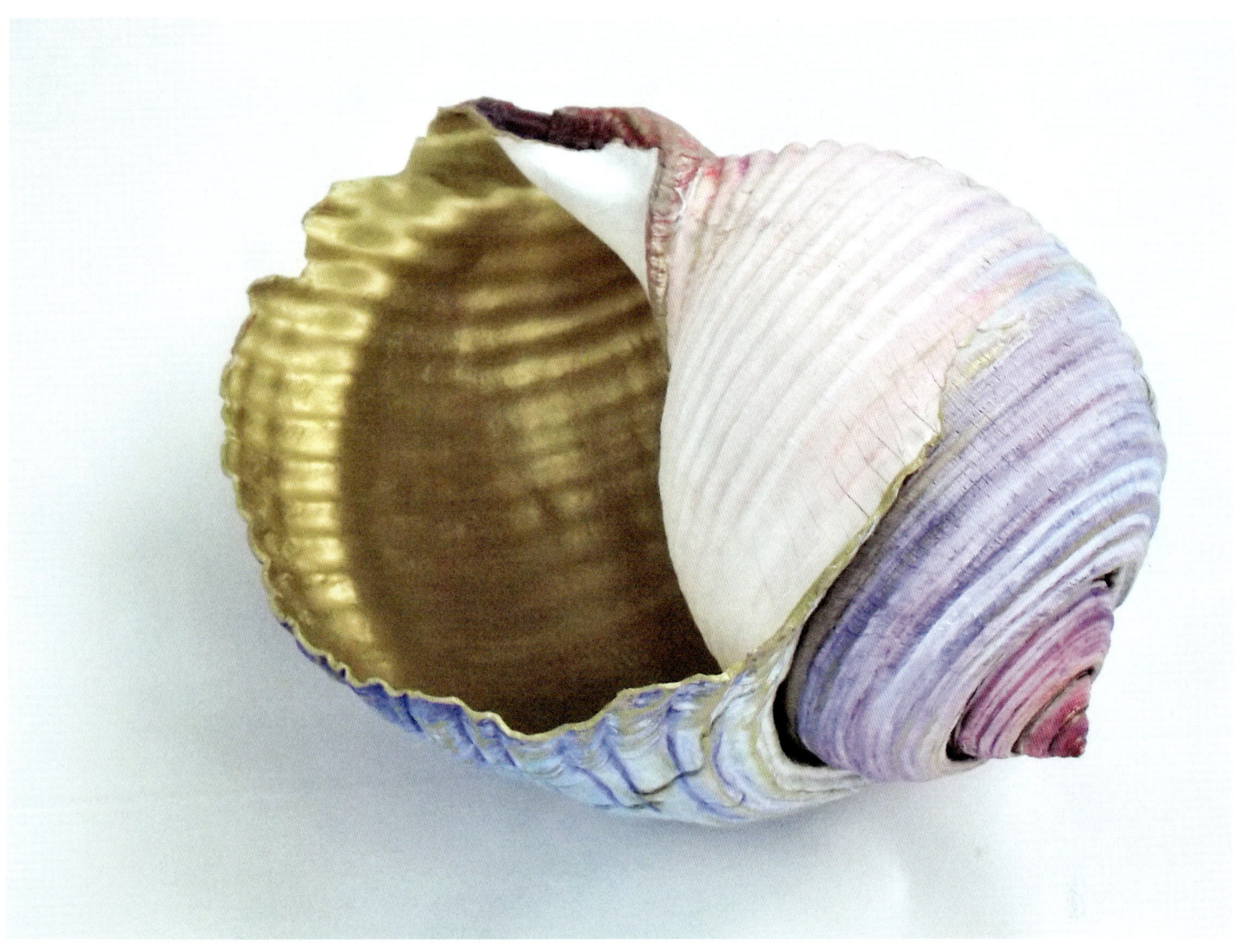

Kintsugi Grace

Nature is the creator and sculptor of each Kintsugi Grace collectible art shell. Time, wind, waves, sand, and sea creatures all exert their force upon a shell to transform it into something unique. There is a fascinating beauty to every shell that is broken, worn, decayed, bleached, and sometimes dyed by the ocean floor. Kintsugi Grace aims to work with the results of this process to accentuate the new beauty created in each shell.

Kintsugi Grace is inspired by the Japanese art of Kintsugi and the message that value is found in embracing both the beautiful and broken places, that with the touch of grace, broken places are mended and can become even more beautiful. There is value in the journey, and those rough places can teach and add beauty.

While shells are quite strong, the years of being tossed about in the ocean wear down the original beauty. Revealing the inside structure presents a new fascinating beauty. It is the artistic goal of Kintsugi Grace to work with the worn and weathered shells, highlighting this natural beauty and transforming them into unique art pieces that showcase the idea of "redemptive beauty" that is called Kintsugi Grace.

Sanctuary
Acrylic on natural Tonna Galea seashell
7.5 x 6 x 5 in.

kintsugigrace@gmail.com
kintsugigrace.art
@kintsugigrace

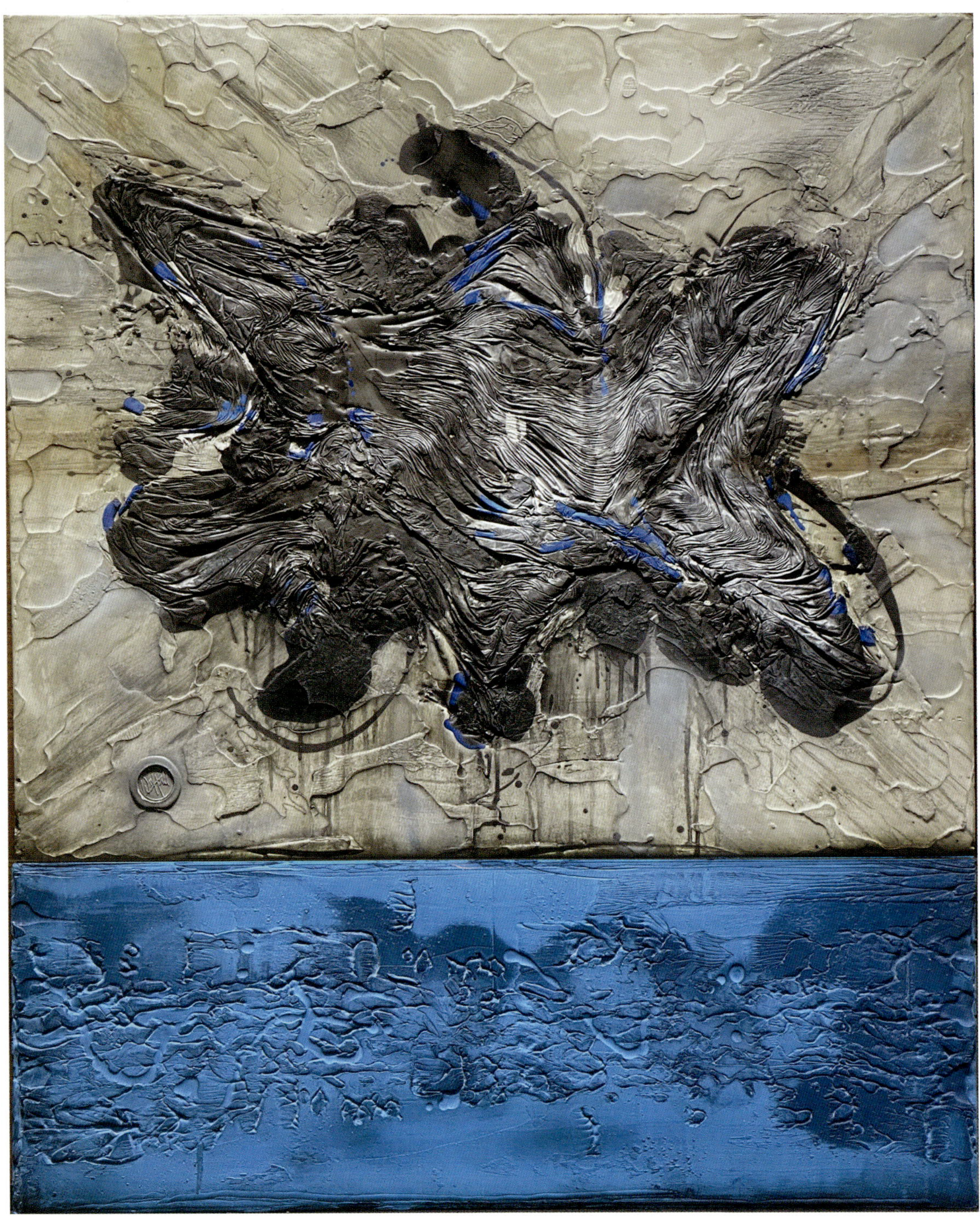

William Hall

With a gritty disregard for symmetry and perfection, William Hall's work mimics the evolutionary process of time, decay, erosion, and regeneration. His original poured, pigmented grout castings exhibit extreme texture and a refreshing industrial feel. His choice of constructs that allow random chance to function much as it does in nature when forming fossils and sedimentary stone, is an active one. His adherence to the Japanese aesthetic of *wabi-sabi* allows his mediums to stay true to their inherent capabilities. This reliance on serendipity ensures that his work continues to be as exciting to him as it is to his collectors.

Dark Angel
Pigmented Grout
46 x 36 in.

william@williamhall.com
williamhallart.com
@williamhallart

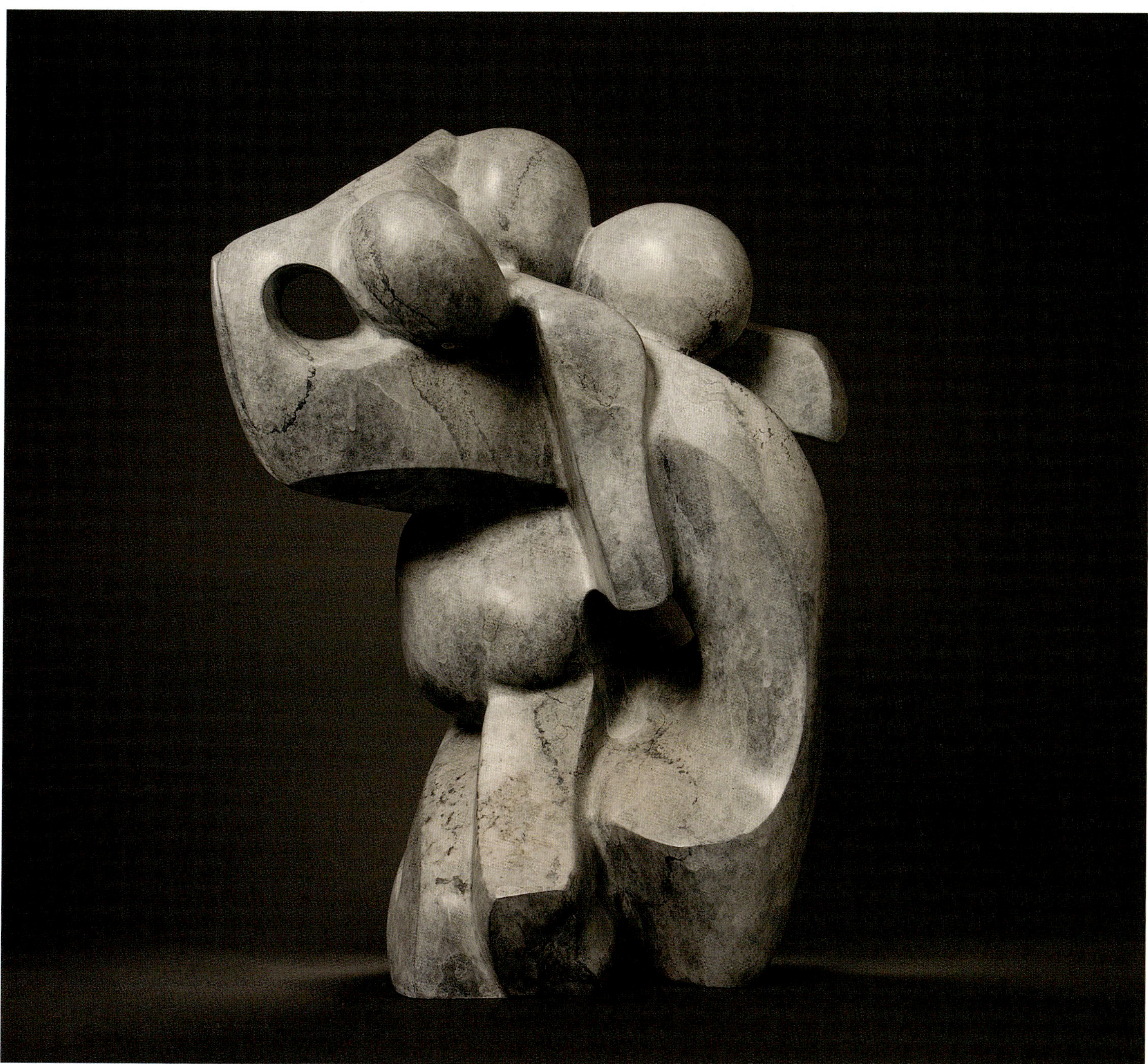

Mark Yale Harris

The purpose of Mark Yale Harris's artwork is to invoke an awakening of the sensual, stimulating a perceptual, internal, and intellectual response for the viewer—a visual that speaks to life's experiences. Creating symbols of universal connection underscores the relationship that one has to another and to nature.

"Art conveys my nonverbal view of life," Harris says. "It is an ongoing portrayal of myself, my behavior, adventure, exploration, risk-taking, and nonacceptance of convention and the status quo. I am constantly in search of the new and different and am fascinated with the unconventional. Life has a hard, aggressive side, as does much of my work, represented by rigid, angular lines. However, the soft side is also apparent, visible as curves and soft forms."

Using the invaluable experience of the mentorship of Bill Prokopiof and Doug Hyde, along with his own vision, Harris has created an evolving body of work in alabaster, marble, limestone, and bronze.

Chaos
Bronze
22 x 10 x 10 in.

markyharris@
artworkinternational
.com
markyaleharris.com
@markyaleharris

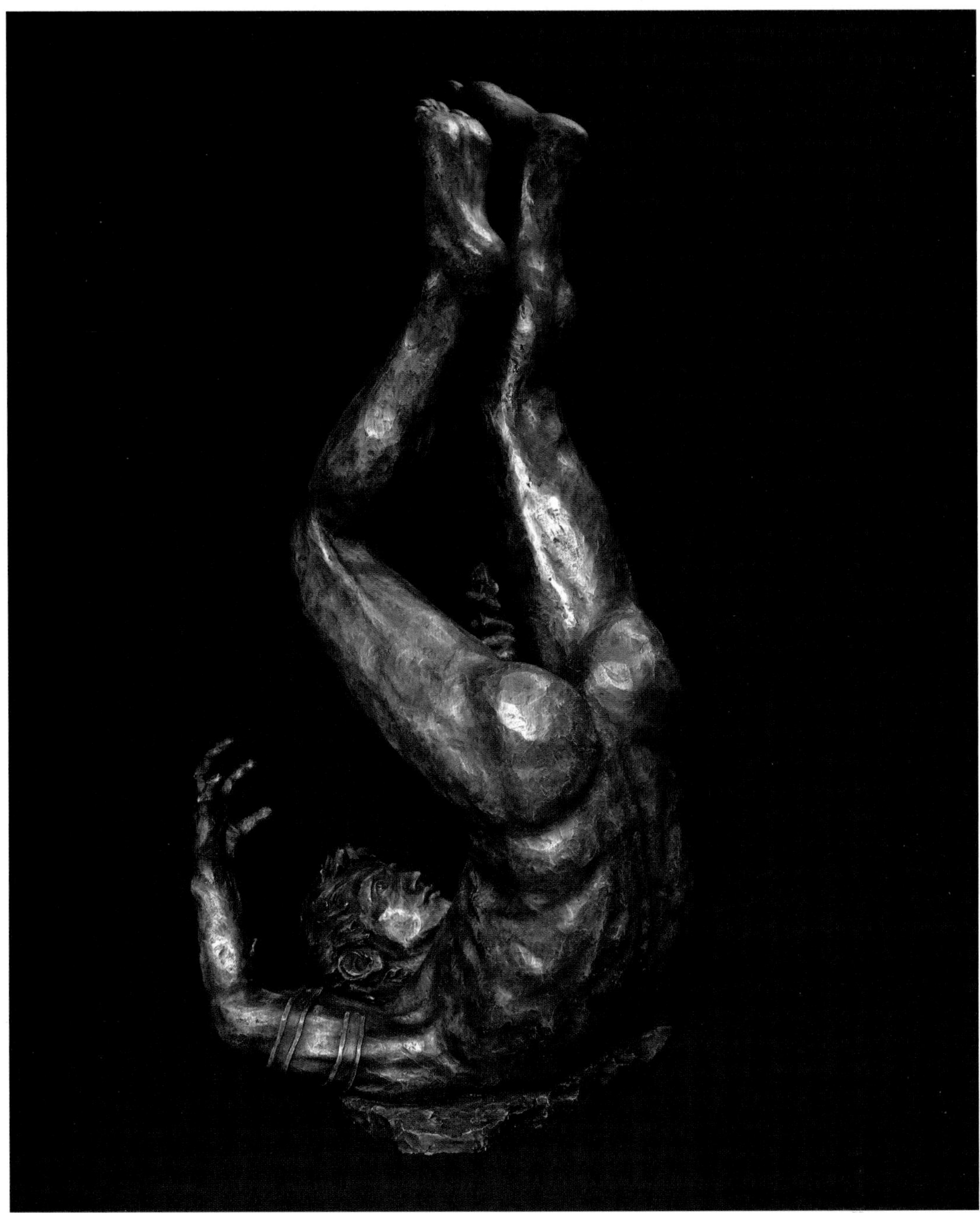

Alexandra Kapogianni-Beth

Alexandra Kapogianni-Beth has been painting and drawing and producing material objects for about twenty years. The last eight years have been mainly focused on sculpting.

For her pieces of art, she uses a wide range of raw materials, making use of the perspective of a Greek artist now living in Germany. Her own experience living in both countries, as well as the unique histories of both countries, force and allow the artist to choose and connect what best serves her intentions.

When considering her objects, the artist is focused on turning dead materials, such as hard rock, or soft matter, like gypsum and clay, into something vivid that offers a contrast between unhewn surfaces and soft, flowing worked surfaces.

"The delight I enjoy, hopefully, finds its way to the beholder and stimulates their reflections of what they see and experience," the artist says.

Falling Icarus
Resin
41 x 20 x 18 in.

kontakt@
bildhauerwerke-ak.de
bildhauerwerke-ak.de
@kapogiannibeth

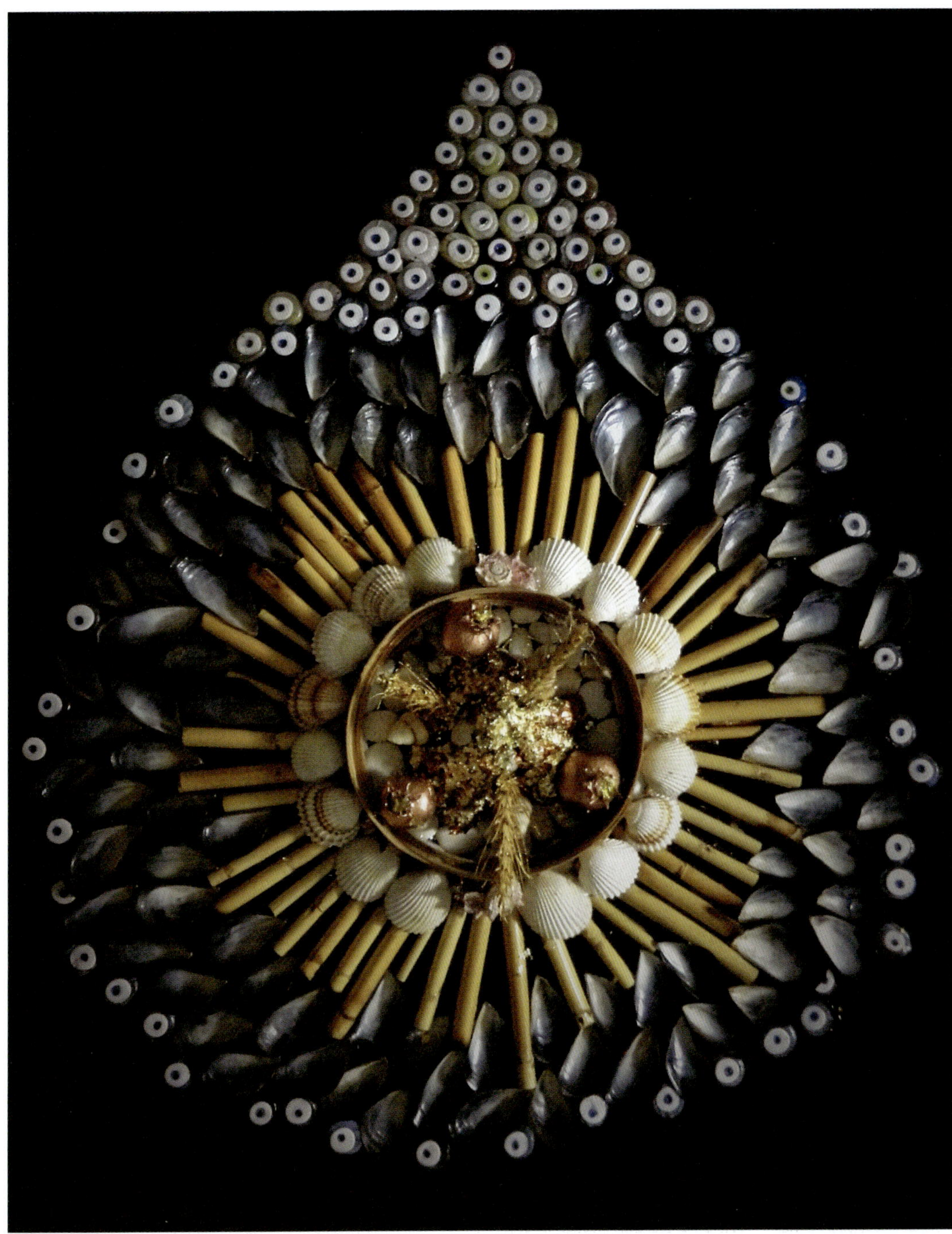

Kenan Koçak

Kenan Koçak says: "It seems that life is an illusion to be fulfilled as joy and/ or pain in line with an individual's purpose in the world. Then, art, as a higher level of illusion, should be able to contribute to advance or increase the degree of consciousness for all. As a creative process, art should contribute to life with culturally aesthetic and refined values articulated through time and nature. By doing so, it becomes more meaningful, not only for what it is but what it serves."

In terms of motivation, Koçak believes that destruction is one of the biggest issues to be tackled in today's world. In terms of technique, Koçak tries to explore his inner world for the harmony of means and ends, using experimentation through the door of intuition.

A Life Drop
Mixed Media on Metal Board
29.5 x 36 x 3.5 in.

absart@outlook.com
kenank.art
@kenank_art

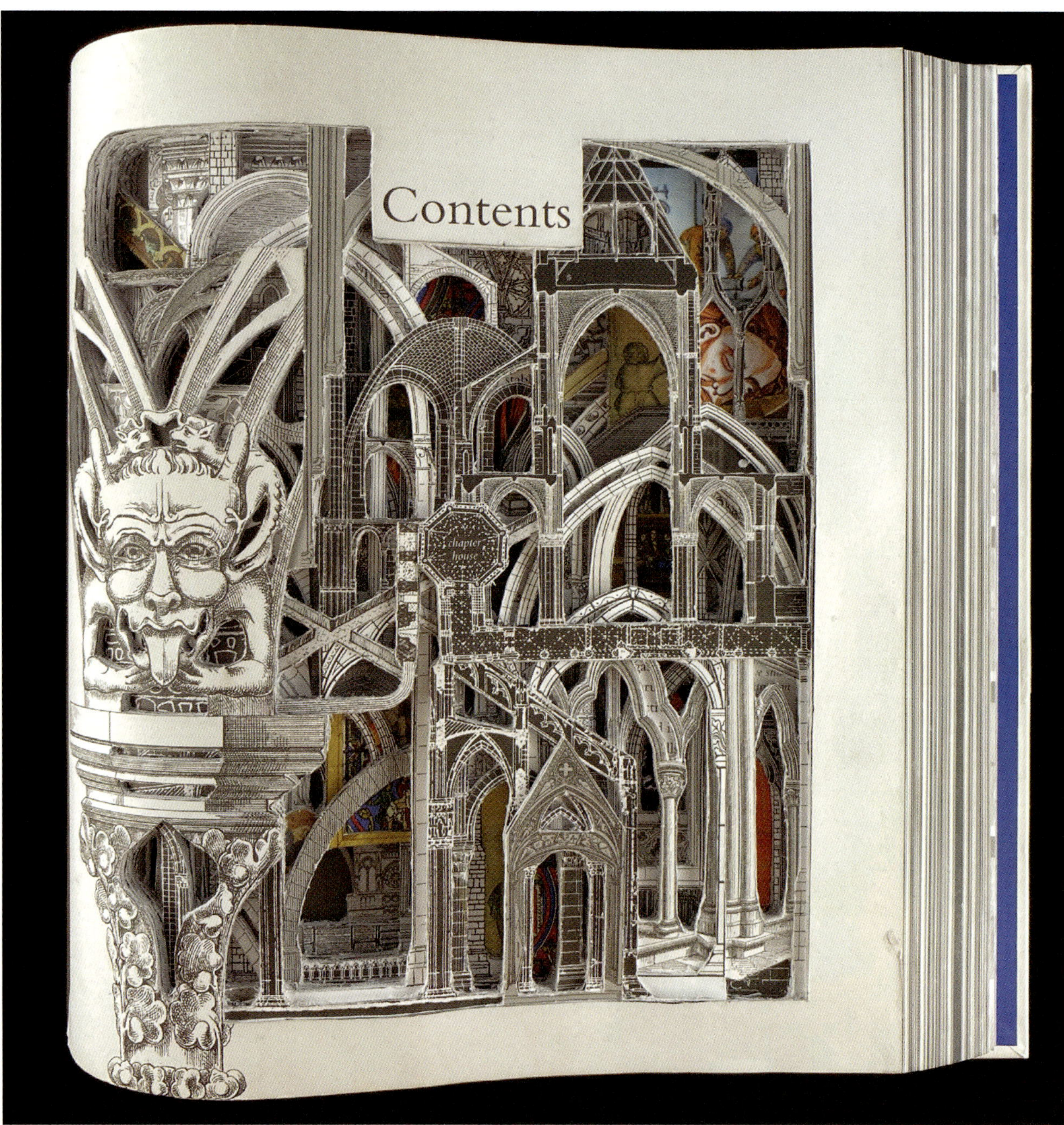

Keith Kriegel

Keith Kriegel takes old books, such as outdated encyclopedias and textbooks found at resale stores and garage sales, and repurposes them by carving them into pieces of art. He is a dentist by profession and discovered that his attention to detail and tactile skill with a surgical knife, along with his creative impulses, provided a perfect segue into carving books.

Kriegel seals the pages of the books before cutting. Thereupon he cannot turn the pages and, thus, he cuts blindly down into the books, one to three pages at a time. Not knowing what will be revealed as he cuts away unwanted material is part of the challenge and excitement of the process.

Kriegel allows the theme and content of each book to guide its unique design. He adds no paper nor any other material to the books; he only removes paper, transforming the old books into three-dimensional pieces of art.

Gargoyle Cathedral
Carved book - Paper
10 x 11 in.

the.kriegels@tx.rr.com

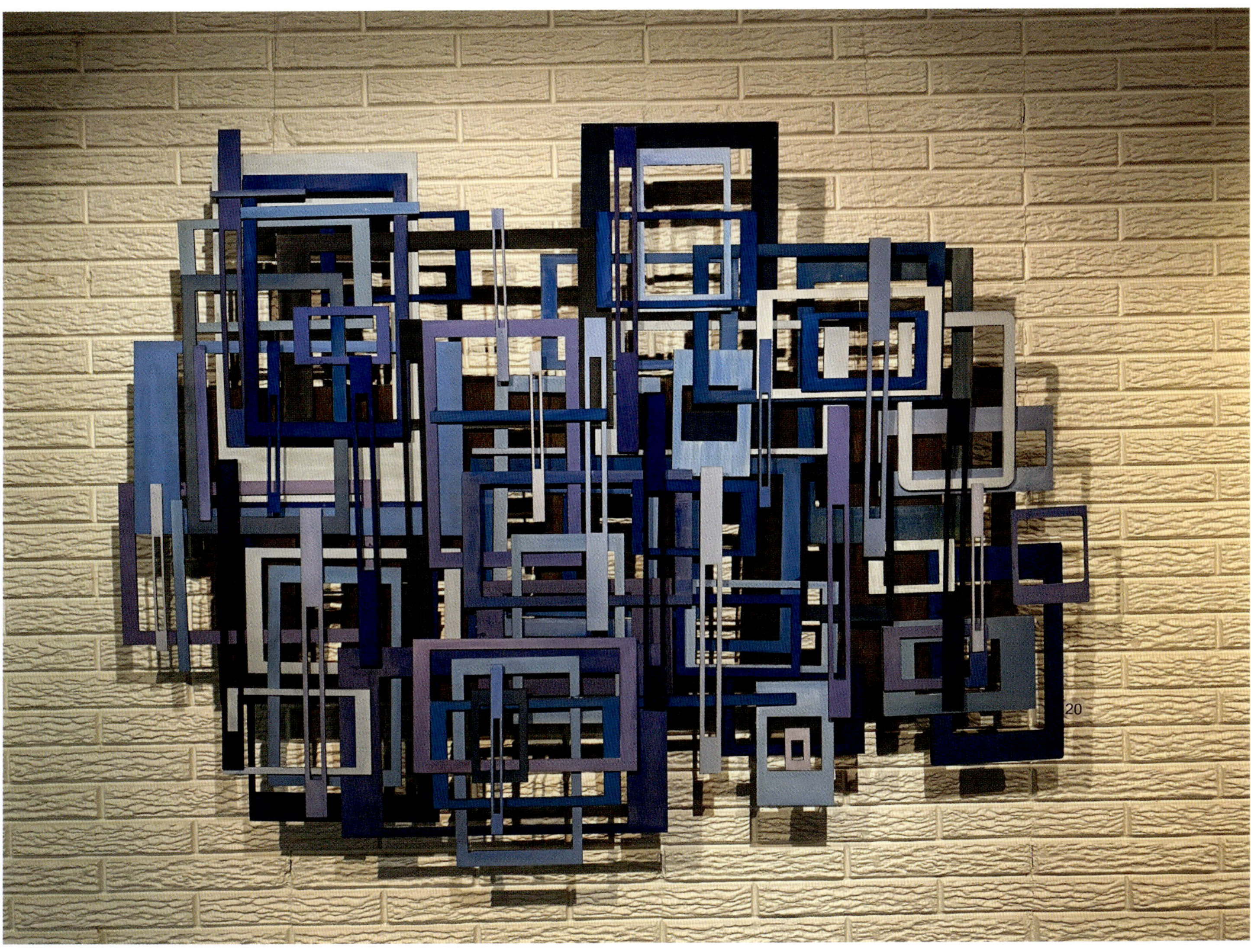

Denise Lion

As an artist who works in a diverse variety of media, Denise Lion experiments with an aleatoric process to create strong personal moments by means of rules and omissions, acceptance, and refusal, and by enticing the viewer to go round and round in circles. She often allows the inventive process to be decided by the hands of fate.

Lion's art is associated with her preoccupation with the acceleration of technology and its multifaceted advances in our lives. In her art, she tries to draw her audience to both the negative and positive outcomes associated with our daily uses of technology.

Her works do not place an identifiable form, rather the results are taken apart to the extent that significance is shifted and possible interpretation becomes multilayered. Lion uses a visual vocabulary that addresses many diverse social and political issues. Her work incorporates time as well as space, allowing an imagined and experiential universe that only emerges bit by bit

Geometric Space
Wood
4 x 6 ft.

dlplano@msn.com
deniselion.com
@dlplano

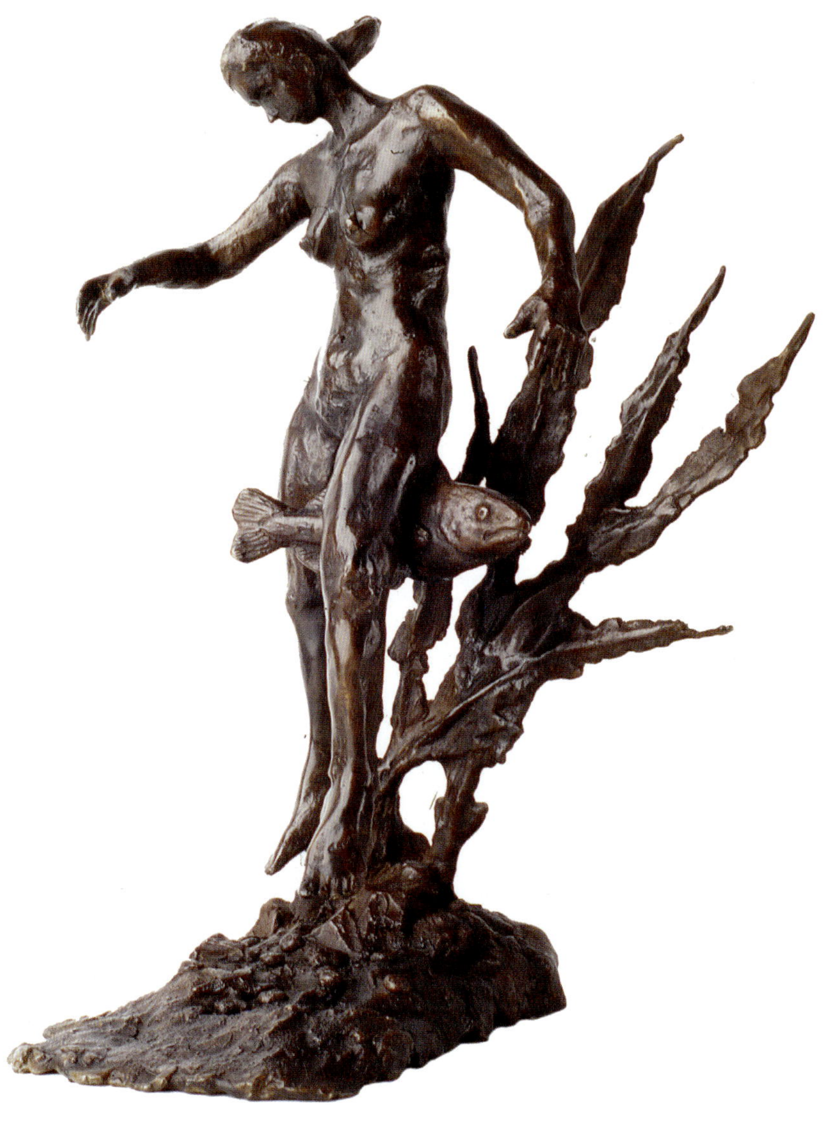

Jim Maunder
Jim Maunder has spent most of his life living by the sea, witnessing the toll on nature and humankind caused by the demise of the once abundant fish stocks. His sculptures, whether figurative or semiabstract, express his deeply held views on the environment, the frailty of the human condition, and the resilience of the human spirit.

Human nudes and fish often appear in his work. The fish represent the vulnerability of nature. By combining the human form with fish, he suggests the vulnerability of humans as a species as well as human responsibility to the earth's ecosystems. With the naked body, he expresses the temporary and vulnerable yet also the joyful nature of life.

Recent advancements in the science of genetic engineering, and the ethical and existential dilemmas they present, have added another layer to his continued exploration of the complexities of the interaction between humans and the environment.

Buoyancy
Bronze
17 x 9 x 13 in.

jimmaunderart@gmail
.com
jimmaunder.ca
@jimmaunderartist

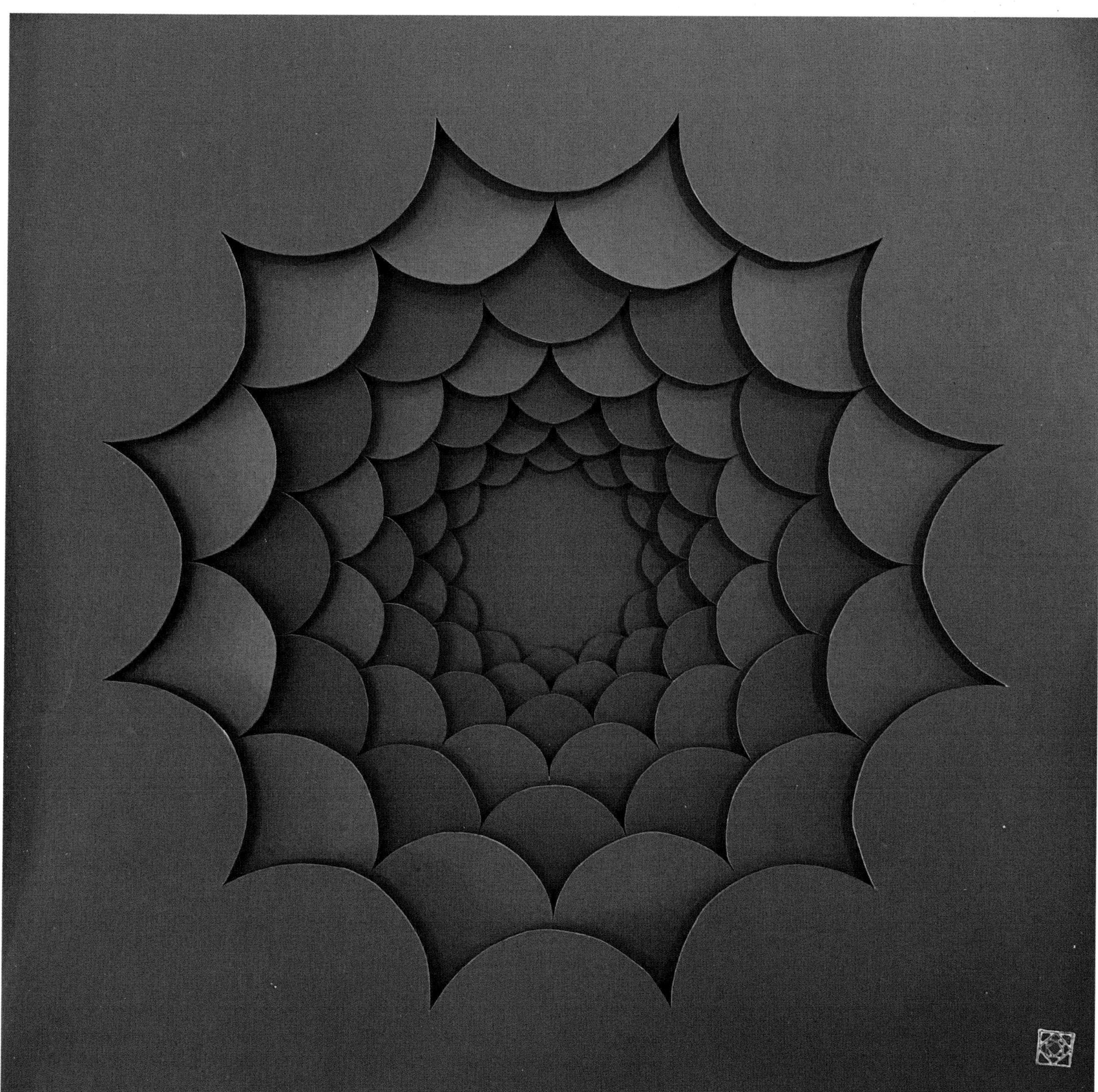

John Meacher

John Meacher, aka Johnny Papercuts, started with a dream—a dream that he could fuel his creative outlets while making beautiful works of art. All of his pieces are created in the Kirigami style of Japanese art and designed to not only be beautiful but also to utilize the fascination and visual appeal of intrinsic designs.

Although he works as a law firm data analyst by day, by night, he transforms into a Kirigami artist who desires to bring fantastic paper art to the world. All of his art is hand-designed and lovingly created in his home studio. It is with love and dedication that he creates this Kirigami art.

Noir
Paper
12.6 x 12.6 x 2.4 in

johnnypapercuts@gmail.com
johnnypapercuts.com
@johnnypapercuts

SCULPTURE/DIMENSIONAL

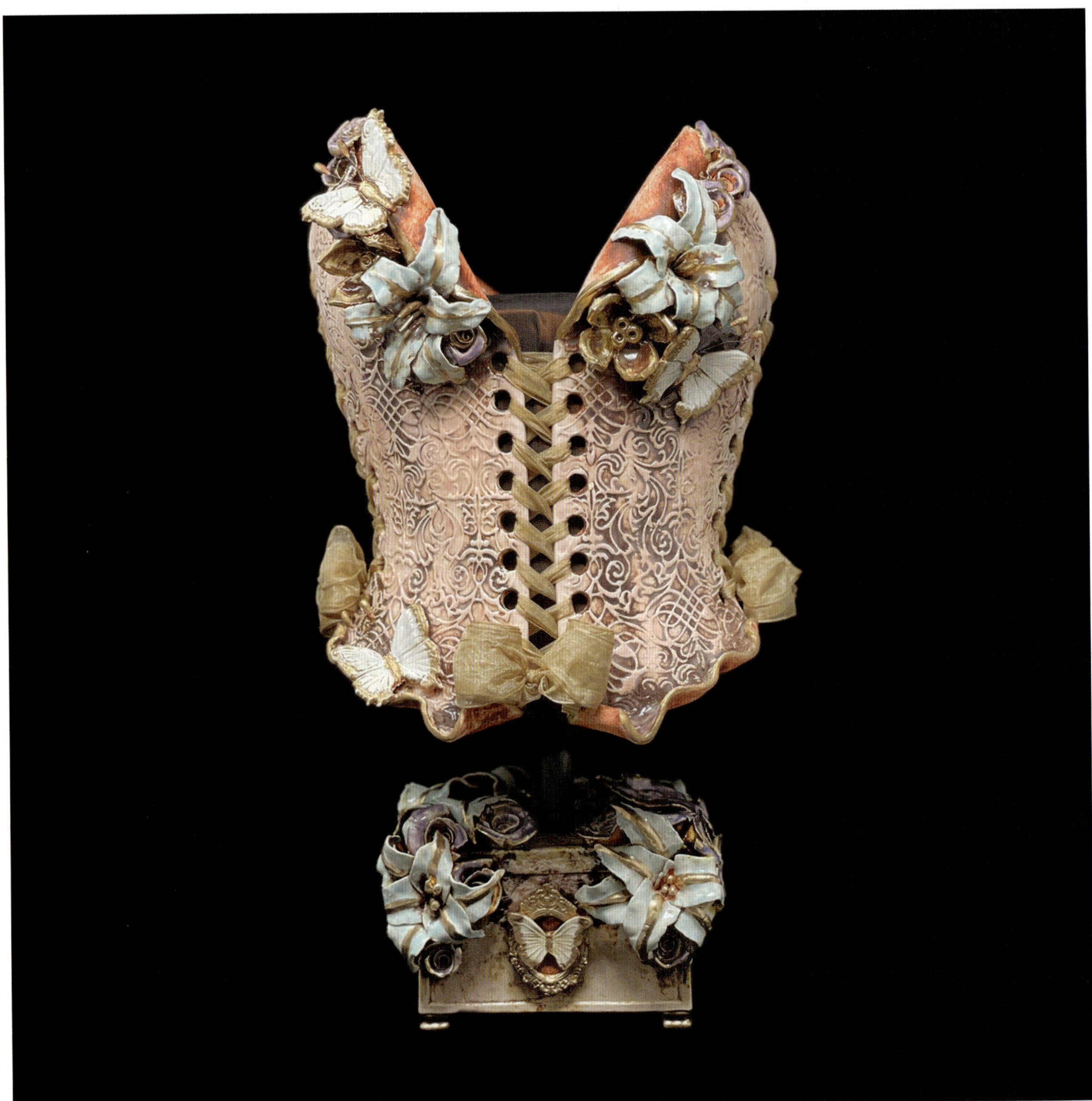

Nicole Moan

Nicole Moan is an environmentally conscious artist, repurposing materials and powering her studio with solar energy. As an active, exhibiting artist, Moan also does board and committee work and teaches art to inner-city kids. For over twenty-five years, she has created work for runway shows, large tile installations, and museum exhibitors.

Touch is a critical aspect of Moan's work. The brilliance and texture of her work doesn't just invite viewers to brush their fingers over the crevices and curves, it demands it.

Born into a family of artists, Moan continues to soak up a vast array of imagery to incorporate into her wearable ceramic corsets and high-relief tile. The clay structure allows her to emulate anything from marine life to floral porcelain attire.

Tabula Rasa wearable ceramic corset
Porcelain clay, vitreous enamel, sheer organza ribbon
20 x 13 x 13 in.

nicolemoan@gmail.com
nicolemoan.com
@nicolemoan

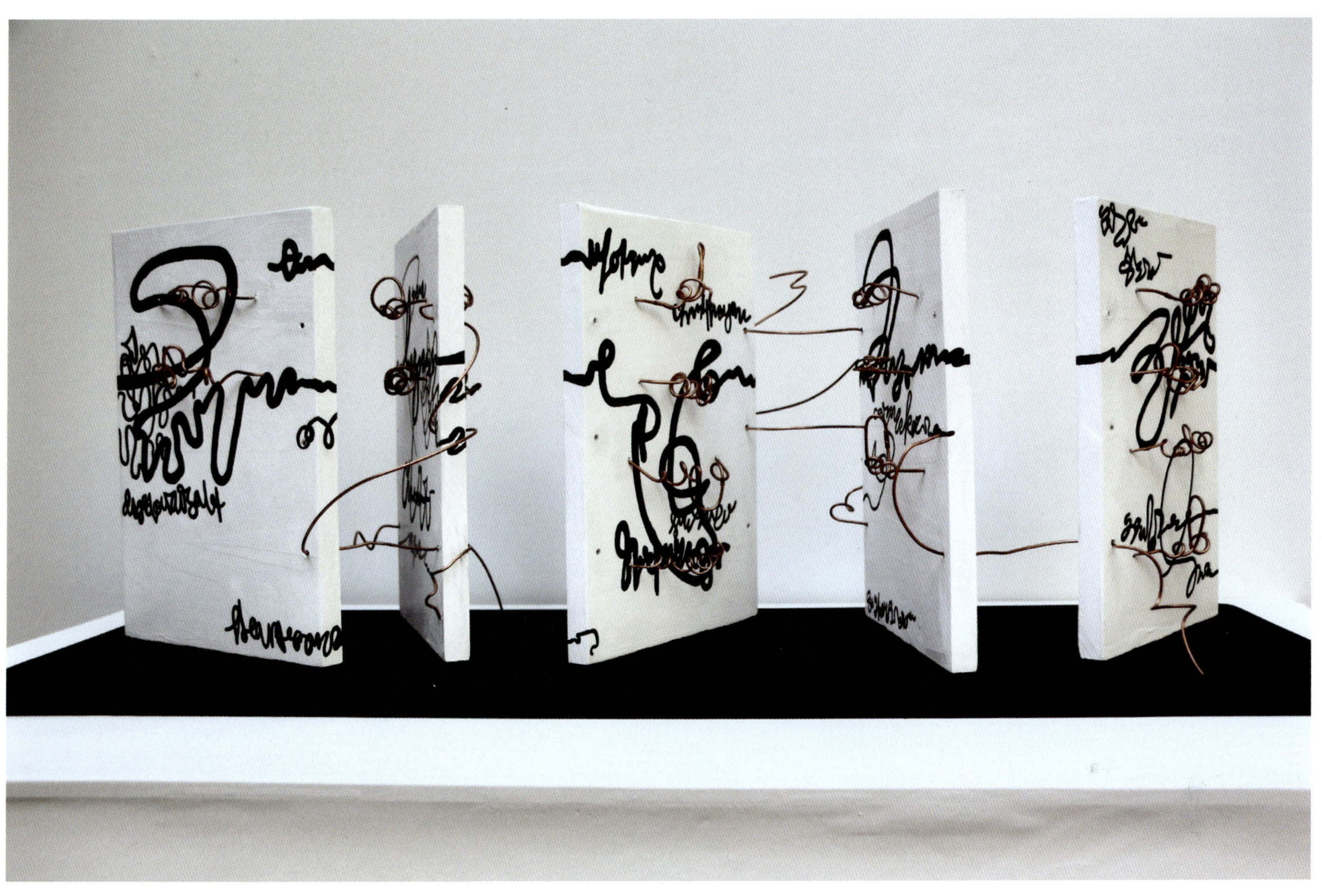

Cecelia Moseley

Cecelia Moseley's work intends to bring awareness to the trials of living with dyslexia. She intends to depict the intangible mental struggles that are not visible to the everyday person by creating a new form of visual communication. This new language breaks down the traditional writing components into three-dimensional planar forms by using fabrication and rearranged letters.

Moseley's works are composed of materials such as sheet metal, acrylic, copper wire, and wood. She is drawn to these materials because of the possible complexity and fluidity that each material is capable of achieving. By bringing all these materials together, she creates various compositions that reflect some of the challenges associated with dyslexic learning. For those people who do not know what dyslexia feels like, she hopes to reflect those frustrations and help create a better understanding for the viewer. The importance of bringing more awareness to this issue is so that, hopefully one day soon, society can better assist a person who needs intervention and accommodation.

Unbound
Wood, copper wire
35.5 x 13.25 x 11.25 in.

cecemoseley@comcast
.net
cmoseleyfineart.com
@cc_art_design

SCULPTURE/DIMENSIONAL

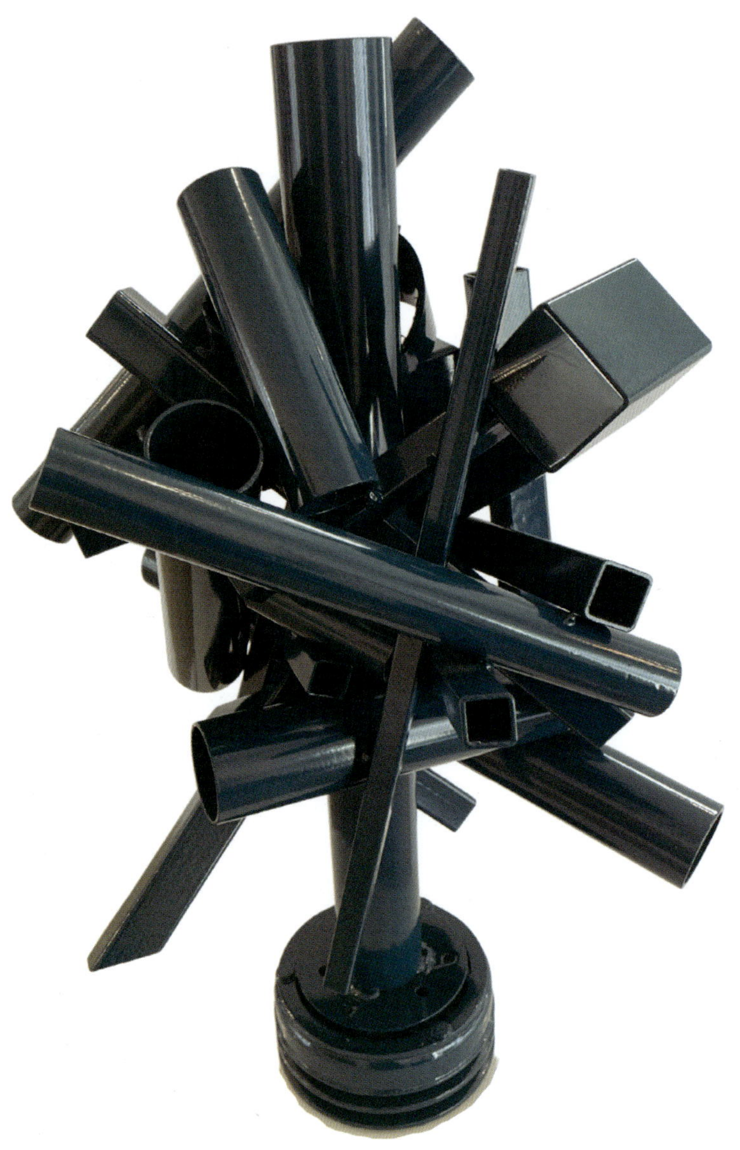

Remains, Inc.
Remains, Inc., a collaboration between artists Deborah Hartigan Viestenz and Gary Buckner, exists to create powerful sculptures with an empowering message. Reconstruction and reuse are the basis for all their works. The *Unchained* series is fabricated exclusively from steel scrap metal.

Hartigan Viestenz and Buckner are both passionate about creating beauty from waste, and they donate a portion of all sales proceeds to organizations actively working toward the preservation and correction of the physical, ecologic, and socioeconomic landscape of today's world. Their sculptures, ironically named *Unchained*, fuse waste materials together to form a body of strength, granting freedom to those with vision. Their works demonstrate strength in unity, solidarity, and commitment in form and action. Remains, Inc.'s mission is to demonstrate how, with very little effort, we can all positively affect the environment for all to experience and enjoy. The founders' core message is: "Experience the beauty in art; experience the beauty in the art of giving."

Unchained
Steel
37 x 22 in.

deborah@dhvartorks
.com
dhvartworks.com
@dhv_artworks

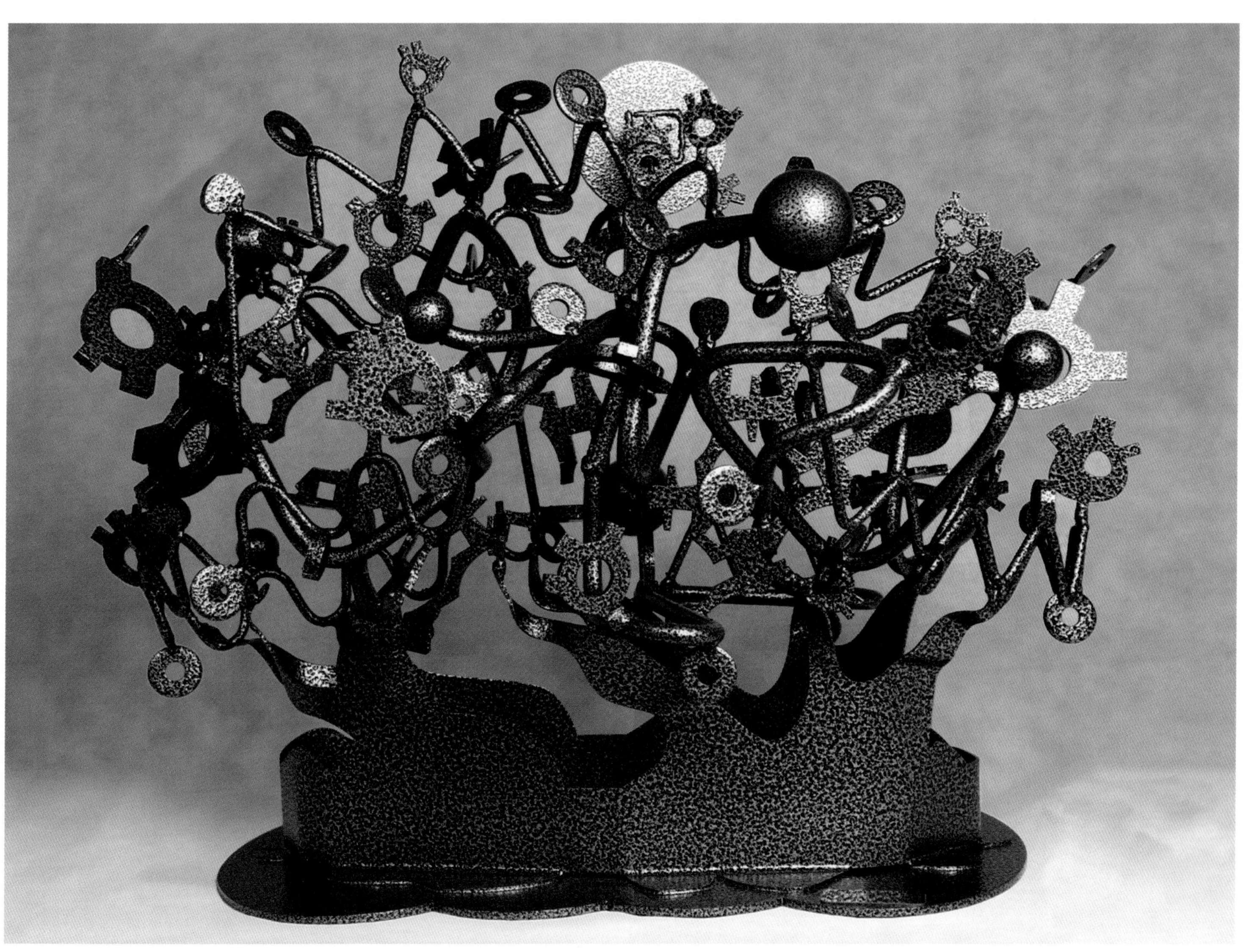

Emmanuel John Santos

"If you can imagine what you want and manifest your desire in bringing them to life, then the magnet of prosperity and 'Superabundant is in you," says sculptor Emmanuel John Santos. *The Superabundant*, one of the sculptures in Santos's *Money Tree* series, has brought our imagination and desires, whether in health, wealth, love, or joy, to reality. "This work brings us one step closer to the endless possibilities of fulfilling a vision to become a reality," Santos says.

The interchanging complexities of symbols and currencies that root the tree's formation as symbols of unlimited prosperity and abundance have taken their place in the form of sculptures. It gives a more vibrant and realistic appearance to the artist's structured dreams in symbols of wealth. A symbol that attracts positivity best describes each of the tree's distinct formations.

Superabundant Tree
Metal
25 x 25 x 18 in.

emansantos1@gmail
.com
@emanm.santos

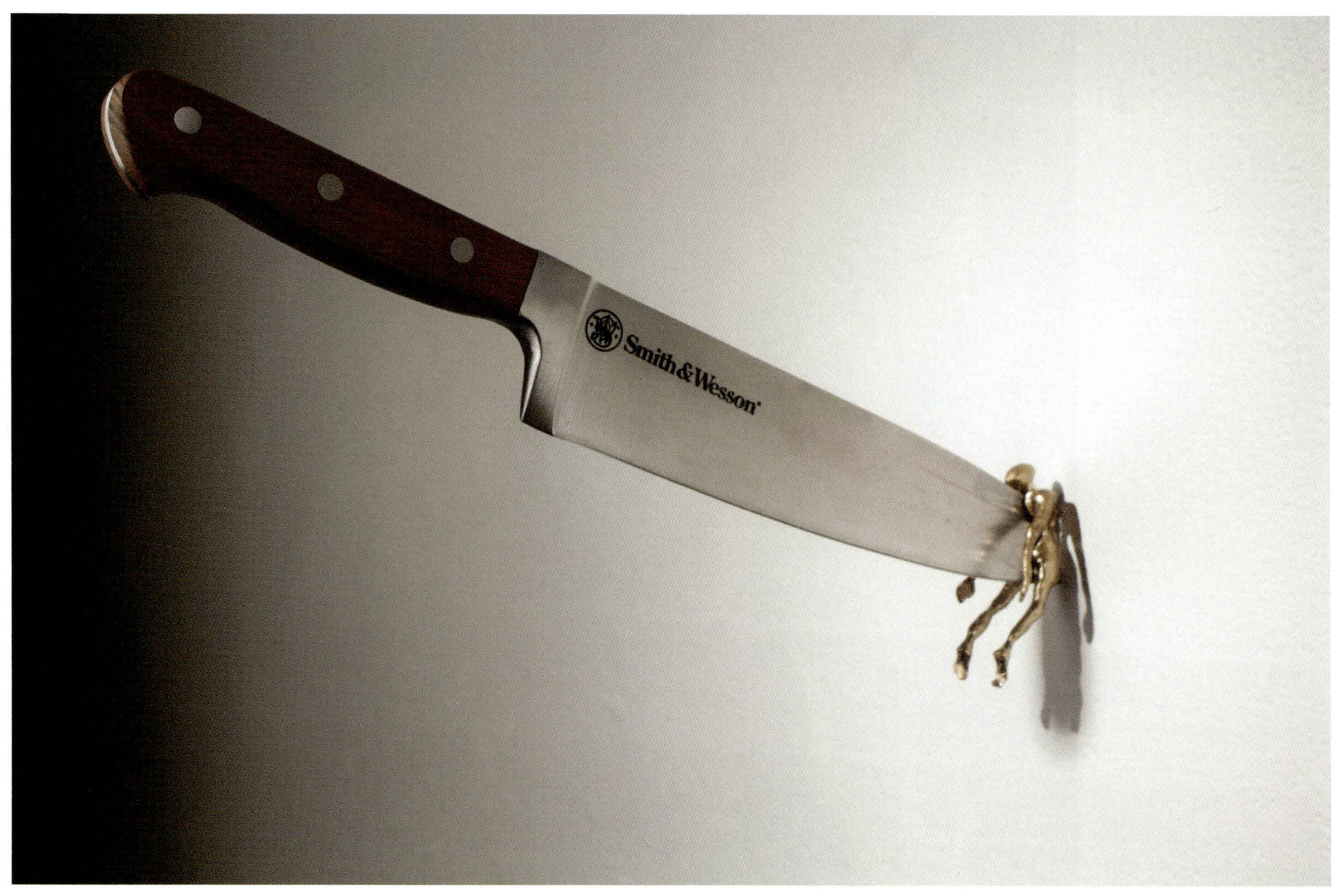

Bernardo Vallarino
Human suffering, violence, abuse of power, politics, control, and hypocrisy are themes Bernardo Vallarino explores in his work. These topics are all part of a larger social commentary regarding the disposable way human life is treated. Vallarino's work describes this disregard for human lives by overlaying concepts of the perceived worth of "the others" with metaphors related to vermin, a common analogy used throughout history to strip others of their humanity. Vallarino designs the installations and sculptures to be emotionally immersive and morally engaging with the intent to pay tribute to the victims, bring awareness to their suffering, the issues that affect them, and ultimately inspire action or activism.

Though Shalt Not Kill is meant to visually represent the hypocrisy between the sentiment religious and secular doctrines have toward the sanctity of human life and the reality of how humans treat other humans. History, past and present, demonstrates that the privilege and preciousness of life only applies to those who hold power. The label "Smith & Wesson" on the knife is not meant to isolate the weapon's producer as the sole provider of killing tools, but rather it's meant to be a recognizable gun icon that could embody all similar manufacturers.

Thou Shalt not Kill
Laser engraved knife and bronze
9.5 x 8 in.

bernardo@
bernardovallarinoart
.com
bernardovallarinoart
.com
@bernardovallarinoart

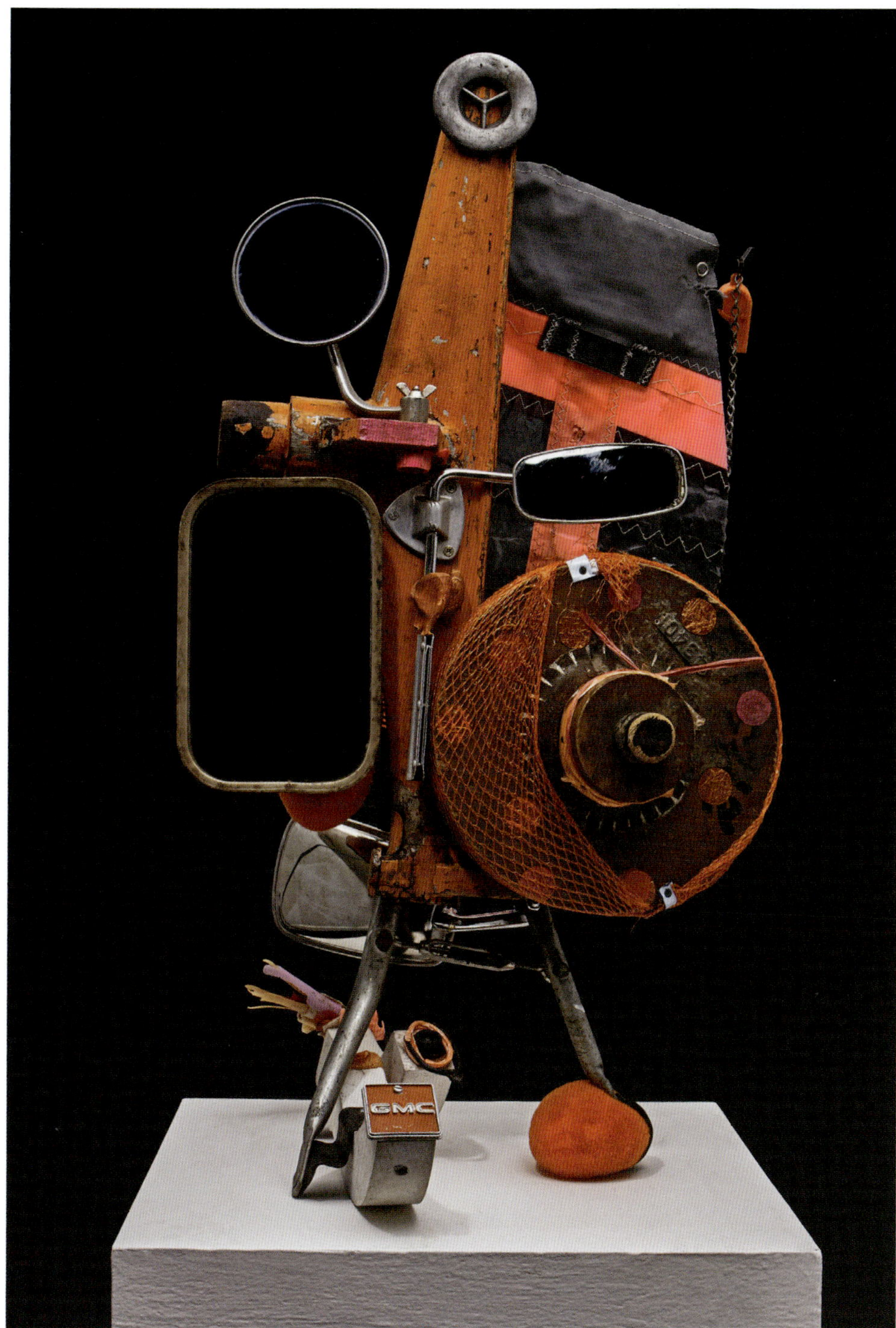

Gwen Waight

Working with found objects is an aesthetic that evokes memories and nostalgia, sometimes common or often unique to each individual viewer. There is a knowing and a genuine understanding that Gwen Waight uses to create her work. She collects specific objects that speak to her and that are part of her memories. She assembles pieces that are wholly new but strangely familiar. Recognition of everyday utilitarian objects gives a viewer a simple, perceived understanding, but when combined with each lived experience and her assemblage of varied objects, the piece becomes much more complex and layered.

"At first glance, people tend to play a sort of 'I spy' game with my work, but over time, I hope the interplay of the assembled pieces makes them want to know more," Waight says.

Plainsailing Weather
Found Object
Assemblage
32 x 20 in.

gwaightee@yahoo.com
@gwaightee

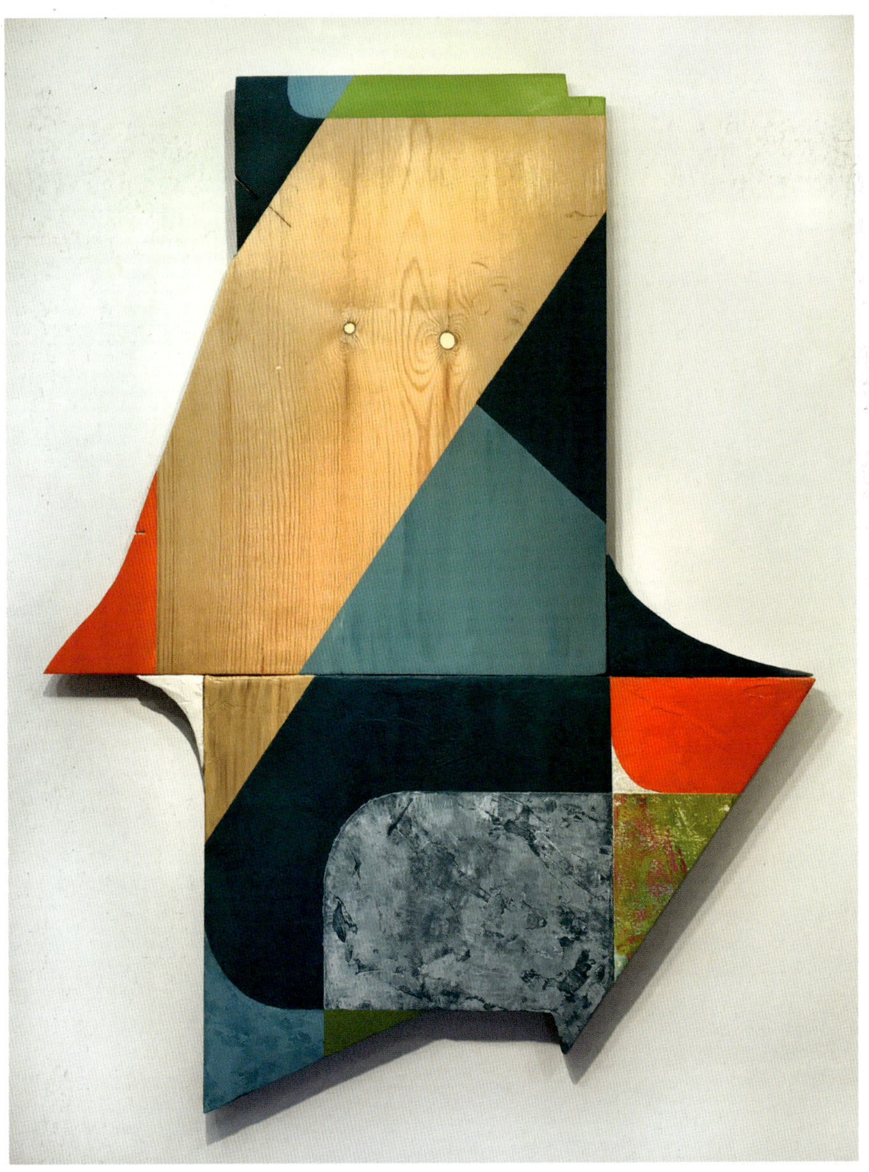

Valerie Wilcox

Valerie Wilcox is a mixed-media artist working with common and salvaged materials to present reimagined connections between our constructed environment, everyday lives, and how our brains work to piece together diverse elements. She likes to push the surreal with quirky and ambiguous shapes that hover between a two-dimensional plane and a three-dimensional structure. Often nuanced by the effects of light and shadow, her work plays with the concept of space and perception but not necessarily the reality of it.

Wilcox incorporates the ideals of *wabi-sabi* into her working process. This aesthetic is centered on the acceptance and beauty of transience and imperfection. It refers to quirks and anomalies arising from the process of construction, which add uniqueness and elegance to both natural and man-made objects. She embraces the mistakes and gives them a new life, with bits and pieces that appear as if they were casually cobbled together, off-kilter and with an imperfect resolution. This reveals her process and addresses our ideals of perfection versus inherent human fallibility.

Wilcox's *Constructs* at once become referential and whimsical, managing to transcend their base materiality as her source materials are elevated and imbued with newness of form and function.

Tinkering
Acrylic, paper-maché, plaster, foam core, salvaged wood
36.5 x 26.5 in.

vwilcox59@gmail.com
valeriewilcox.com
@valeriewilcox_art

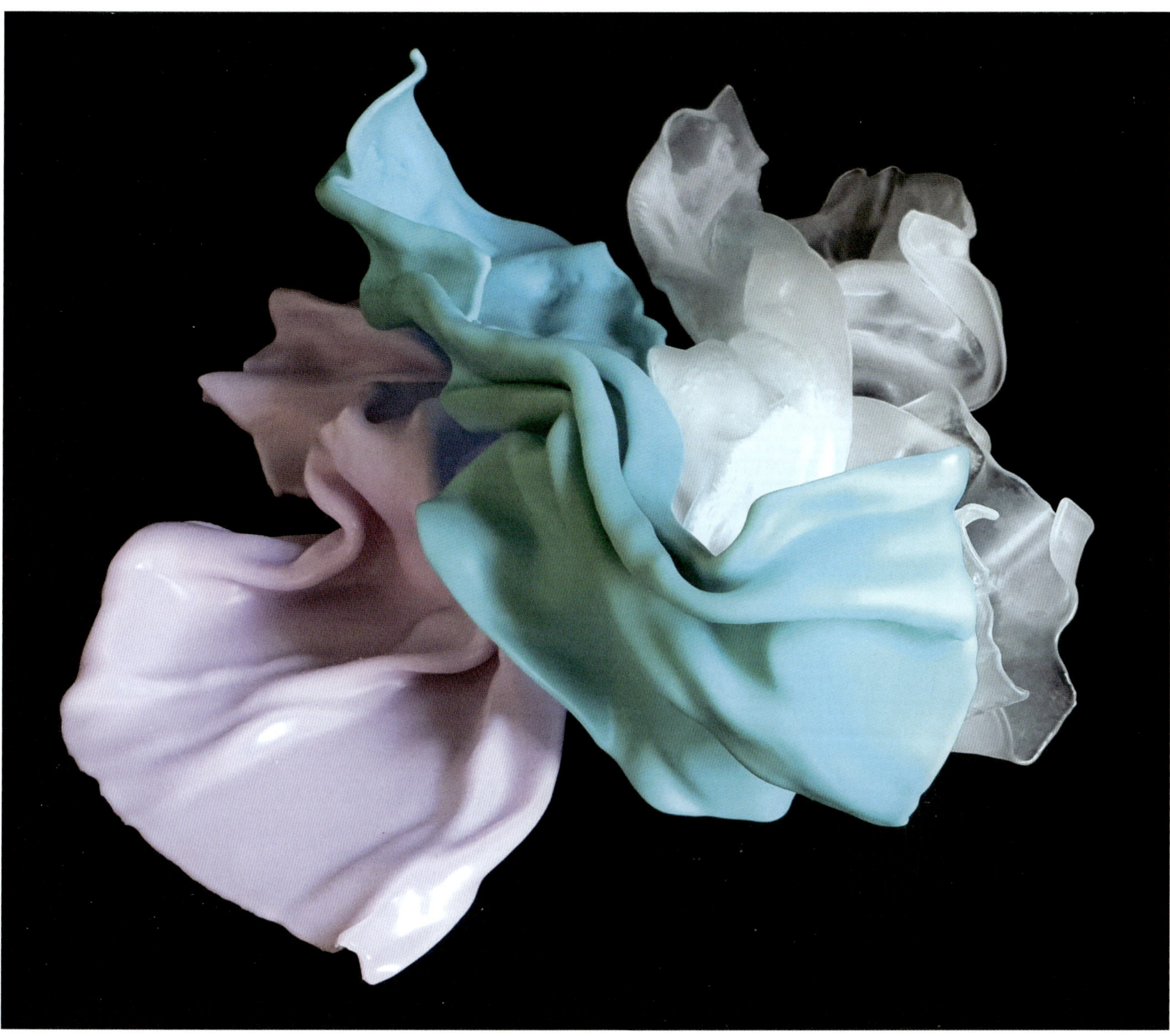

Silvia Zimerman

In her art, Silvia Zimerman likes to capture the beauty of glass. Different techniques allow her to express different ideas. She is interested in creating works that excite and touch the viewer.

"I'm enchanted by the play of light and color, the complexity of the material, and the challenge involved in creating something soft and caressing from a material so sharp and cold as glass," Zimerman says.

Zimerman's father was a tailor and passed away very young. She has a strong and beautiful memory of his workshop, including flashbacks of him seated and sewing, surrounded by fabrics. The artist now transfers those memories into the glass. "I honor his memory by creating work about fabric," Zimerman says, and her work gives the glass the qualities of softness and movement of fabric.

"For me," she say, "creating things connected with my childhood around my father is a way to keep him with me."

Fabrics
Glass - multiple foldings
19.5 x 19.5 in.

glassart@silvia-zimerman.com
@silvia-zimerman.com

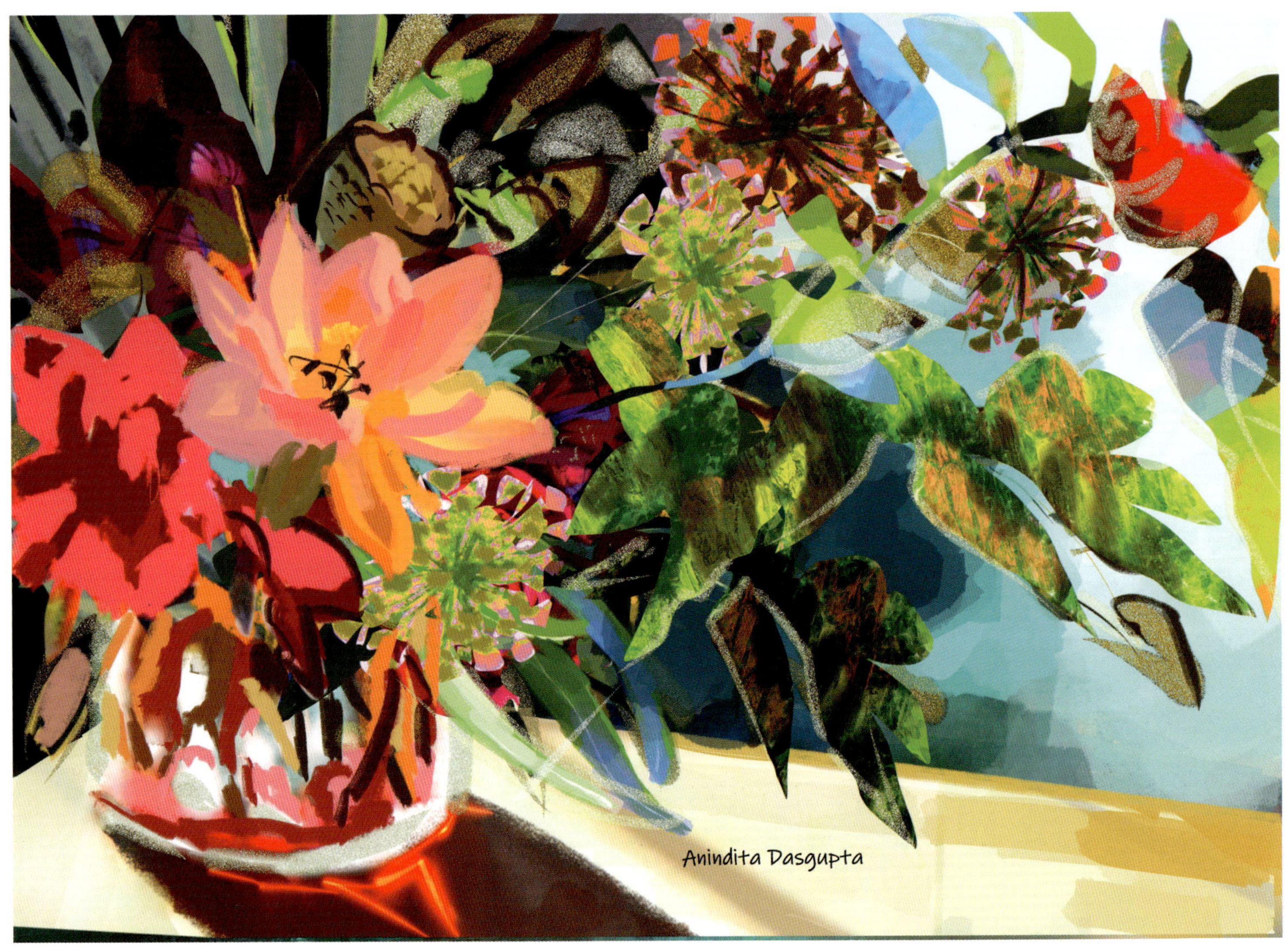

Anindita Dasgupta

A self-taught artist, Anindita Dasgupta makes abstract, intuitive, and impressionistic art. She creates energy through her art. Her work is primarily focused on the portrayal of real things but painted in a way that is outside of the realm of realism and shows how she perceives reality to be. As an artist, Dasgupta tries to find creative ways to paint flowers while learning and discovering different techniques along the way. Her love for florals has guided her through this journey so far.

As an avid traveler, Dasgupta is constantly inspired by nature and its abundant beauty. Her new landscape series explores what she sees during her travels across the United States. "My art is totally abstract and intuitive," the artist says. "I create the way I feel at a certain time yet maintain uniformity in all my creations. Right now, I am exploring and trying to reinvent this tactile medium of digital art with my creativity. I hope to spread happiness through my work. Being able to create art full time is nothing short of a dream come true for me, and so I just want to use my gift to create and express my love for all the beauty around."

Beauty in Shadows
Digital art on photo paper
20 x 30 in.

OPPOSITE
Belles Fleurs 2
Digital art on photo paper
24 x 24 in.

asguptaanindita11@gmail.com
artsywanderlust.com
@anindita.art.etc

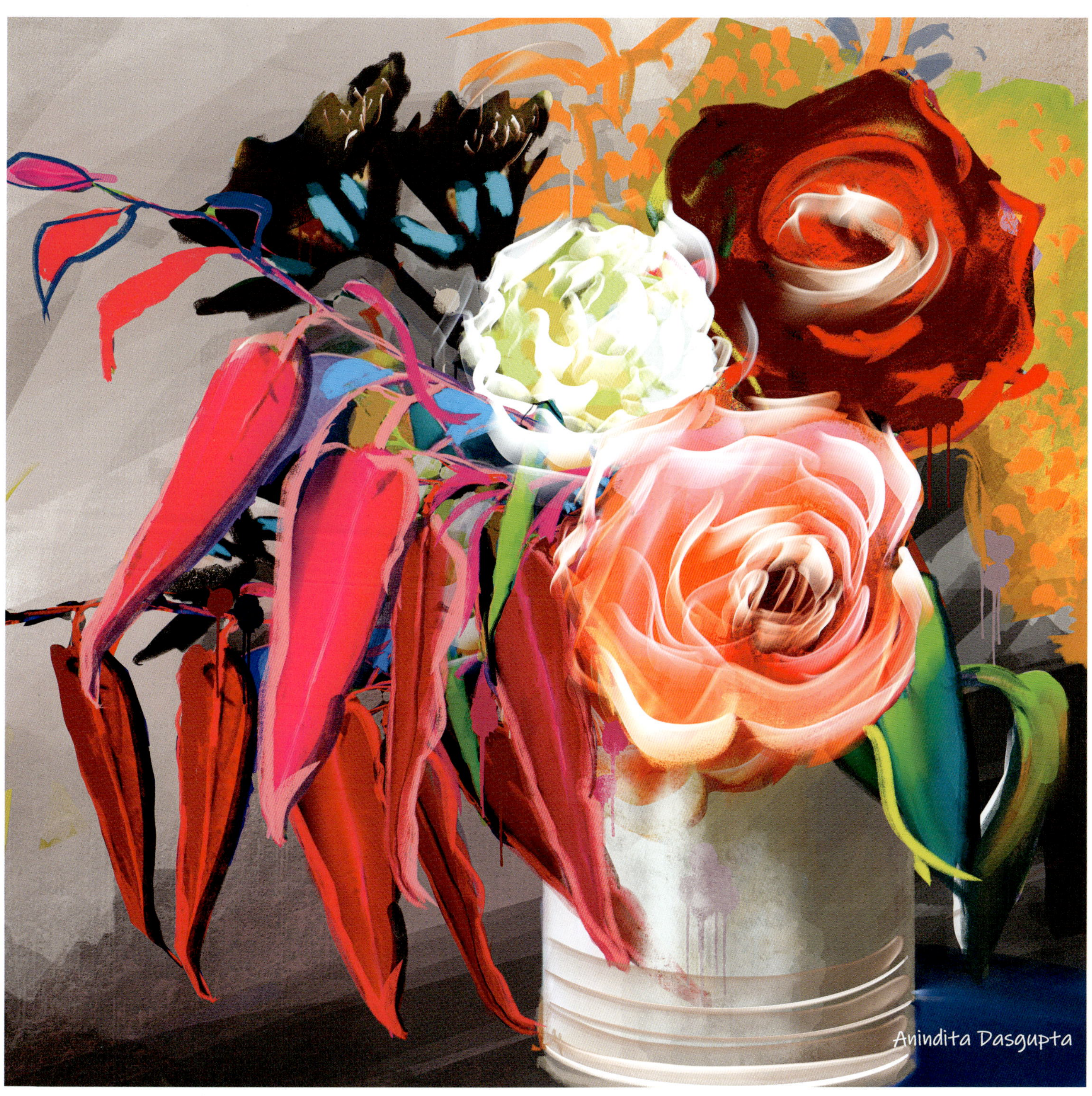
Anindita Dasgupta

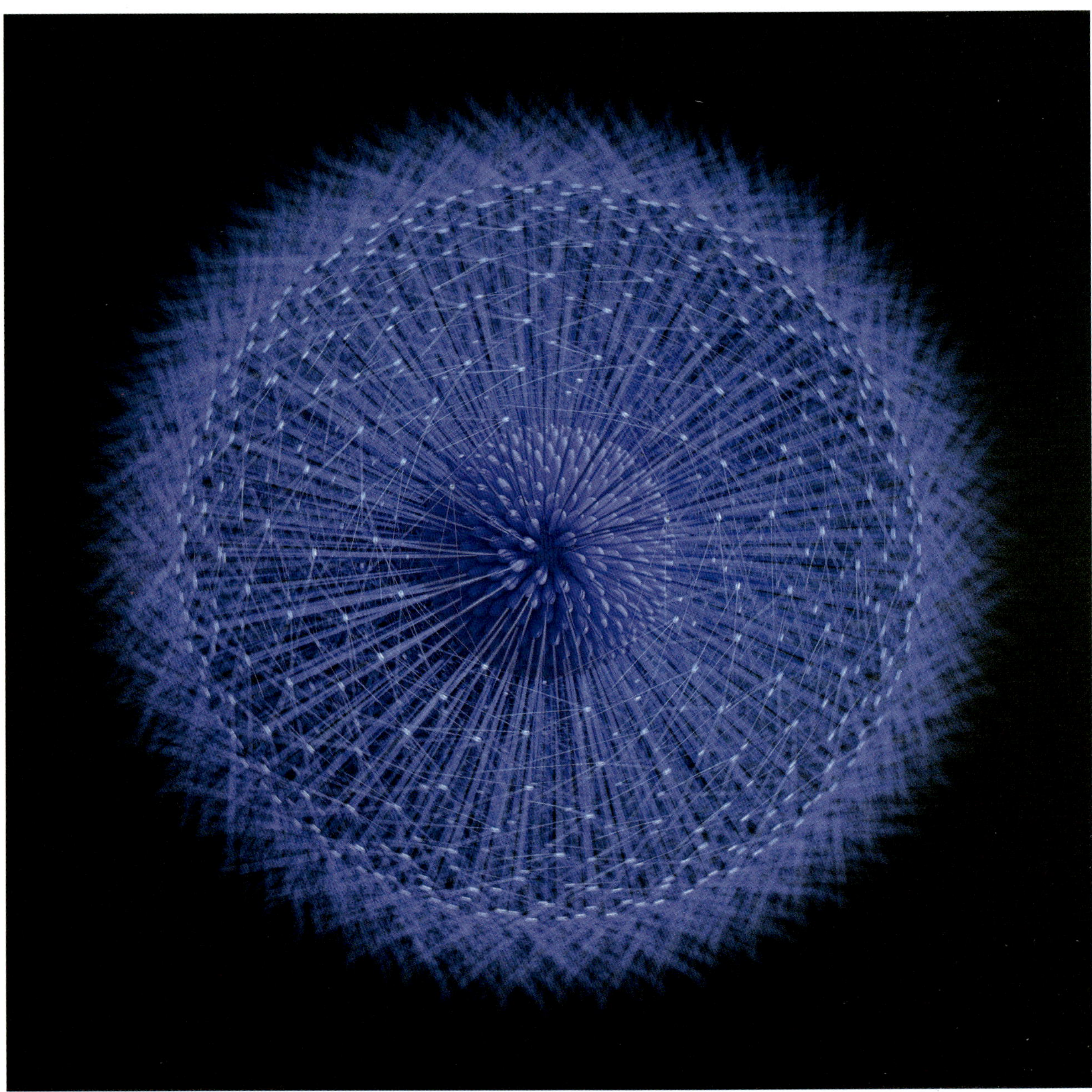

Richard Devonshire

Artists have always been among the first to reflect on the culture and technology of their time. From the 1990s to the early twenty-first century, the digital medium has undergone technological developments of unprecedented speed, moving from the "digital revolution" into the social media era.

UK-based artist Richard Devonshire utilizes cutting-edge technology to give a modern interpretation of fine art photography, painting, sculpture, and drawing. He is creating a body of work that focuses on the deeper meaning of the amazing shapes, patterns, and principles that exist in nature and the relationship with mathematics that informs us of our view of the world around us.

Devonshire's creative process involves creating textured three-dimensional models, virtual cameras, and lighting systems that mimic real-world settings and characteristics. While the work suggests a form of photorealism, its visual qualities also radically differ from that of photography and lend a heightened level of detail, implying unlimited possibilities.

Beautiful Thought
3D rendering, giclée print on smooth cotton rag paper
18 x 18 in.

Richard.Devonshire@ yahoo.com
richard-devonshire.com
@richard_devonshire_art

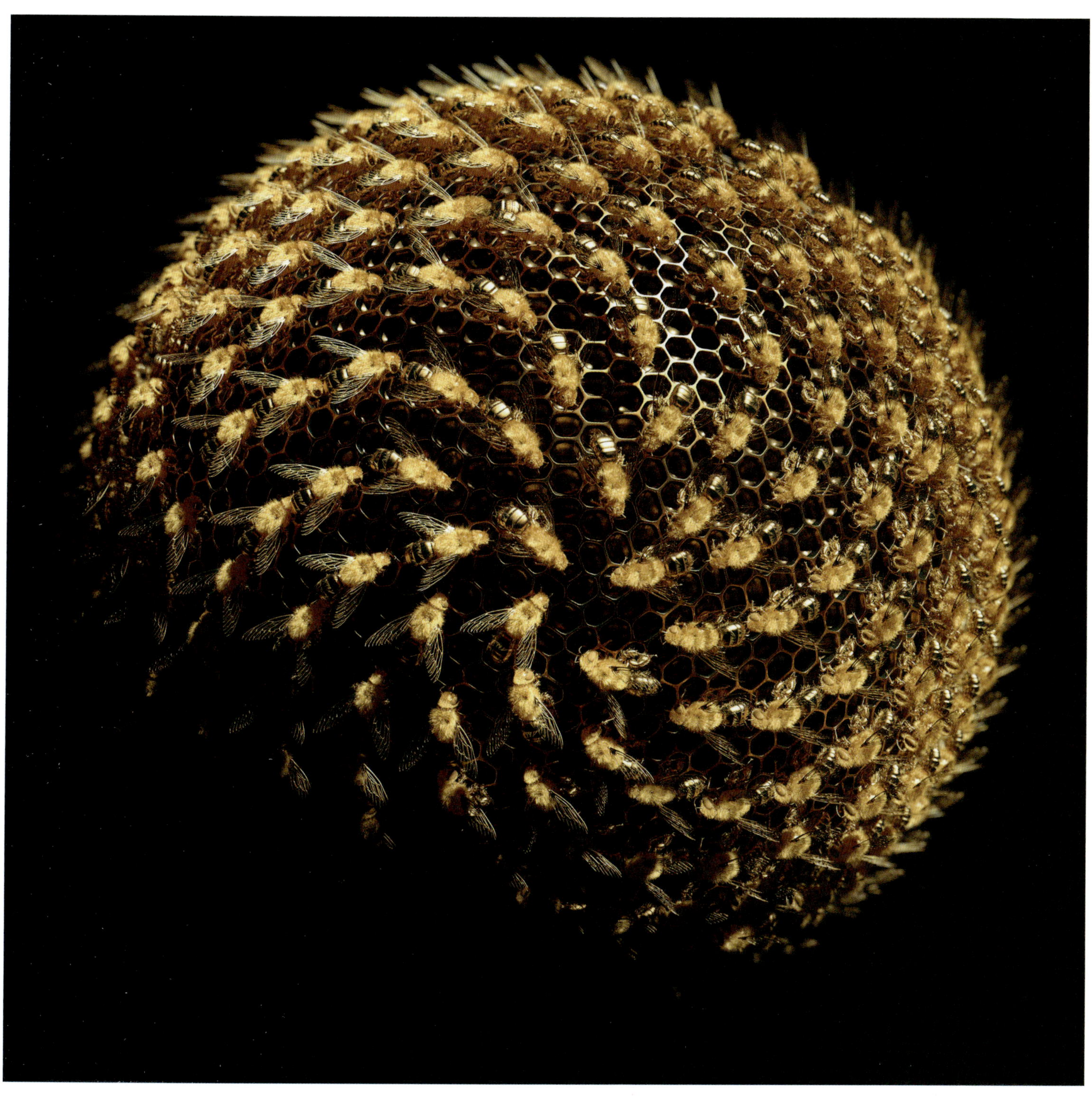

The Hive
3D rendering, giclée
print on smooth cotton
rag paper
18 x 18 in.

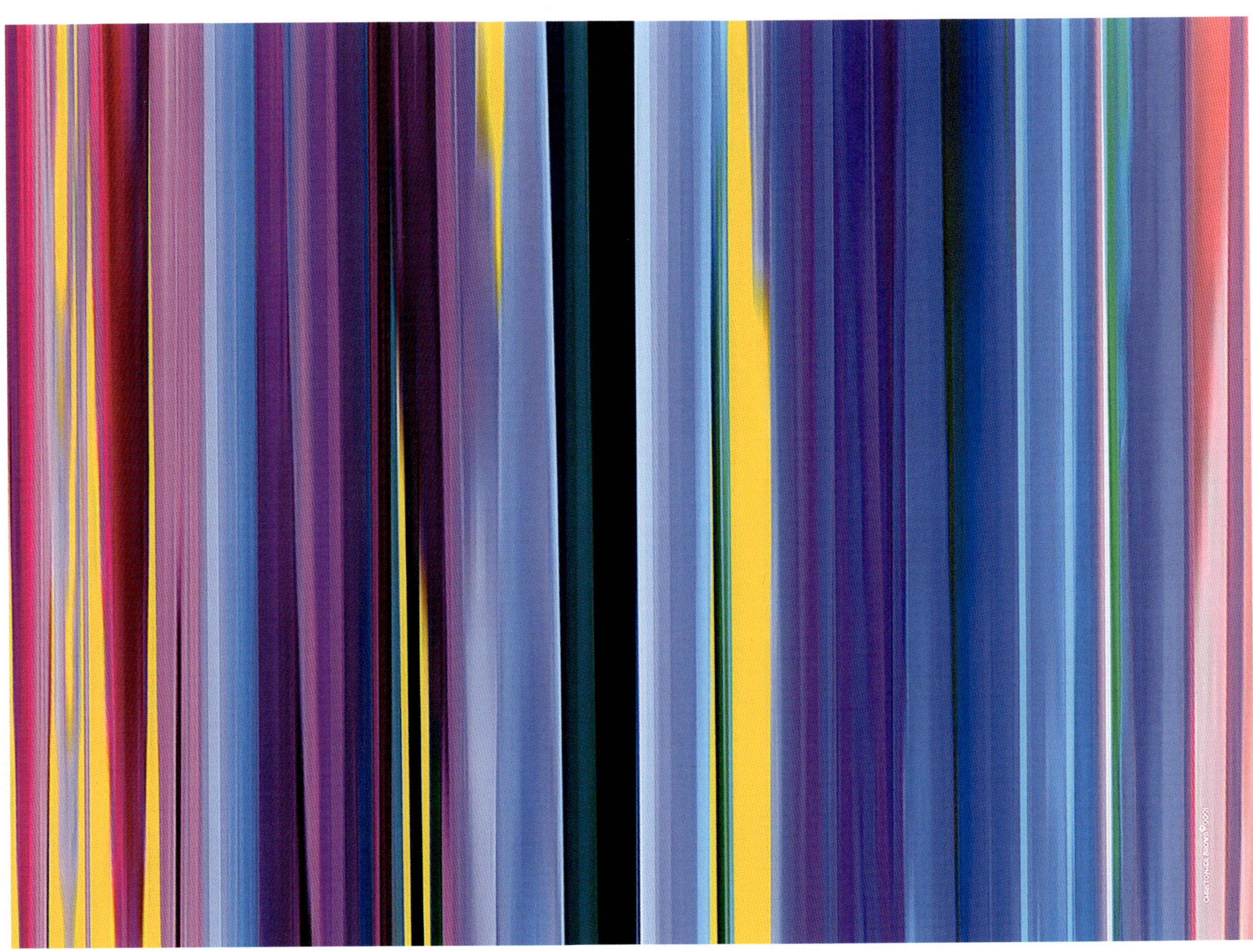

Christopher Brown

Christopher Brown is a Dallas, Texas-based artist with degrees in fine art and architecture. He creates digital abstract art that pushes the limits of color until it has a visual energy of its own. He wants to immerse the viewer with visual sensations of vibrant color.

Color is his obsession; he switched from painting to the computer in 2019 to explore ways to manipulate color. Digital technology allows for limitless experimentation of color combinations. Brown's work is a mix of photography plus abstraction plus digital media, which represents a new progression in the ever-evolving abstract art movement. It is representational but photo-manipulated with the latest in digital technology. Like a DJ that samples different types of music, Brown samples textures and colors, then dissects and reconstructs these images using photography and digital media to create compelling and surprising new abstract forms.

Color Variations
Digital
18 x 24 in.

chrisbrownartist@att.net
@christopherbrownstudio

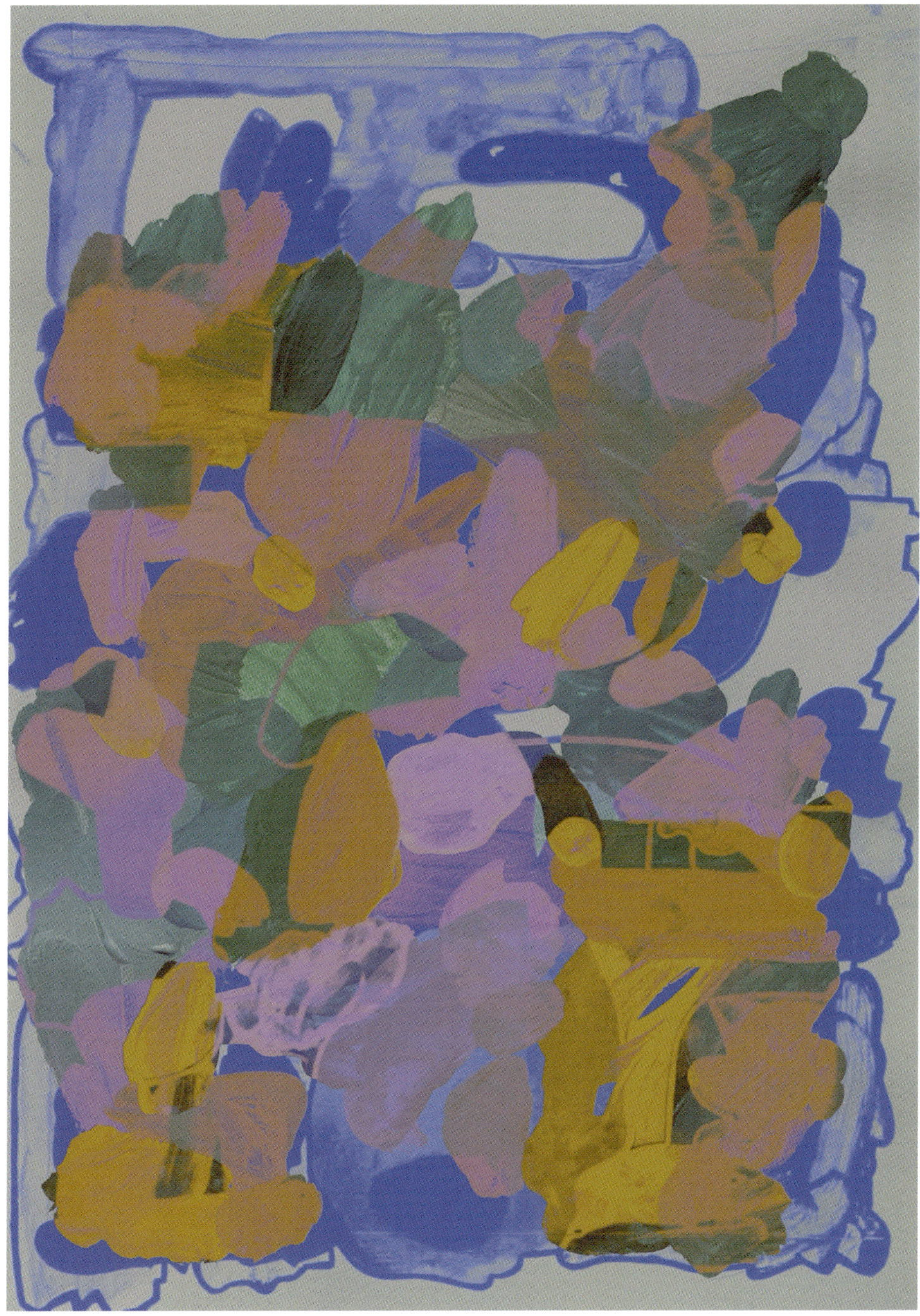

Kat Evans

Kat Evans was once told that the best way to describe herself as an artist was as an image maker. Twenty years later, Evans now prefers to introduce herself as an interdisciplinary abstract expressionist.

Evans chooses to work in many mediums, mixing paint, ink, enamel, crayon, and oil pastel onto reclaimed wood, paper, canvas, and book pages. She often abstracts the imagery she creates using digital applications in an intuitive way, building layers/trapping time.

"I work obsessively to fulfill my desire to understand the meaning of life and to create memories to leave behind," Evans says. "My obsessive behavior includes a fascination with art history. From an early age, I have meditatively chosen to absorb the image and not the blurb, as to who, what, where, and why."

Evans's artwork is a celebration of the contemporary, a fascination with what's next, and a time capsule of the marks she has made, others have made on her, and the irrelevance as to why.

Tangled Up In Blue
Mixed media and digital composition
8.25 x 6 in.

ktheo2010@gmail.com
katevans.art
@kat_evans_artist

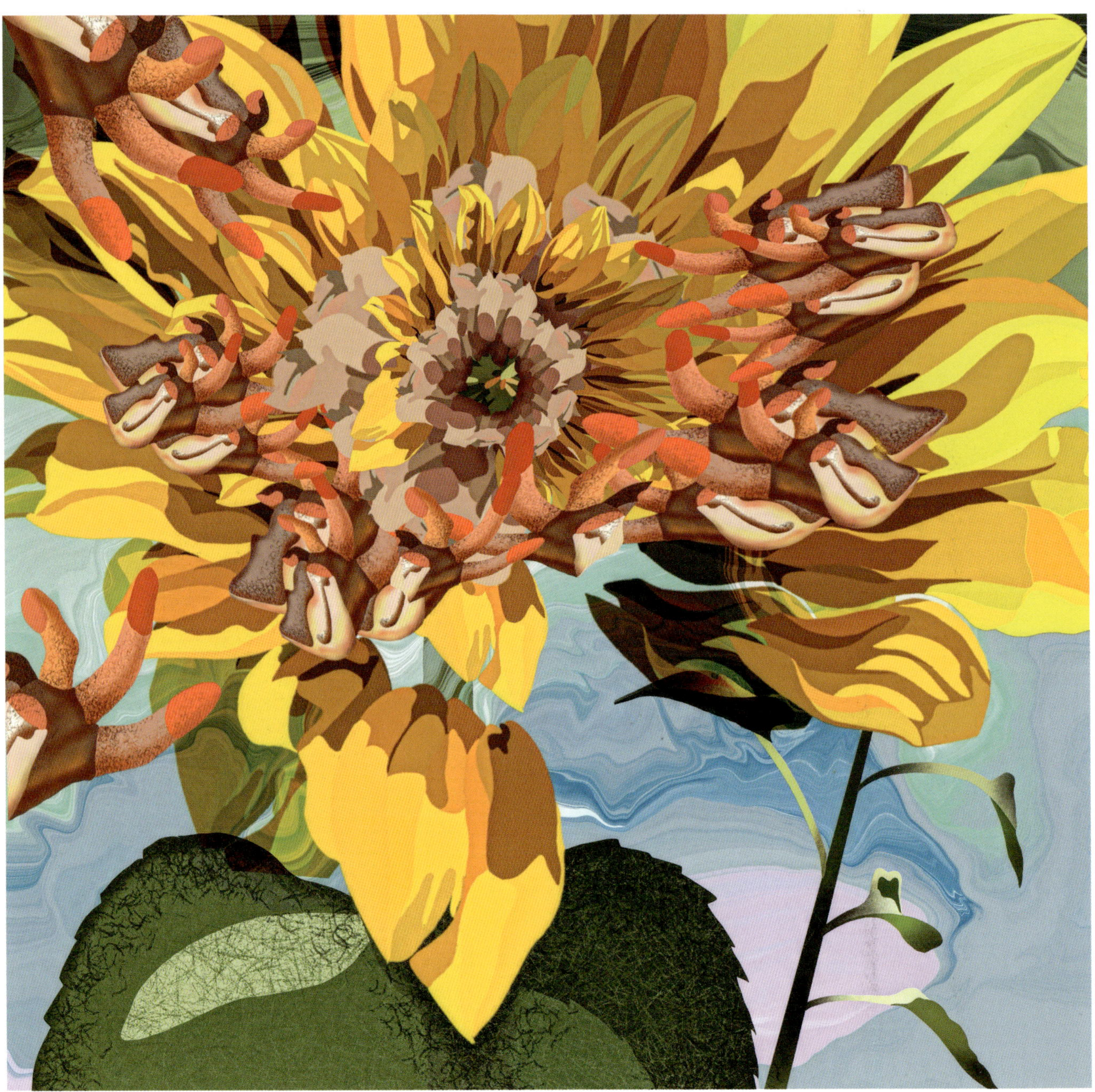

Jenny Jiyoung Han
Driven by curiosity, Jenny Jiyoung Han poses the question of how societies construct their original functionality in creative domains. Han, a multidisciplinary visual artist, has gained international recognition from gallery representation since the summer of 2020, when the COVID-19 pandemic hit across the world.

Currently, she works by taking some whimsical abstract figures and cartoon-based illustrated resources into one particular two-dimensional format and then reformatting the subjective images, remaining equivocal resemblances, and familiar symbols. Her adoration of the sunflower became her loveable symbol of creation.

Every piece of Han's artwork has been created as a range of sunflower series that explain her personal depiction of the human story. The sunflower represents multiple creations that contain the whole validity of what it means to be human beyond what the eyes see.

Life Expansion
Digital painting
15.75 x 15.75 in.

jenjiyoung09@gmail
.com
jenny-jiyoung-Han
.format.com
@jennyjiyounghan

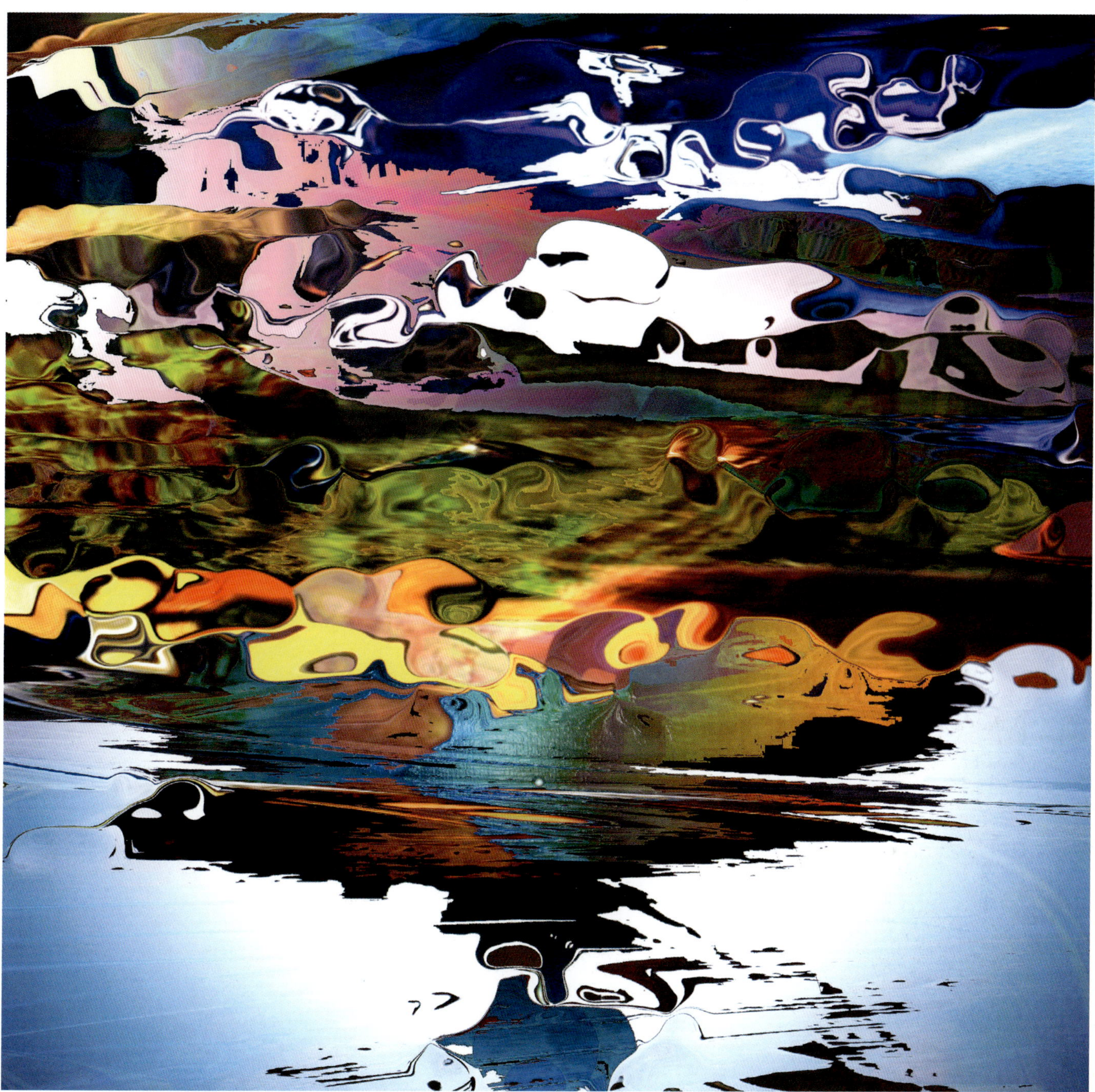

Pierre-Hugues Hétu

Artist Pierre-Hugues Hétu, aka Puguess, evolves constantly—changing and moving other directions, and always questioning his art. This is what allows his art to be expressive, eventful, exploratory. The original touch of the artist is everywhere in his works. From curves to straight lines, from rough textures to smooth surfaces like glass, Puguess's works lead to exploration; we see what we want and interpret what we see according to our state of mind. This is the strength of the abstract: to allow the observer to see for himself what his heart or his head dictates according to the moment.

Un dégradé des plus cosmiques
Oeuvre lumineuse
40 x 40 in.

puguess@gmail.com
puguess.com
@puguess

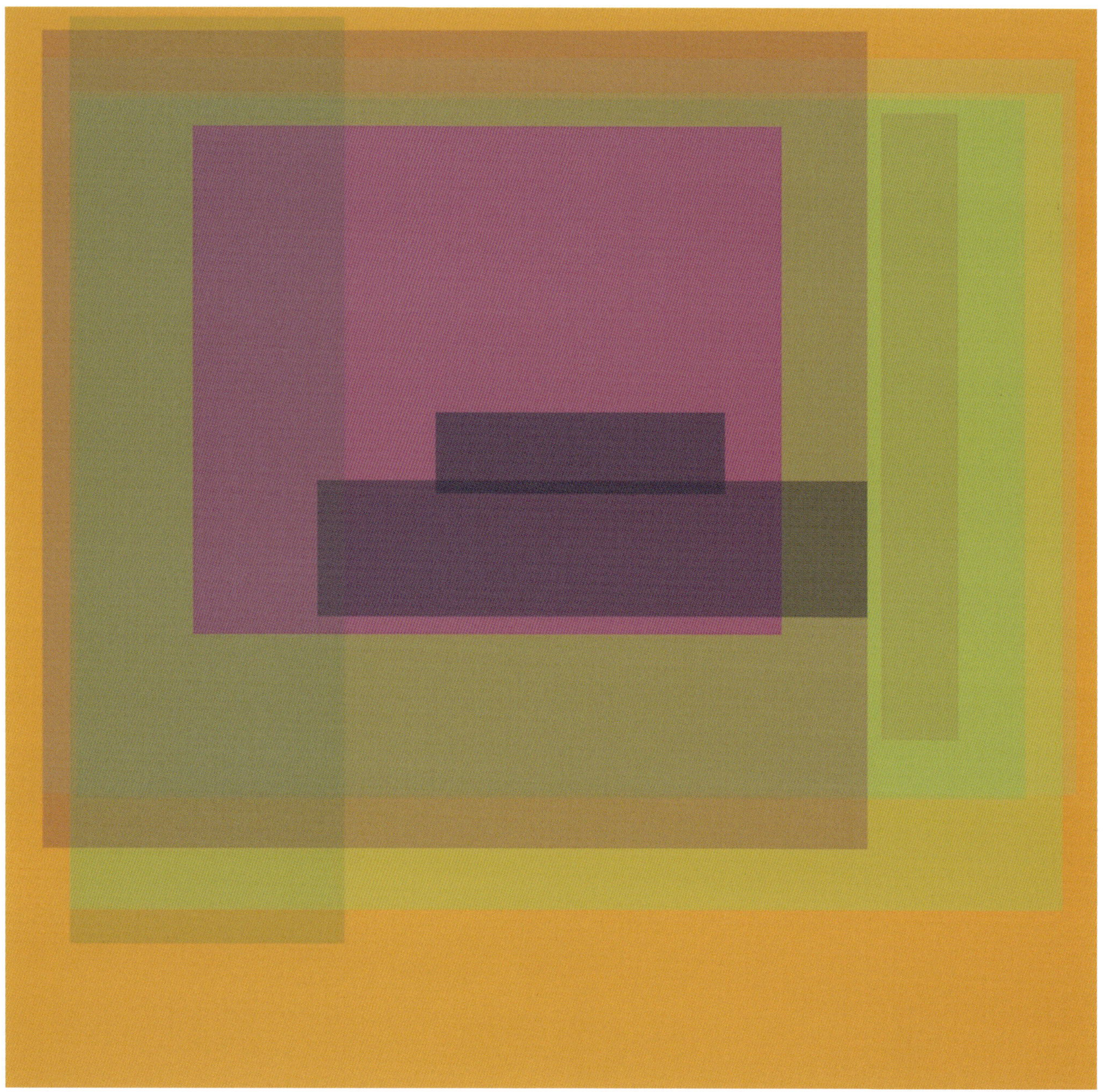

Tyler N. Horton

Tyler N. Horton's art explores the themes of purpose and meaning and whether these things even exist in what we see, hear, and feel. His work is meant to reflect on whether anything has meaning, whether there is a reason behind any given occurrence, and whether life and its many events are all just unavoidable happenstance. The main aspect of life on which his art intends to focus is the interactions with others. Horton's art is based on asking questions such as: What is our relation to other beings? Why is it significant? Was the interaction meant to happen or is it a product of sheer coincidence? What is next for this interaction? What other interactions will occur? His art does not reveal any answers to these inquiries, but it offers the idea that there may not be any attainable answers and to continue searching for them would prove futile.

Quadrilateral Gathering 002
Processing
2000 x 2000 px

tnhforum@gmail.com
tnhortonforum.com
@tnhortonart

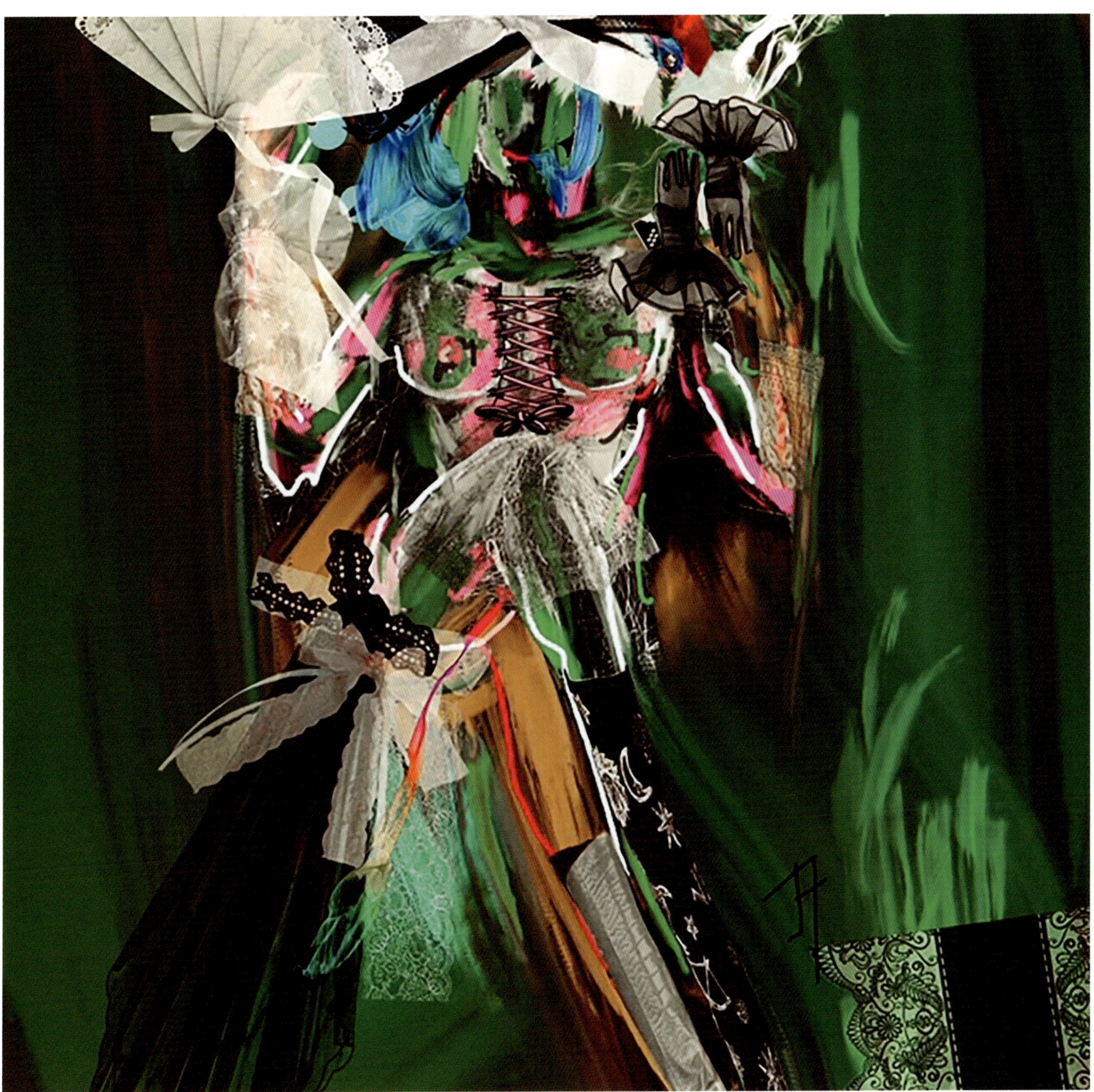

Joanne Huxford

Joanne Huxford began her art career two years ago at sixty-six years young. Some would call her a late bloomer. She works in many styles of art, from traditional and abstract to street art and digital art, and with different mediums. Digital art gave Huxford the feeling of the darkroom experience.

"My art mixes a certain feeling of fantasy and surrealism," Huxford says. "I began in the most traditional sense with watercolor, acrylics, and pastels. As I began art, my sense of freedom from the everyday mundane began to emerge. At first, I played with color strokes, the playful aspects of art."

Huxford's earlier works were symbols of what she loves: flowers, sailboats, oceans. As time went on, the artist experimented with color and abstraction. "I believe my art goes beyond the everyday mundane to bring a sense of joy, color, movement, and freedom to the observer. My work has a certain edge to it, perhaps from a life replete with loss and certain tragedy."

Victoria
Mixed media
14 x 11 in.

jkhuxford@gmail.com
@jojohuxford2

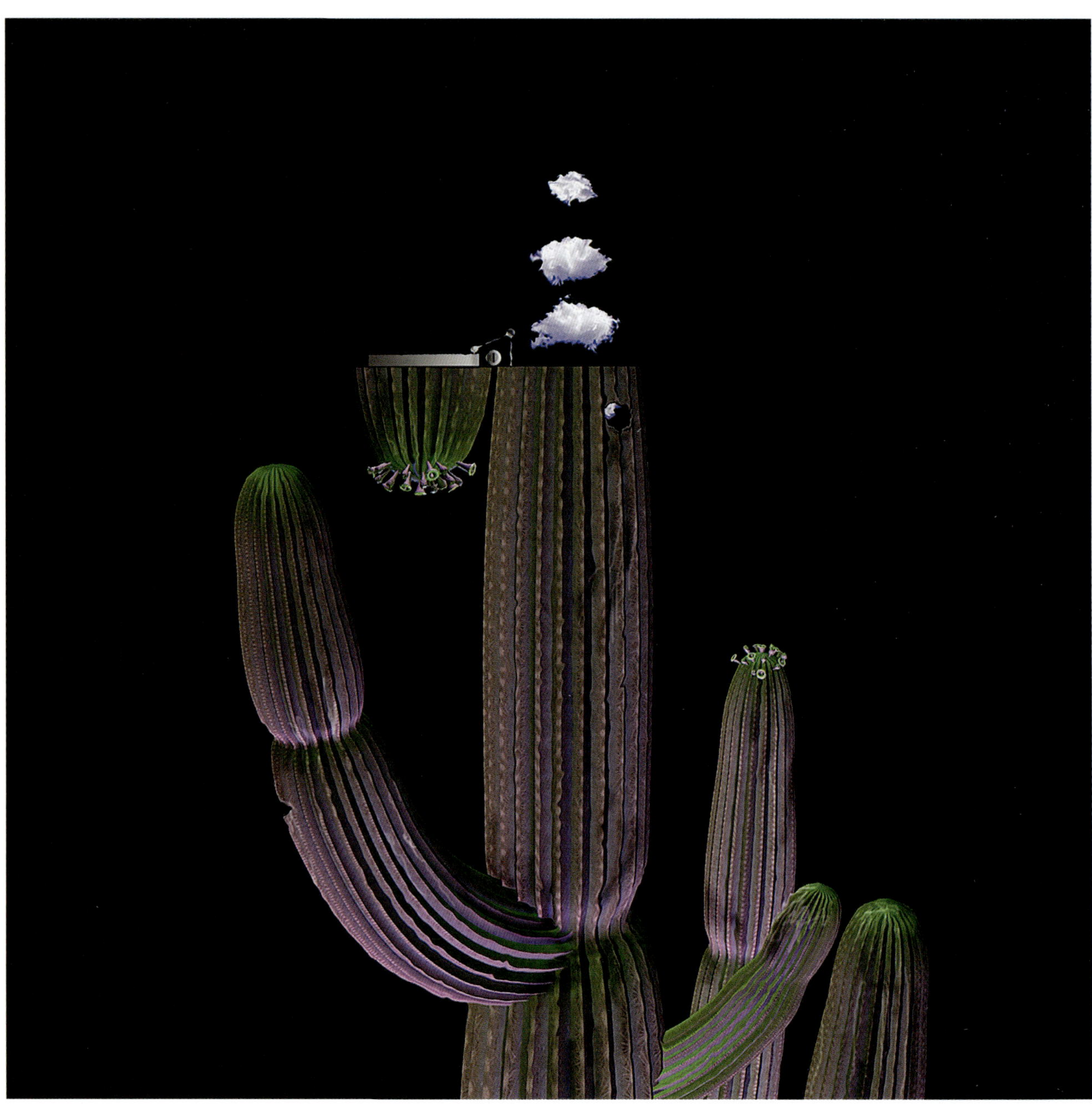

Lawrence Lee

It has taken fifty years for Lawrence Lee to finally understand one basic truth about all art: People get out of art what they bring to it. "No matter what an artist is trying to communicate through a work, it will always be perceived through the life-lens of the observer," Lee says. "Everything they have ever seen or done has created a filter through which they now experience life—and art. So, each person experiences a work of art differently, and it is as though some art can create a door where no door had been. If the art resonates through the life-lens of the viewer, that door will open, leading not out to some alien place, but inward: to self. And when a person is fortunate enough to experience a resonant piece of art and to open that amazing door, there is no end to what they can learn about themselves."

Thus, Lee creates art for himself. The viewer will not see what he, as the artist, created in the same way that he does. Even so, his creations might open a door within the viewer.

Steamer
Digital
Variable

lawrence@
lawrenceleeart.com
@lawrenceleeart.com

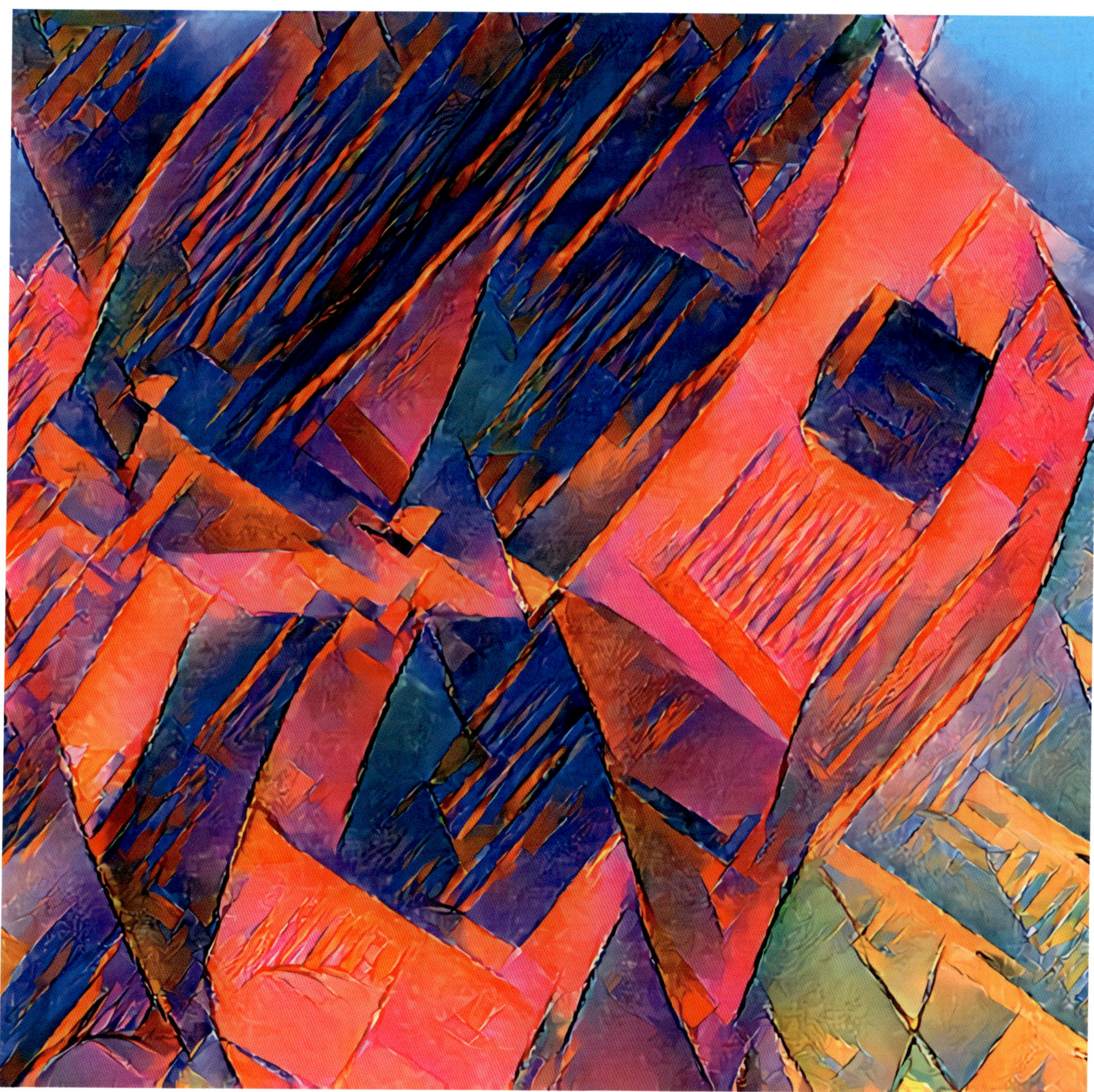

Michael Pierre Price

"Our universe is so much grander than we realize. We go about our daily lives within a very limited range of existence that too often hinders our appreciation for the fractal-like tapestry of the abstract reality beyond our senses. To truly understand the universe, as well as ourselves, we need a profound shift away from the narrow and skewed perspective of old notions," artist Michael Pierre Price says.

Price's artwork presents just such a shift, integrating elements of chaos theory, quantum mechanics, cosmology, neuroscience, and dreams, along with Indigenous and Buddhist wisdom, into a cohesive artistic framework.

Price's pixels are his Lascaux; animals on cave walls are now neural network-induced marks deciphering modern physics. His art is about contemplation, seeing our humanity in the abstract and surreal beauty of a universe too often beyond our imagination. A beauty found in supercollider collisions, a crawling ant, and a spiral galaxy.

Complex Manifold In Red
Archival pigment print
22 x 22 in.

michael@
michaelpierreprice.com
michaelpierreprice.com
@mpp_digital_art

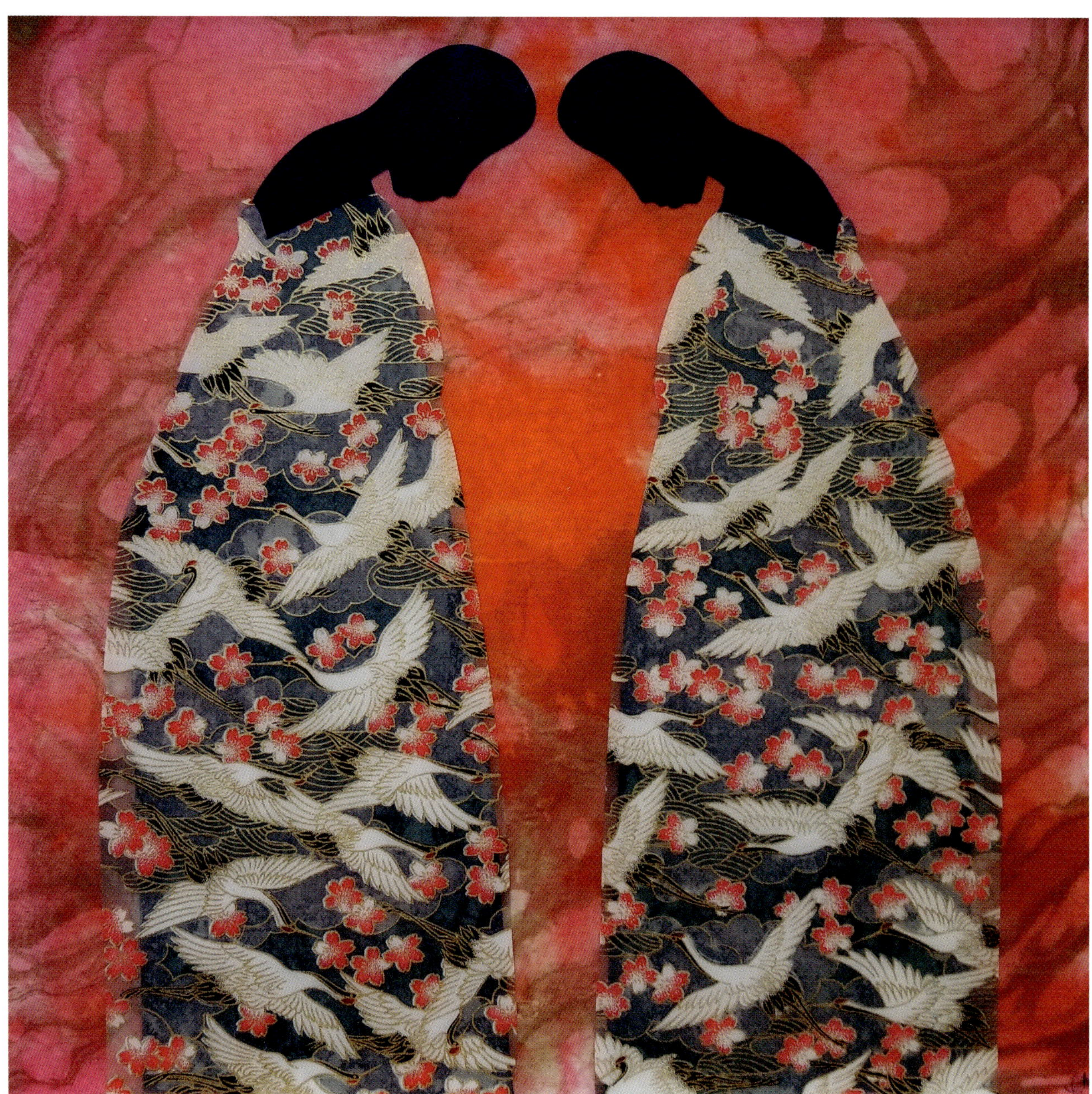

Tracy Murrell

Tracy Murrell's work is a celebration of the beauty and grace that she sees in the female form. Her intent is for the viewer to slow down, take their time, and find their connection to the portraits before them. Often, the reflective surfaces of the work invite the viewer to see themselves in the silhouettes.

As a woman of color, Murrell is drawn to images of women that look like her, and it is their silhouettes that are of particular interest to the artist. "I see and feel the poise and energy we exhibit in the world, which is so often commodified in popular media. In response to this, I offer counter symbols of women as figures personifying grace and strength," Murrell says.

In her work, Murrell explores the use of silhouettes by recontextualizing images from popular culture to use as entry points for deeper conversations on gender, race, and the perception of beauty. In her current body of work, Murrell focuses on themes of identity, migration, and displacement in the human narrative by collaging hand-cut patterns, encaustic, and specialty papers with the silhouettes, which she then finishes with resin.

Sumaya, On Their Wings We Will Fly
High gloss enamel, chiyogami papers, marbled paper and resin
12 x 12 in

tmurrellart@gmail.com
tracymurrell.com
@tracymurrellart

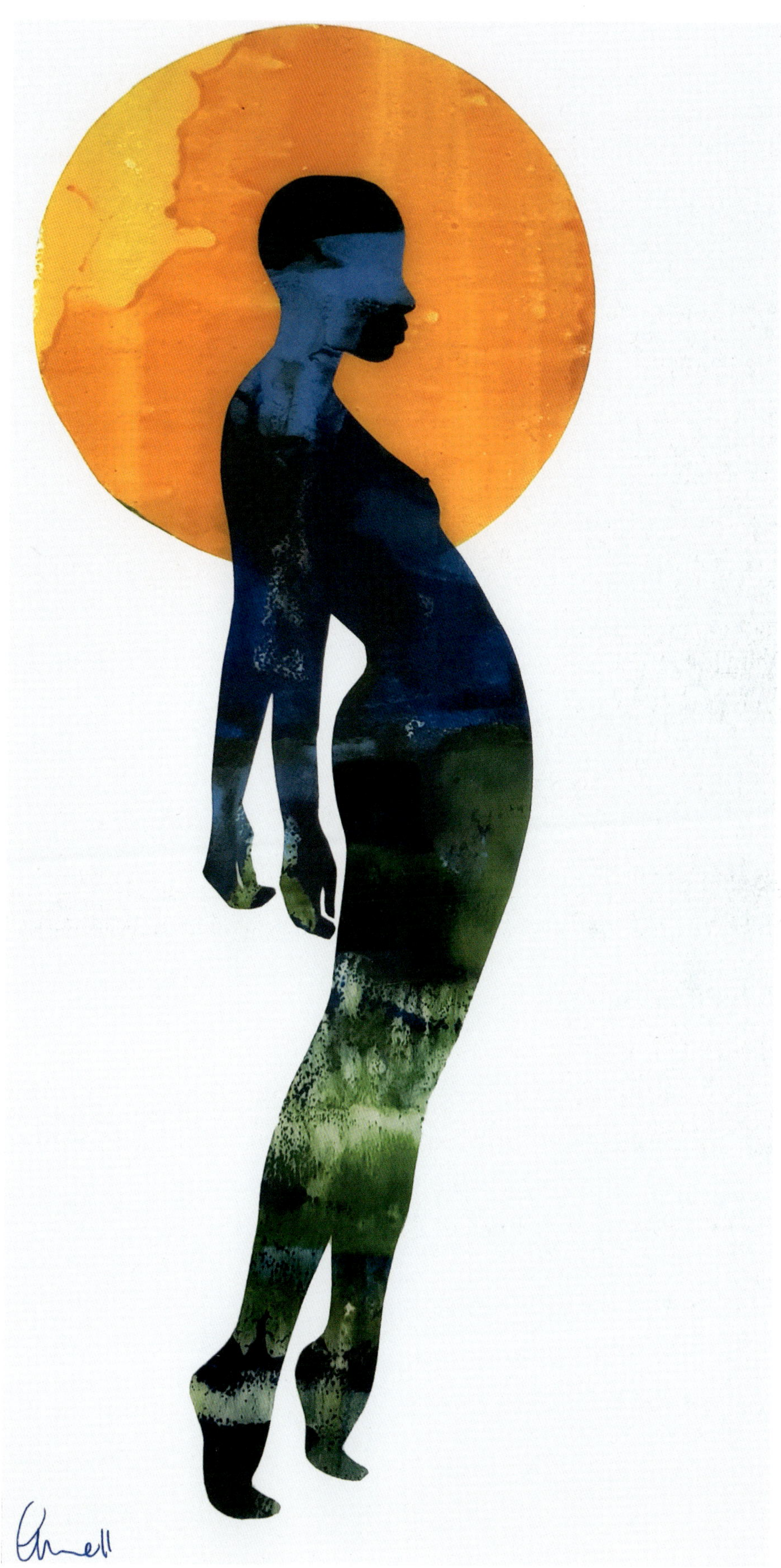

Surrender I, Consciously Opening Myself to Grace
Encaustic rice paper and resin
24 x 12 in.

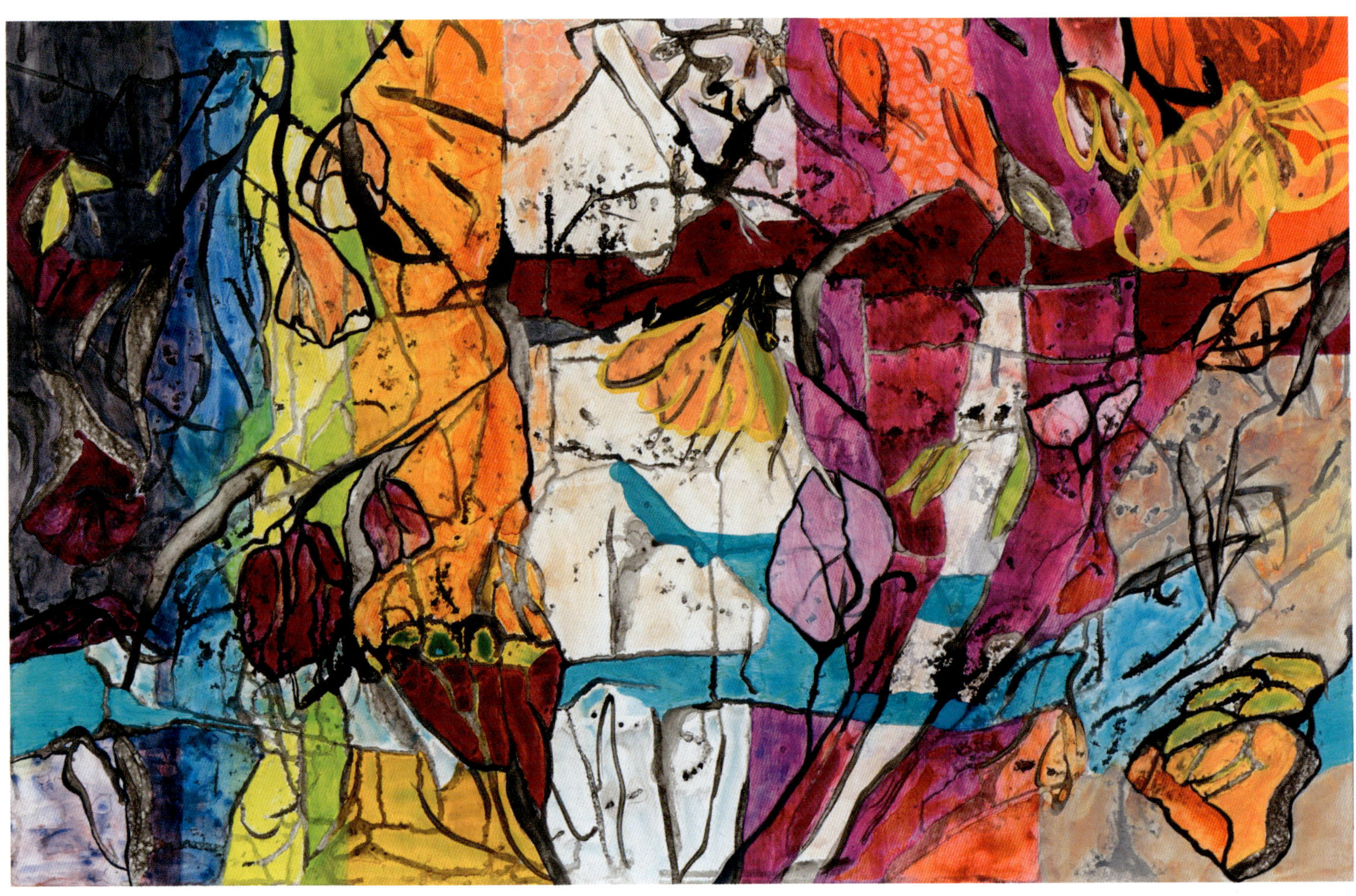

Julie England

Julie England's paintings are experiences of outdoor places from observation, memories, or imagination. During 2020 and the global pandemic, we spent more time outside, seeking safety and connection with neighbors to overcome isolation. Outdoor rooms in front yards, backyards, or the street were our gathering places. We heard about isolation from loved ones, job loss, stress from working at home and schooling at home.

Being outdoors can be a link to childhood. England was raised on a rural Wisconsin pine tree farm, where trees beckoned to her as imaginary childhood friends. Her connection to outdoor energy is comforting, like being with family.

England paints with natural, organic imagery as her focus, followed by mark-making and use of material transparencies. Her work includes botanical forms and gestures, using color as a vehicle to convey energy from nature. England creates images of imaginary botanical environments, inviting viewers to visit.

Mary's Trumpet Vines and Blooms
Ink, watercolor and oil on Yupo paper
26 x 40 in.

julie@julieenglandart
.com
julieenglandart.com
@julieenglandart

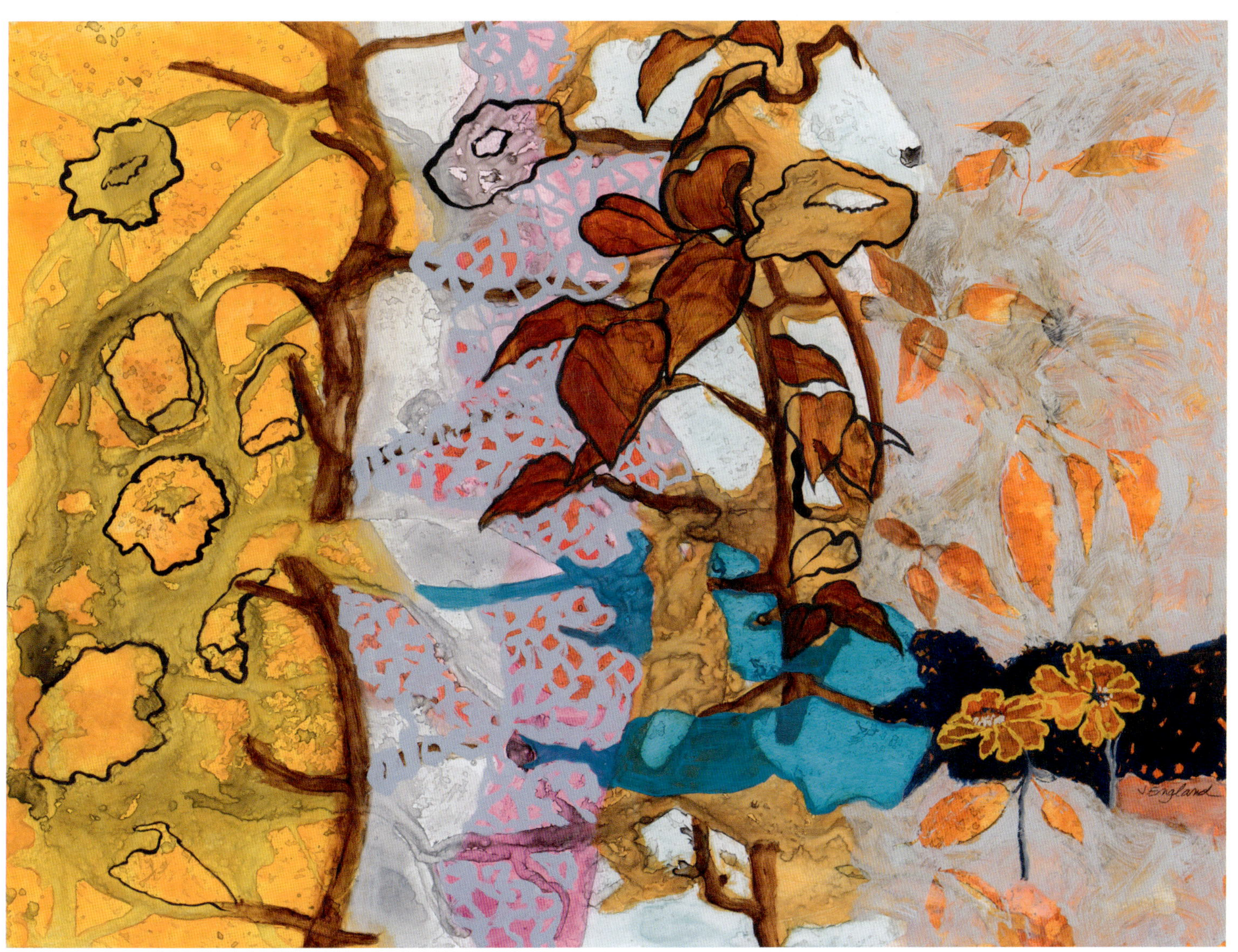

Summer Leaves 3
Ink, watercolor and oil on
Yupo paper
20 x 26 in.

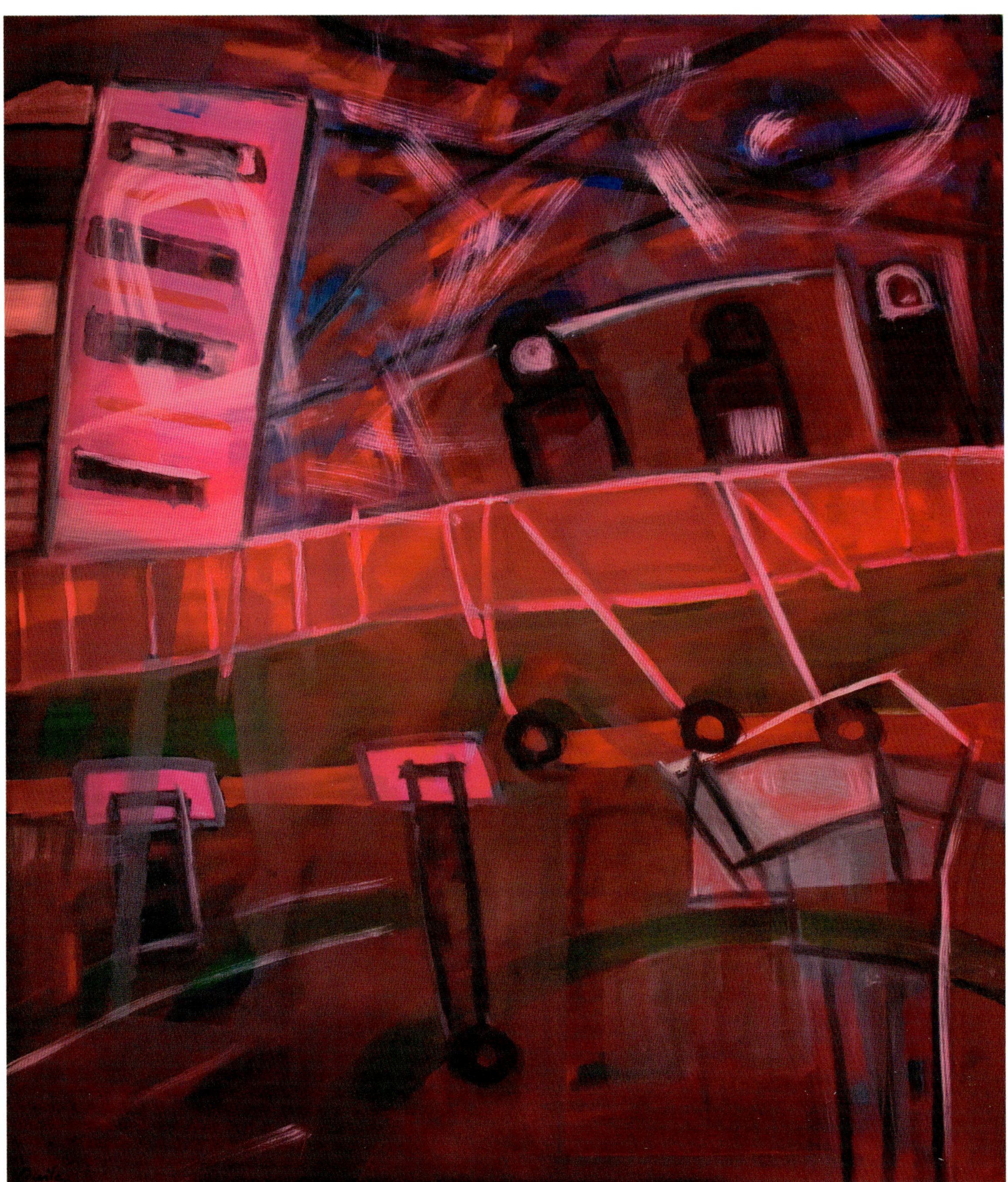

Gaby Avila

Gaby Avila is a Mexican artist. Her relationship with art started at a young age. She used to sneak into her uncle's office and spend countless hours analyzing all the art material she could get her hands on.

Her projects start by using photography to capture the objects that later will be put on canvas or paper. Throughout time, her art has adopted a personal language that is reflected in all the different themes she works on.

Recently, her work has evolved around urban art, interpreted in her own personal style and in the way she perceives her surroundings. Each place represents an opportunity to capture the scenery, energy, and emotion through her personal perspective. There are always beautiful things around that she wants to share with others.

She hopes that every piece can bring joy to people in the same way that she enjoys creating art.

Bridge at the Park
Mixed media
47 x 39 in.

gabyavila2401@gmail
.com
@gabyavilasanchez

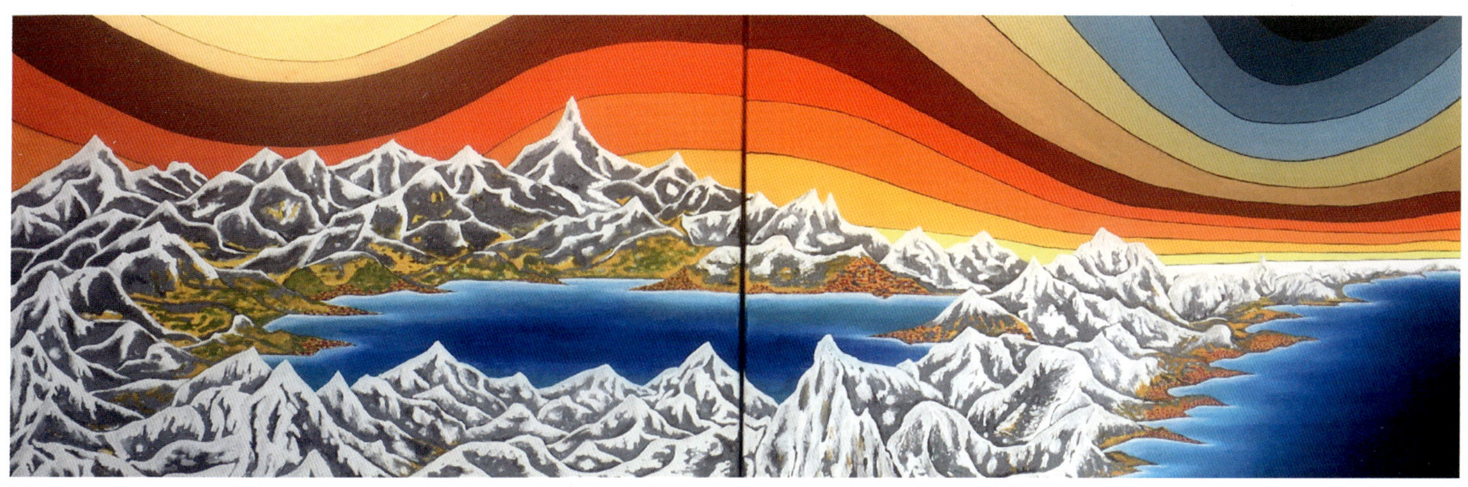

Franco Baldazzi

Franco Baldazzi expresses himself with strong and contrasting colors, using phosphorescent enamels and acrylics. His particular creative vein pushes him to use, as pictorial supports, heterogeneous tools and materials of everyday use: plywood, fabrics, polymers, plaster. His latest creations have as their subject human figures and landscapes in unnatural colors. Behind this group of works is hidden research toward the knowledge of the mystery of life and ultimately of the most impalpable and mysterious chords of the human soul. The brush responds only to the language of the soul, translating into lines and shapes with vibrant textures in which art becomes a mirror of the spirit. The artist succeeds, through painting, to give a soul to his emotional perceptions, to make tangible his fears and his intimate, dreamlike visions. The genesis of the work thus becomes a cathartic process of liberation and purification of his own states of mind.

Immaginazione
Acrily and enamel
27.5 x 78.75 in.

frabaldo69@gmail.com
francobaldazzi.com
@francobaldazzi

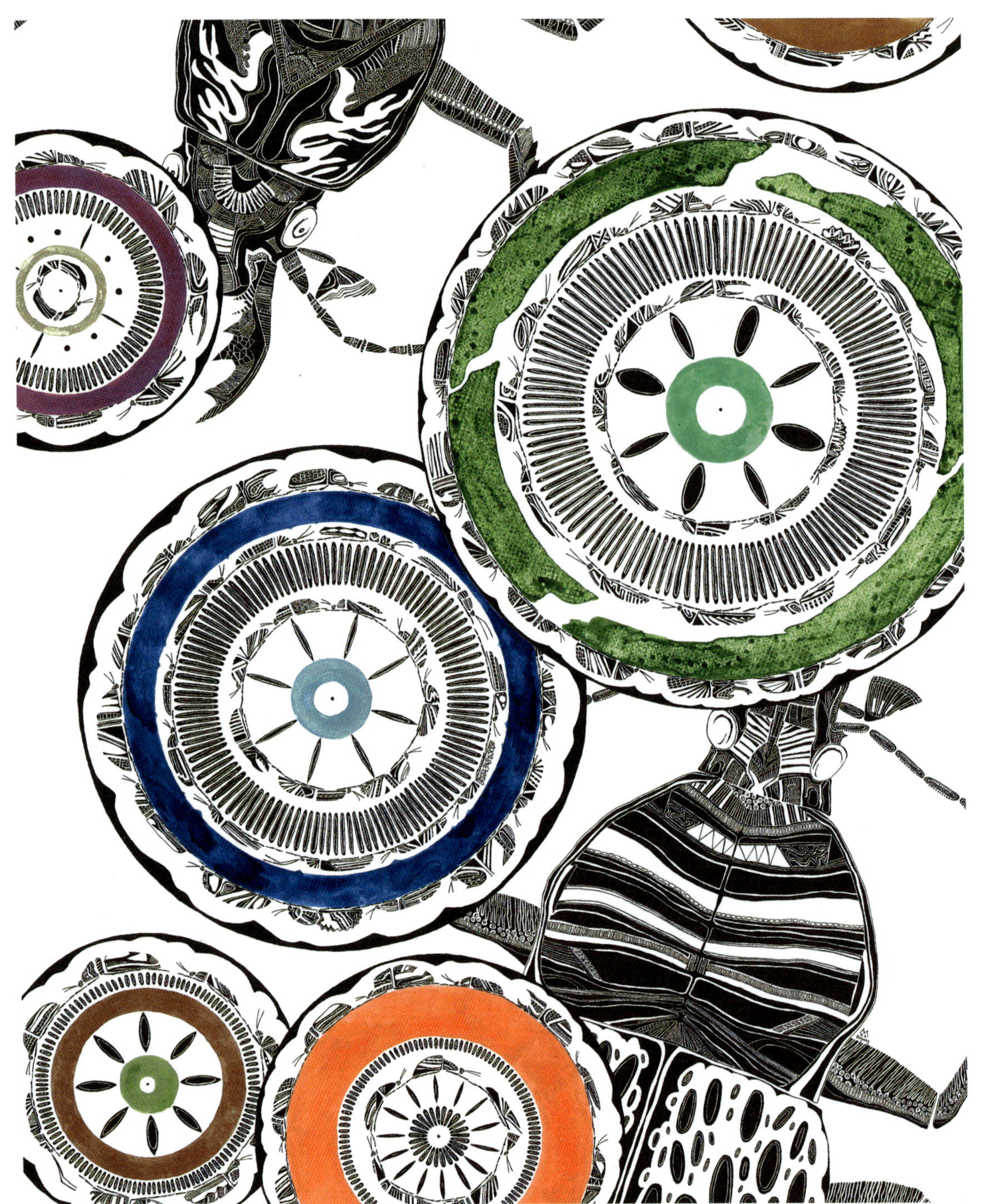

Max Boyang

As Max Boyang has grown older, he has found that his views and values have altered. From a pursuit of success in spite of personal reflection, Boyang found himself trapped in an endless loop, a swallowing pit that enveloped his thoughts and poisoned his motivation. From these times, he found meaning not in the comforts of his own self-detained bonds but beyond that. Meaning in a more raw art form, in objectivity.

"I've felt the swelling in my chest, the touch of pride in success," Boyang says. "I've seen the effects that have come from art as an expression, and I have seen the lasting impacts that it has had, even when the vestiges of its outline are long gone. I create not in the hopes of tracing its shape, but in making my own, slightly dented, fraying patchwork."

Bug Wheel
Quill pen and ink with watercolor on paper
24 x 19 in.

boyangtwins@gmail.com
boyangtwins.com
@boyang_twins_art

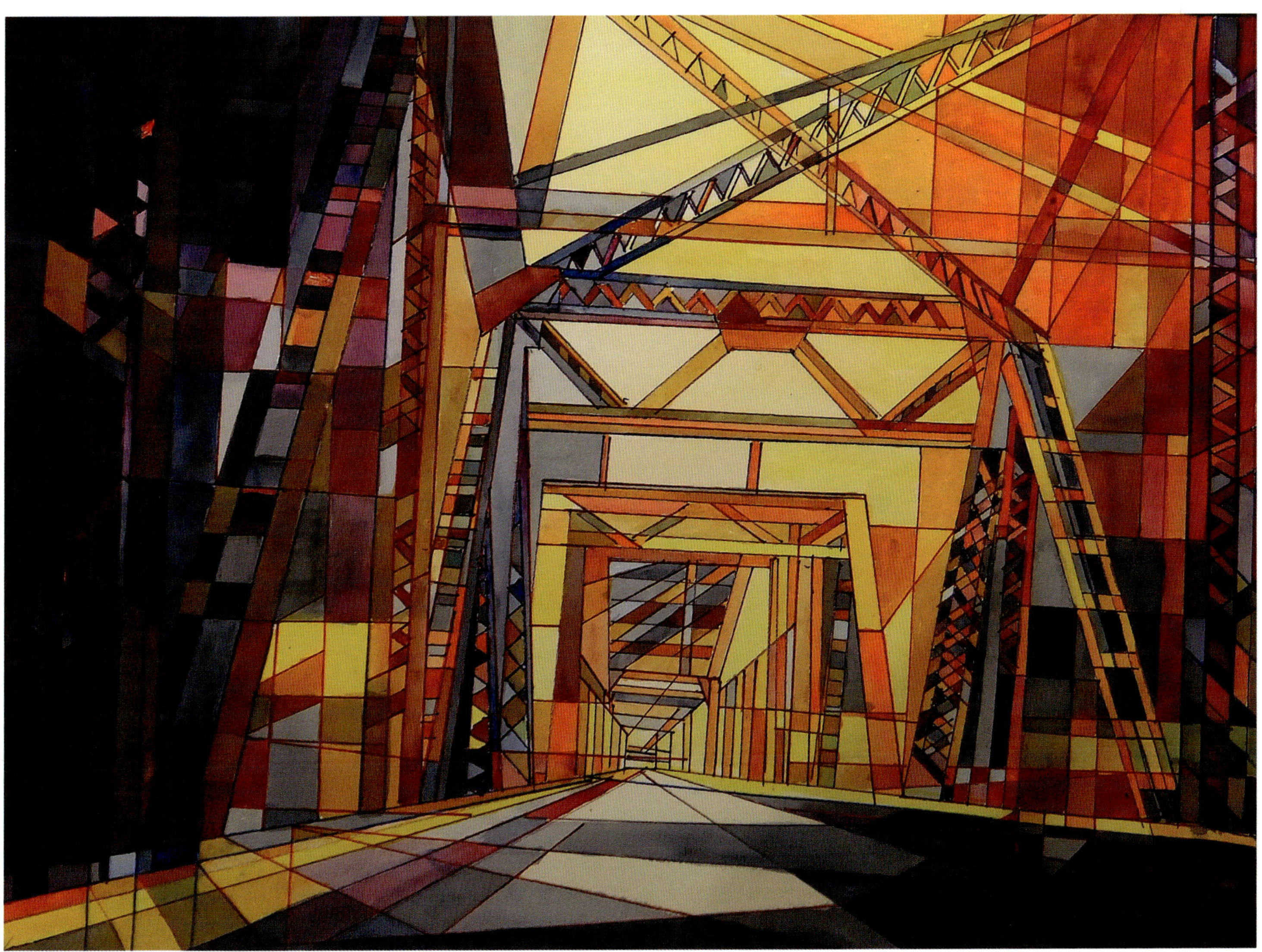

Marilynne Bradley

Sometimes changes happen when you least expect them. After years of approaching her art in a traditional way, something monumental happened and Marilynne Bradley is now exploring new visual paths. Her compositions evolve by reconstructing overlapping planes created by straight lines and tangents. The straight edge depicts precise, sharply defined spatial environments within the context of architectural and natural elements. Bradley sees structured lines, angles, edges, and shapes. Within the structure of lines, light becomes abstracted into layers of values. Patterns of shapes evolve and add depth.

"I now know what Josef Albers's theory of color means," Bradley begins. "Cool colors recede, and warm colors come forward. The intensity of colors within the geometrical spaces creates a depth of field. The gradations of values and shades of colors and the buildup of overlays of pigment pull the viewer into the composition. The paintings shimmer with a mystic energy, and the viewer is transformed into my reconstructed world."

Bridge Deconstruction
Watercolor
15 x 22 in.

mgbrad@aol.com
marilynnebradley.com

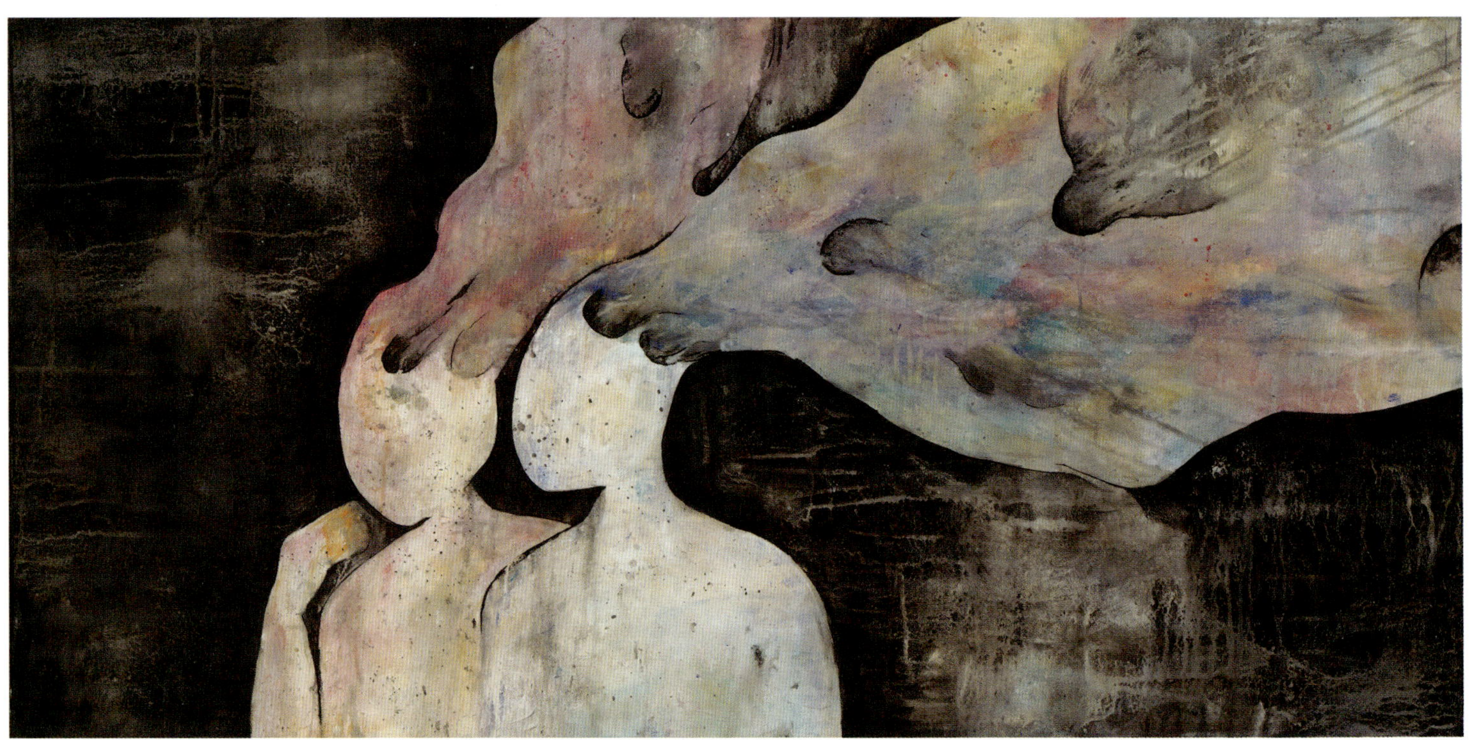

Laura Castro

If you asked Laura Castro to describe her work, she would say it's about the process, and what she does is an abstract form of sculpture on canvas. "I start with just simple direction flow and texture until I find a pattern that interests me. From there, I'll use paint and other mediums to emphasize and enhance the underlying base," Castro says.

The result of this approach is a cacophony of color and compositional inconsistency that examines the symbiotic nature between order and chaos. Over time, Castro's work has changed, fluctuating between concrete and abstract subjects. Her particular focus has always been on the creation process, the workflow. She utilizes a wide variety of media in her work, including concrete, silicone, plaster, and Plexiglas. Castro is constantly exploring new forms and never hesitates to violate conventional norms in this pursuit. The end result is open for interpretation; the artist just wants the viewer to want to reach out and touch the work.

Moments Passed
Mixed media
24 x 48 in.

castro@lauracastroart
.com
lauracastroart.com
@castrofineart

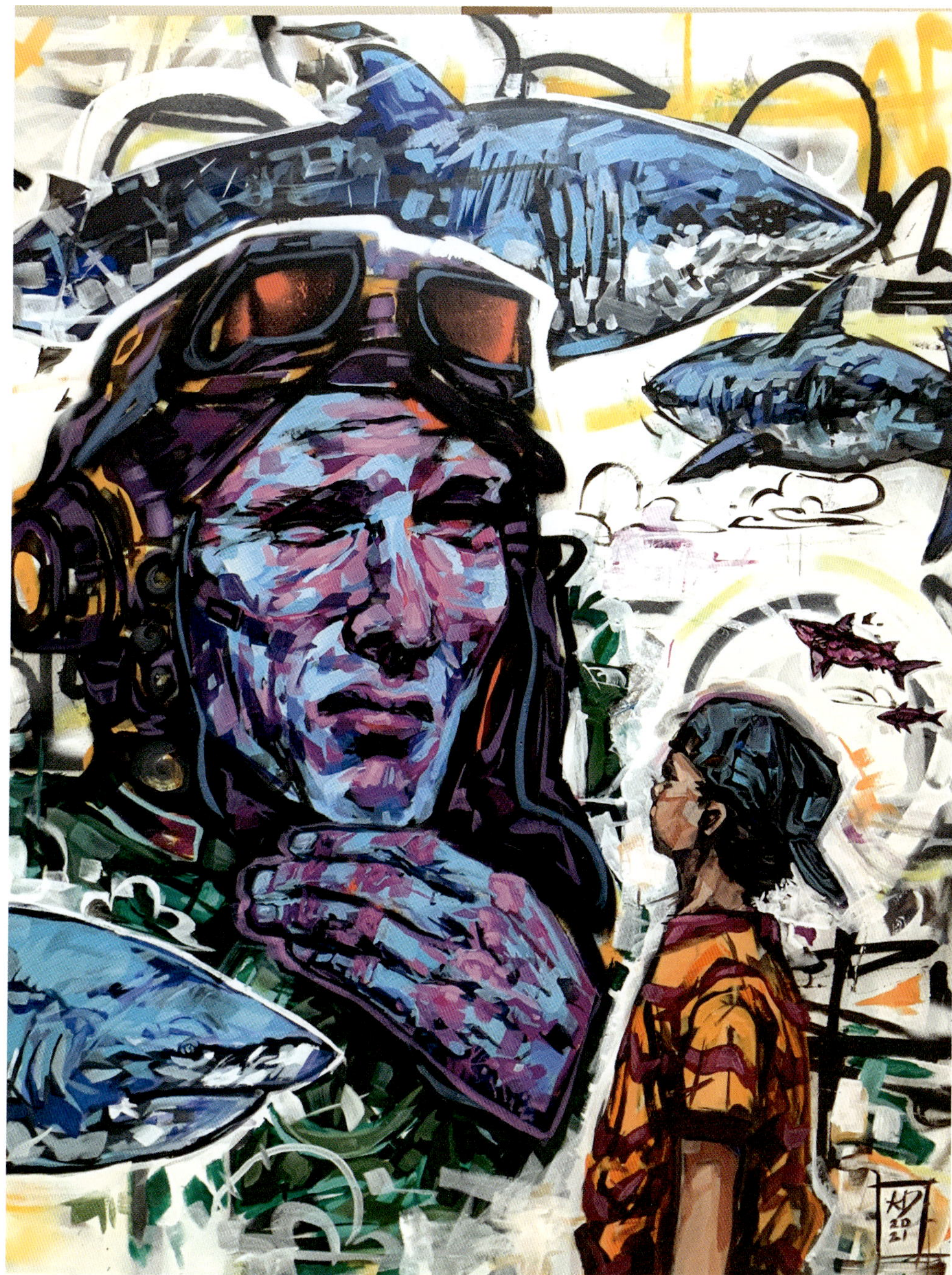

Alec DeJesus

Born in Illinois, artist Alec DeJesus turned to art as a means of escaping a rough upbringing. Although troubled and withdrawn due to his trials growing up, art was always a means to connect with the world around him. As the years moved on, his obsession with art became exactly what connected DeJesus to the world.

DeJesus's use of symbolism directs the narrative, while his use of color and composition relates to the emotions and purpose of the subjects. Focusing on these explains the painting, but it's the controlled and chaotic marks that tend to make them stand out. By combining expressive gesture and graffiti techniques, one can truly understand the balance by which the artist strides.

Influenced by both classic and street art, DeJesus uses bold colors and surreal compositions to convey a very real message of "strength and pride through perseverance" in his vibrant paintings.

Daydream in Deep Waters
Spray paint and acrylic
48 x 36 in.

adejesus708@gmail.com
alecdejesus.com
@Youcancallmealec

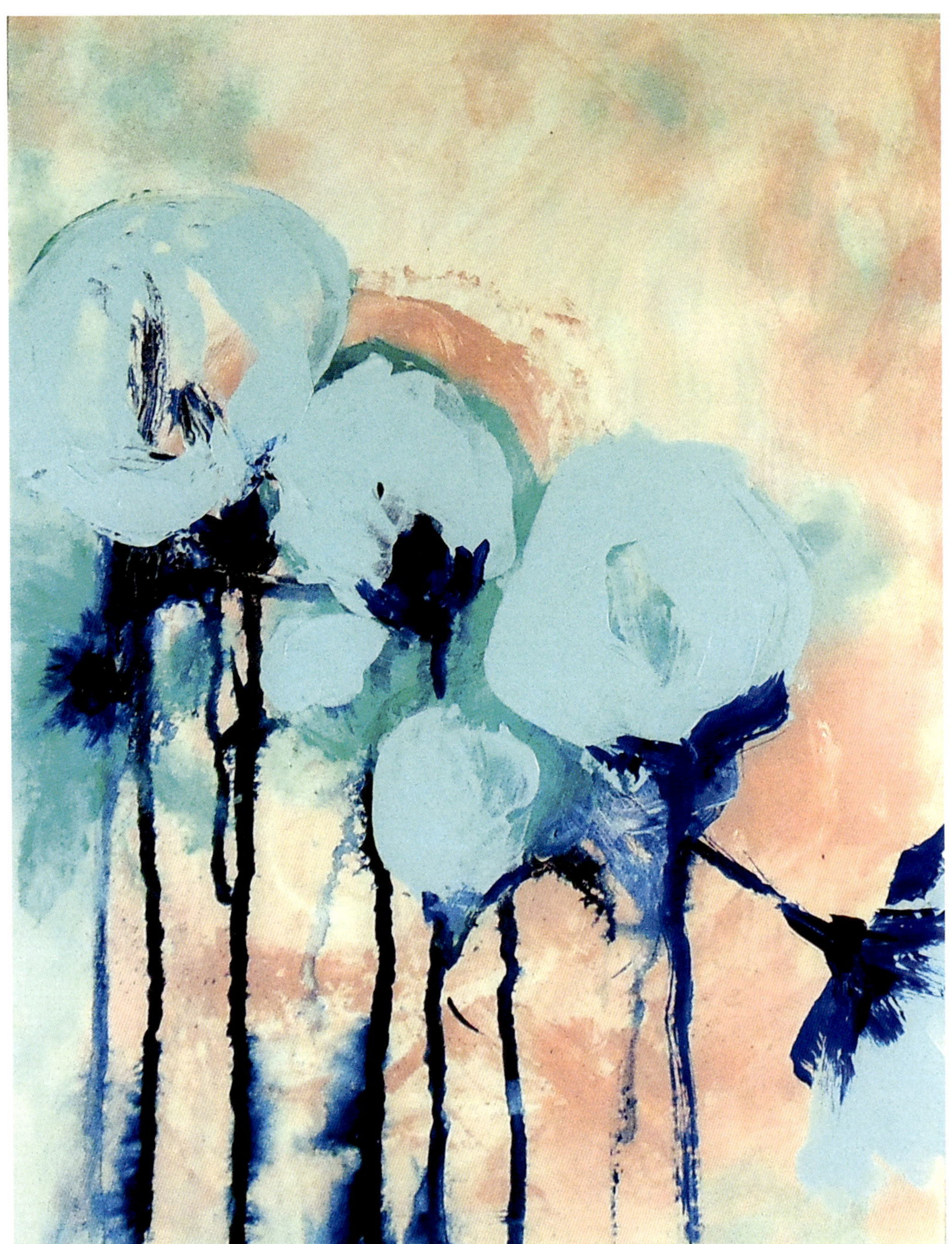

Patty DelValle

Patty DelValle is an abstract, expressive artist working out of her home studio in Woodstock, Georgia. Her process is that of creating intuitively from a place of spiritual connection. That connection brings a sense of joy and hope that translates into her work. Using an expressive, intuitive approach, through gestural mark-making, abstracted shapes, and serene color stories, allows an authentic expression of herself, her faith, and her interpretation of life.

Usually drawn by exploring a particular color palette, the work will develop a sense of tone or emotion. Shape and line continue to express the story as the work unfolds. DelValle believes that each painting has a story of its own to tell that unfolds as the layers and marks take shape.

Garden Whimsy - Blossoms
Acrylic
12 x 9 in.

Patty@PattyDArt.com
pattyd.art
@pattyd.art

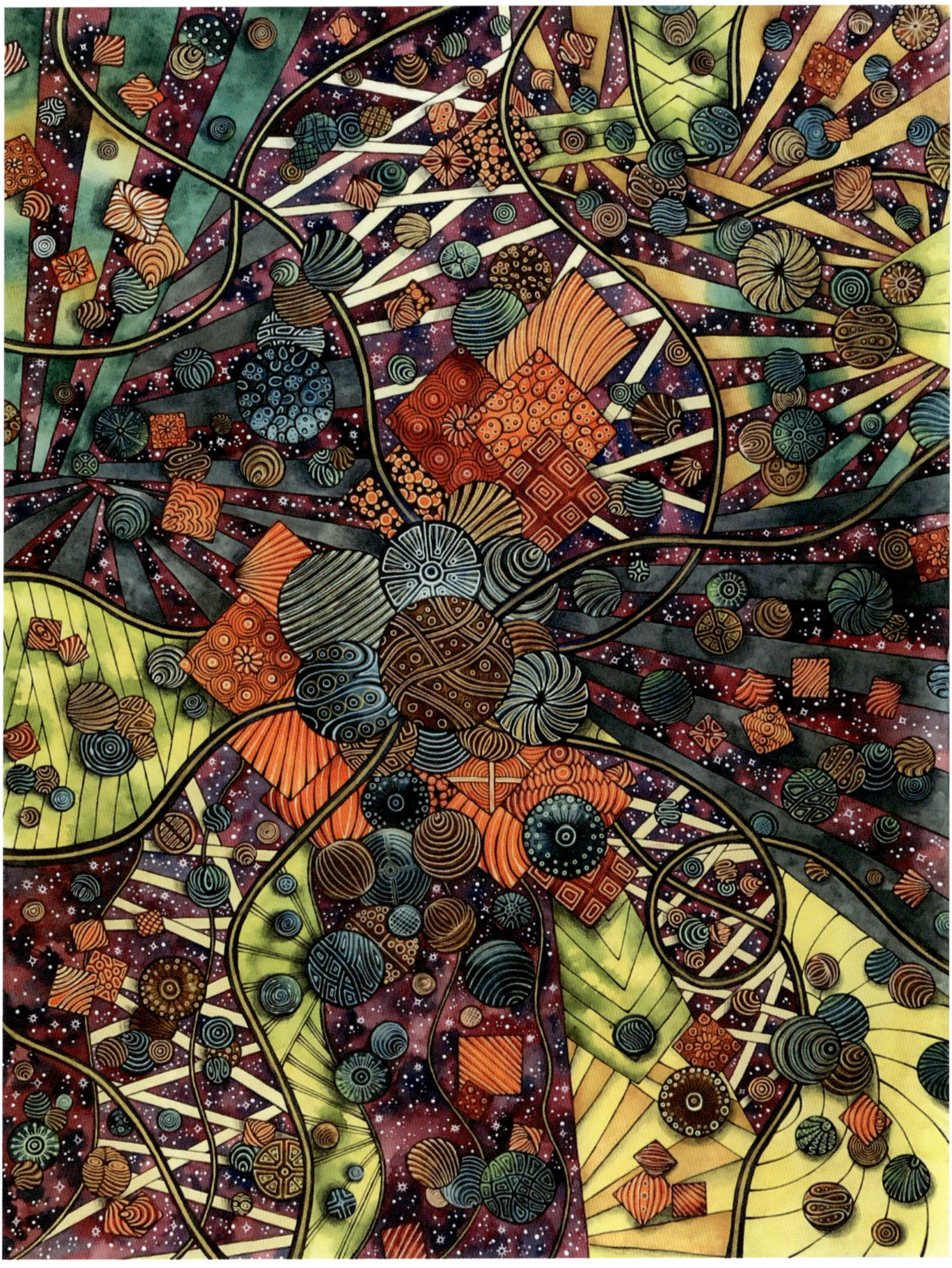

Amylia Faizal

Amylia Faizal is a self-taught modern, contemporary, mixed-media artist and illustrator residing in Brunei Darussalam. She creates her work primarily using watercolor, gouache, ink pens, colored pencils, and pastels.

Each piece of artwork she creates has a story behind it that is based on her emotions and intuitions. "Having an appreciation for my intuition, I allow this element of my life to transform all kinds of personal emotions and consciousness into an art form. It is my cathartic way of telling my story and also helping to bring more joy, peace, love, and understanding into the world."

Faizal also has a deep appreciation for shapes, particularly spherical in nature, as it allows her to bring depth, dimension, and meaning into all her artworks. She loves creating vibrant, bold, and intricate art pieces.

My Whimsical Dream
Mixed media
30 x 22 in.

amyliafaizal@gmail.com
amyliafaizal.com
@amyliafaizalart

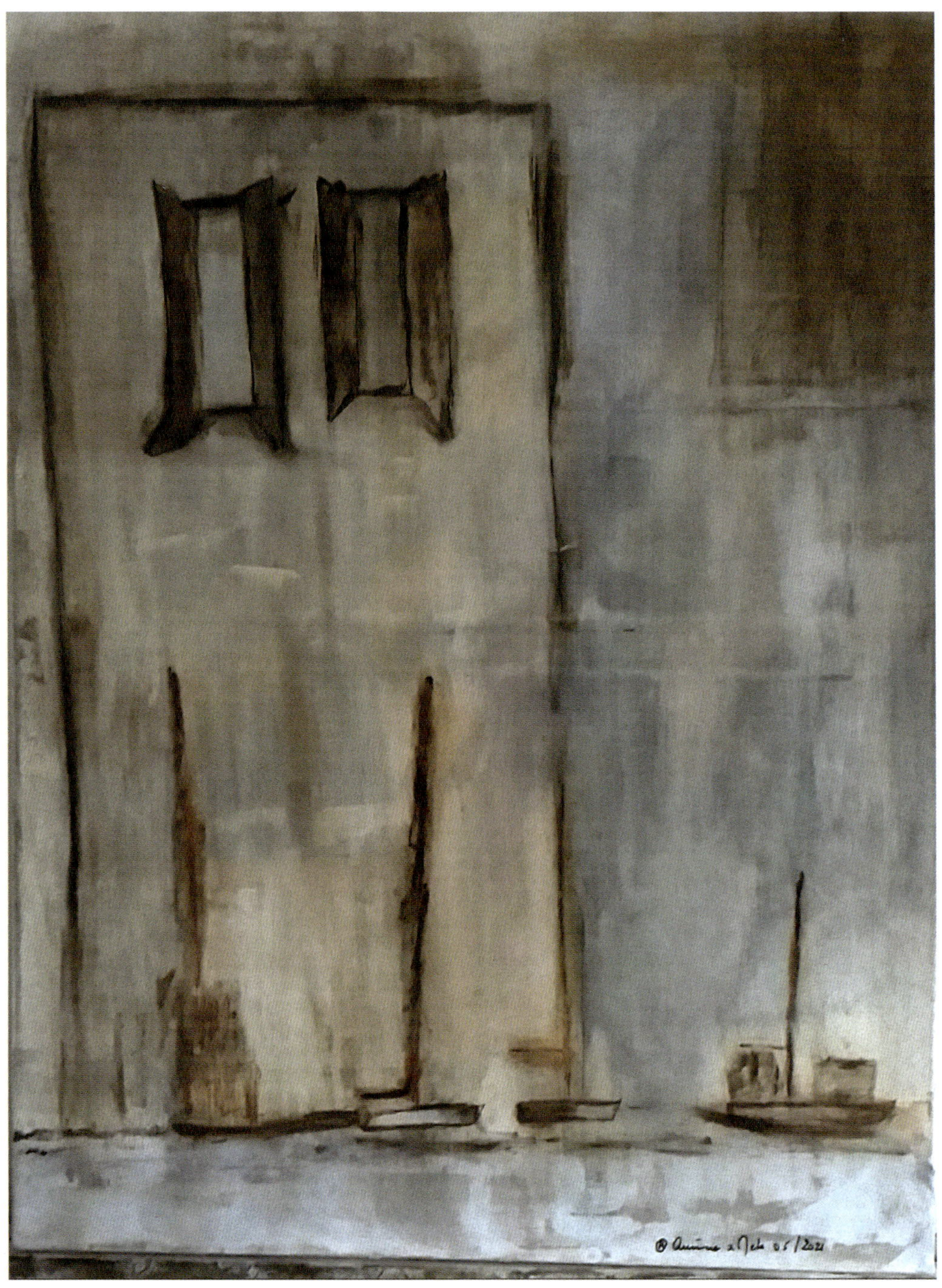

Claudia Fischer

Claudia Fischer, aka Anima e Mela, is a German painter who spent most of her life in France and now lives on the Mediterranean coast. Self-taught, her passion for painting came out following an extremely strong emotion that changed her life.

Fischer is interested in lots of things, such as society, philosophy, nature, psychology, the human being, and spirituality, which she tries to make the observer think about when looking at her work. Her painting process is purely instinctive and inspired by life, readings, and observation, and most of the time, she paints in a more or less subconscious state of mind. When a painting comes to its end, Fischer suddenly feels the title come to her as if it was fated.

Fischer is extremely curious and always exploring new techniques and tools for a permanent evolution.

Early Morning on the Docks
Acrylics on canvas
32 x 23.5 in.

cldfischer12@gmail.com
@animaemela

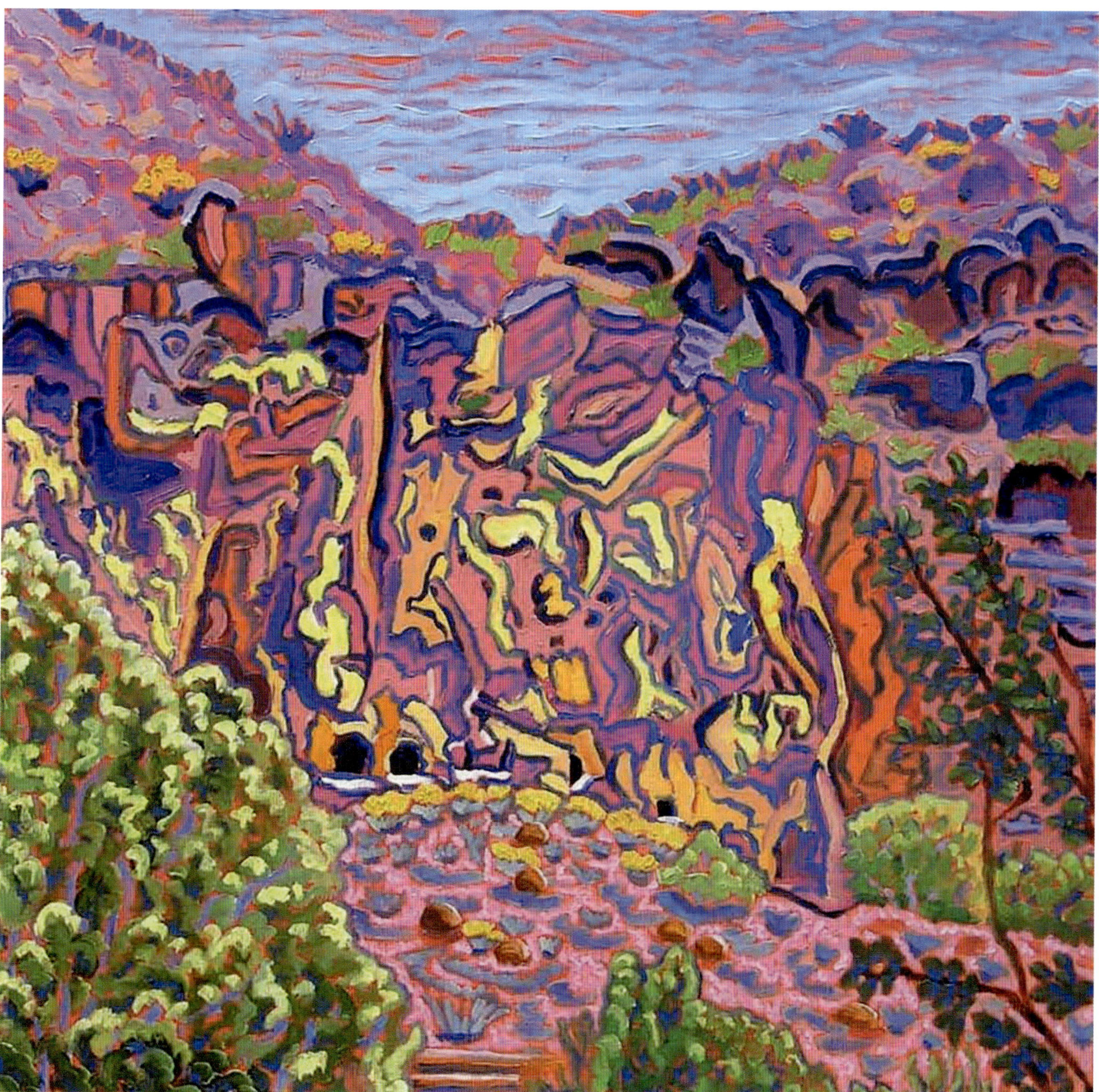

Kathleen Frank

Having been an art teacher, wood-carver, and a printmaker in her formative years, Kathleen Frank emerged as a painter, joyously overwhelmed by color and searching for patterns. A pattern in nature is primal to the artist, which fuels her desire to find a glimmer of logic in the vastly complicated, confusing, and tumbled landscapes. She also seeks out the vibrant hues in landscapes.

Frank's oil paintings begin with a saturated red-orange backdrop. This is overlaid with the main imagery, applied with distinct brushstrokes of brilliant color. Hints of the red background peek through like a woodcut, creating subtle impact without drawing attention away from the primary subjects.

Several times a year, Frank travels throughout the Southwest, hiking and photographing vistas for future paintings. Her goal is to catch the light and design in these scenes in all their strangeness and beauty. It is a lofty goal, but the artist finds when the quest is shepherded with paint and brush, it is a delightfully daunting adventure.

Bandelier
Oil on canvas
30 x 30 in.

k.frank@
artworkinternational
.com
kathleenfrankart.com
@kathleen-frank

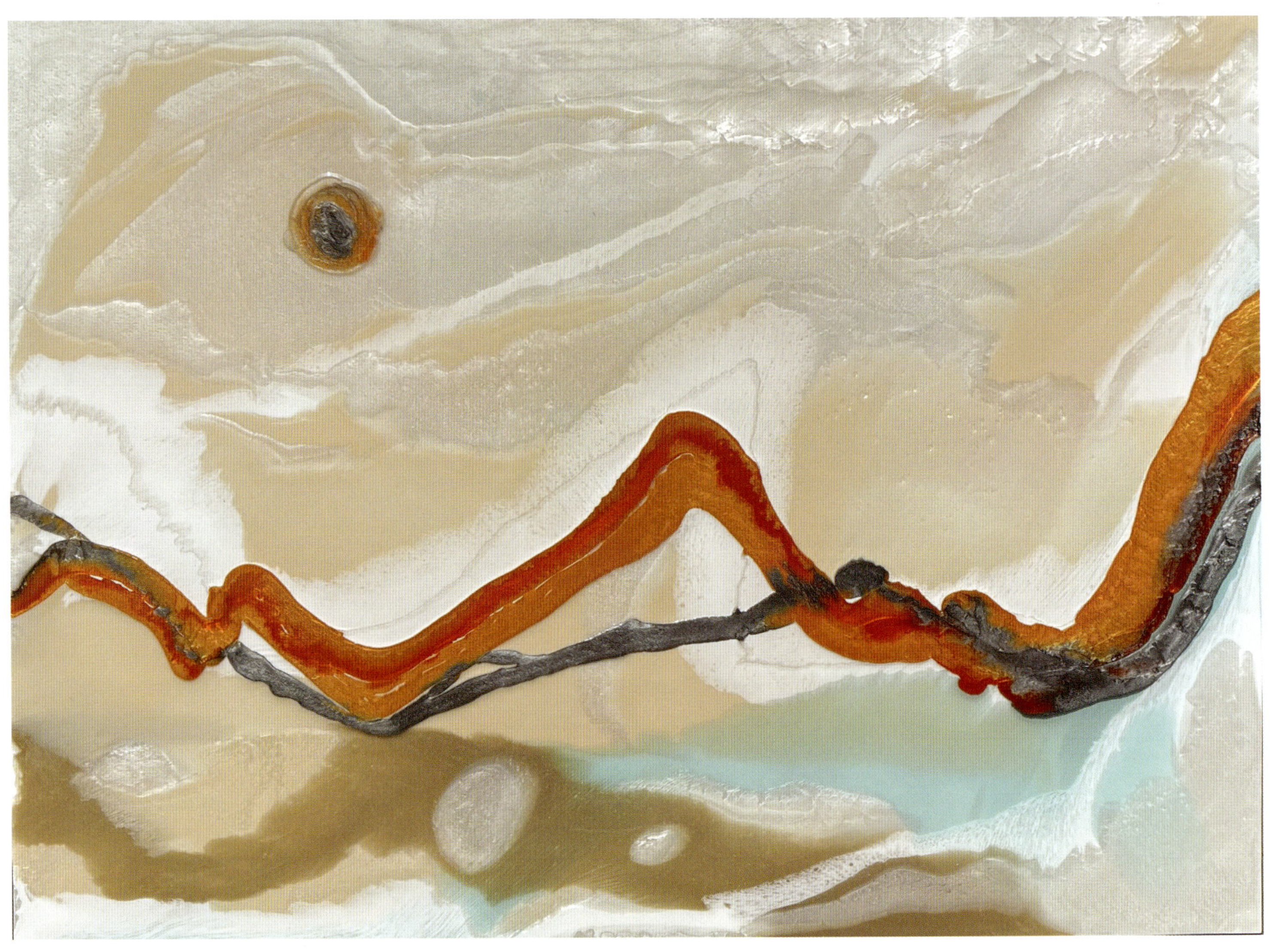

Kelly Gowan

To Kelly Gowan art is an endless, always-evolving experience, like life. She uses a wild palette of colors and mediums to create freely, and she continually discovers new ways of expression, through all mediums and surfaces, without limits. Gowan's creations are a mixture of scenery, memories, and emotions. They are the places she has been, wants to go, and the dreams that she has. Her style of work is modern and contemporary abstract expressionism. "I feel this style allows more space for collectors and art lovers to enjoy my work. With my work being more abstract, this allows the viewer's mind to wander a bit and come to their own conclusion about the painting," says Gowan.

Often Gowan's art includes resin, but she does not confine herself to one medium or style, which allows her creations to appeal to a wide range of collectors. When she is not working on one of her own painting inspirations, she collaborates with designers and collectors that want to commission a piece of artwork for a collector.

Salmon River
Resin
30 x 40 in.

kellygowanart@gmail
.com
kellygowanart.com
@kellygowanart

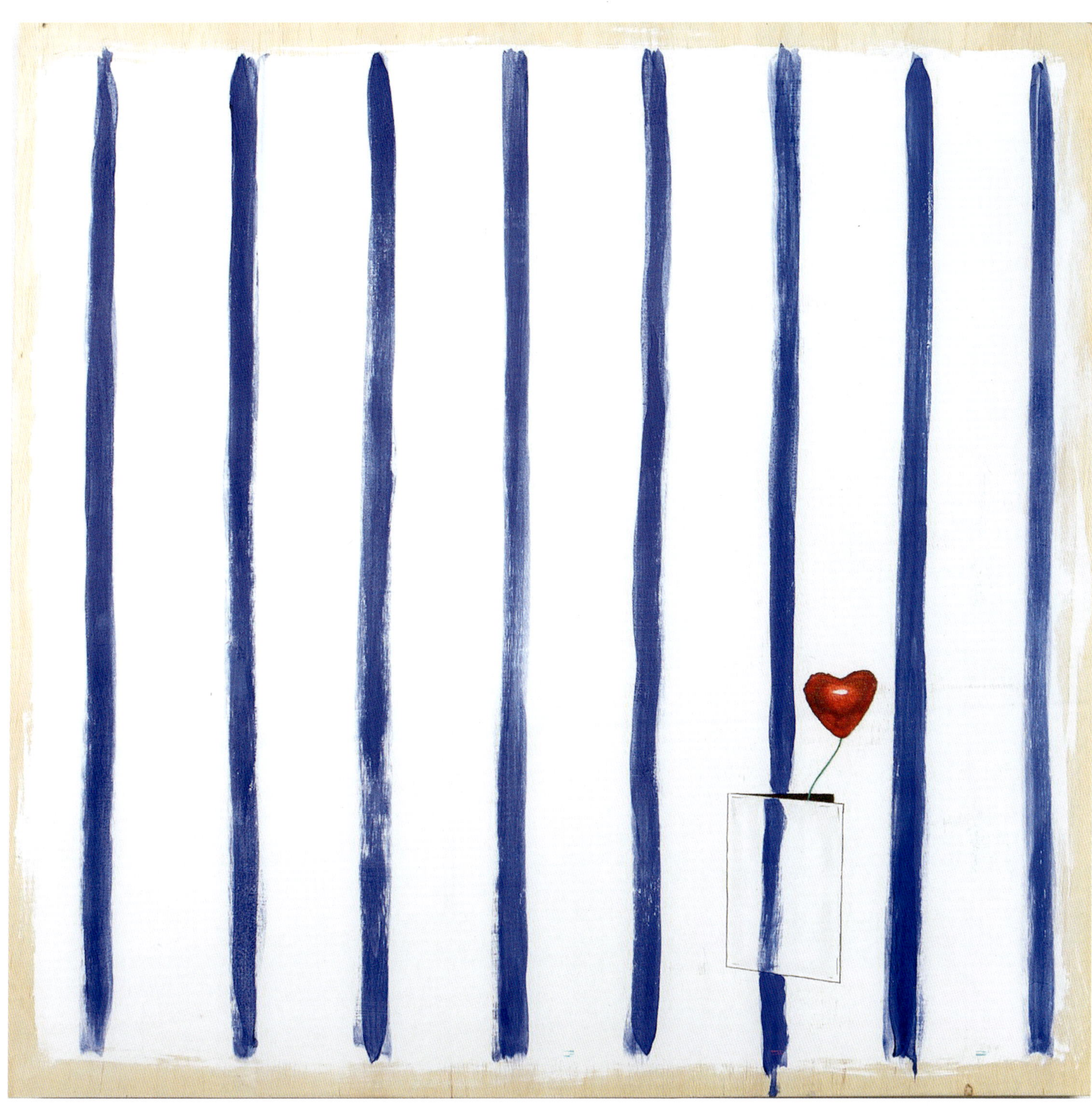

Annie Griffeth

Hailing from Oahu, Hawaii, pop artist Annie Griffeth's ink, acrylic, and oil artworks reflect her empowered perspective and worldly style. Griffeth combines realism and illustration in modern works that are meant to inspire, entertain, and connect us through shared experiences.

"My work is a conversation about things that give our lives purpose. No matter how different we are, we all share experiences that make us feel vulnerable or fierce, that give us strength or cause us pain, and are the reason why we are who we are today," Griffeth says. "I use symbols, colors, and words to communicate my thoughts, and if you find yourself understanding, relating to, or just 'getting it,' then we've both found a friend."

A Crack in the Wall
Acrylic and ink
33 x 33 in.

anniegriffeth@gmail.com
anniegriffeth.com
@anniegriffeth

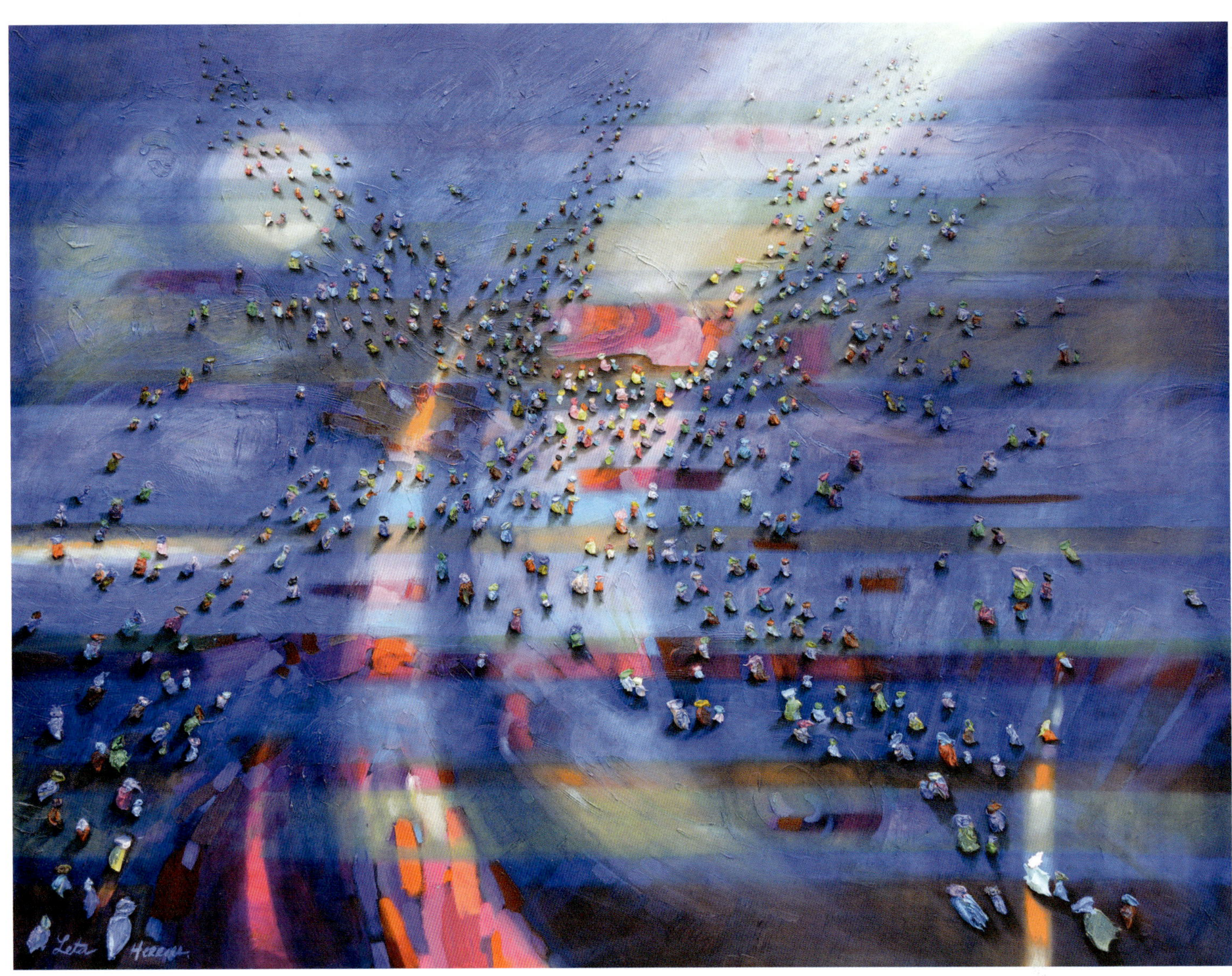

Leticia Herrera

"I consider myself an evolving artist because I am always transforming. My work walks with me and changes with me," says Leticia Herrera.

Herrera is a prize-winning and published Mexican-American artist who seeks to explore what it means to be human in her art. Painting mostly with oils and a palette knife, she masterfully captures perspective in her pieces. She refers to the three-dimensional oil impasto figures as "walkers."

In her *Walkers* series, the tiny figures are searchers of beautiful emotions; they are travelers of the universe and the world. They are catchers of dreams. They are explorers of aspirations, searchers of unity and of freedom, asking always: Who are we? Where are we going? What are we looking for? What do we want? Who do we love?

In her paintings, Herrera tries to transport the viewer to those places in her imagination. "I want to touch your soul, open your heart, and invite you to walk with me," Herrera says.

Stages of Life
Oil
48 x 60 in.

leticiaherrera@
leticiaherreraart.com
leticiaherreraart.com
@leticiaherreraart

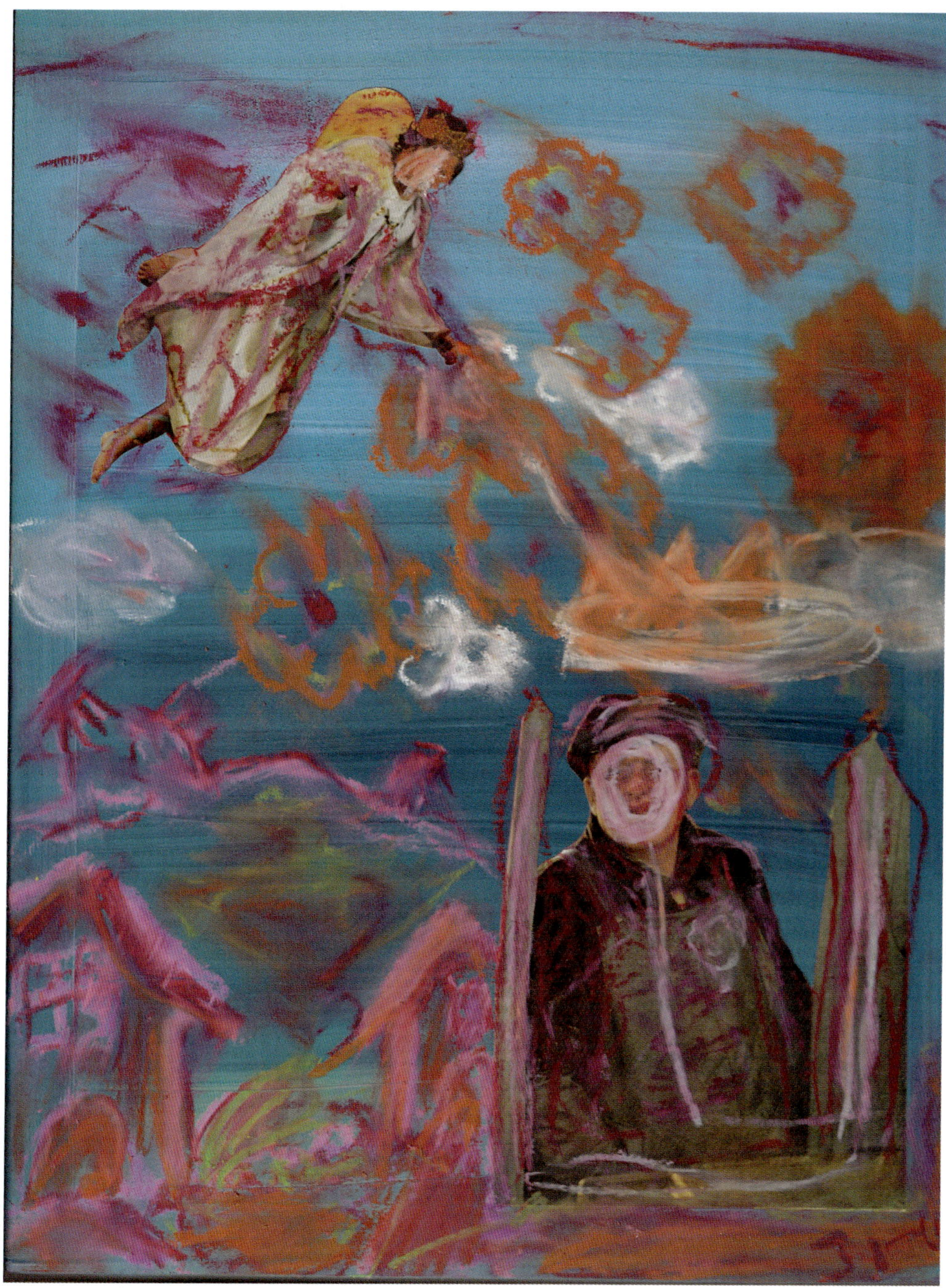

Jay Hodgson

On the 3rd of August 1980, the French brutalist Jean Dubuffet, then nearing eighty-one years of age, croaked to a young reporter what, in Dubuffet's estimation, was the sum total of all his years doing weird things with weird artistic materials to create his peculiarly brutal vision of art. Dubuffet said, "I believe in all my works that I have been concerned with representing what makes up our thoughts—to represent not the objective world, but what it becomes in our thoughts."

Jay Hodgson does much the same with his art. Hodgson, too, remains an outsider to the artistic culture, insofar as he only very recently decided that he would consciously take part in it. "I enjoy the exchange almost as much as the painting itself. From my work, you can see that I am clearly a fan of the brutal artistic genre," the artist says.

Alongside a thriving career as an analog collage artist, Hodgson has devoted himself almost completely to creating and advancing that culture.

Hyper-Lysergic
Acrylic, oil stick, paper and glue on cradled wood
12 x 16 in.

jayhodgson@mac.com
jayhodgsonart.com
@jay_hodgson_
analogcollage

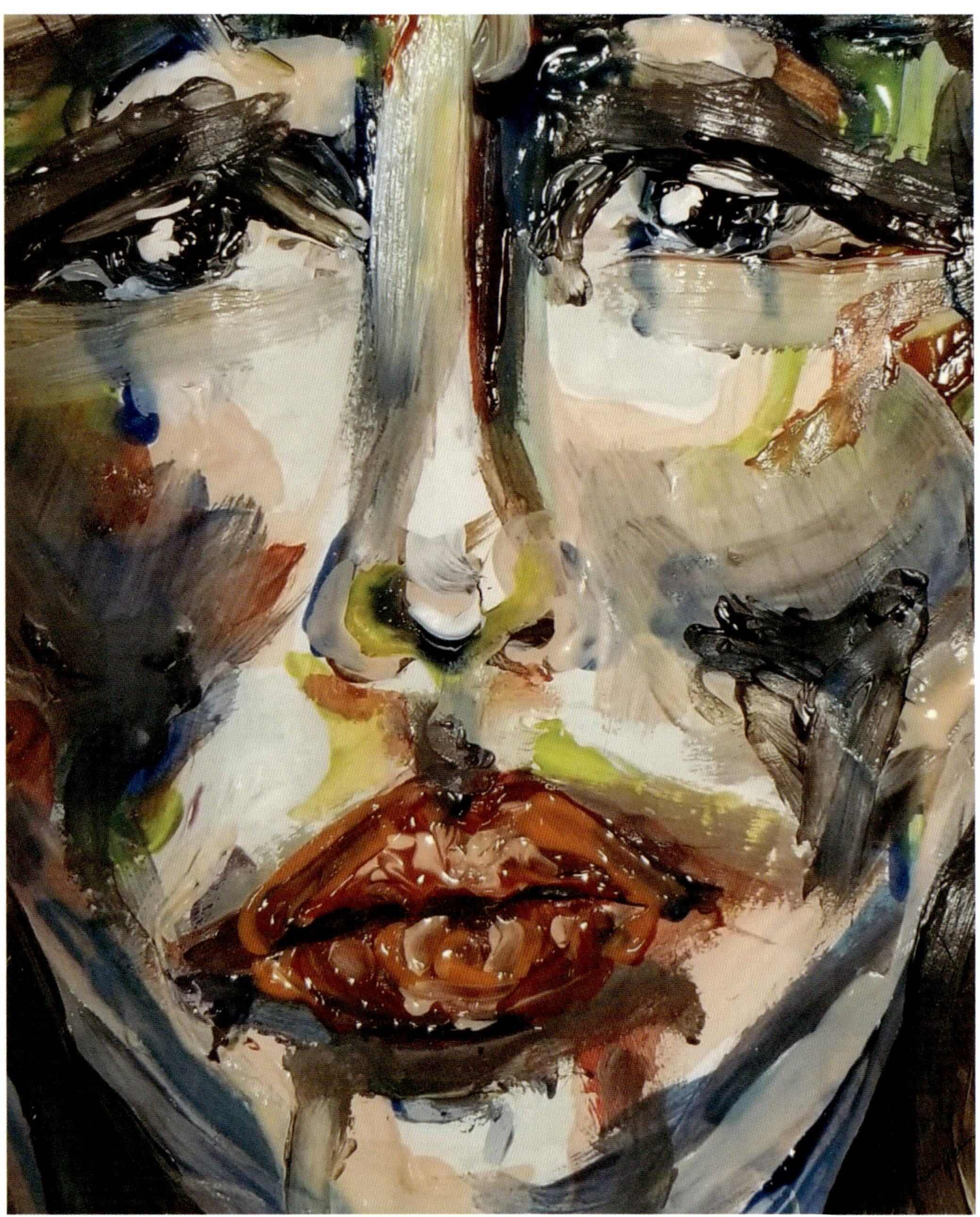

Deana Jackson

Deana Jackson is a traditional, contemporary self-taught artist. She created her first painting in 2016 while attending therapy for post-traumatic stress disorder. What began as a coping mechanism became her life's passion. With each painting, Jackson hopes to bring awareness to mental health.

Her painting style is spontaneous and thought-provoking. She dips her paintbrush in emotion and lays it down on life's canvas, sharing it with the world. Each brushstroke is charged with intense feeling and provides a raw, unfiltered glimpse into the underbelly of the human condition.

Jackson does not limit herself to any one methodology. Rather, she prefers to create hybrid portraits that incorporate the use of both conventional painting methods and digital technology. Her paintings blur the line between traditional and present-day artistry. Each portrait is created with the intention of delivering the viewer into a world of emotion that's often hidden behind a smile.

The Cloud I Carry
Mixed media on paper
42 x 22 in.

emtcanvas@gmail.com

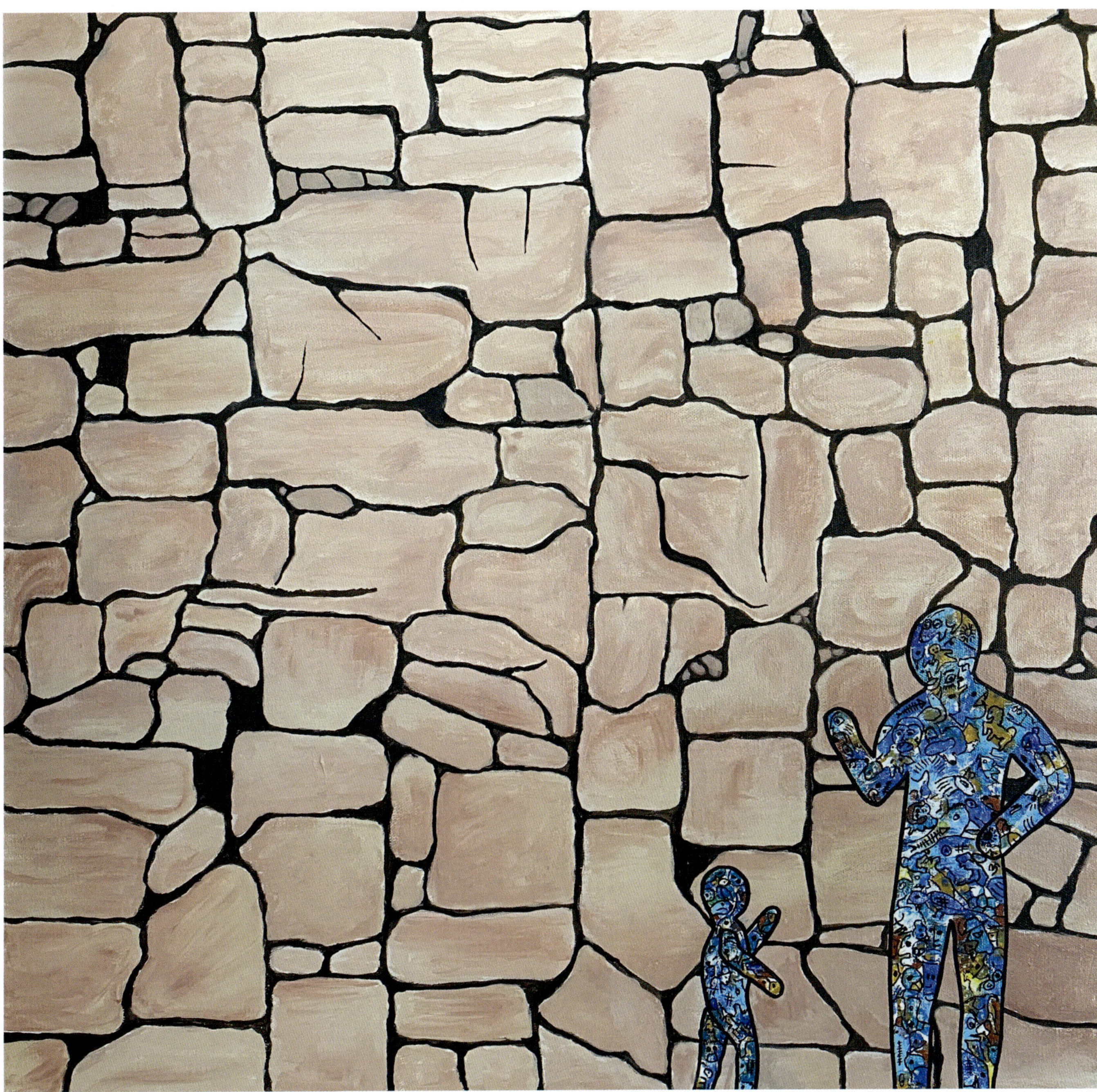

Amogh Katyayan

Amogh Katyayan's painting technique can be compared to looking for images in the clouds. She begins with a blank canvas, and as she layers on the initial coat of paint to create textures and colors, she begins to see shapes and figures emerge from the paint. This is the foundation from which her paintings develop. With the freedom this open-minded approach brings, her painting takes on a life of its own. From the images Katyayan initially sees, her paintings take on stories, issues, and experiences to which others can relate.

"When you look into my work, you will see the story falling into place. With this process, what is currently around me influences what I imagine in a painting, and I finish sketching it out on canvas," Katyayan says.

The Dialogue
Acrylic
24 x 24 in.

amogh@amogh.art
amogh.art
@amogh_art

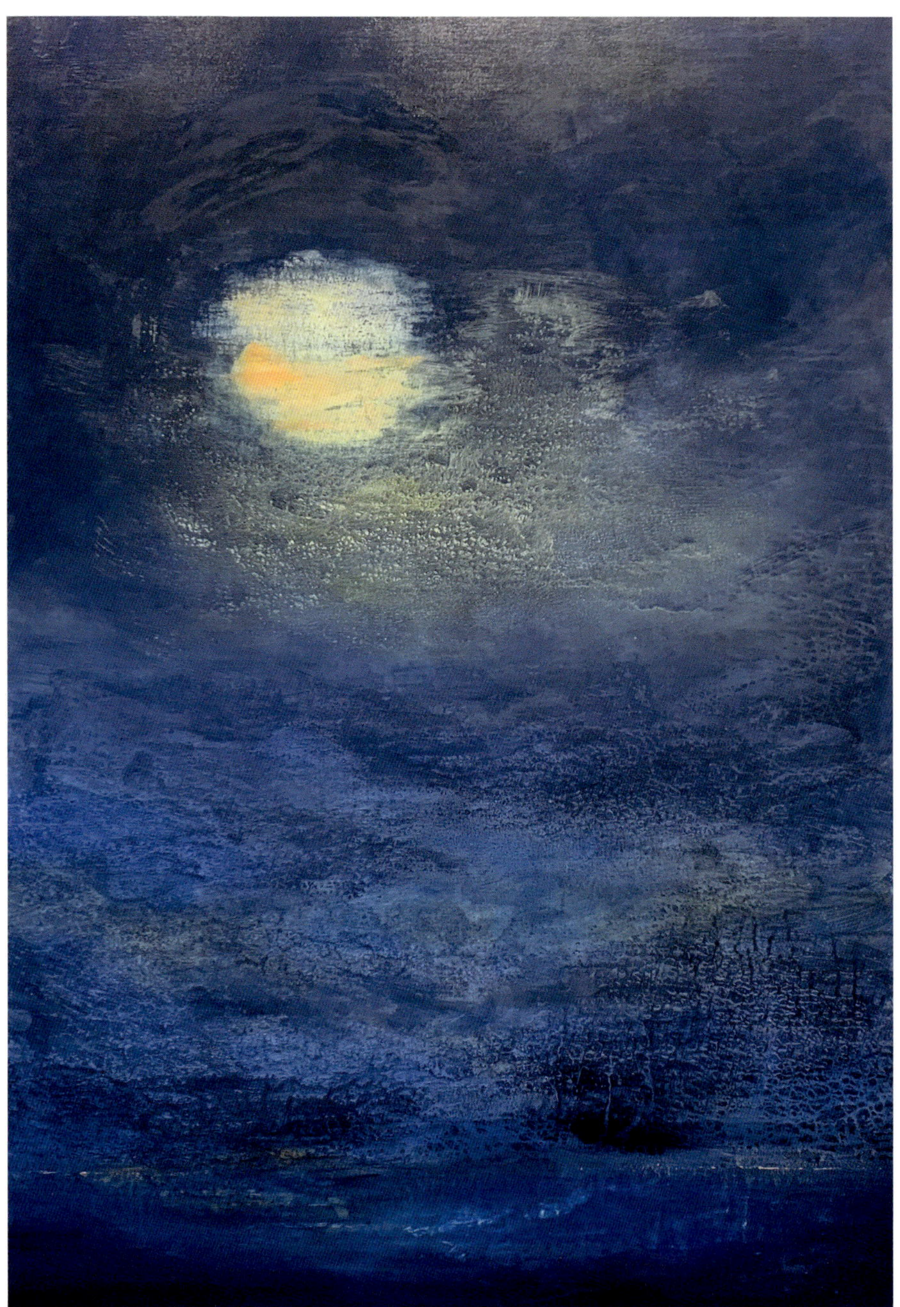

Rebecca Katz

Rebecca Katz's inspiration comes from the beauty of the atmosphere—of the sky and how it's connected with the earth. Every time she looks at what nature is presenting in front of her—the clouds, seductive with the constant movement of the atmosphere—she is reminded that life is constantly shifting and never stagnant. "I get that calm feeling when I look at the horizon and resonate with translating the vast spaciousness and mystery to the canvas," Katz says.

Katz works in acrylic and graphite, using many layers of glazes to achieve the luminosity of the atmospheric quality in her work. She also works wet on wet and uses drips to create texture and atmosphere, which alludes to what's beneath the surface. Layers and layers of paint are applied on the canvas before Katz even knows how the image will present itself in its final form.

Her paintings are asking viewers to step into a world of possibility, mystery, magic, and atmosphere, and to be transported through color, light, and texture.

Moondance
Acrylic
57 x 36 in.

rebecca@rebeccakatz
.com
rebeccakatzart.com
@rebeccakatzart

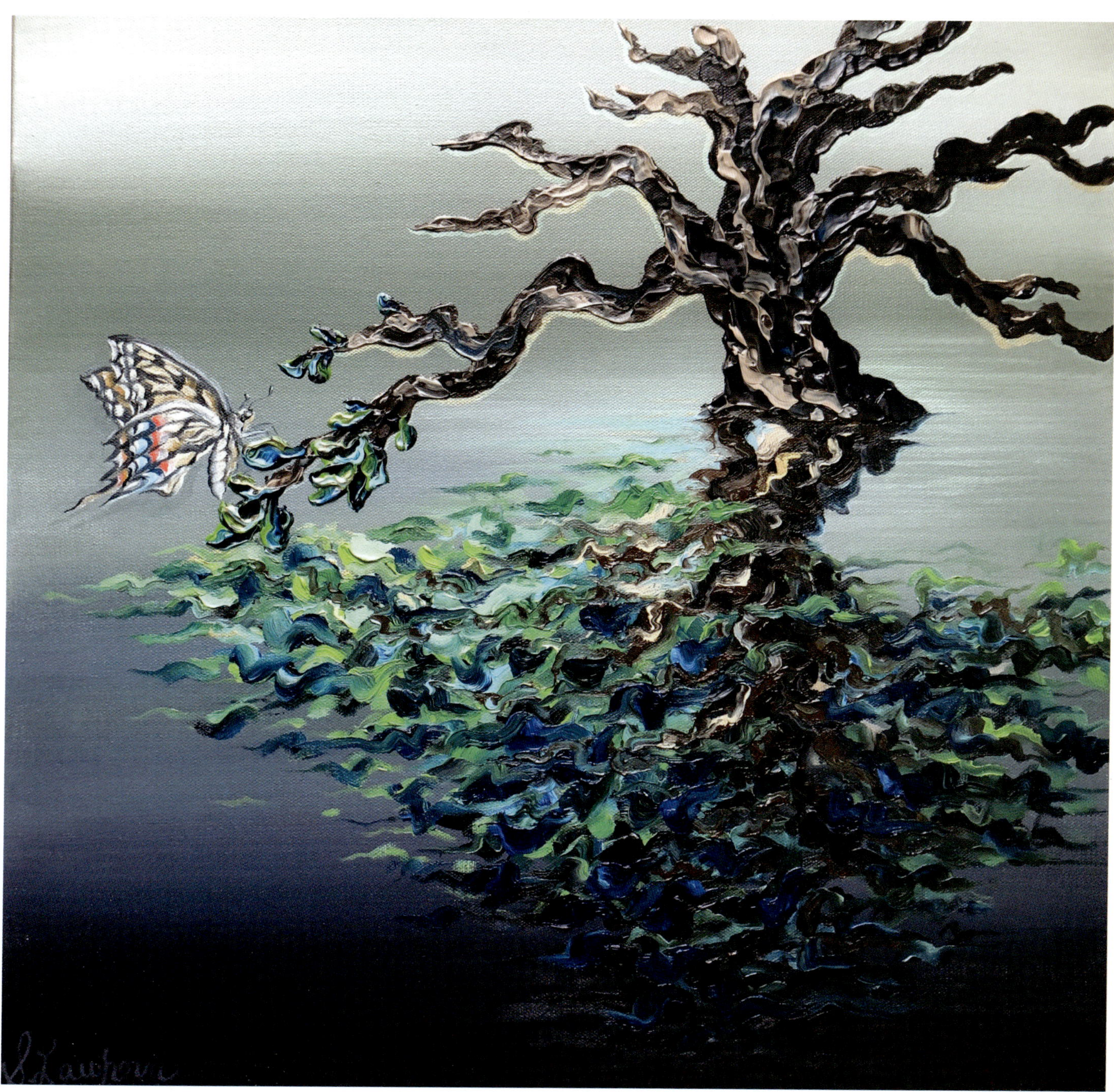

Stephanie Lawhorn

Stephanie Lawhorn is a teaching artist who is inspired by colors, textures, and movements of the natural world as seen through the lens of her Christian faith. She manages her art business, known as Inspired by Him Fine Art, and seeks to share the beauty of her faith and God's perfect love through all her works.

Each piece, while consistent in inspiration and vibrancy, becomes an entity of its own, depending on the message the work is meant to convey. Lawhorn explores a variety of mediums as she feels that developing these foundations helps improve her skills over time. Her paintings, the medium she is most known for, are created in oils and heavy acrylics with palette knives and coarse brushes, and her own fingers are often used as well to create the resulting textures. Although she currently works as an art educator in Texas, she herself is self-taught and enjoys exploring the creative freedom of her own intuitions.

Forever Quenched
Oil and acrylic
20 x 20 in.

inspiredbyhimart@gmail
.com
@inspiredbyhimart

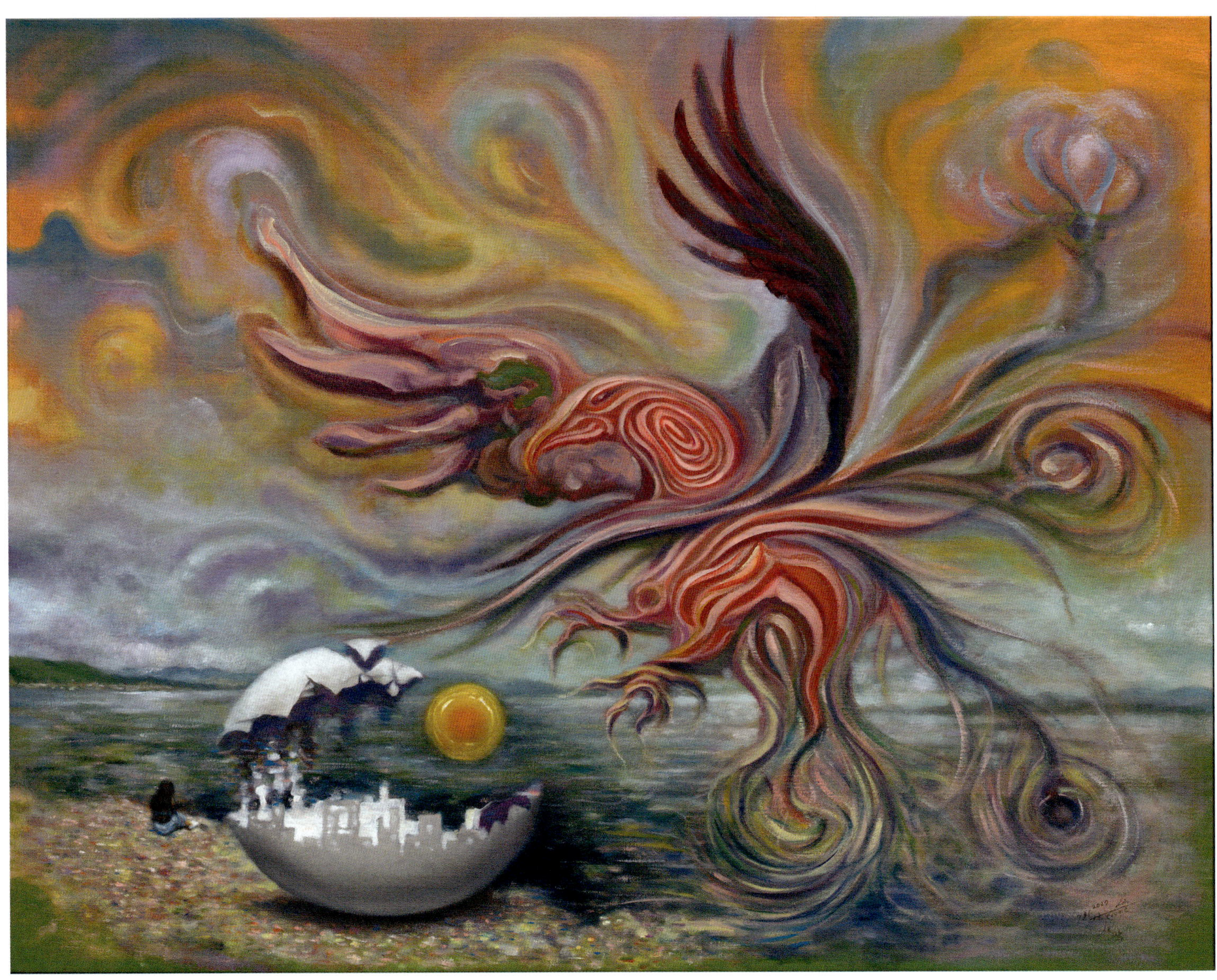

Jerome Chia-Horng Lin
Jerome Chia-Horng Lin believes that art is a state of mind. "Artworks showcase the vibration of our mind in a tangible way. They are the bridges connecting the external and internal world. I like to explore how my mind functions as well as others'," the artist says.

Lin is fascinated by the wonders of Mother Nature. Moreover, he is also attracted to the vastness of the human mind. While he finds scenarios in nature captivating, he believes the exploration of the images generated by each of our minds is sometimes more mysterious and enticing.

For Lin, art is an excellent means to express his ponderings about the universe. "My works reflect what's in my mind. They seem to be surreal. I like to think of it as a spiritual journey for me. I explore my life using art as my main tool," Lin says.

Remembrance is a Form of Meeting
Oil
31.5 x 39 in.

jeromelin2006@gmail
.com
jeromelin.net
@jeromechiahorng

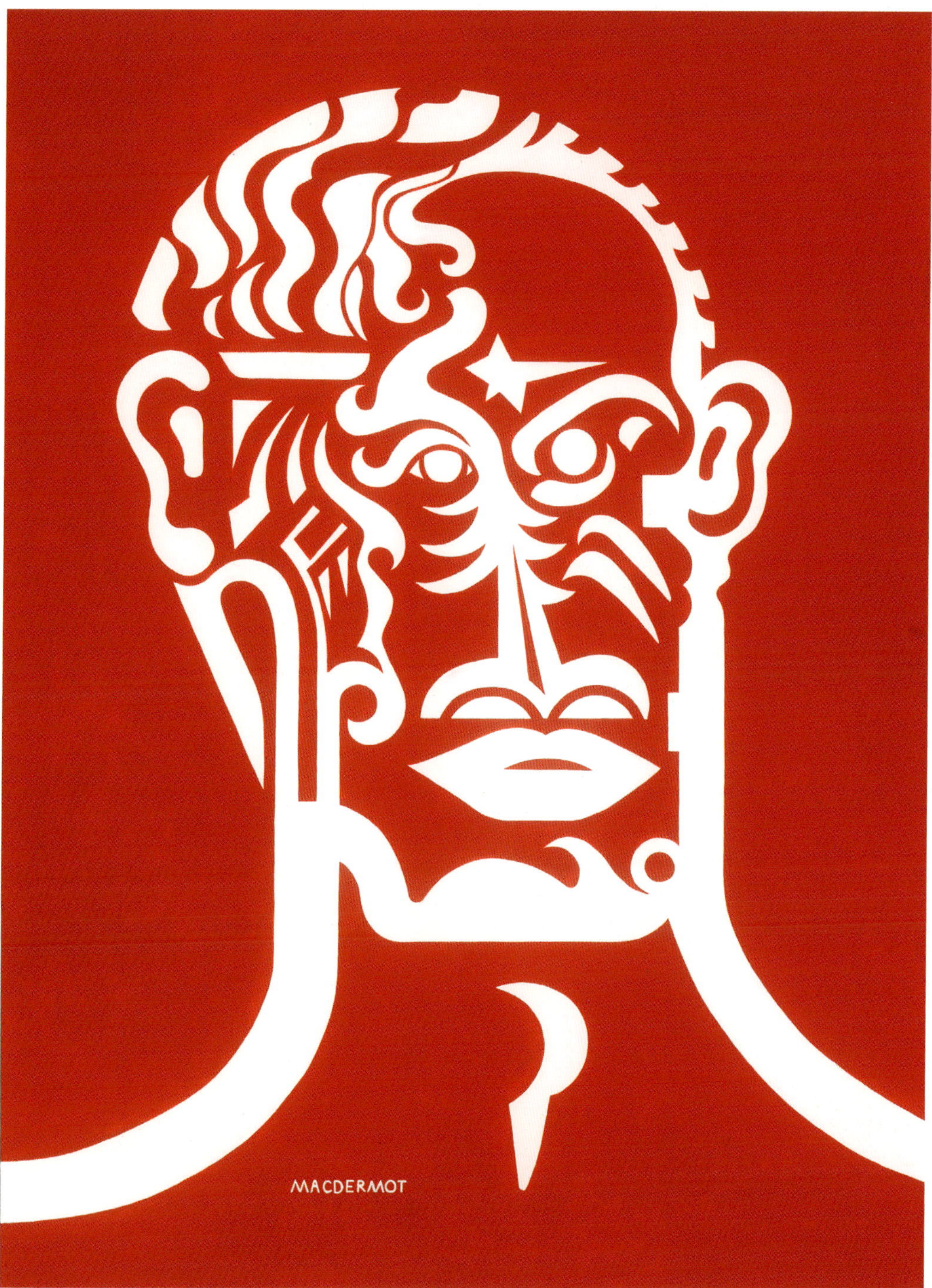

Vince MacDermot

Vince MacDermot began The Big Red NYC series with a few observations. "I was taught by my father, a composer, that it is necessary to tell a story in art. The stories I want to tell are about the characters I meet in New York City, working people, friendly people, and the things I see," he says.

MacDermot feels that we are bombarded with images all day long—advertising, television, cell phones, etc. The images are sophisticated and complex. He wanted the opposite: to work in a very simple format. It became a "one image" type of story. MacDermot chose to work in red and white as these are his favorite colors. The colors contrast to make a clear statement. Ultimately, each painting will hang on a wall, and the artist wants each of his paintings to be a "good companion" to the room and the people of the house.

Spiritual Spartan
Acrylic
84 x 60 in.

vincemacdermot@gmail
.com
vincemacdermot.com
@vincemacdermot

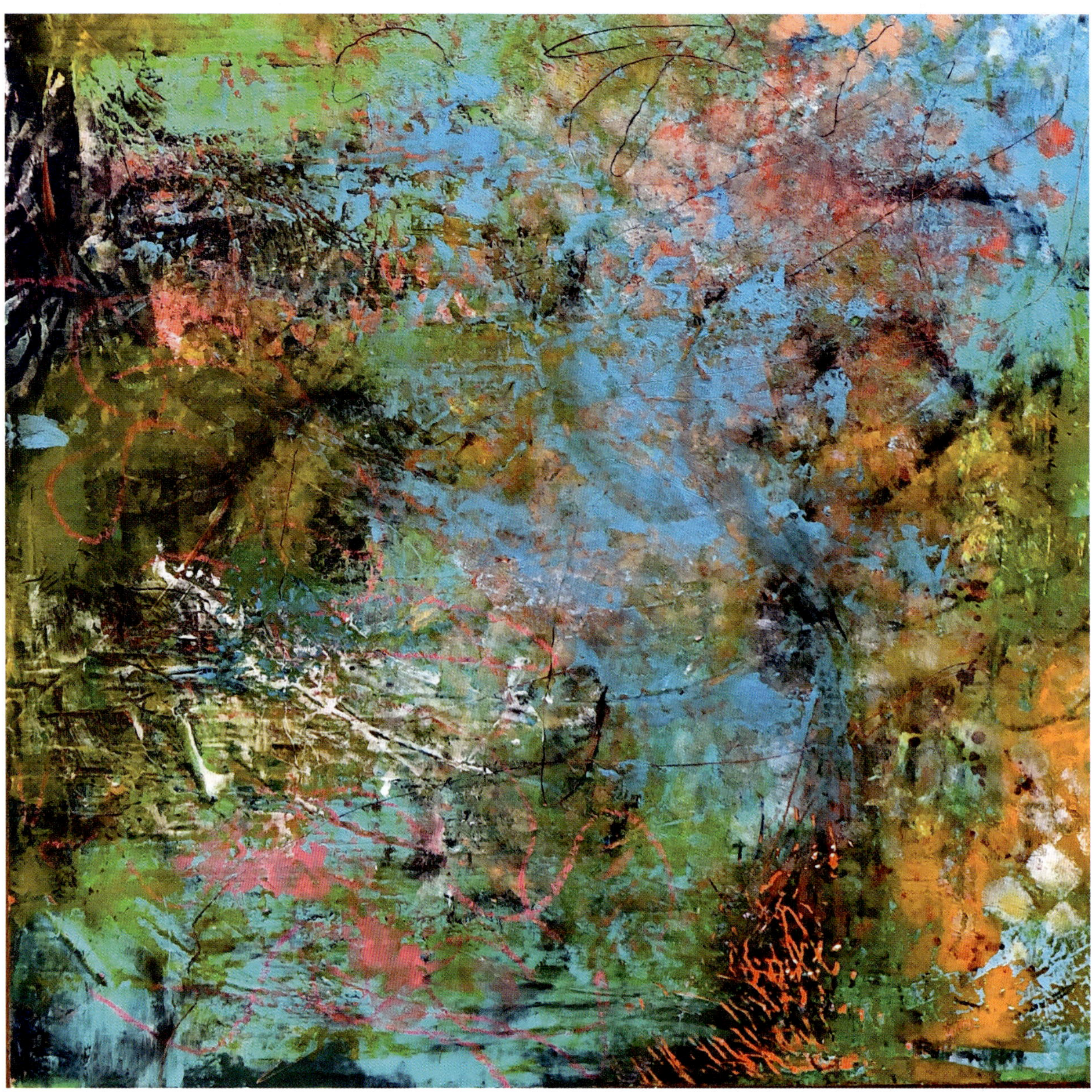

Gini Mallory

Gini Mallory believes art should be just as life is—interesting, textured, and multilayered. She begins every painting with layer upon layer of pigment, Italian plaster, beeswax, mark-making, texture, and patterns. As she works to create a final piece, she incorporates textiles, ink, and other materials. During the process, Mallory regularly plays hide-and-seek, scraping to reveal the history of earlier layers—just like elements of personal history exposed in daily life.

Mallory's inspirations include the colors, shapes, and textures found in nature and in life. From the Gulf Coast beaches to the Blue Ridge Mountains to the Marrakech Medina, Mallory finds inspiration all around her.

Mallory is attracted to renditions of gestures and memories, particularly those found in her own photography, her first artistic medium. Her diverse interests are shown in her paintings, where animals, women, and patterns feature prominently. The more unique the medium, texture, or color combination, the more Mallory is inspired. Most recently, she has been incorporating tar into her paintings.

Peripetia
Oi and mixed media
24 x 24 in.

ginimallory@gmail.com
ginimalloryart.com
@ginimalloryart

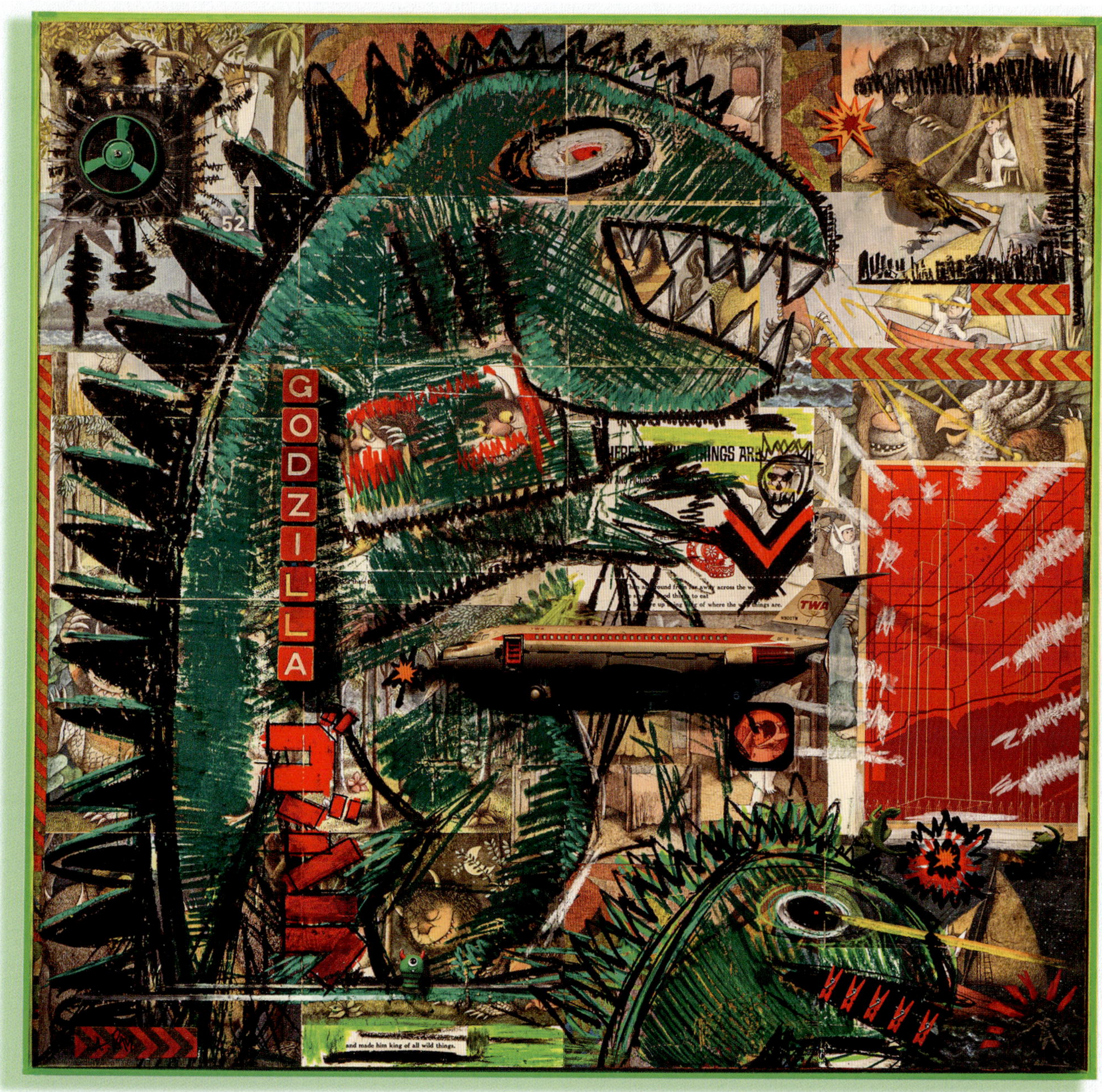

Andrew Manocheo

The thrill of experimenting with new-found materials, the curiosity that comes from discovering salvaged objects, the insatiable quest to discover new techniques, and the delight that comes from making truly original artifacts are what define Andrew Manocheo's work as an artist.

By embracing a creative process that is driven by experimentation, exploration, and discovery, there is never a need for contrived or fabricated inspiration. The work of producing countless artistic iterations that are essentially the same is of little value to Manocheo in terms of being true to his creative drive.

Incorporating a variety of three-dimensional objects into two-dimensional paintings creates a compositional dynamic that draws in the viewer and sparks an immediate response. Each object placed within Manocheo's artwork brings with it a tremendous amount of information for the viewer as it relates to color, material, shape, symbolism, and literal meaning. The allure of capturing just a portion of the infinite combinations of colors, materials, textures, and curated objects is the artist's personal crusade.

Godzilla
Mied media and collage
40 x 40 in.

andrew@notboringart
.com
notboringart.com
@notboringart

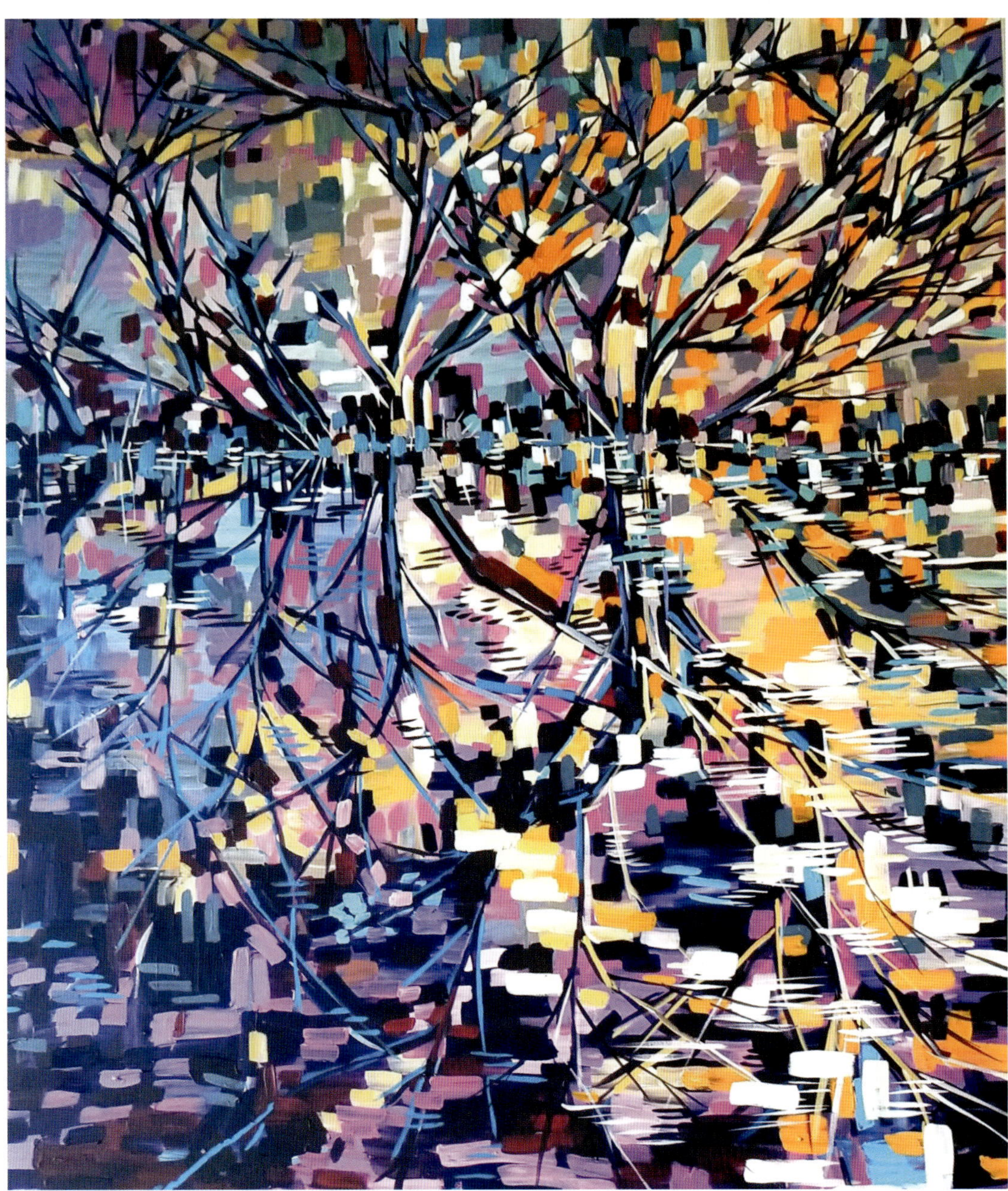

Janak Narayan

"I paint sometimes as I see it, other times as I imagine it, but always because I am loving it," says Janak Narayan.

Art to Narayan is about a beautiful journey of self-discovery and painting is a medium to articulate her inner glee. Narayan would like her art to be experienced through all five senses by transporting the viewer to a place that evokes a certain feeling of joy and a sense of being in the moment. She wants the viewer to step into the canvas and breathe in the world within the composition.

"The numerous facets of my visual experiences of nature and landscapes while growing up in India and traveling abroad have translated into ideas for my compositions," Narayan says. "I also tend to notice patterns and gravitate toward their abstract rhythm. Botanical elements, especially trees, have become my muse. They take on human forms in my imagination, a continuity to my core belief that we humans have to become one with nature. Finally, color is the language of emotions and the medium of my expression."

Submerged
Acrylic
60 x 48 in.

janak202130@gmail.com
janaknarayan.com
@janaknarayanartist

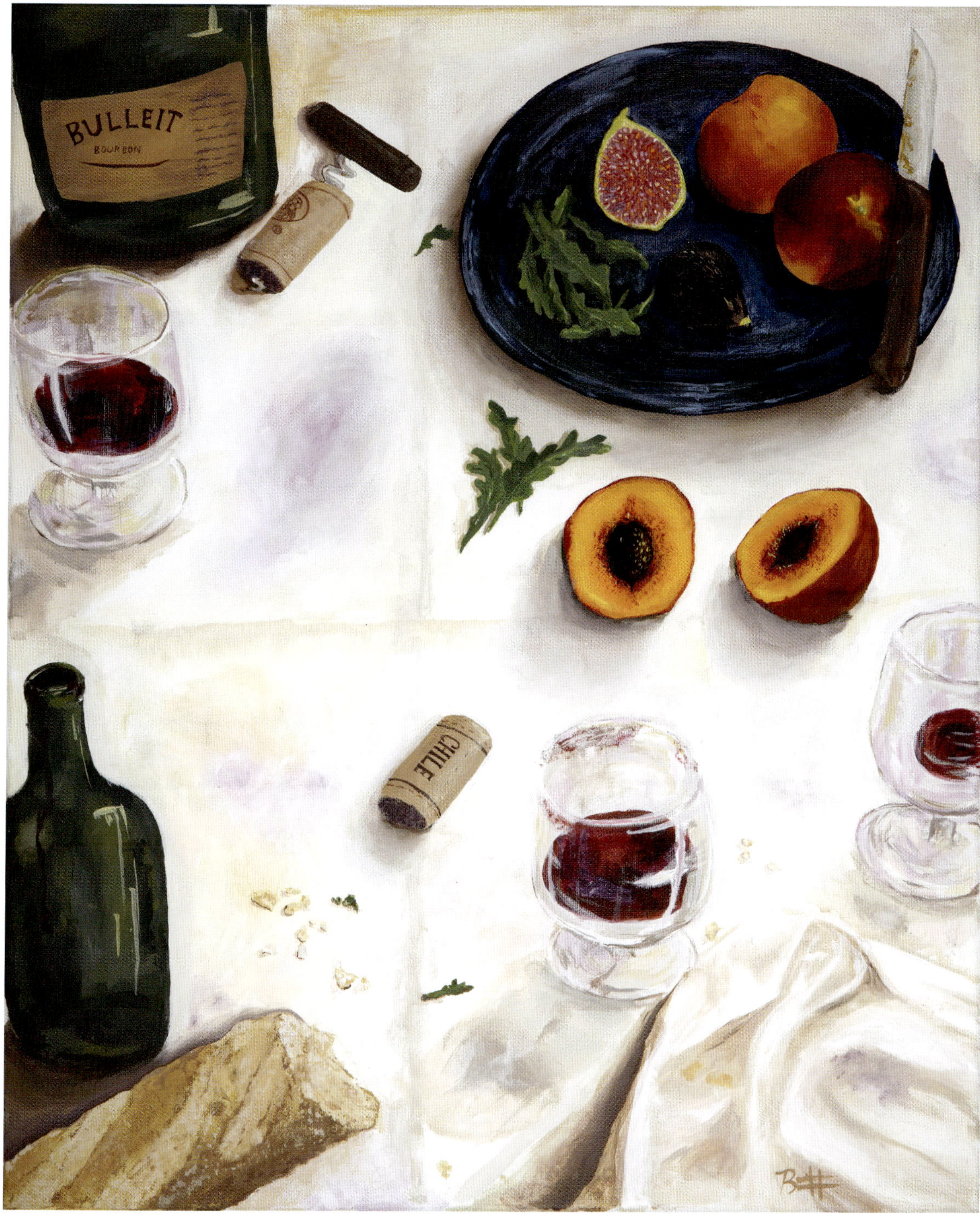

Isabella Penner

Life and culture are at the heart of the subject matter of contemporary artist Isabella Penner. The artist examines and responds to her natural surroundings and the culture that makes up the fabric of society. In particular, the vibrant, colorful, and energetic culture of South America captivates and inspires her imagination.

Penner describes her work as vibrant, and she frequently uses pattern and contrast throughout her pieces. Her aesthetic is influenced by her time spent living in Bolivia. "I lived in Bolivia for a significant amount of my youth, and it was here that I fell in love with the use of color and the influence art has on people, community, and culture," she says.

Her preferred mediums are acrylic on canvas and ink on paper.

Party Isn't Over
Acrylic
20 x 16 in.

isabellapenner.artist@
gmail.com
isabellapennerart.com
@bellalona.studio

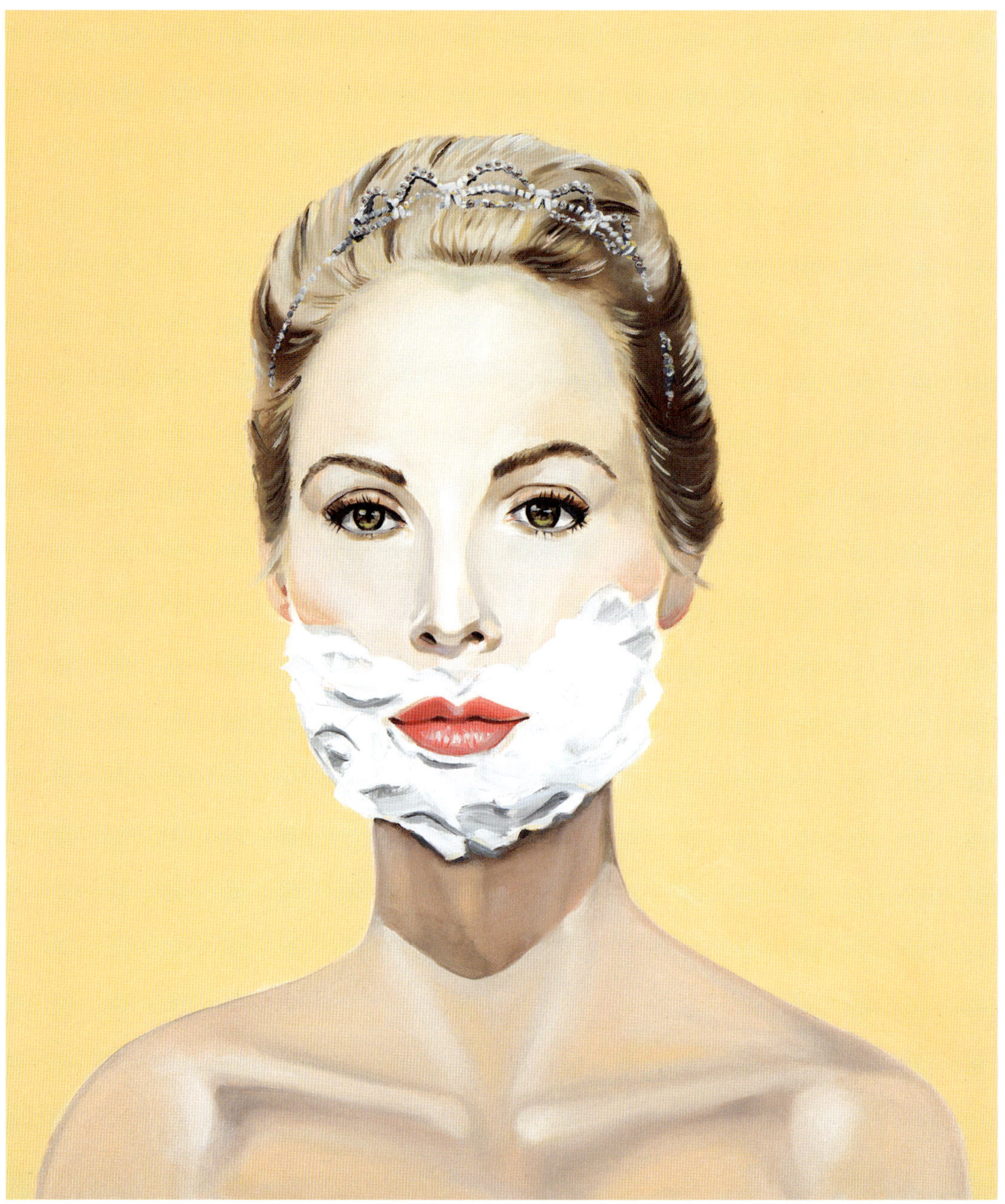

Vedrana Pinjo

People's lives have always fascinated Vedrana Pinjo: why they happen, where they take us, and how they end up being a story. "I am a pop-art story painter. A woman who tells stories through portraits," she says.

Pinjo's art is not self-centered, nor is it an expression of how she feels while creating it. Instead, her process consists of the careful selection of an iconic figure, instilling contemporary relevance in some aspect of their image and incorporating modern topics into their otherwise outdated presence. Essentially, she uses her subjects to represent a current event or statement as a means of exploring particular political or social issues. Using an icon's face as a medium allows Pinjo to expose truths about topics through a lens that lets people see the issue from a different angle.

There is a provocative cynicism in all of her work. "I like to cause discomfort, challenge stereotypes, awaken curiosity, shame, and humor, and engage passive people in productive discussions," Pinjo says.

Grace Kelly: Shaving
Oil and crystals on canvas
36 x 30 in.

vedranapinjo@gmail.com
vedranapinjo.com
@vedrana.pinjo.art

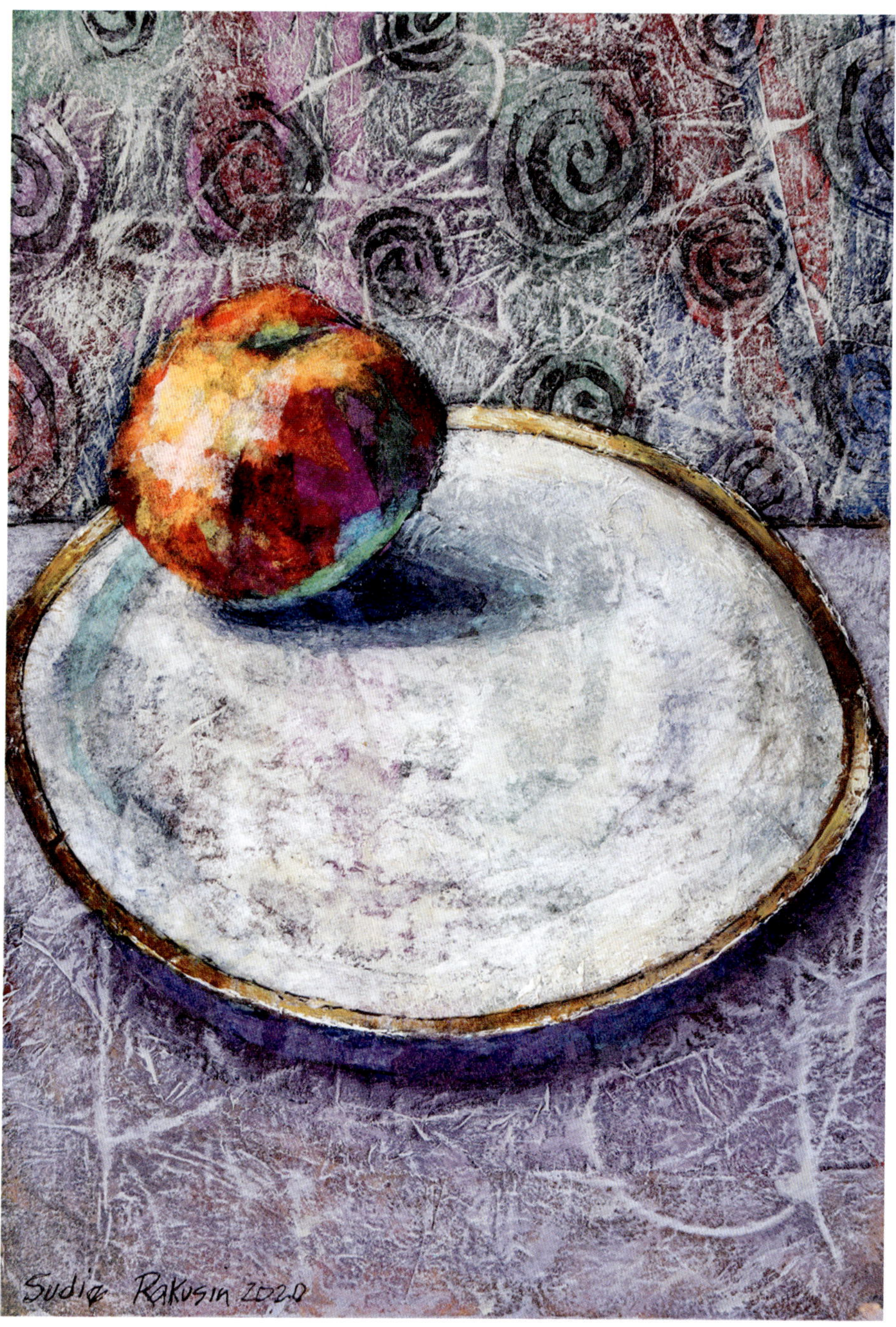

Sudie Rakusin

As an animal activist and feminist, Sudie Rakusin creates artwork that flows from what moves her and from where she finds beauty: women, animals, the earth, color, pattern, and light. Her art represents the deep connection she feels with these elements. "Art is where I go for refuge, replenishing, and how I pay homage to what sustains me," she says.

Line drawings inspired her collection of small collages/ paintings of women's portraits, plants, fruit, and vegetables. Rakusin found herself painting with tissue. Each work is created with layers of tissue, paint, and line. Layers of emotion, layers of memory and dreams. Layers that are hidden and secret, brave or wild. Layers that are always variegated, always colorful.

Peach on Plate
Tissue collage, pen and ink, acrylic paint on archival board
11 x 8 in.

info@sudierakusin.com
sudierakusin.com
@sudie.rakusin

PAINTING: TRADITIONAL/CONTEMPORARY

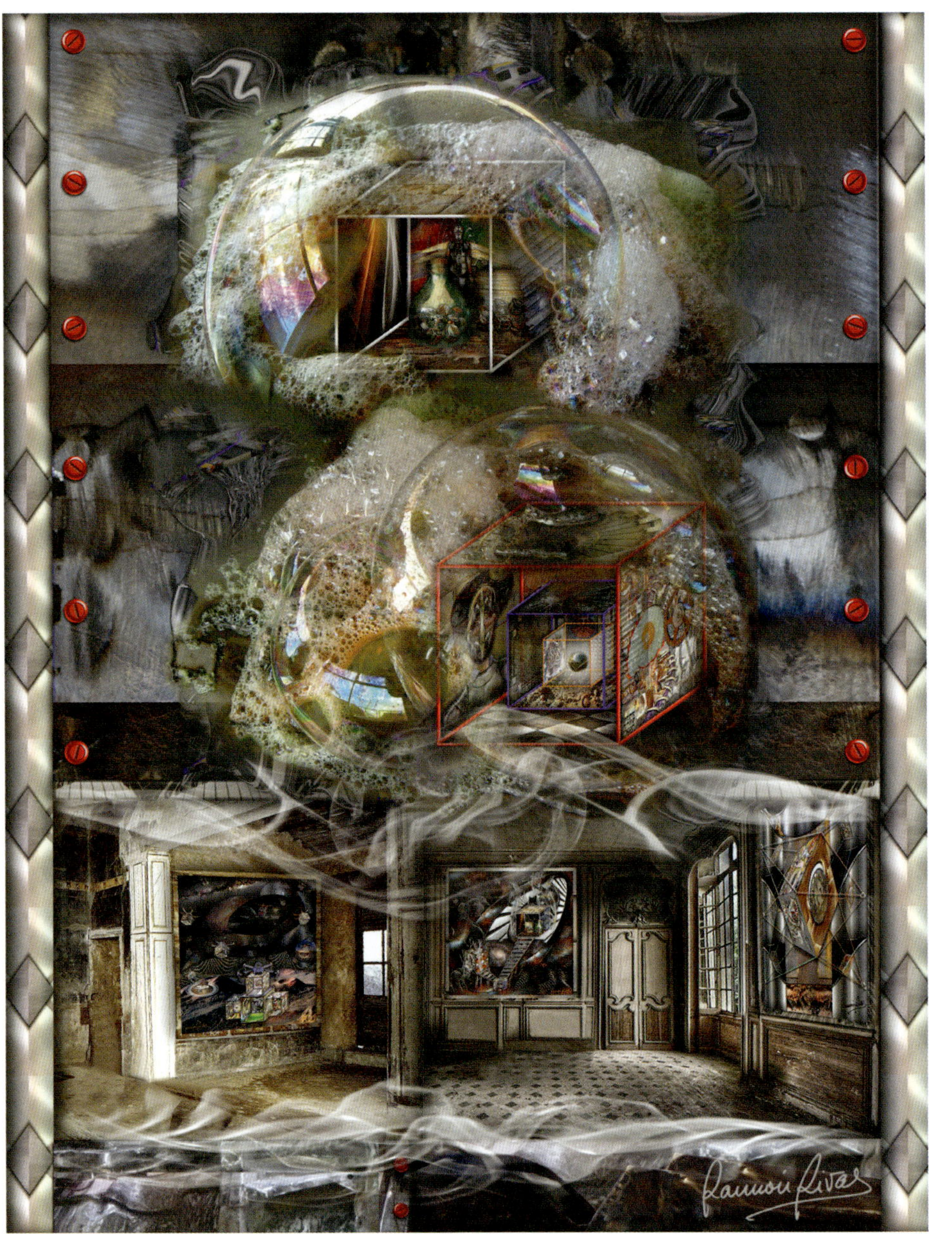

Ramon Rivas
Ramon Rivas's work has a marked personal seal of identity that he applies freely and without limitations. He uses his creativity to be different and look for new artistic proposals with the purpose of surprising and exciting the viewer.

"My imagination has been and is fundamental to developing creative, novel works that interact positively with the observer's eyes. My training as a project and organization engineer makes me work in an orderly, methodical way, studying the best alternatives, supervising good execution, introducing scientific topics, balancing the composition, and making the painting a walkable space for the viewer," Rivas says.

The results are images produced with elaborate precision, with impressive density and depth that visually captivate. Rivas prefers to work in a large format. For him, the artist's work is the embodiment of his inner self in a tangible form.

Rivas's works are not intended to be mere decorative objects but a skillful source of provocation that encourages the viewer to participate.

Art Explosion
Mixed media
78.75 x 59 in.

ramonrivas2012@yahoo.es
rivismo.com
@ramonrivas_rivismo

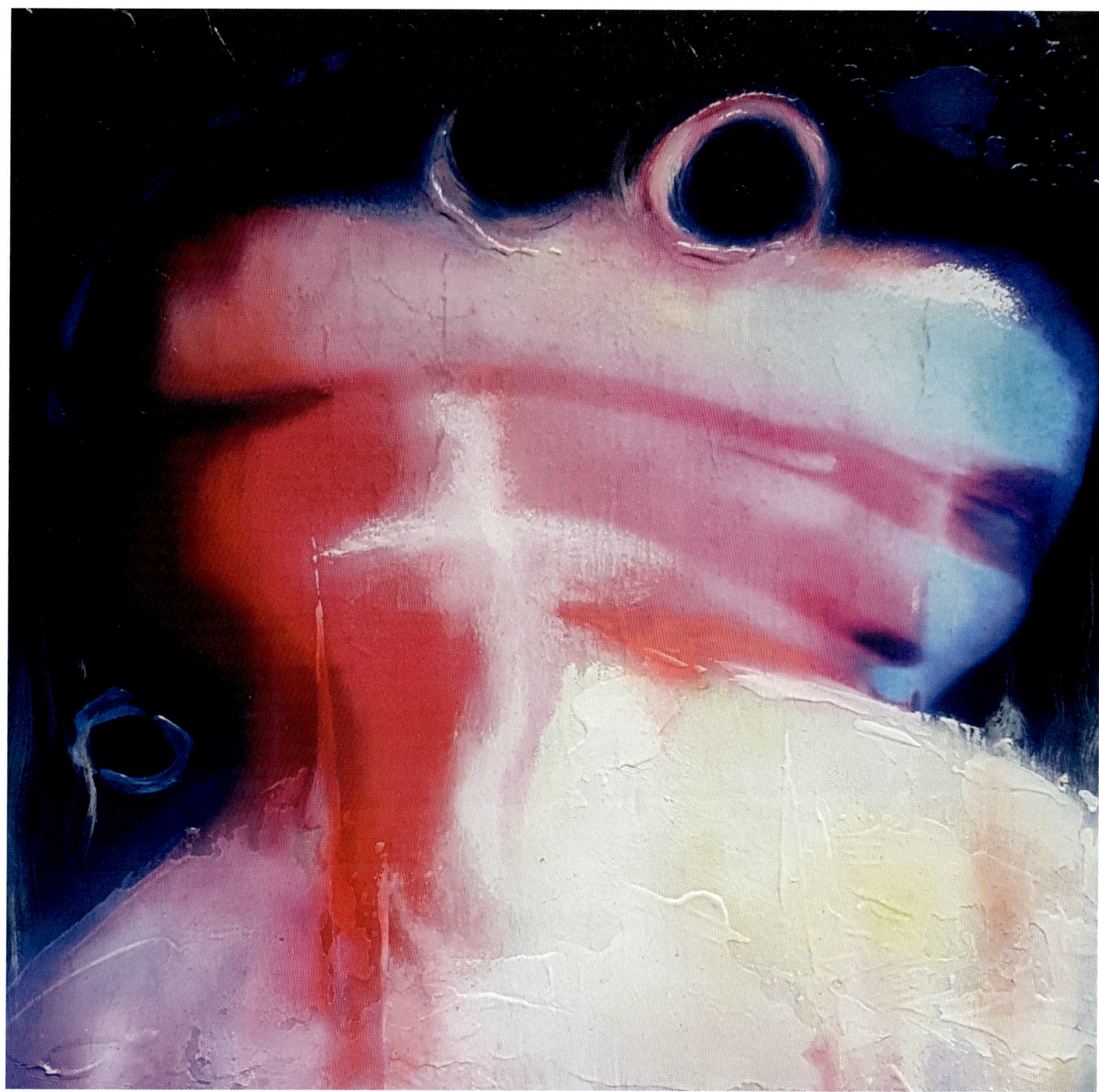

Stewart Russell

Stewart Russell has always had an interest in consciousness and the countless states of mind one can experience. Through exploring his own sense of self and the many different forms that reside within him, he finds he can express his true self.

The work created through this exploration conveys Russell's willingness to communicate with the viewer. However, the introverted desire to hide from view is always present. The work displays shades of himself that are still not fully familiar to Russell and conjure feelings of vulnerability and exposure. This tension is presented to the viewer in a distorted and often abstract and symbolic way, allowing the viewer to get a glimpse at Russell's consciousness.

Russell's aim is to have the viewer question their own inner being and remind them that we are all enduring a conscious experience both inside and outside of ourselves, while expressing this is unique to oneself. It is through a mixture of methods and mediums, from painting and printing to digital photography and videography, that Russell finds the appropriate way to reveal the inner moment to the viewer.

Subdued
Oil, printed image on MDF Board
7.8 x 7.8 in.

russells187@gmail.com
stewartrussellart
.bigcartel.com
@stewart_russell_art

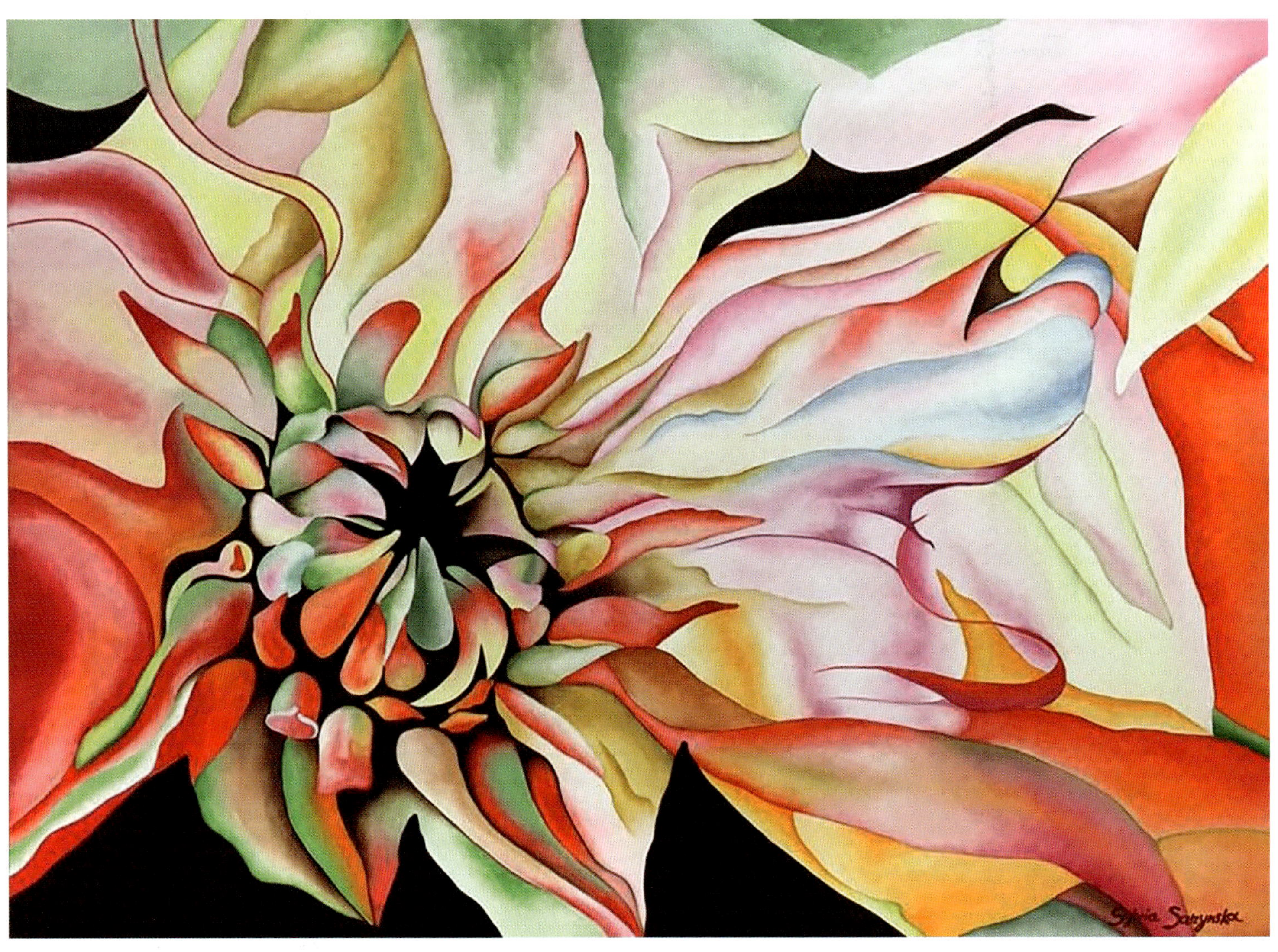

Sylvia Sarzynska

Sylvia Sarzynska is a self-taught, Polish contemporary abstract artist based in the United States. In college, Sarzynska's artistic pursuits led to a degree in fine art/graphic design.

With a fascination for the floral form and an instinct to capture it on canvas, and with a knack for drawing and a whirlwind of possibilities in her head, she admits she found inspiration in unexpected places. Her artistic trademark is to capture the timeless yet elegant and delicate feel of the flower, allowing the viewer to better identify with each painting.

Over the years, Sarzynska has been taking her paintings in an innovative, new direction that is really beginning to show who she wants to become as an artist. Her strongest inspiration is derived from her personal experience in the female form, which dove her into the idea of creating almost three-dimensional female torsos. The new pieces allow her to convey texture, design, and abstraction with a freedom she has never known until now. She has fallen in love with the expression the pieces create. The female form has the ability to be empowering and beautiful.

Dahlia Goddess
Oil on canvas
30 x 40 in.

sylviasarzynska@yahoo.com
sylviasarzynska.com
@sylviasarzynska

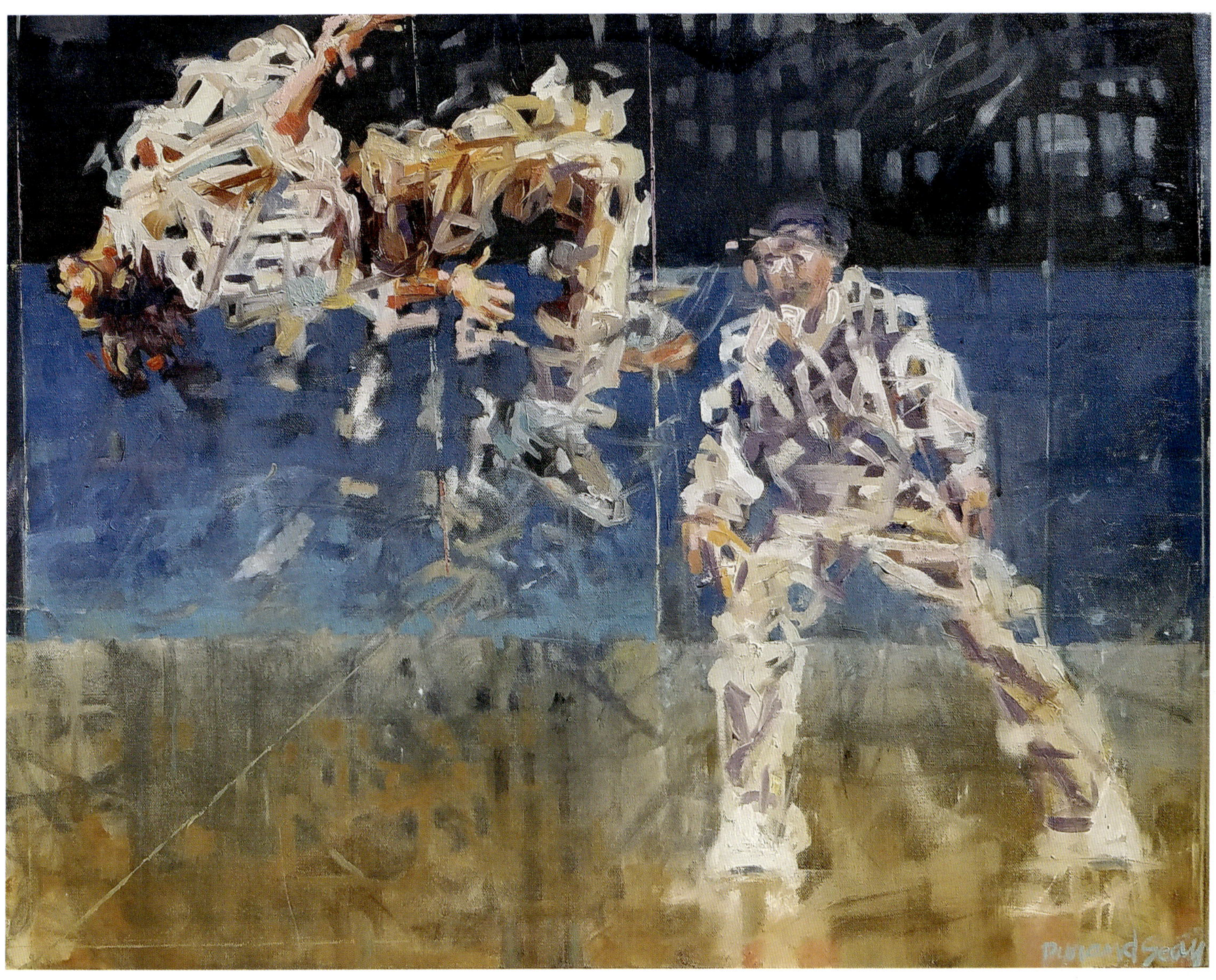

Durand D. Seay

A deep-South Alabama artist, Durand Seay escapes from traditions that label artists by location. His paintings search for a flowing and unpredictable expression, ever-changing, like water in a stream or the fluidity of waves. There is a search for a connection to the soul. Time and movement are essential factors that affect the participant. As an architect, Seay builds these expressions from structures intuitively found in nature. There is a language with a quantum perspective, past, present, and future all at once. Seay harnesses a viewer's subconscious to instill awareness, insight, achievement, and the ascendancy of understanding.

Seay employs symbols such as horses for freedom, blue roosters for vigilance, and dancers for human emotions like satisfaction or regret. All of these are in some form of movement in time and space.

"When we as viewers respect our acceptance of our own place in the fabric of nature and our rejection of stability in favor of balance, we begin to understand nature's chaos in structures," the artist says.

Taking Flight
Oil on canvas
24 x 30 in.

durand@durandseay
.com
durandseay.com
@durandseay

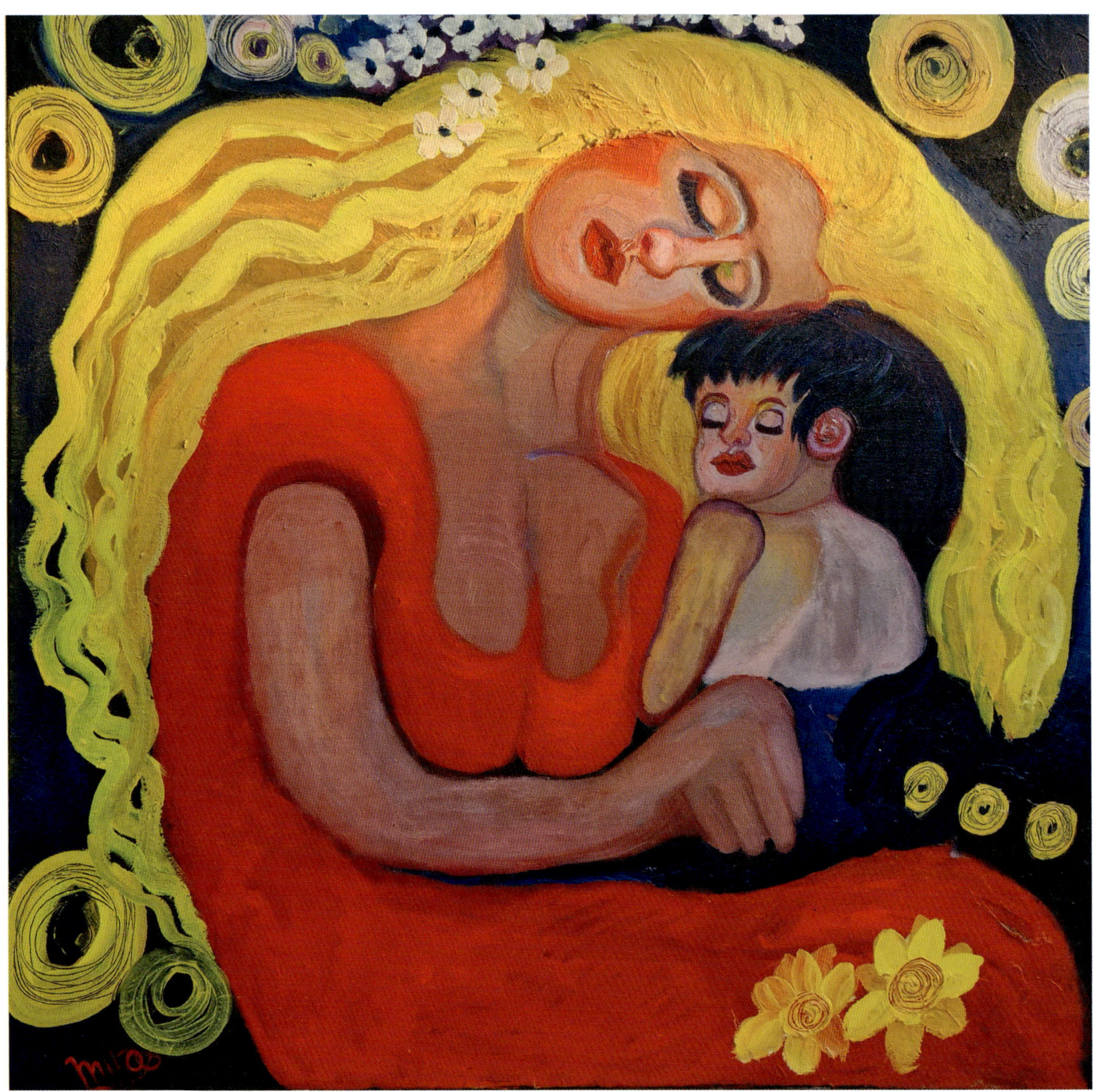

Mira Seeman

Mira Seeman has been painting since her youth. Her art presents the vitality and beauty of nature, the pure nature that she loves so much as it is, and her universal love for people without deference to religion, race, or gender. "This is an essential component of what I am choosing to express in my paintings," Seeman says. "I am not repeating the same topic of my paintings. All of my art comes from the depths of my soul."

Some of Seeman's paintings come through visions she has, through her dreams, as well as other sources of inspiration. Her works are executed spontaneously in the alla prima technique with impressionistic notes.

Softness
Oil on canvas
31.5 x 31.5 in.

mirasee121@gmail.com
miraseeman.com
@Mira Seeman

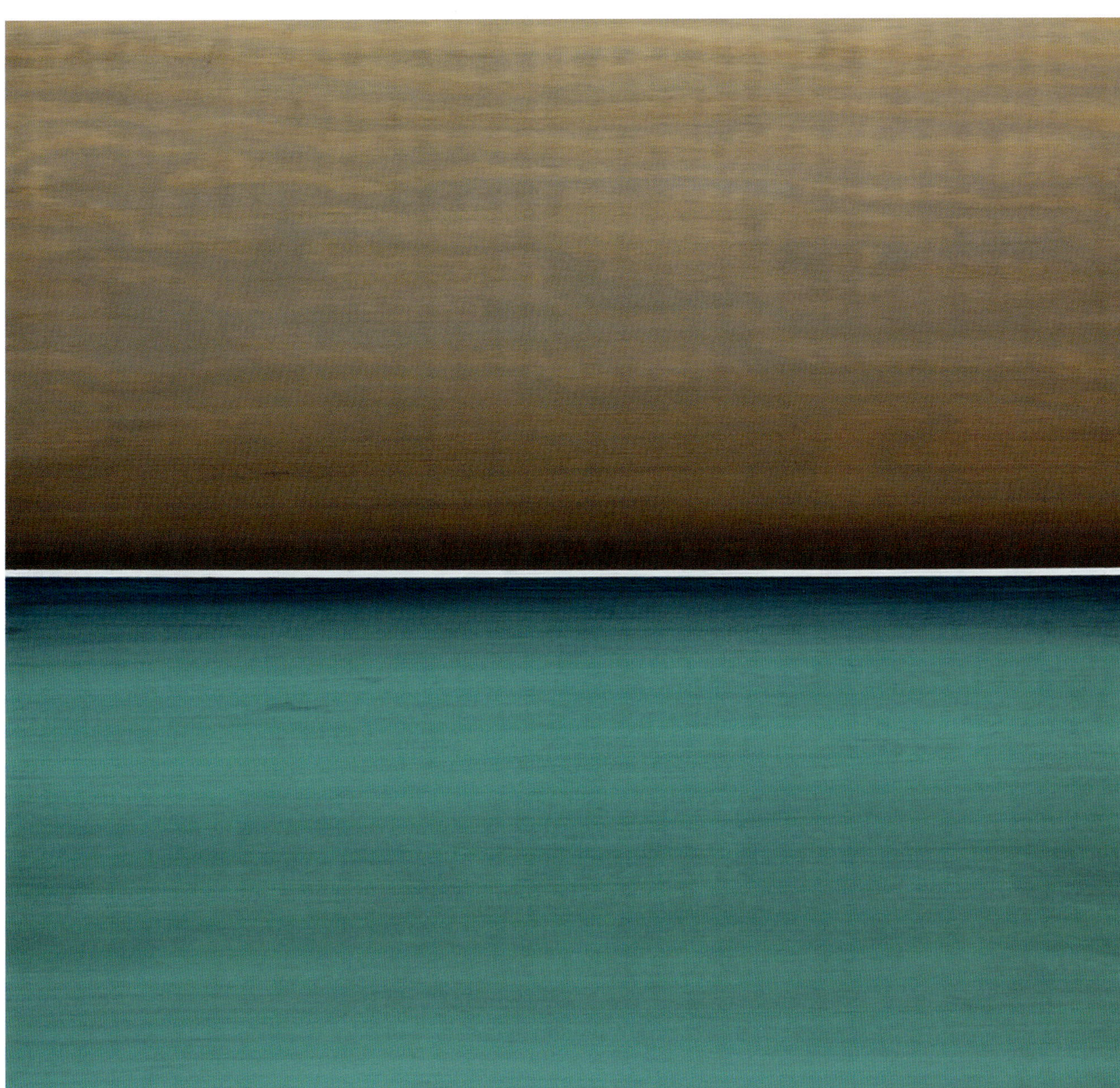

Gordon Skalleberg

Gordon Skalleberg paints faces and eyes, or sometimes only sections of a face, because he is trying to see beyond the surface. Often, he paints from old photographs of people he has never met. This allows the artist the freedom to depict the face as he wants because he is not trying to capture what he knows about the individual, but rather only what he sees. Some of Skalleberg's paintings inspire the viewers to create their own stories from their own perspectives. This thrills the artist.

A recent relocation to Santa Fe, New Mexico, with its desert landscapes and open skies, has inspired new imagery in a semiabstract landscape style that draws on quintessential Southwestern features. Skalleberg's faces and landscapes are painted in oil on untreated plywood and other types of wood. Unique wood grains become part of each painting, often in serendipitous ways. The process and the result often surprise the artist, and he likes to surprise the viewer as well. Imperfection is often found in his pictures—a crack in the plywood, trickles, scratches, roughness—all are welcome additions by the artist.

Horizon 23-20
Oil on board
16 x 16 in.

skalleberg@
artworkinternational
.com
gordonskalleberg.com
@gordonskalleberg

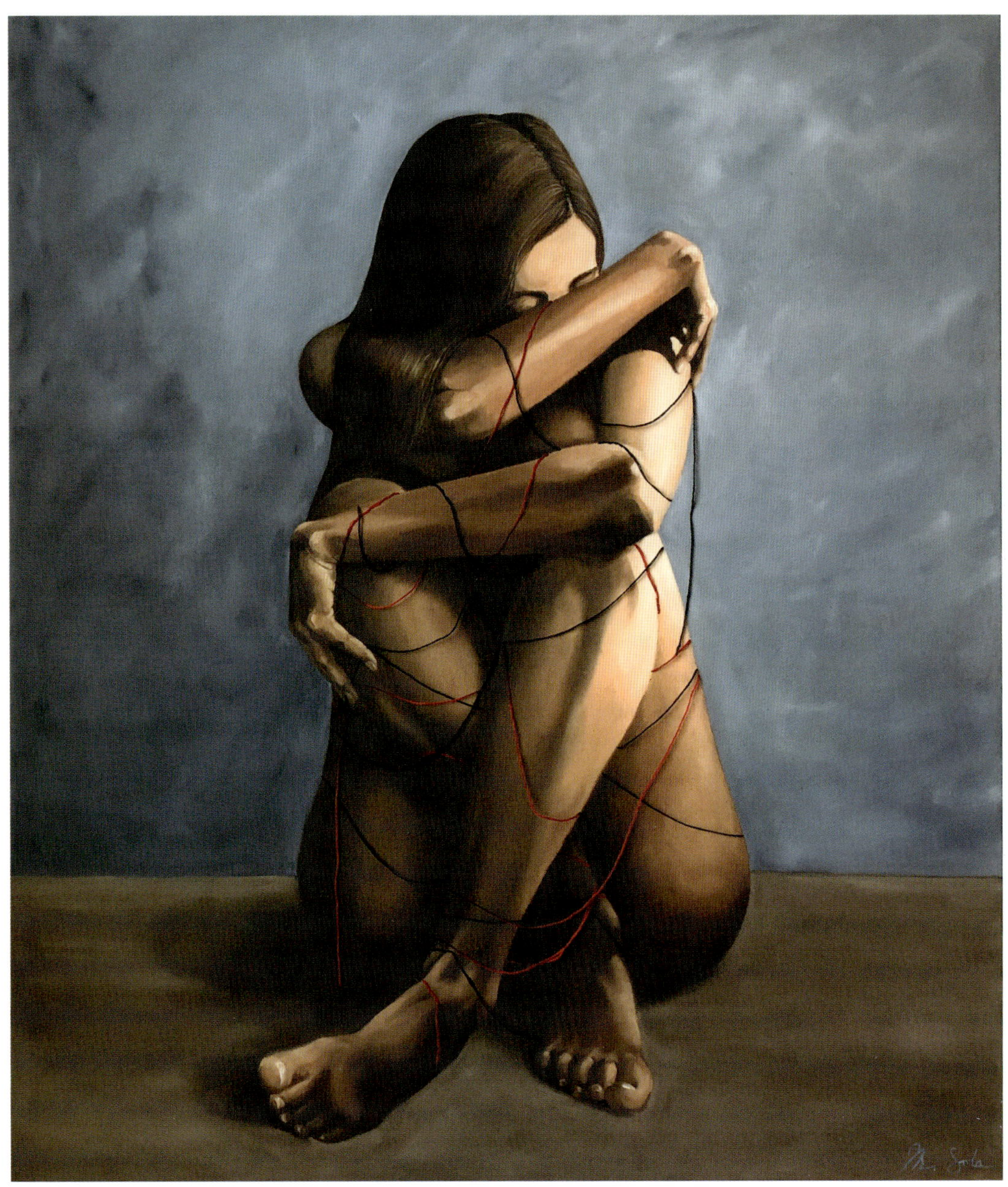

Meghan Sola

From an early age, Meghan Sola was drawn to visual art for its therapeutic and expressive value, something that still is central to her practice today. She continues to produce work that expresses her own emotional struggles and depicts her life experiences in both a metaphorical and literal way. Having a strong episodic memory, much of her work is tied to specific memories and events from her past and has a nostalgic quality. Sola's more metaphorical pieces tie to broader themes and emotions of loss, loneliness, isolation, depression, and lack of control. Regardless of the subject matter, the majority of her drawings and paintings have a sense of placelessness; the figure, memory, or metaphor hover in a space with little attachment or belonging.

An avid traveler and a Baltimore transplant now living in Dallas, Sola's struggle to feel at home has followed her throughout her life and is evident in her work. Despite the very intimate and personal quality of her work, she strives to create imagery that elicits visceral emotional responses in her audience, thus creating a universal narrative of loss and struggle that speaks to the human condition.

Unravel II
Oil and embroidery thread on canvas
38 x 32 in.

solameghan@gmail.com
solameghan.wixsite.
com/mysite
@msolaart

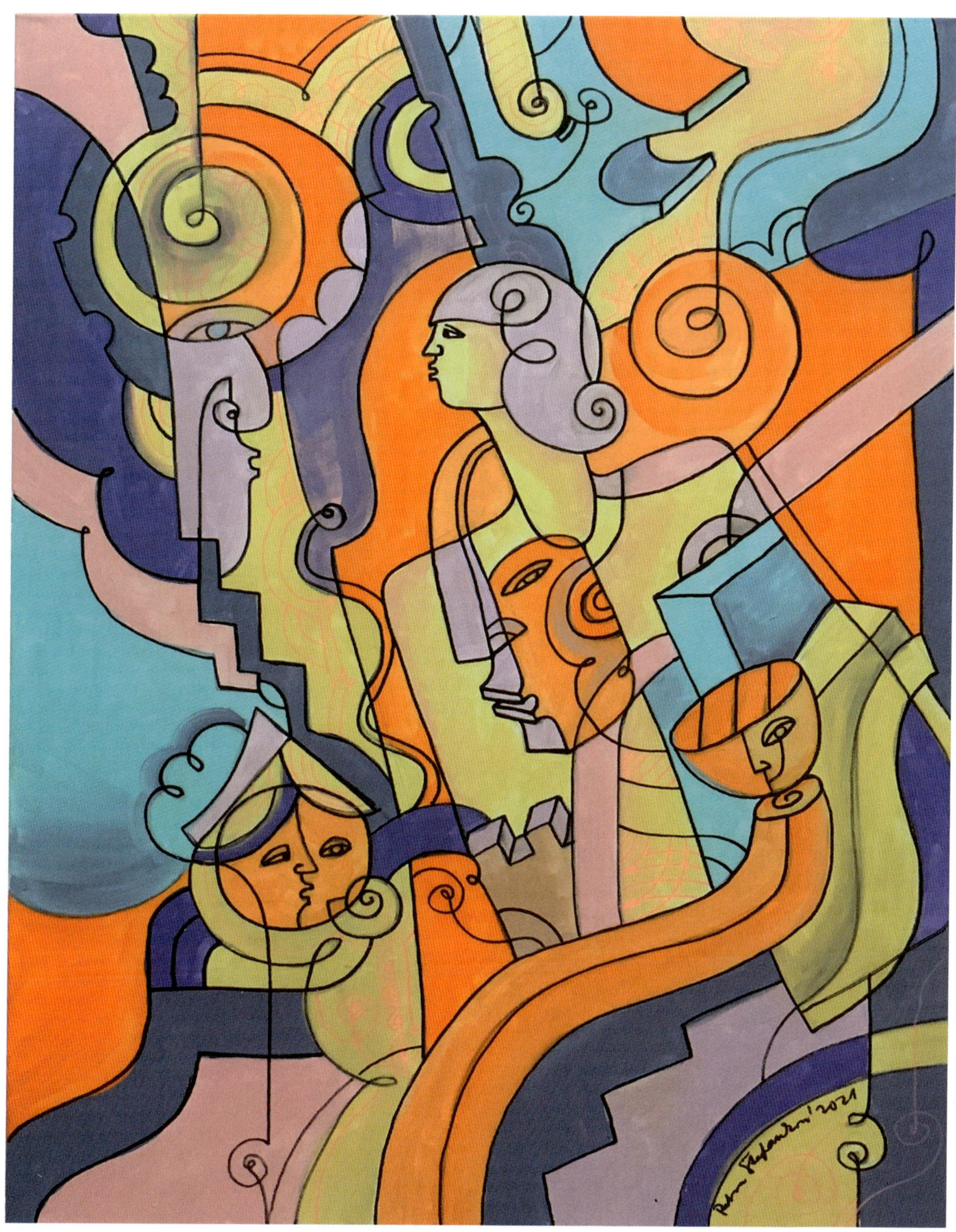

Petra Stefankova

Petra Stefankova is an award-winning fine and digital artist who is published all around the world. Now based in Slovakia, she spent some time living in London and traveled to the USA, Australia, France, and Germany to develop a professional artist presence. Her work reflects her travel and life experiences.

She often uses the automatic drawing method, which is her way of collecting experiences, memories, feelings, and situations depicted in her drawings. She uses computer tools, especially vector graphics, to redraw and aesthetically improve her doodles, but her work also represents traditional modern painting and acrylics on canvas. Her color palette is vivid and fresh, but at the same time, it is very feminine. Her visual artwork refers to introspection rather than simple observation of reality. As she studied graphic design, she tends to simplify shapes and objects. A strong black outline is a natural signature of the artist.

Games of Life
Acrylic on canvas
35.5 x 27.5 in.

petrastefankova@gmail.com
petrastefankova.com
@petrastefankova

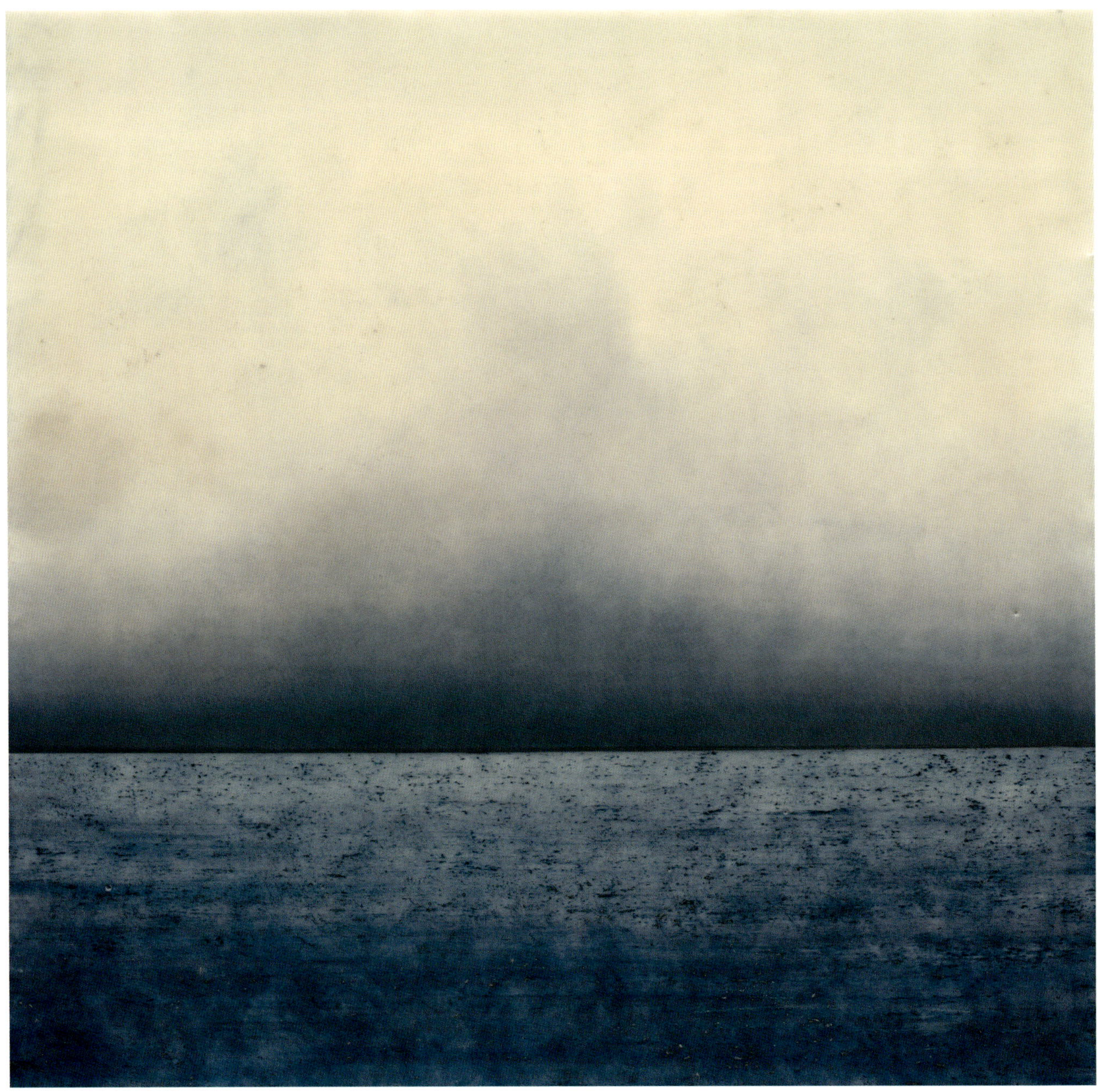

Tricia Trinder
Tricia Trinder is an encaustic artist known for her atmospheric *Porthole Horizon* series.

In her garden studio, she creates her ocean horizons using beeswax, damar resin, and dry pigments. Trinder concentrates on how the light reflects on the water through different times of the day and types of weather. Her horizons give a sense of inner calmness and serenity and also encourage the viewer to contemplate what is beyond.

"I like to create the illusion of distance in my paintings using light and dark," Trinder says. "I use texture to create the idea of waves and water, and light on the horizon to distinguish between times of the day. Encaustic lends itself beautifully to images of water because the natural element of beeswax reflects the natural texture and translucency of water, also the unpredictability of how the wax responds each time I burn in the color reflects the unpredictability of the ocean and skies."

Brewing
Encaustic and dry pigment
23.5 x 23.5 in.

tricia@trinder.net
triciatrinderart.com.au
@tricia.trinder

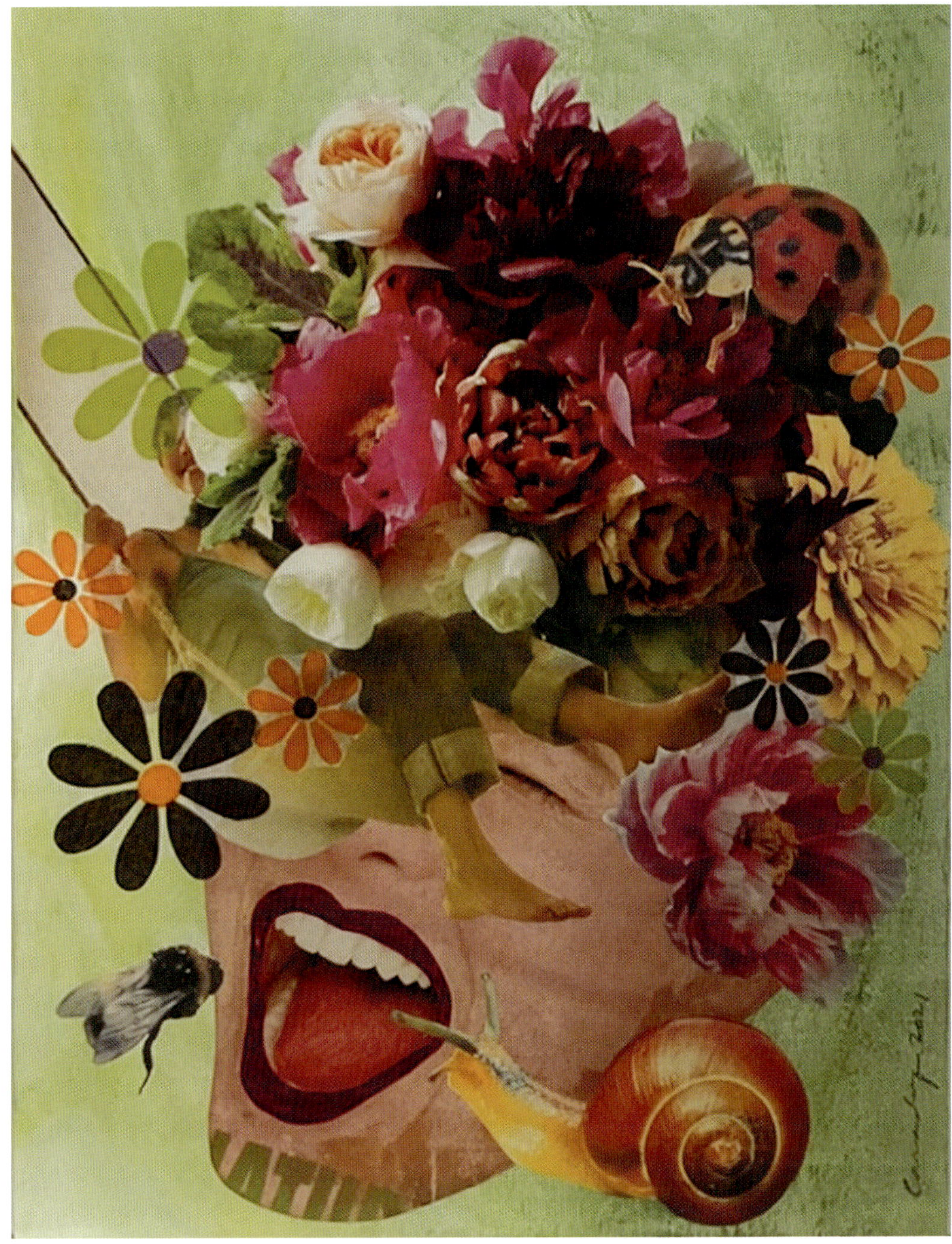

Carmen Angela Yandoc
Carmen Angela Yandoc creates mixed-media collages from magazine cutouts, public domain images from the internet, her own artwork, and photographs, combined with acrylics, gouache, and colored pencils. Cutting, piecing together, placing, and gluing images by association and bisociation allows the artist to explore new interpretations, often unanticipated. Collage lends itself to the transformation and expansion of her ideas beyond the initial intentions, which make for wonderful surprises. Hence, besides the artistic process, it is the exercise in fresh and fertile thinking that appeals to her. She finds the possibilities afforded by collage both exciting and freeing. She considers collage to be her playground, where imagination and reality meld effortlessly. Her work is inspired by the Old Masters and contemporary artists, as well as fiction and film. For Yandoc, creative self-expression and the sheer pleasure of making enriches the ways she experiences the world.

Swing
Magazine cut-outs, table napkin, acrylic on canvas board
12 x 9 in.

cara.y.duque@gmail.com
@cara_duq

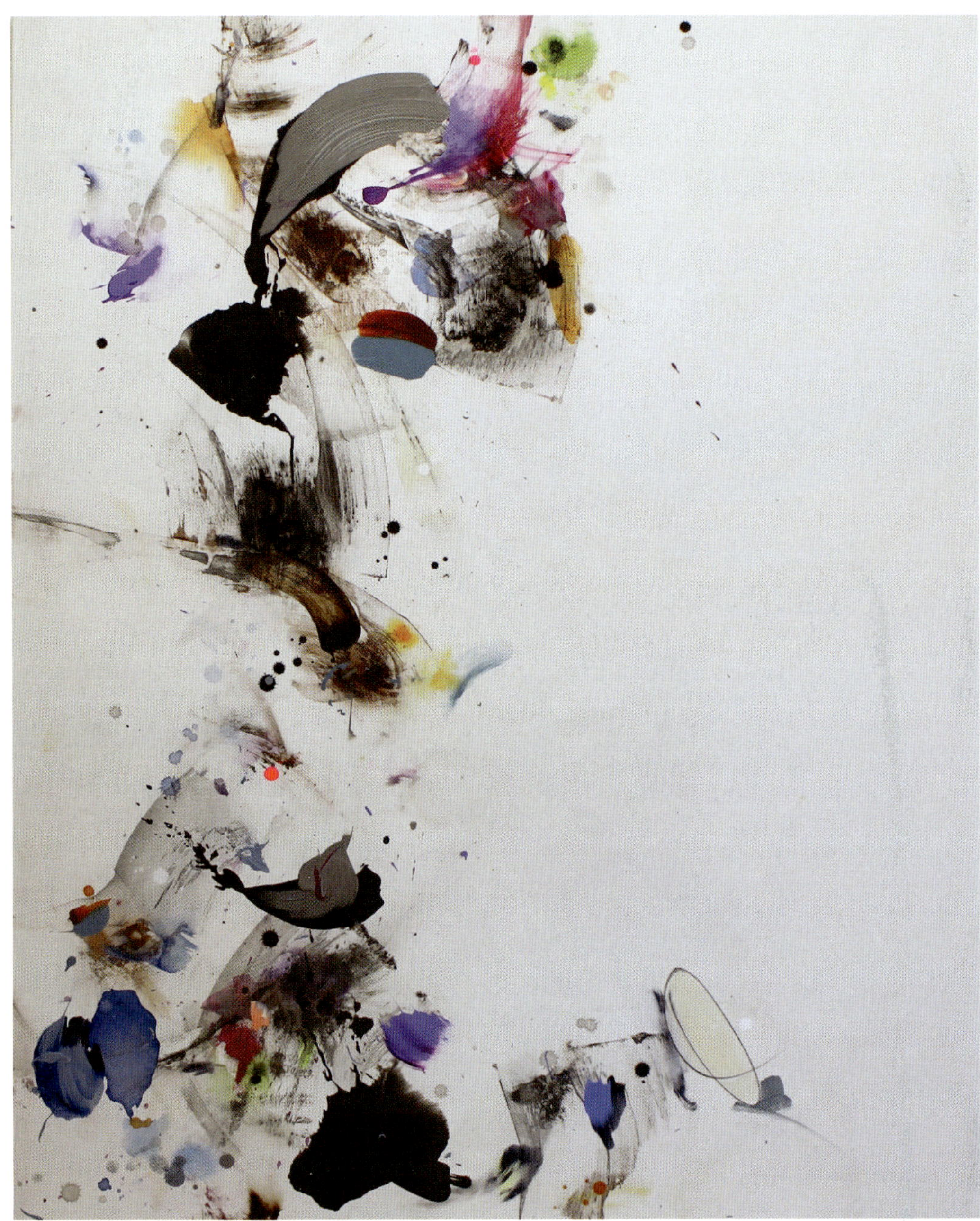

Nikki Hill-Smith

"The joy of being a painter is the daily challenge to conjure a dynamic formal language," says Nikki Hill-Smith. For the artist, that means combining lines and color in a particular way, as well as the constant rearrangement of forms and structure. "I attempt to hold in check order and chaos and when to embrace unplanned events," says Hill-Smith. Sometimes this requires losing the focus on a painting in order to find it. Hill-Smith uses negative space to set off the calligraphy portions of her work with an emphasis on the process, continuously facing more questions than answers while always working in a state of flux.

"The continuity of the fluid process shifts from point to point in my work," Hill-Smith says. "I am governed by self-imposed rules formed by the intense debate between everyone that has ever painted before me and myself. Creating the best composition is my highest priority." In Hill-Smith's work, the subject matter is the paint itself.

Infinnitely Interruptible 1
Acrylic on canvass
60 x 40 in.

OPPOSITE:
Infinnitely Interruptible 2
Acrylic on canvass
60 x 40 in.

n.hillsmith1@googlemail.com
nikkihillsmith.art
@nikkihillsmith

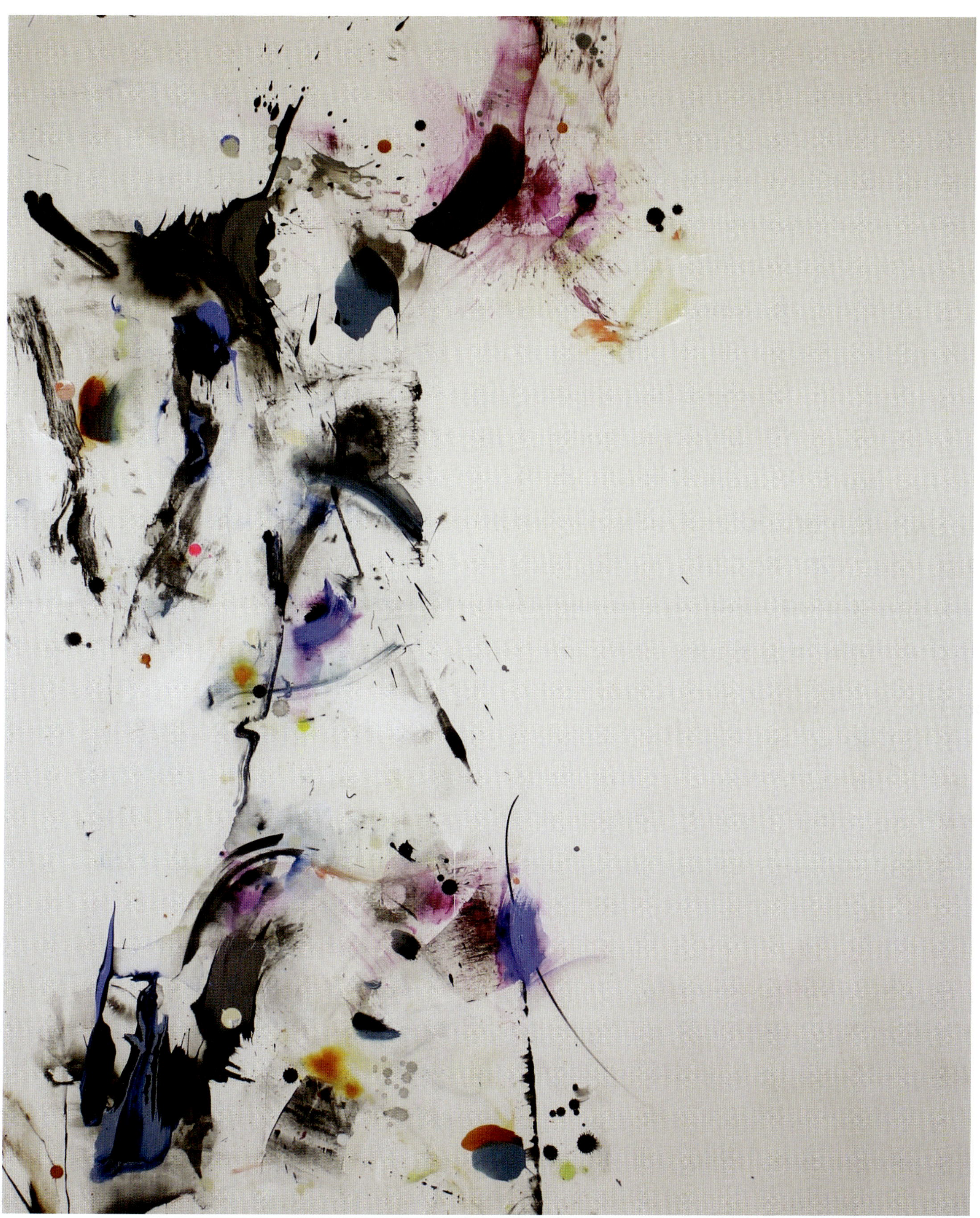

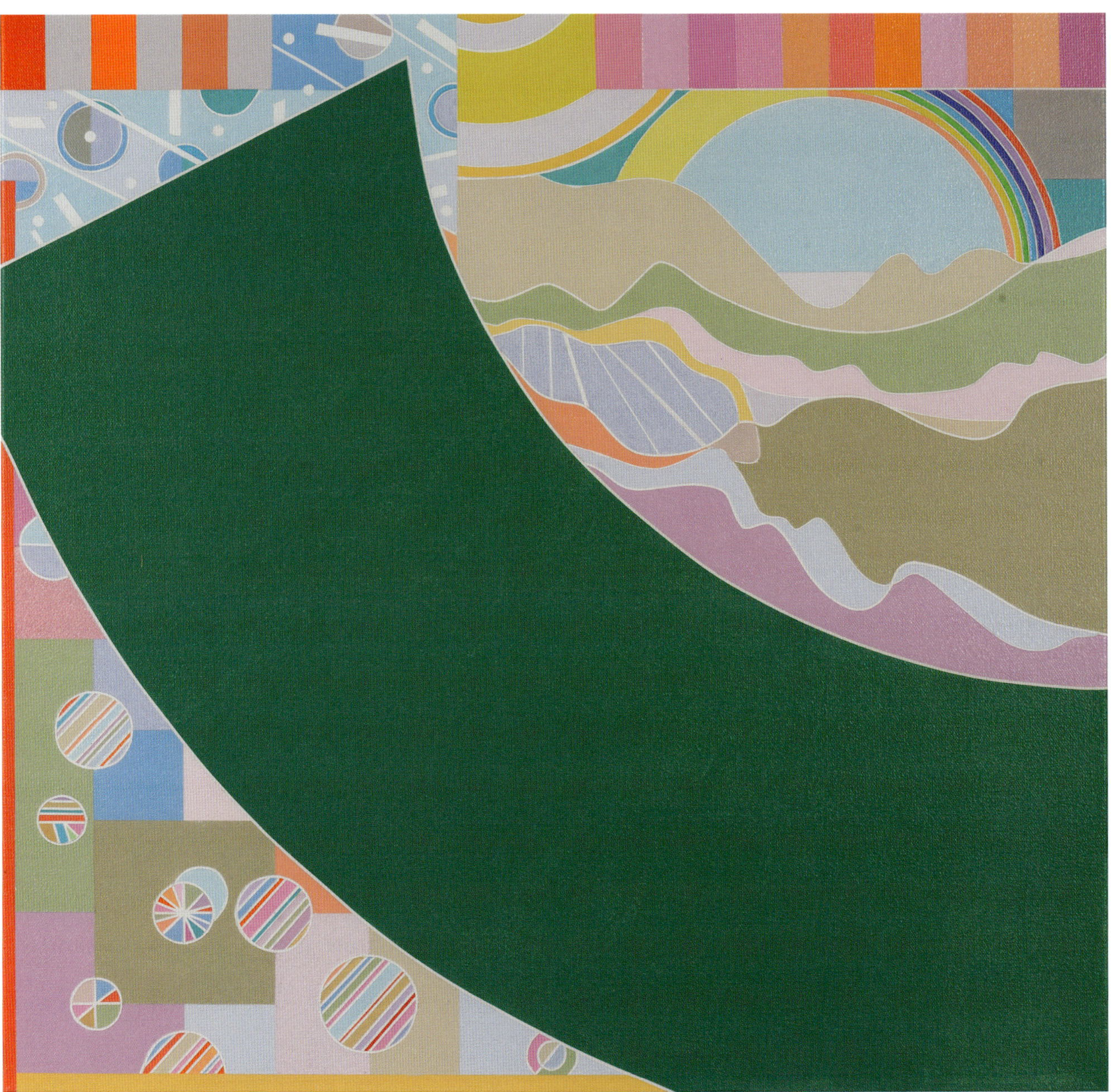

Ai-Wen Wu Kratz

Coming from an Eastern culture and having no background in Greek mythology, Ai-Wen Wu Kratz found it difficult to follow Homer's *Odyssey* and *Iliad*. Thankfully, because both texts are part of the literary canon, the artist was able to listen to them via LibriVox.

"As I listened, it didn't disappoint me at all for not being able to capture the stories in good order. Instead, I found what I heard to be absolutely beautiful. It was the excellent use of language with words and phrasing that electrified me," Kratz says.

What the beautiful writings of the *Odyssey* and *Iliad* did for Kratz could be what the small strokes of colorful paints in Monet's painting of haystacks did to Kandinsky. Kandinsky did not recognize that what he saw in Monet's paintings was about haystacks. Instead, he saw something far more intriguingly powerful—the interplay of colors, forms, lines, volumes, and movements.

"I associate realism in visual art to journalism and abstract art to poetry," Kratz says. "I strive to make visual poems, and I hope my works will bring happiness and peace to others."

Five Sonnets. No.1
Acrylic on canvas
24 x 24 in.

kratz@
aiwenwukratzartstudio
.com
aiwenwukratzartstudio
.com
@aiwenwukratz

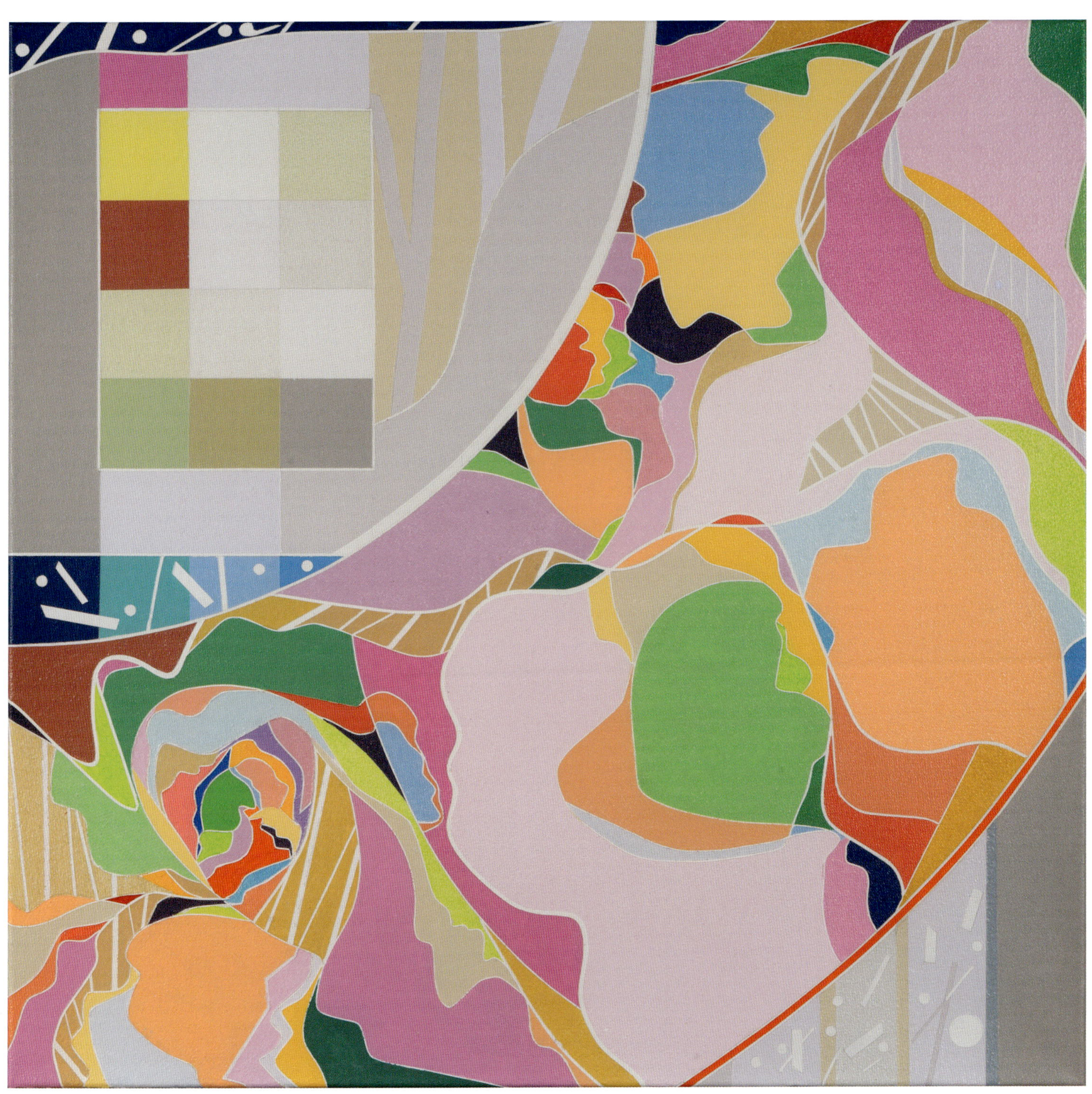

Five Sonnets. No.3
Acrylic on canvas
14 x 14 in.

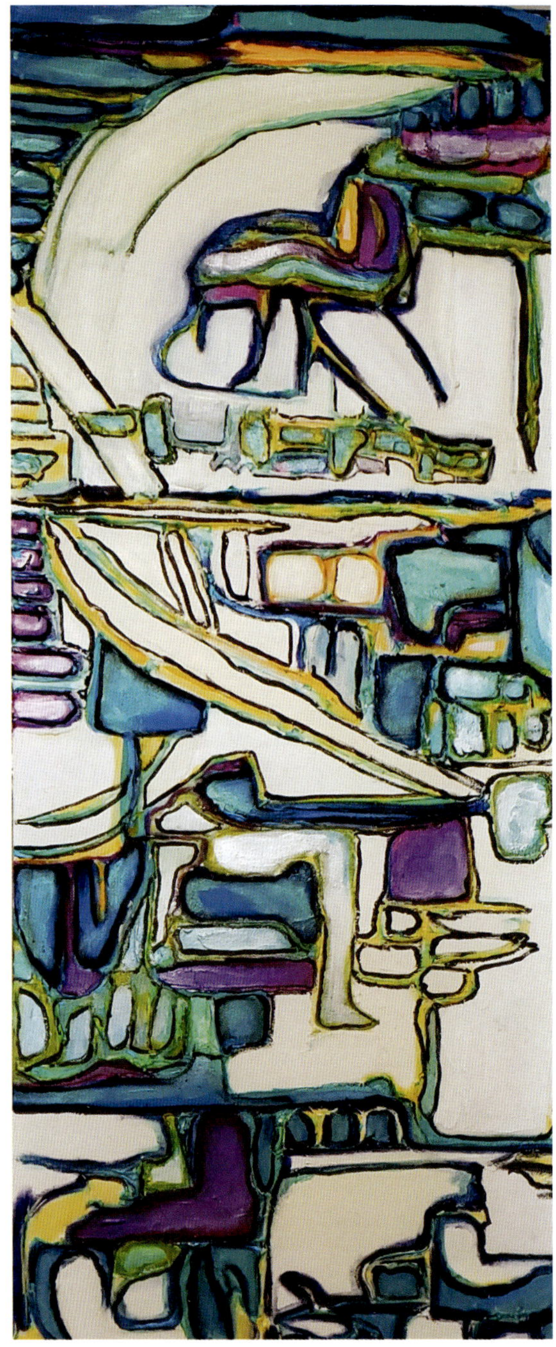

Caren Akers

Caren Akers loves painting abstract works of art because it allows for infinite possibilities of what can be achieved with paint. "We live in a colorful and ever-changing world, and I try to capture that vibrancy, movement, and texture in my pieces," Akers says. Being an abstract artist, Akers enjoys hearing what others see or perceive in her work. She often asks of her viewers, "What do you see, and if I change the way it is hanging, what do you see now?"

One of the greatest things to Akers is the conversation that the piece brings, the different ideas or visions that each person sees. If someone stops, views, and discusses the art, it is much better than no discussion at all because it prompted something in them. With all her work, Akers paints so the viewer can display them however they choose. The beauty of the art is solely in the eye of the beholder.

Travel into Another Dimension
Acrylic
40 x 16 in.

carens.art@gmail.com
caren-akers.com
@carenakers

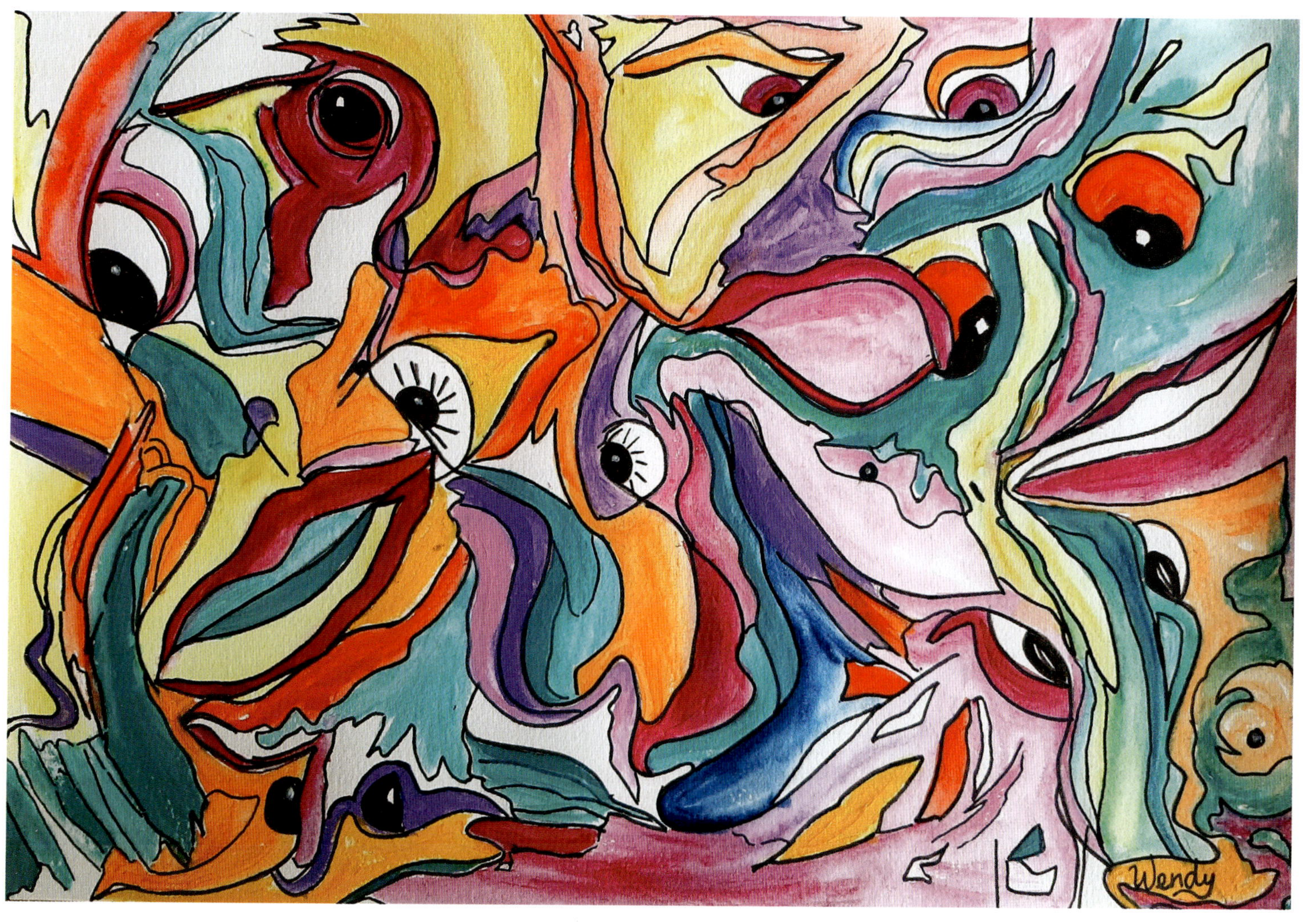

Wendy Alber

Wendy Alber is a Mauritian artist, currently living in Germany. Due to COVID-19 travel restrictions, Alber cannot fly back home and has found painting to be the only way she can translate her feelings, which calms her soul. Her works are a depiction of her inner self. Through each brushstroke, Alber has the intimate feeling that she is releasing energy from her soul, all the pain and mistakes, and seeking to find her real self in her paintings.

Alber's main medium is acrylic, and she enjoys using vivid and contrasting colors. Through her work, she creates an encounter with that part of herself that stayed in Mauritius. "I paint with my heart and soul, and my themes are mostly landscapes, seascapes, figures, body parts. However, I always create an abstract work when I start a painting related to my country, mainly to express my present feeling," Alber says.

Often the artist will use a fork, her fingers, or bold lines in the pursuit of self-expression. Showing her paintings is exposing part of her soul to the world, and she feels complete as long as her work can bring joy, peace of mind, and a positive mindset to the viewer.

Regards sur le passé et l'avenir
Mixed media on paper
16.5 x 11.6 in.

wendyalber@hotmail.com
wendyartworld.weebly.com
@wendy_artworld

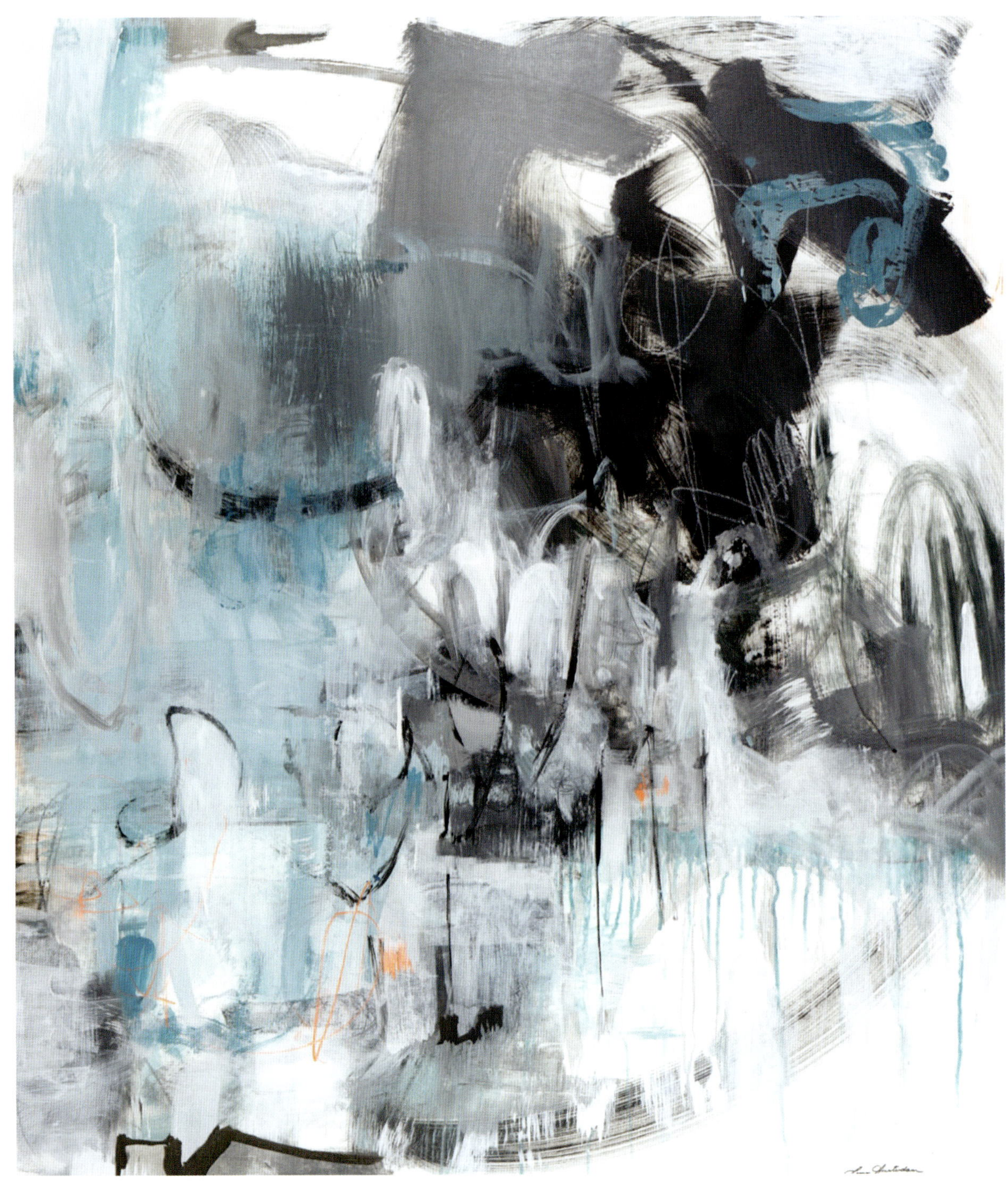

Lynn Amsterdam
Lynn Amsterdam's interests are wide and varied and include literature, movies, and art. The same can be said about her artwork. To some critics, this may be an issue, but for Amsterdam, it is a freedom that allows her to explore the many realms of creativity within herself. She tries hard not to put limits on her exploration, seeking out various mediums like paper, canvas, and wood. From these substrates, she ventures further in her exploration by deciding if she wants movement or stillness, bold colors, or shapes. Sometimes Amsterdam allows the environment she is working in to influence her process. "Not every venture turns out a masterpiece, however, I always discover something new about the process," she says.

Acquafredda
Acrylic on Rendr paper
40 x 34 in.

lynn.amsterdam@gmail.com
@lynnamsterdam.com

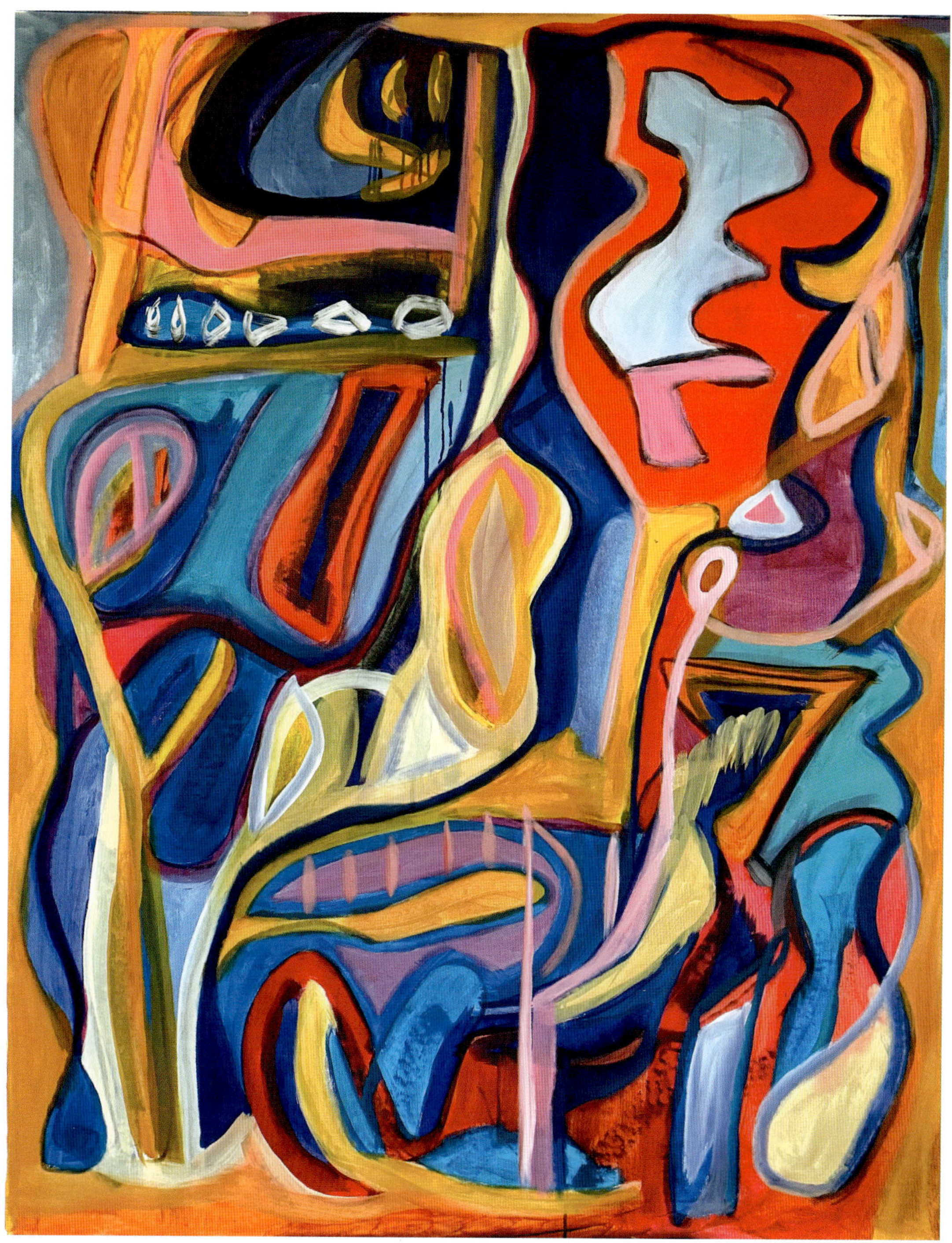

John Bacon

"Being an avid collector of abstract art since the early 1990s eventually led to creating my own abstract works," John Bacon says. His works are largely nonrepresentational. His paintings are characterized by a distinctive use of color and form that make for a unique style. Bacon is always seeking to develop new techniques and colors, which leads to a large variety in his work.

Bacon's process for creating his work is largely intuitive without predetermined plans. The paintings proceed from beginning to end by letting the canvas speak and show the way. This leads to a style that is totally uninhibited and presents infinite possibilities. His art is not only visual but also emotional. It is meant to be felt as much as seen.

"In abstract art you see with your mind instead of your eyes. I hope to have the viewer feel first then see," Bacon says.

MadHatter
Acrylic on canvas
57 x 47 in.

johnwb67@gmail.com
@baconmodern

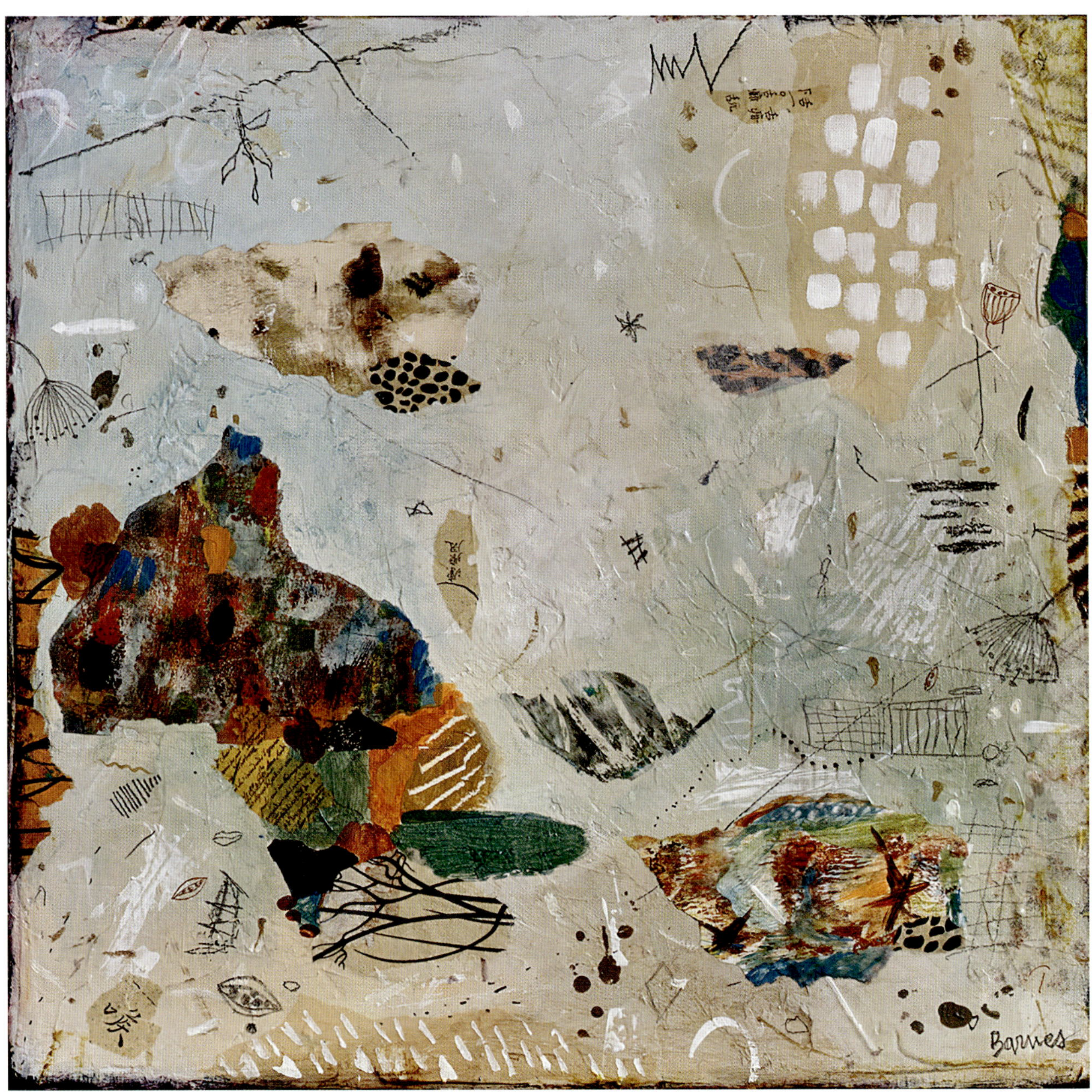

Françoise Barnes

While Françoise Barnes cares deeply about the profound issues facing our world, when making art, she does not seek to convey any specific message. Instead, what draws her to her studio is the almost primal need to create something that will record on paper or canvas what she has observed and loved, what has moved her. And it is her hope that, if the work is successful, it will bring to others a moment of joy, beauty, and a sense of wonder or surprise.

She draws her inspiration from nature, especially observed from very close up, from the lacy details of a dragonfly's wing to the dots, flecks, specks, and the artful unevenness of stripes and marks found in some plants, flowers, insects, and animals. She also draws upon her profound love and admiration for the awesome art of indigenous cultures, whether here or far away.

Petite Symphony
Mixed media on canvas
16 x 16 in.

franswazz@gmail.com
franswazzart.com
@franswazzart

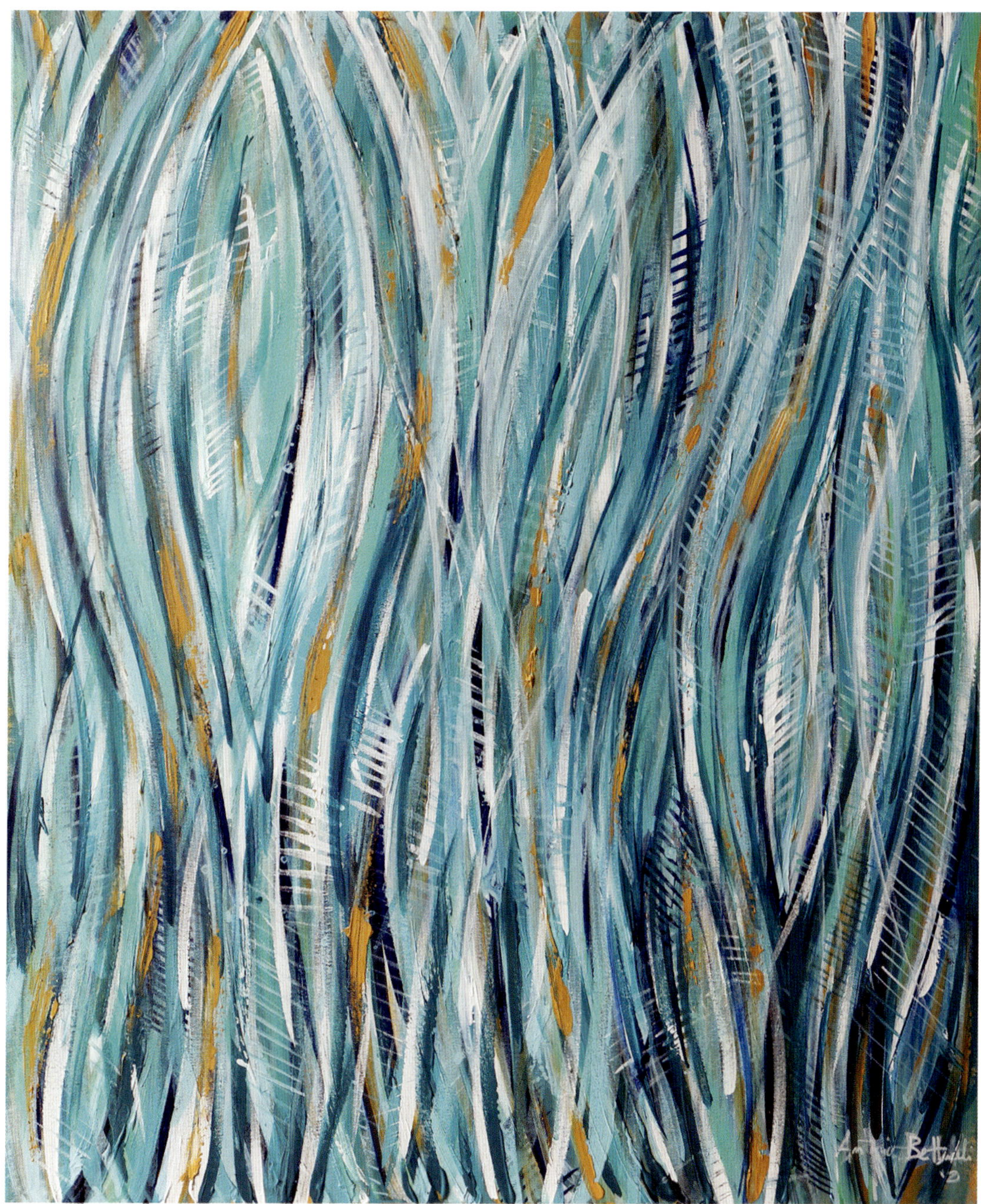

Antonio Bettuelli

Antonio Bettuelli was born in Genoa, Italy, and graduated from the Faculty of Architecture of the University of Genoa. He worked for a decade in important professional studios that allowed him to take part in the design of numerous interventions of strategic importance both in Italy and across Europe. After this "apprenticeship," Bettuelli founded the Bettuelli architecture studio BBarchYacht with his brother, specializing in yacht design and architectural design.

"The years of my schooling, with an artistic focus, combined with a great passion for drawing and materials, have catapulted my interests into everything creative," Bettuelli says. "I love to use simple tools, to transmit on a sheet of paper all that goes through my head, depicting a landscape, a still life, passing from the design of a building to the concept design of a yacht to the scribble of something ephemeral. I love to use all artistic techniques. The important thing is to create."

Sea Traces
Acrylic on canvas
39 x 31 in.

art@antoniobettuelli.it
@antoniobettuelli_art

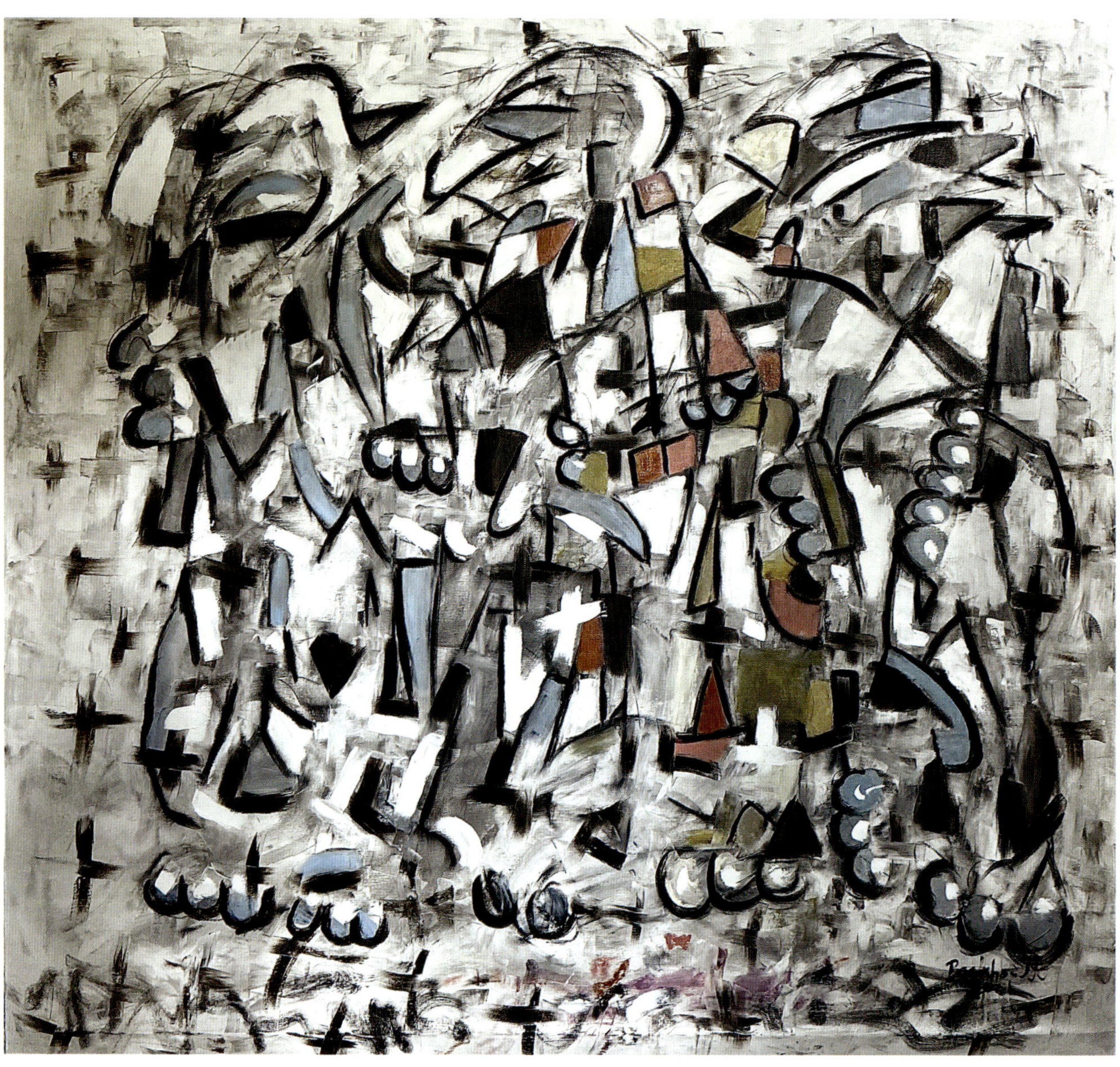

Johannes Boekhoudt
"The theory or practice is nothing more than my desire and interest of wanting to communicate with the public through my paintings," says Johannes Boekhoudt. "My work carries a simple philosophy focusing on social criticism. The painting as a method of communication in itself transforms the panorama of art into a different perspective. Its contours and colors displace the primary artistic plane towards a complex physical creation. The importance of this work provides a voice confronting the atrocities that occur in this world. Fortunately, the colors, as complementary elements of the painting, blend into the work itself. Without risk, they collaborate in the vision of its creator."

Boekhoudt's artistic language is definitively an expressive abstraction. There is a complete submission onto the canvas, which understands and feels the artist's emotions. The magnitude of the image's development in itself fills the void from which it came. Each stroke evokes multiple sentiments. Whether good or bad, the strokes want to resolve the judgments generated by the injustices of our social rights.

Colada
Oil on linen
60 x 57 in.

johannesfineart@
me.com
johannesboekhoudt
.com
@johannesboekhoudtoficial

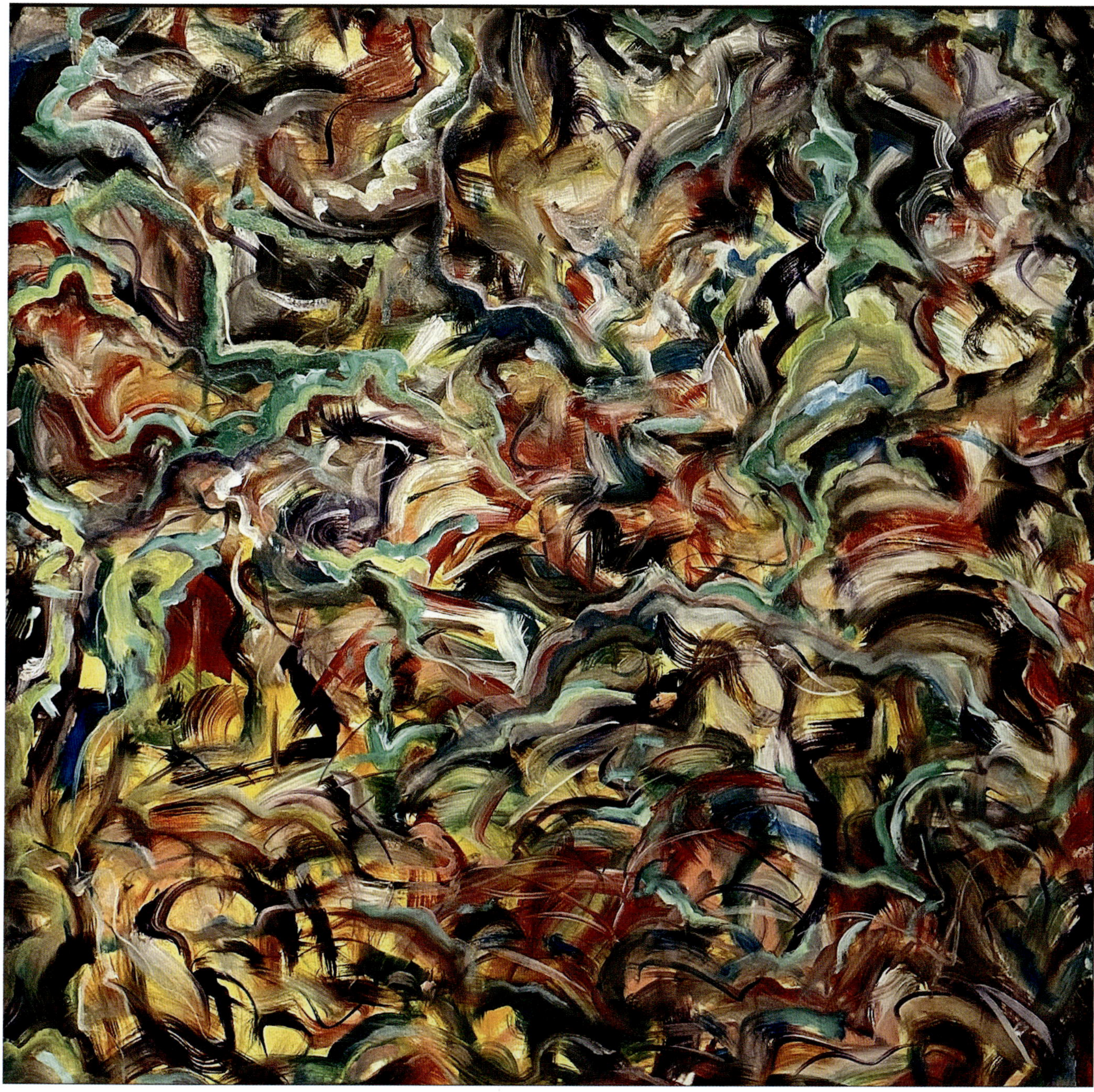

Alessio Bonini

Alessio Bonini is inspired by relationships, and his work focuses on the links between interior and exterior, the soul, nature, and the universe. His artwork is predominantly produced using oil paints; however, he also creates mixed-media artworks. At the age of fourteen, he was introduced to the painter M. Bertonati, who taught him the techniques of dripping and lithography. Bonini attended the local art school and simultaneously enrolled in ceramics courses.

In addition to his creative practice, Bonini firmly believes in independent artistic growth and actively helps and promotes emerging artists.

His works are featured in numerous private collections around the world.

Esperimento Di Memoria Eidetica
Oil on canvas
41 x 39 in.

alessio.bonini@hotmail.com
alessiobonini.com
@alessiobonini_artist

PAINTING: TRADITIONAL/ABSTRACT

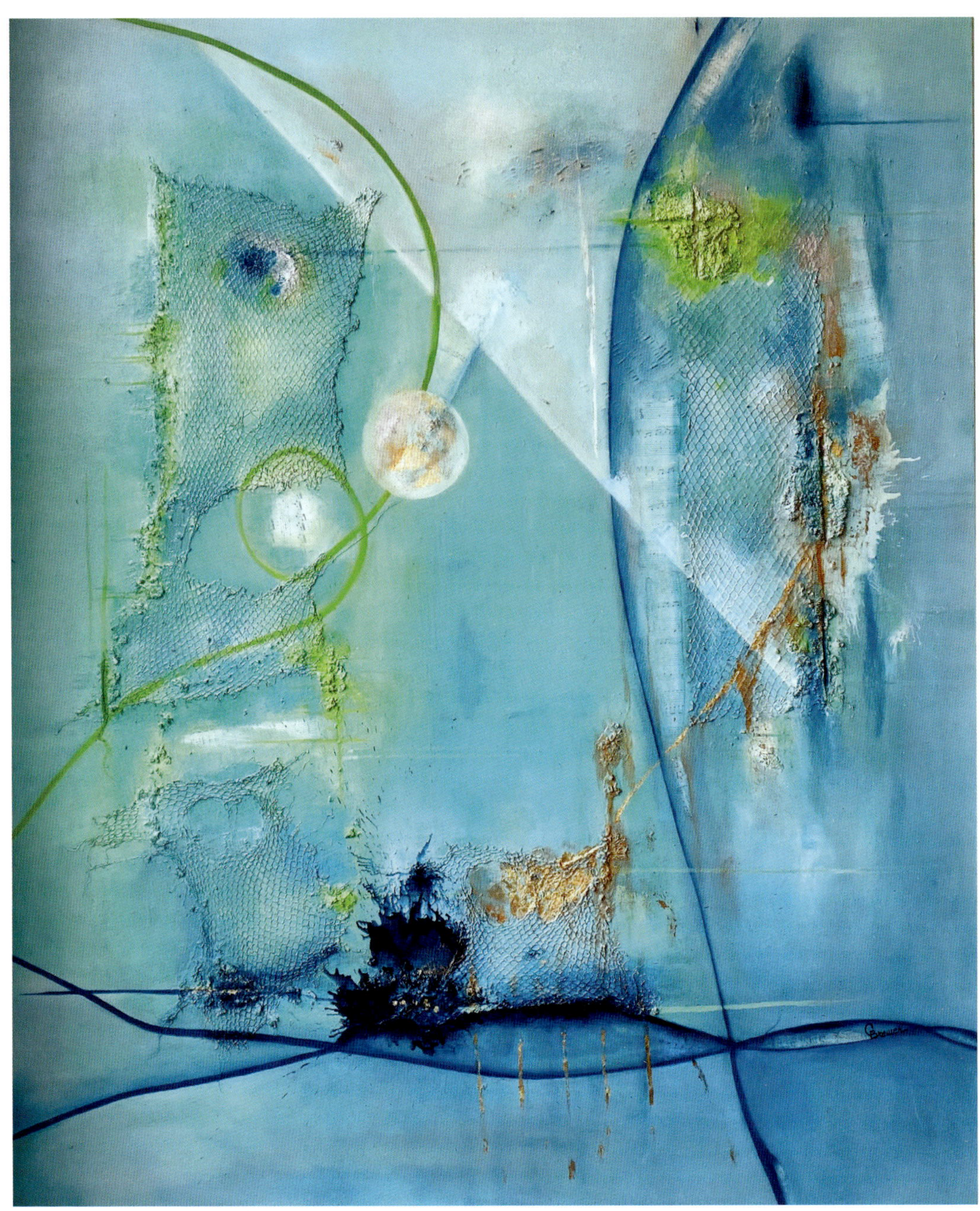

Cindy Brewer

"Painting is a joy and therapy, a creative process for expressing my inner being," Cindy Brewer says. Besides personal expression, evoking a feeling in others through her painting is tremendously rewarding. Painting abstract work offers Brewer the most freedom, whether it's nonobjective, expressionism, or representational. These paintings evolve and emerge through several layers of paint.

Brewer achieves a three-dimensional effect by experimenting with additives, papers, and various mediums. Color, texture, the interplay with light, and the spatial relationship on the canvas create interesting pieces that are often unexpected and surprisingly revealing. Each painting represents one of the many emotional cycles the artist experiences in her daily joy and struggles. "The work brings truth and peace to life's journey. Painting is a blessing and an opportunity to share my inner feelings and thoughts with others," she says.

Cross Roads
Mixed media and oils
60 x 48 in.

cabrewer58@yahoo
.com
cindybrewerfineart.com
@cindybrewer1

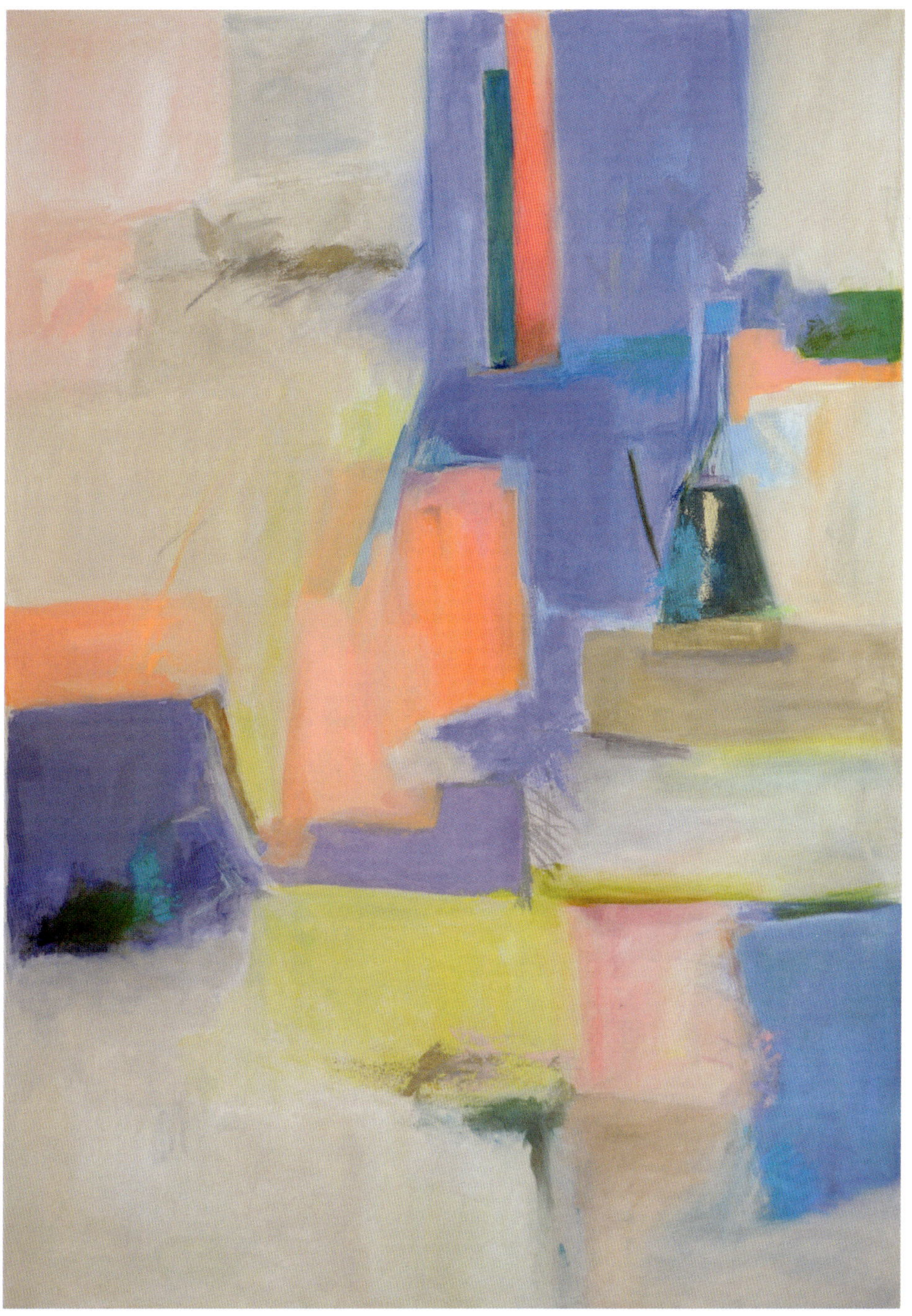

Debby Brisker Burk

Discovery is Debby Brisker Burk's motivation to create and spend time in the studio. Writing and mental preparation pave the way, giving birth to her ideas. For Burk, being in the flow is an act of intuition and of paying close attention to the chosen subject matter.

"I work in series, whether abstract or figurative, to get to the essence of the selected subject and then to distill the greater parts into a new, cohesive whole," Burk says. The tools that she employs—paints, brushes, textural devices, palette knives, charcoal, mediums, pastels, and crayons—are servants to her chosen intention.

There is a bit of wanderlust that inspires Burk in the act of painting. She seeks to discover the undiscovered, to find that which has yet to be found or figured out. Being in a state of "curious intuition" pushes Burk to forge ahead into new lands of exploration, finding answers in the creative process.

Surf's Up, Firmscapes
Mixed media on canvas
69 x 48 in.

debby@briskerburk.art
briskerburk.art
@debbybriskerburk

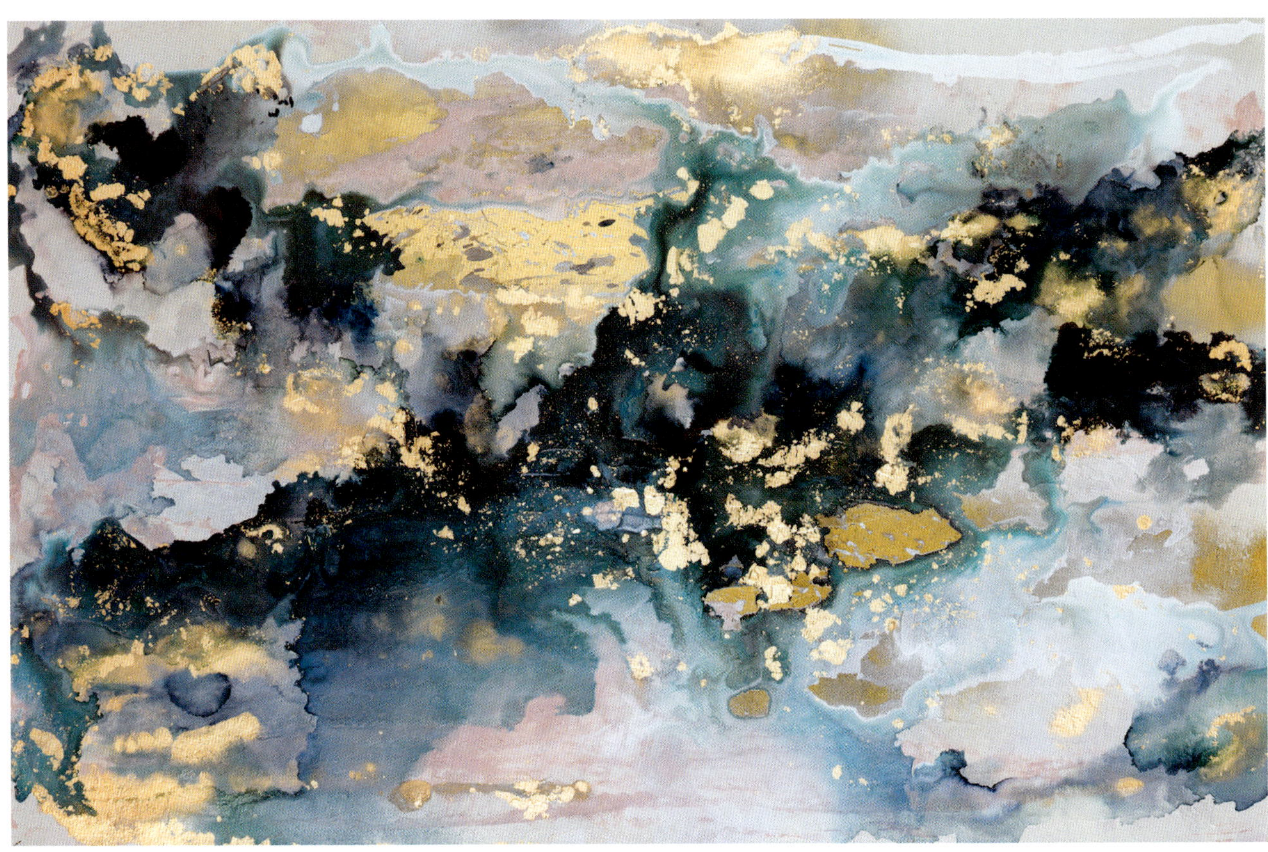

Lori Burke

The pull of creative expression began for Lori Burke at a very young age. She was always captivated by the creative process, and this yearning developed into a passion for painting that has stayed with her throughout her life.

Burke is an intuitive painter, guided by her personal connection to the spaces and people around her and her desire to show compassion for all living things. "When I paint, I am embarking on a journey to tell a story—it usually begins with a strong feeling in my mind's eye that I have a need to express," Burke says.

Being so in touch with the inner workings of her heart and mind, Burke does not limit herself to just one form or style of expression. She feels at home with acrylics but often integrates mixed media, which makes a wonderful, multidimensional impact, blending acrylics with spray paint, integrating gold leaf, adding paste, playing with ink and stains, using her fingers, a brush, or a palette knife. What drives Burke are the strong impulses she feels as well as being present as the emotions come pouring out.

Rolling In The Deep
Mixed media
36 x 24 in.

lori.fickledesigns@gmail.com
fickledesignsartstudio.com
@Loriburke3667

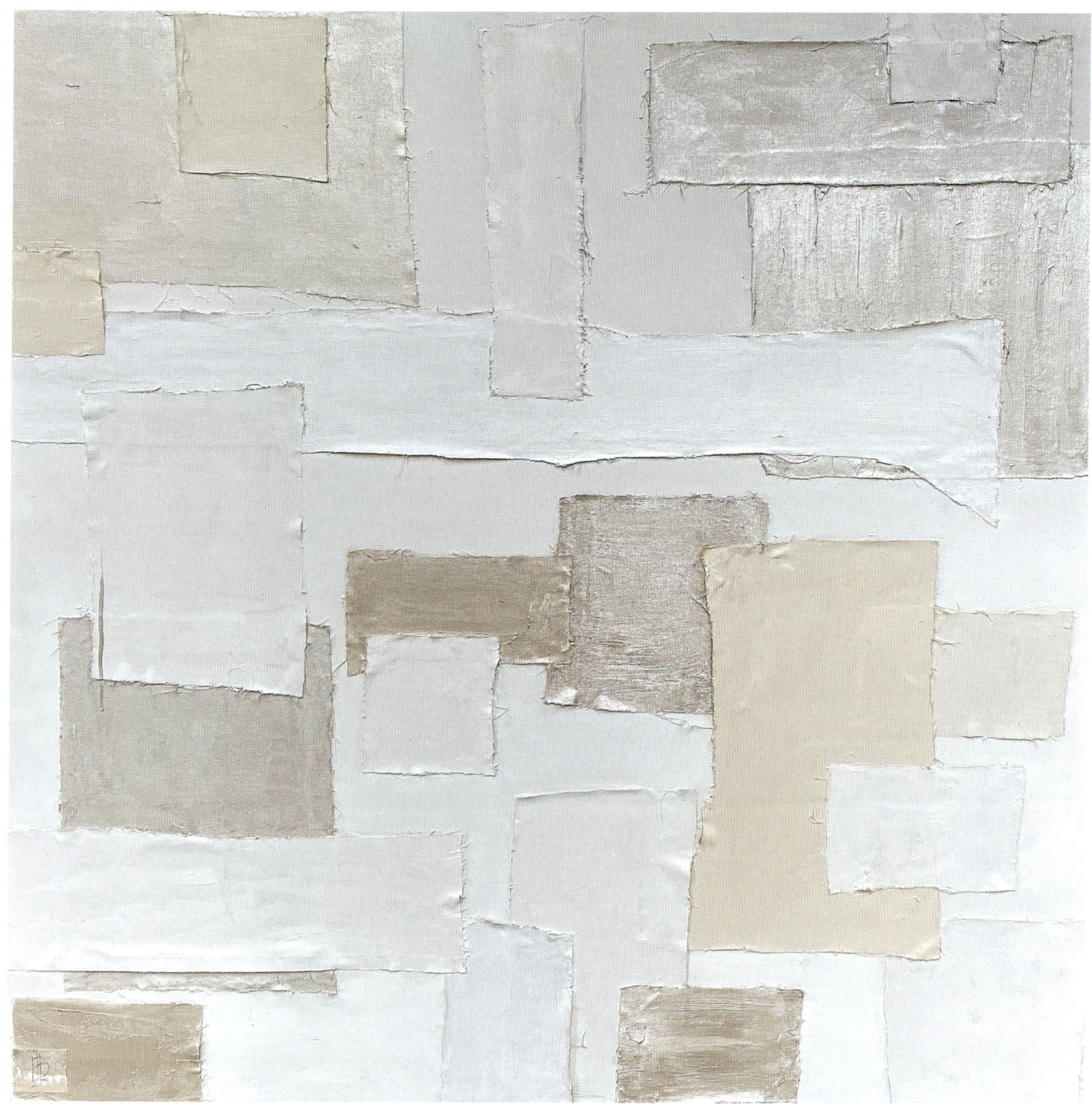

Leslie Poteet Busker
Leslie Poteet Busker's *Raw Canvas Collection* is a body of work that seeks to stir hope by studying beauty in imperfection. All the paintings in the series are formed from pieces of rough, raw material, which is cut and layered. The artist's objective is to preserve the rough and fragmented parts while refining them into a harmonious whole.

The linear compositions are open and honest and encourage the viewer to be still and recognize the good amid that which has unraveled, to find and reflect on beauty in the fray. The artist employs a monochromatic palette that elevates the texture of the original elements and allows glimpses in some places of transparency, in others opaqueness, and in yet others a hint of what lies beneath. The layers, lines, and raw edges, along with the colors white and pearl, further illuminate the artist's work by alluding to ageless concepts such as redemption and renewal.

Bianco
Oil and acrylic collage
on canvas
48 x 48 in.

lesliebusker@gmail.com
lesliepoteetbusker.com
@lesliepoteetbuskerart

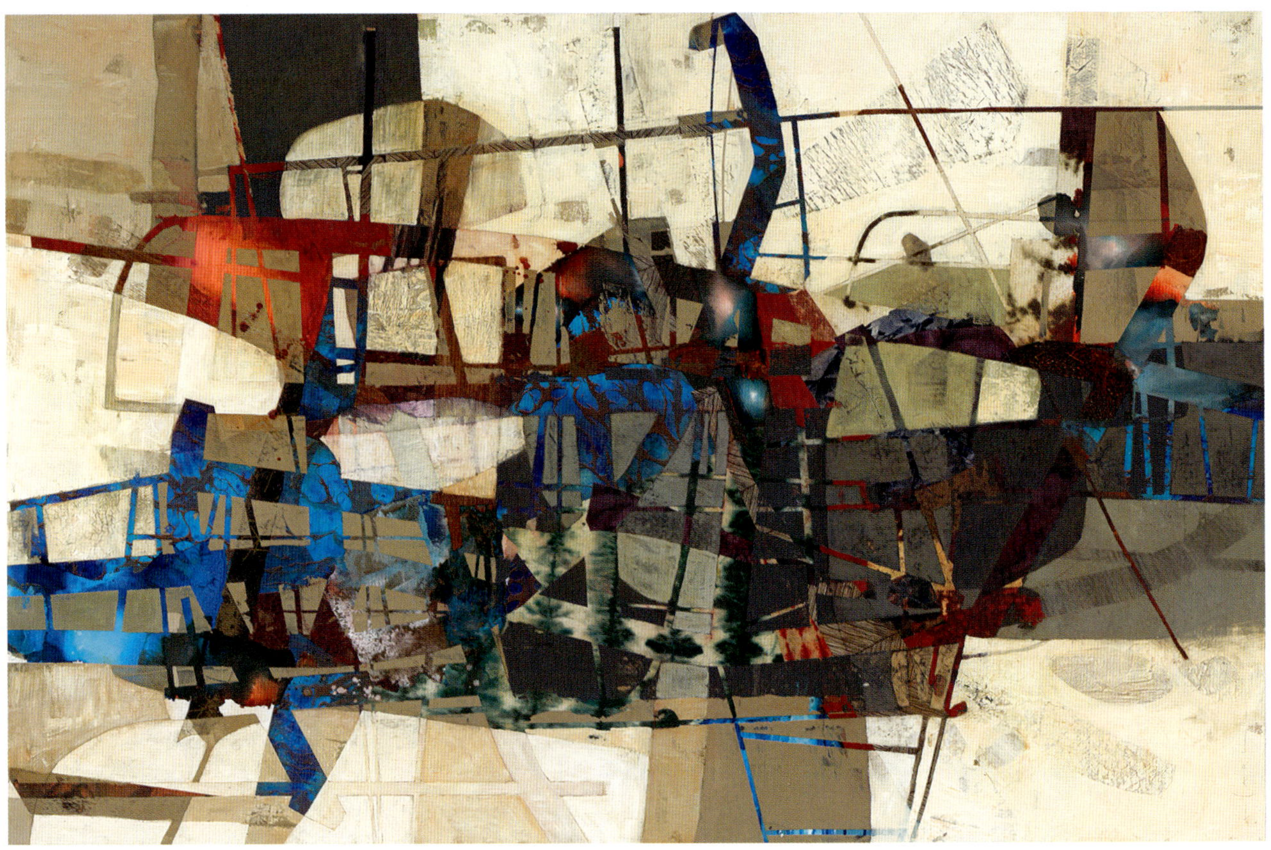

Anna Carll

Anna Carll's abstract work is based on the concept of urban erosion and explores the cycle of city life alongside nature. It is the observation of constant urban expansion that creates a push/pull of reconstruction within that natural cycle that moves Carll. Civilizations are built on top of each other, creating a rich history of efforts to exist within this construct and producing a process that requires constant maintenance to survive.

The *Urban* series examines all aspects of this concept through intense color with a bird's-eye view, and the work is built layer by layer as an examination of this conflict. Carll often uses discarded paintings and collage material on canvas or paper, repurposing and creating new life out of past work. A careful study of structure along with attention paid to negative space completes Carll's creative method. Carll combines painting, collage, and mixed media within a multidisciplined art practice, using her own vocabulary to create powerful visuals that embody her unique vision of the world.

Urban Grid #81
Mixed media on canvas
48 x 72 in.

annacarllfineart@gmail.com
annacarll.com
@annacarllart

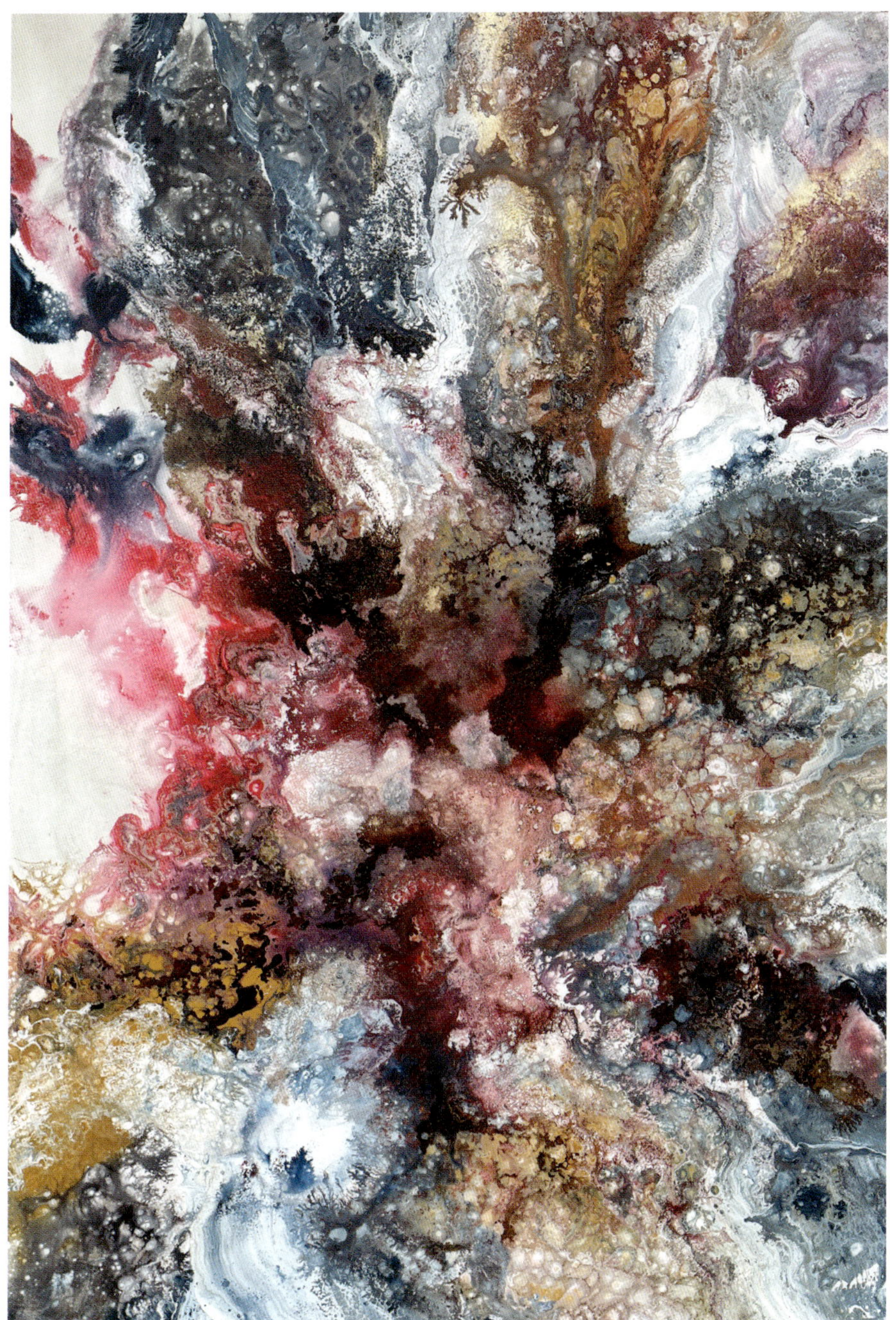

Jessica Chaix

Jessica M. Chaix was introduced to plastic arts at a noticeably young age in her hometown school in Chihuahua, Mexico. Early on, she began experimenting with a variety of painting and drawing techniques.

As a young artist, she moved to Monterrey to pursue her interests more deeply in the arts. She earned a bachelor's degree at the Instituto Tecnológico de Estudios Superiores de Monterrey while simultaneously continuing her artistic studies.

In 2001, Chaix moved to Dallas to expand her art skills; experiment with different techniques, materials, and textures; and experience personal growth as an artist. Since moving to Texas, she has been featured in multiple art exhibitions and recognized by local and international organizations as an artist who showcases her multicultural background and experiences in her artwork.

Chaix continues to explore and experiment with new techniques, allowing her to refine her personal style and differentiate herself in the art community.

Saturno
Mixed media on canvas
72 x 48 in.

jessica_chaix@yahoo
.com.mx
jessicamchaix.com
@Jesschaixart

PAINTING: TRADITIONAL/ABSTRACT

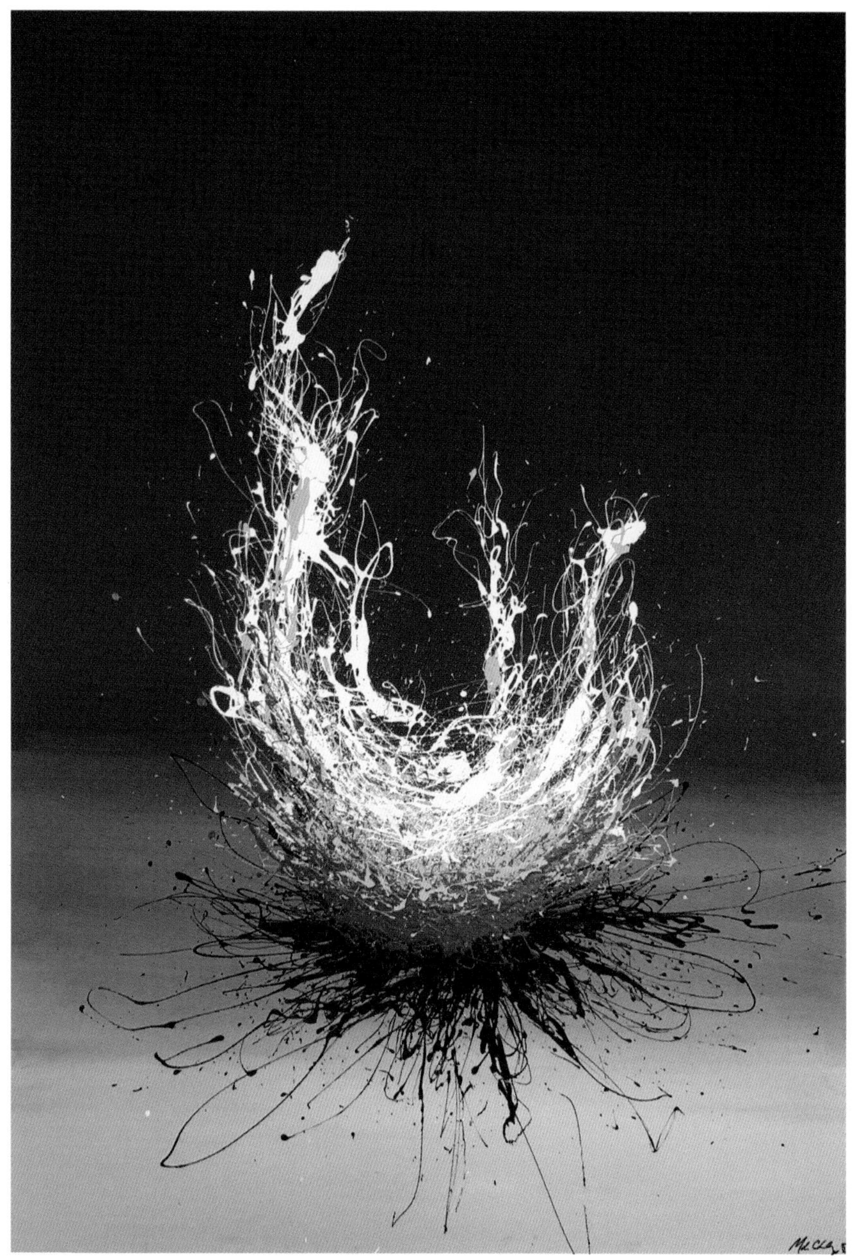

Miles Chumley

The essence of Miles Chumley's art emerges from the restless excitement of a free-flowing mind. Tapping into life experiences, Chumley paints to capture the amazing, whimsical influences in the world and reveal the impact external influences have on our surroundings. More specifically, the artist's work illustrates how classical elements and humans interact and affect the environment around us. Filled with energy, movement, excitement, and depth, his artwork explores the complex, ever-changing world from a "point-in-time" perspective.

"I begin my paintings with carefully chosen groups of colors that are layered to create movement and depth and evoke a subtle ambiance. As I progress, the work embodies my feelings and emotions with descriptive strokes, creating a wonderful synergy and conveying a sense of chaos with a deeper meaning," Chumley says.

Most of his paintings are worked on with the canvas flat on the ground. Chumley is then able to move around the piece, freely working every side and angle, becoming one with the painting.

No. 36
Acrylic on canvas
48 x 72 in.

miles.chumley@gmail.com
mileschumley.com
@mileschumley

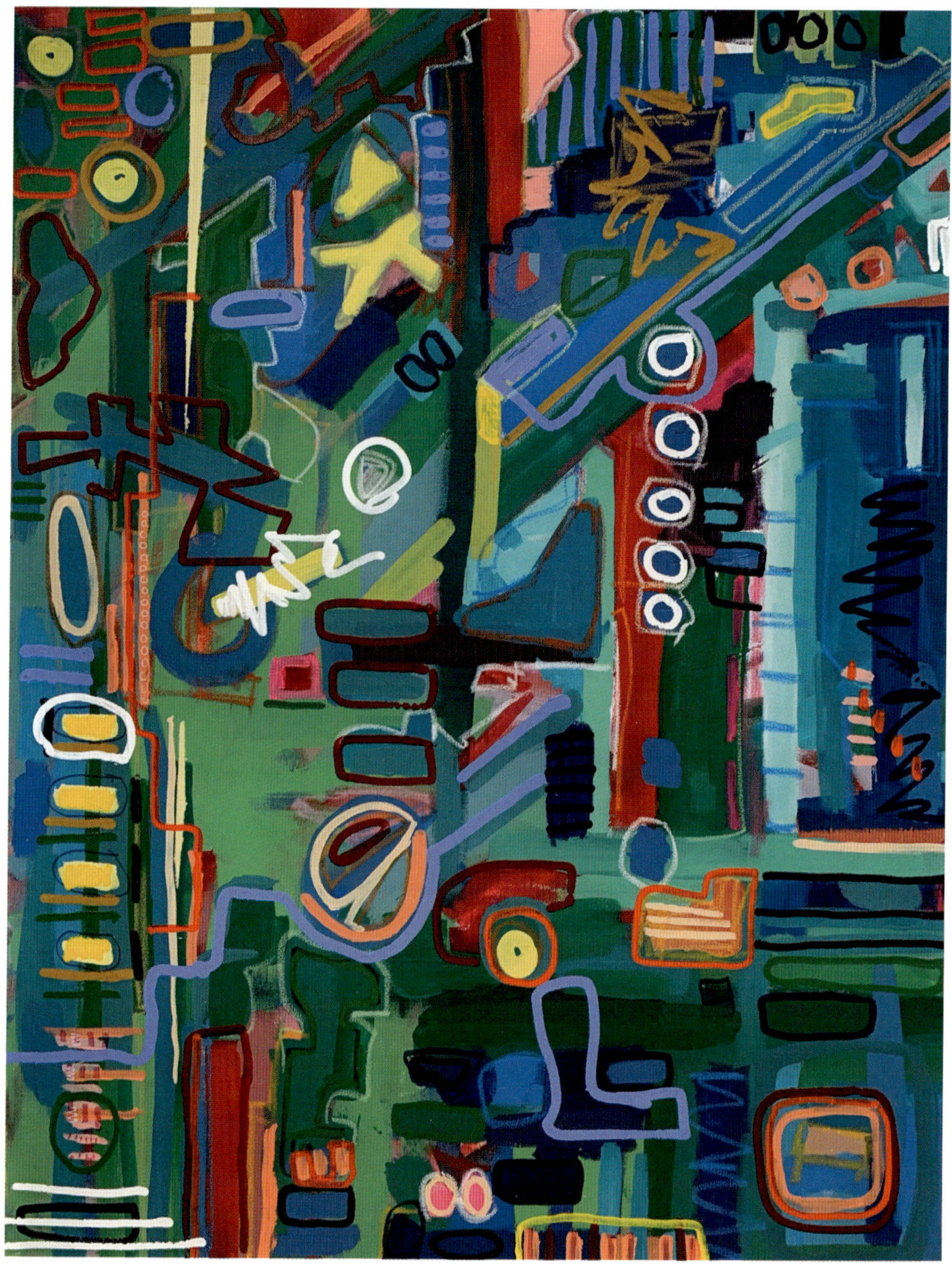

Amy Holt Cline

Amy Holt Cline cares deeply about the issues facing our world but specifically uses her acrylic-based art to explore concepts connected to people and the environment. She uses mixed-media layers of color and textures and is continually influenced by the ocean and a bright color palette. The art she creates is made up of shapes, lines, and figures, using brushes, palette knives, markers, paper, fabric, and more.

Cline seeks new experiences and conversations, which allow her to use new artistic methods to try to answer life's big questions. She believes that being an artist is about expressing the nonverbal part of being human through layers, themes, and color blends. She is inspired by maps and charts of the seafloor and notices the connection between different kinds of spatial data. Cline hopes that making art with bright colors and interesting patterns will somehow create a community of inspired thinkers who see life in possibilities.

The Bustle
Acrylic and mixed media
48 x 36 in.

holt.cline@gmail.com
amyholtcline.com
@amy.holtclineart

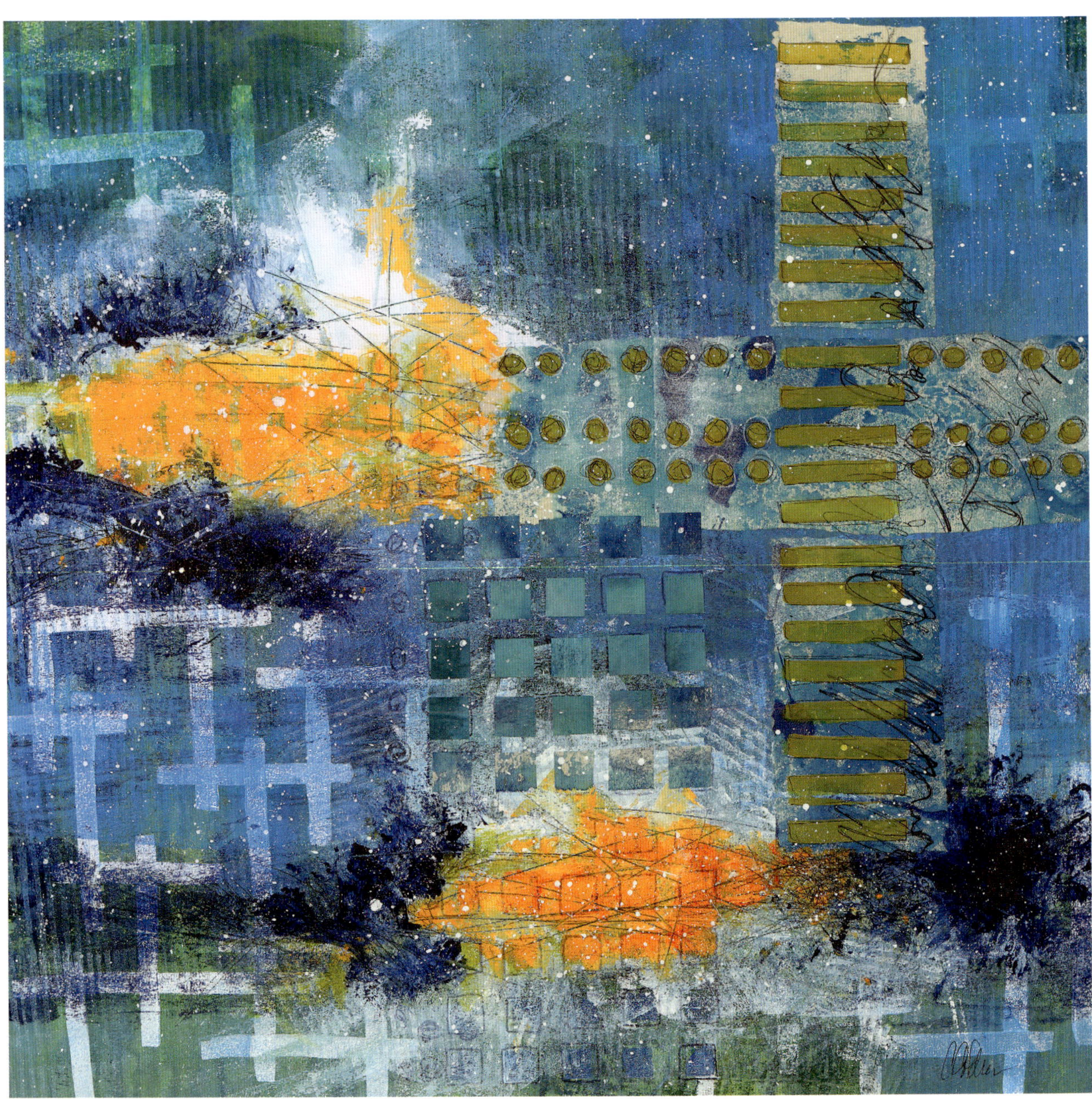

Cynthia Coldren

Cynthia Coldren's paintings embrace abstract language. They are intentional contrasts that join color and line, shape and pattern, texture and layers with paper and canvas. She explores how these random and separate elements can be connected to form harmonious paintings that visually speak to the viewer.

Coldren's creative process is both planned and spontaneous. She enjoys creating new color palettes and abstract studies inspired by aerial landscapes, urban structures, earth patterns, and old surfaces. Using acrylic paints, inks, and pencil on paper and canvas, Coldren creates and scrapes away the layers, adding hand-painted paper or canvas fragments to contrast or complement the developing painting. This blend of the familiar with the ambiguous is a hallmark of her art and gives each viewer a personal way to interpret and connect with her paintings.

Turbulence
Acrylic and mixed media
28 x 28 in.

cynthia@
cynthiacoldrenfineart
.com
cynthiacoldrenfineart
.com
@cynthiacoldrenfineart

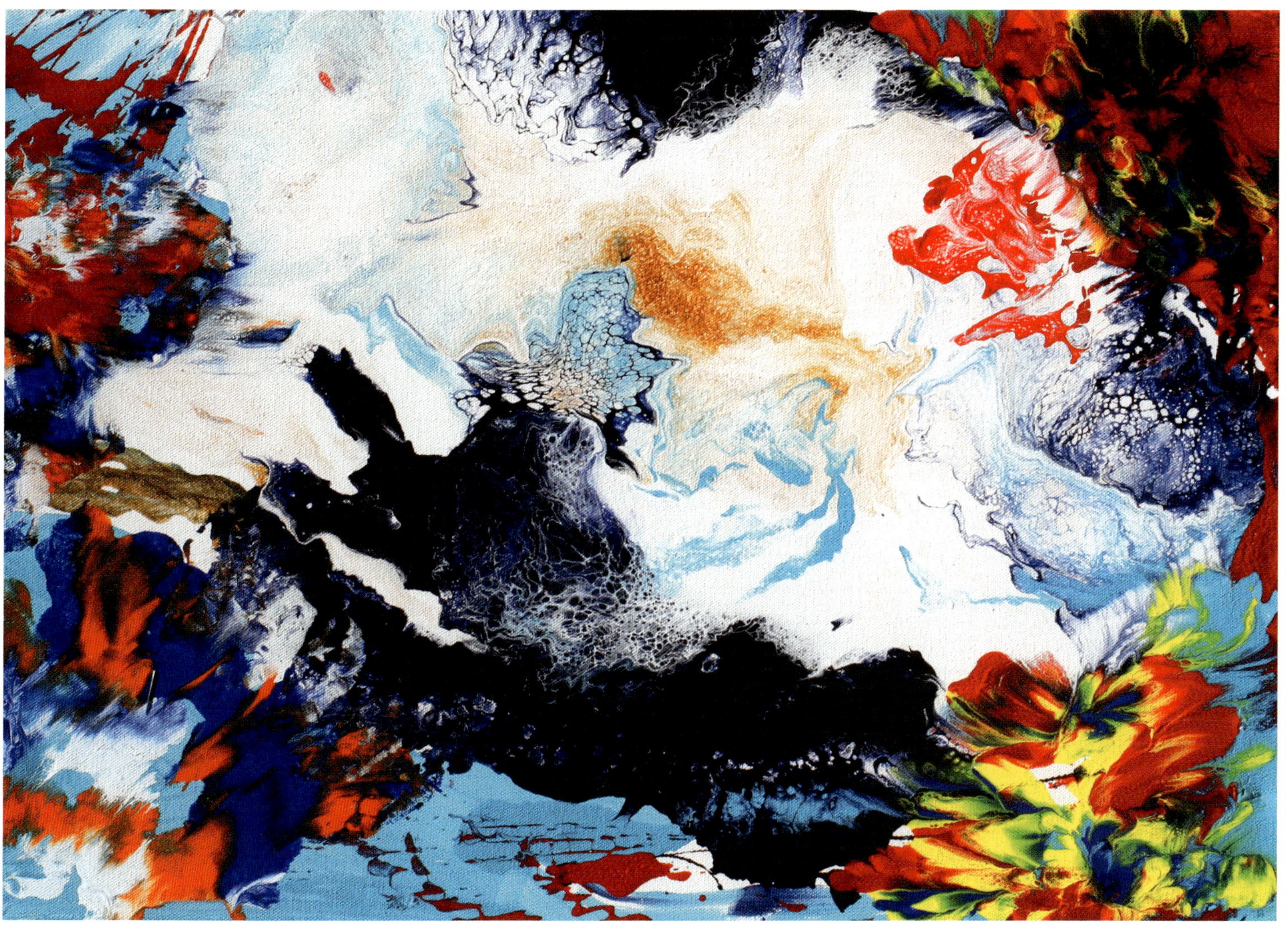

Stephanie Comegys

Stephanie Comegys is an artist inspired by faith, human experiences, concepts, and emotions. When creating, Comegys looks past the obvious to see into the essence of the subject matter in order to tell a story of human experience, emotion, or concept, then translate it into a visual format to give it a redemptive identification. This is expressed with color, texture, direction, and form in a free-flowing yet intentional method. Comegys's work is both abstract and representational and can often be viewed in multiple directions to share another aspect within the story.

The challenge Comegys takes on when she paints is to capture the universal emotion, experience, or concept that many can identify with personally. The result is redemptive in balance, beauty, and unity. The painting becomes one cohesive creation. Comegys strives to communicate that each one of us is connected as a whole while remaining unique and complicated individually.

Overcome
Acrylic
18 x 24 in.

victoriousartworks@
gmail.com
victoriousartworks.com
@s.comegys_art

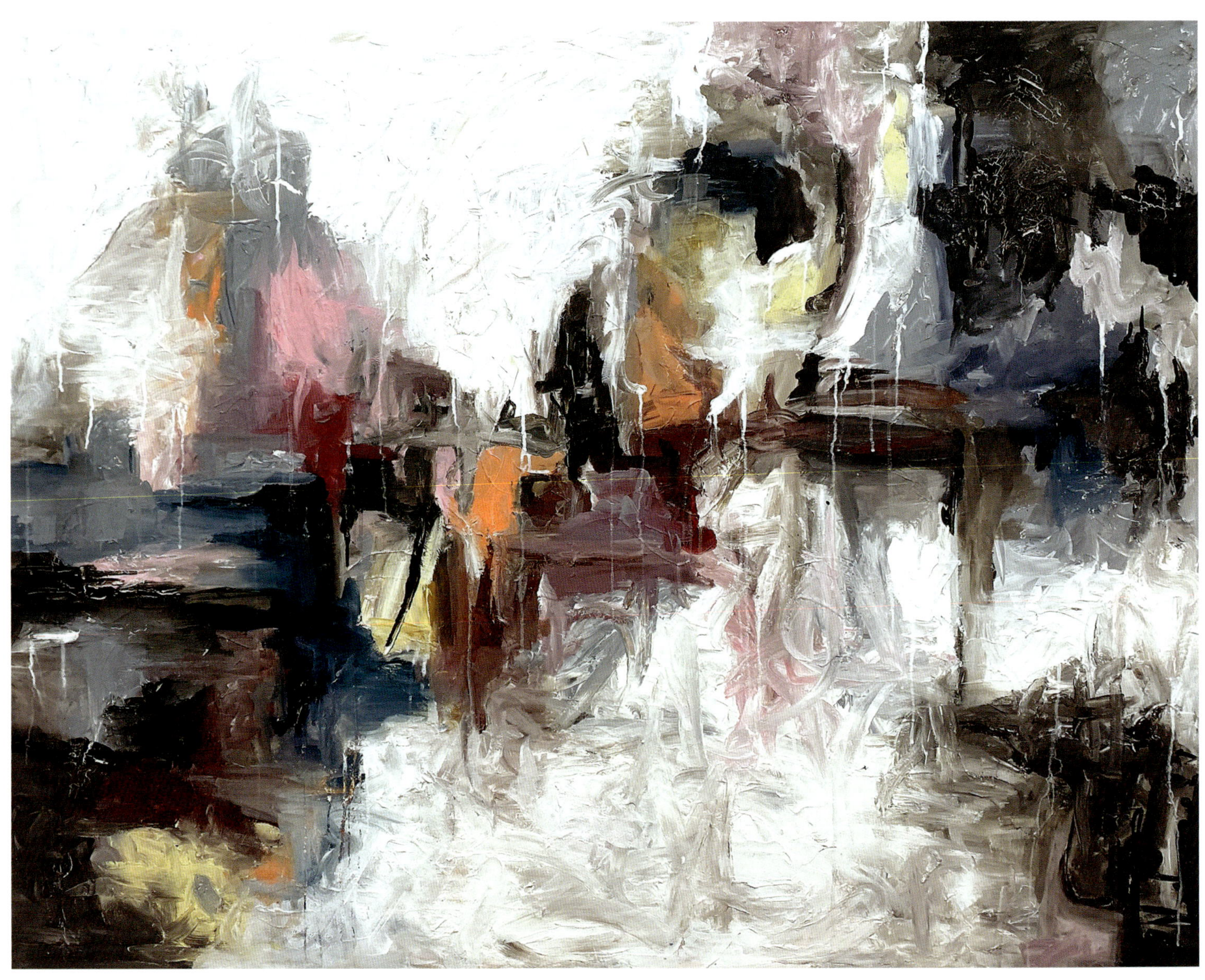

Melanie Crawford

Melanie Crawford has learned that life is complex and in a perpetual state of change and evolution. Nothing remains the same over an extended period. Her optimism, passion for art, and continual desire to create are reflected in every aspect of her work.

"For me, art is about connection, an expression of the journey of life, and offers a higher understanding of communication. I am always curious and experimenting, yet I find my process to be the most integral part of my art-making," Crawford says.

Layers of texture, drips, colors, and welcomed mistakes build the story of her paintings. Crawford's process reveals, conceals, and reexamines what we define as beauty, like collecting evidence of a life lived over time, the peeling of paint on walls, and the hidden potential residing in discarded remnants. She is fascinated by the beauty found in organic marks made naturally without overthinking or correcting.

Trouvaille
Acrylic on canvas
48 x 60 in.

art@melaniecrawford
.com.au
melaniecrawford.com.au
@melaniecrawfordartist

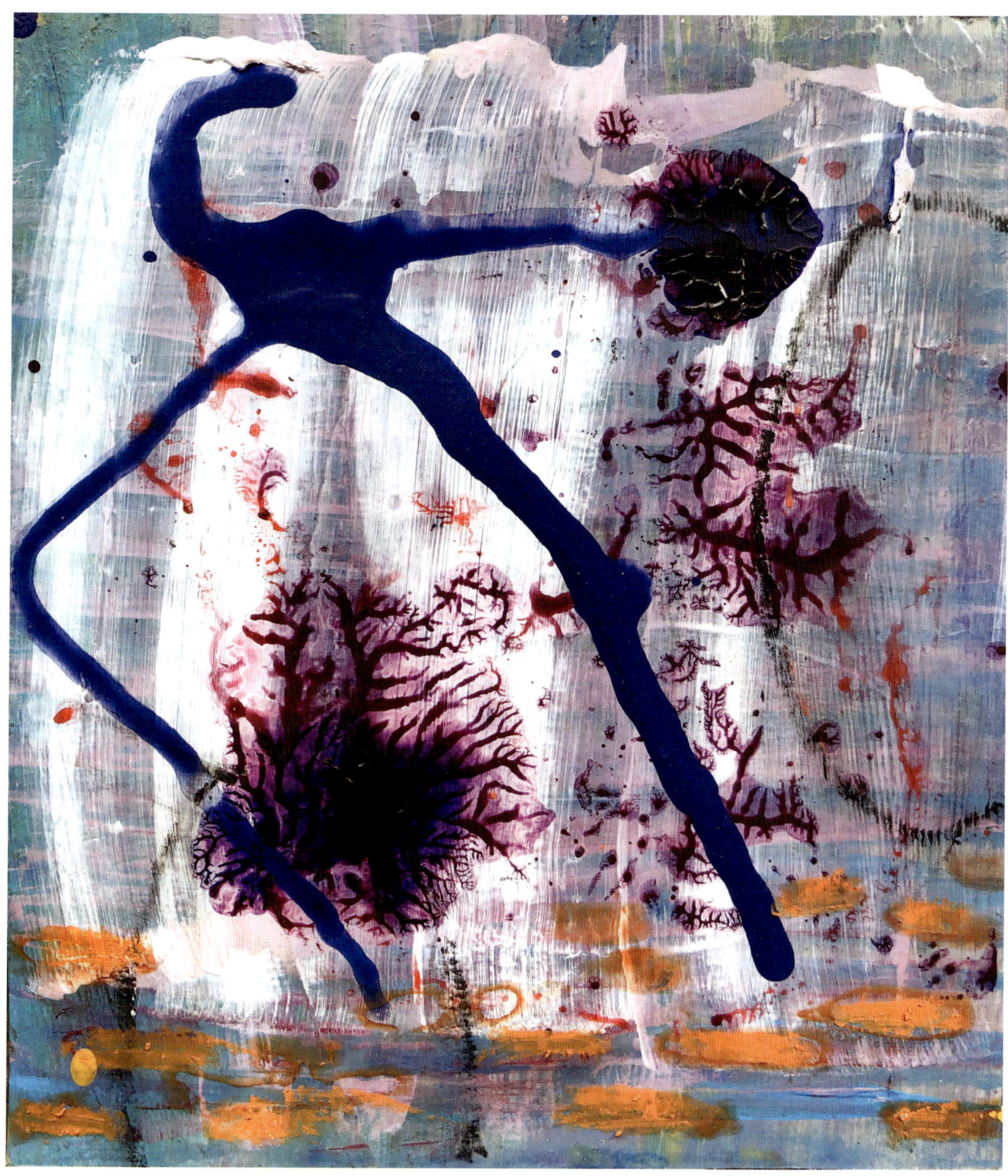

Julia Crosara

Julia Crosara's paintings dwell in the imperceptible boundary between the conscious and subconscious mind and convey a sense of freedom and ingenuity. Her use of color is bold and vibrant, and she creates new pieces with spontaneity and determination that is akin to jazz improvisation. Working in the moment, she communicates her state of being through the expressive use of color, texture, layering, and paint.

Inspired by the automatic techniques practiced by the Surrealists, Crosara continuously explores novel ways of interacting with paint while allowing chance a leading role in the process. She creates unbroken lines by dripping fluid paint and tilting the surface in different directions to find the unexpected. Incidental shapes spring to life after pressing two paintings together and pulling them apart. The resulting images jump off the surface, the nuances demand attention, and best of all, the meaning of each painting is left to the subjective imagination of the viewer.

Breaking Free, No. 3
Acrylic and oil pastel on paper
7.5 x 6 in.

juliacrosara@gmail.com
juliacrosara.com
@julia.crosara.art

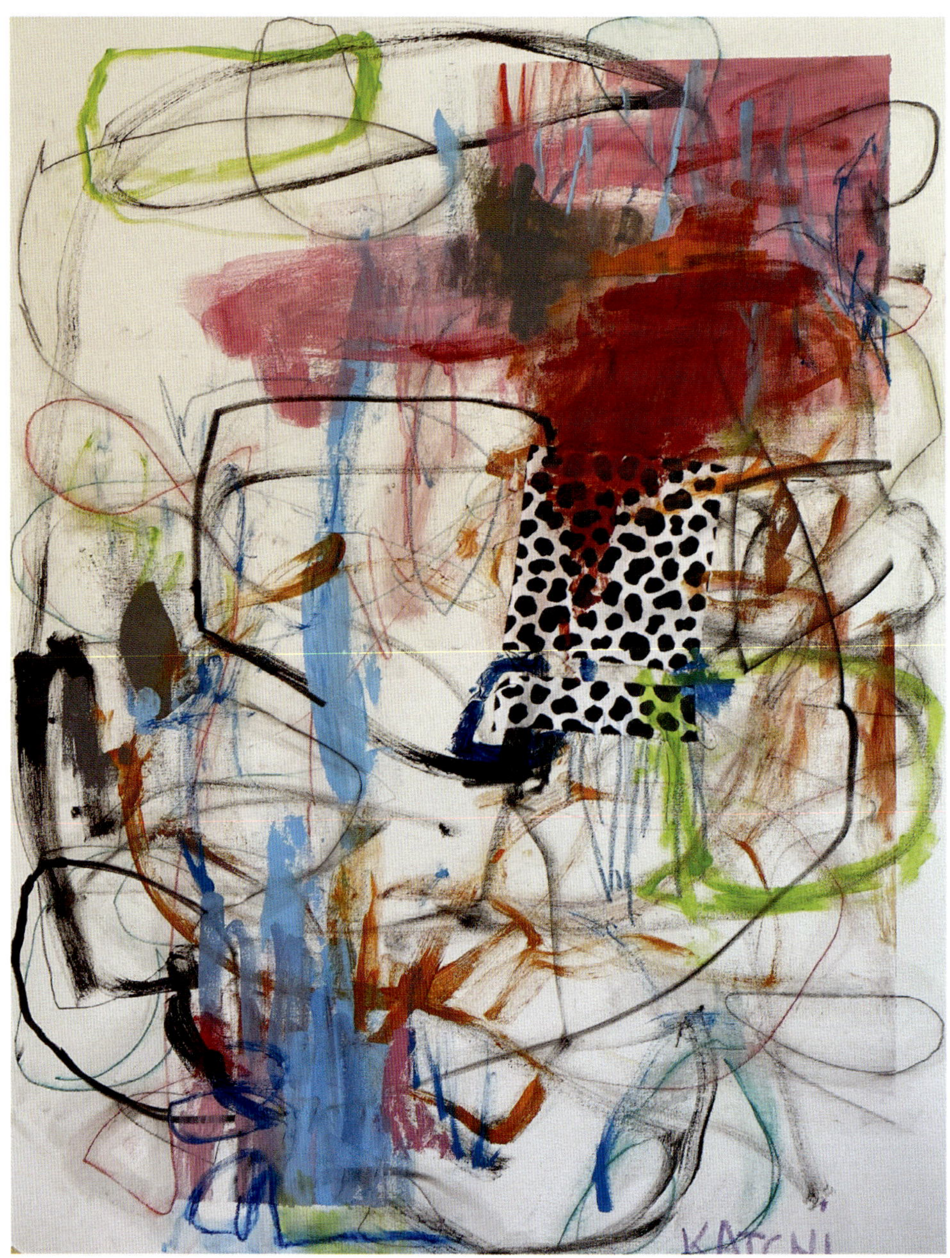

Kathy Crosby
When Kathy Crosby goes into her studio, she always goes with a sense of wonder, asking the question, "What if?"

"Creating my art is like being on a curving mountain road or exploring an unknown path, the ups and downs, highs and lows, twists and turns. I try to approach each piece without fear of doing something wrong. I let the piece shape itself and bring me along for the ride. Like life, my pieces are constant movement, constant change. The creation process is cathartic, allowing my emotions to spill out onto my canvas as a release," Crosby says.

When she starts painting, Crosby never knows what will come out. It's the not knowing that excites and fuels her creative process. When she is inspired to start a painting, the piece usually takes on a direction of its own. Sometimes conflicts have to be overcome, but at other times, when she is in the moment and not really thinking about where the painting is going, she just lets it take her where it needs to go. "That's when it's magical, when I don't have to think, I just have to do," she says.

Soul Kitchen
Acrylic and mixed media on canvas
40 x 30 in.

katcrosby@bellsouth.net
katcrosbyart.com
@katcrosbyart

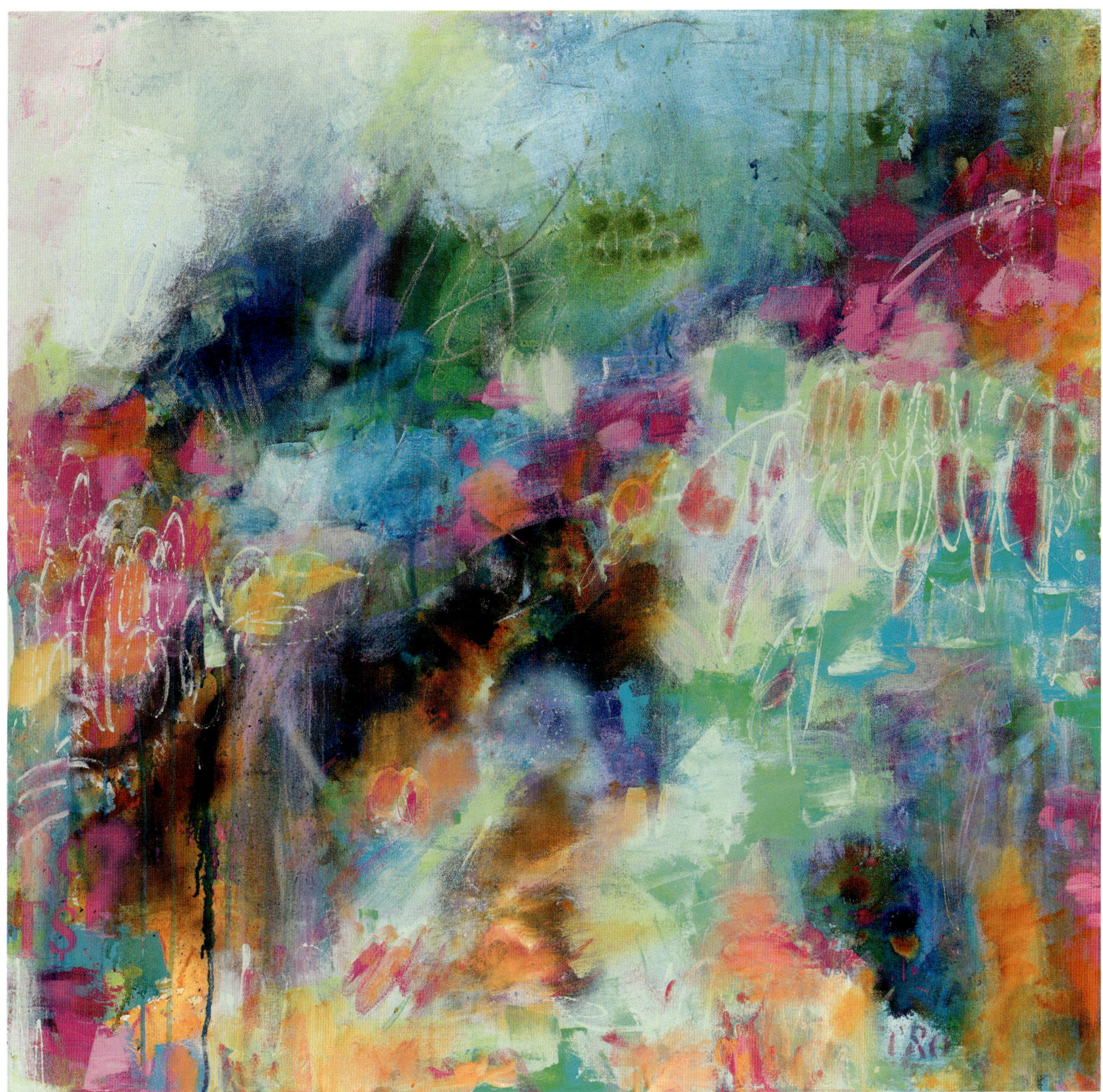

Sami Davidson

The world is different now, and color is Sami Davidson's happy place. Davidson is inspired by the magnificent Florida sunsets, the luscious colors of the flowers in her garden, and the translucent turquoise hue of the ocean. "I want to immerse myself in these colors and create beautiful, joyful paintings," she says. "For me, creating a painting has always been an exciting and unpredictable adventure."

As a nonobjective abstract artist, Davidson works intuitively. Creation comes from within. Her process is one of impulsive and sometimes compulsive experimentation. She begins her paintings with random bursts of bright colors. Then she applies layers of opaque and transparent hues, gestural marks, handmade papers, drips, stamps, and stencils. A final image gradually emerges. Davidson hopes the final image will evoke an emotional and pleasurable response in the viewer.

Channeling Monet
Acrylic
40 x 40 in.

samidavidson@gmail
.com
samidavidsonart.com
@samidavidsonart

PAINTING: TRADITIONAL/ABSTRACT

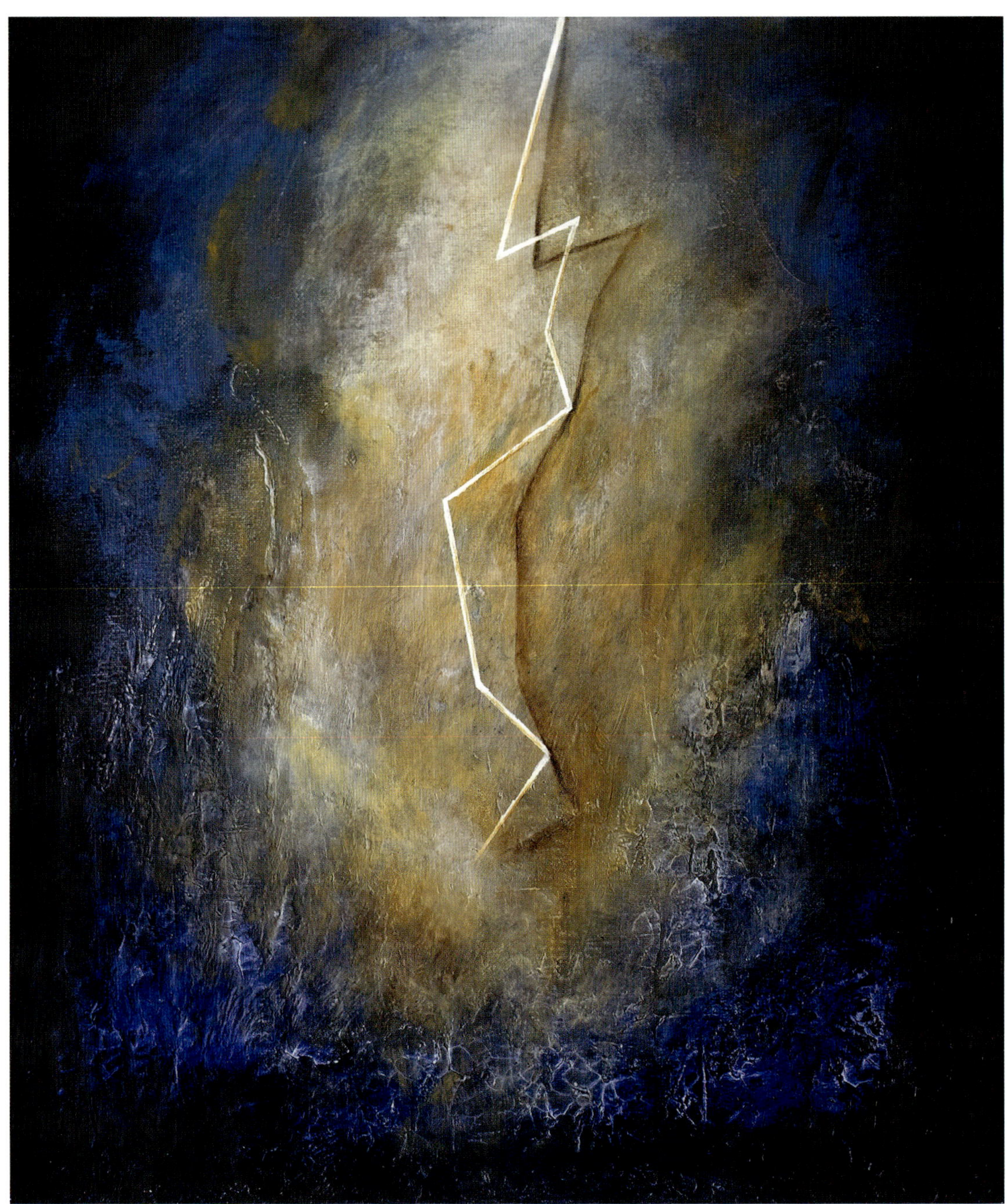

Kinga de Jongh
Kinga de Jongh prefers to explore canvas without limits, loyal to a concept of endless space, opposing her personal "horror vacui." With heavy primers and textures, she creates detailed, three-dimensional, even organic-looking, surfaces that speak their own language about the architecture of the universe. The process is one of construction. There is always a plan, scribbled somewhere in a notebook or on a torn piece of paper. She builds her art with blocks she has, experimenting and combining, exploring the canvas as she goes. It is a map or actually the entire atlas of phenomena around her that she tries to share? The important thing to her is the subjective, individual experience of those who look at it. A statement that through art she channels her feelings is too bold. Instead, she tries to evoke feelings in others.

Untitled 131219
Acrylic and mixed media
19.5 x 15.75 in.

kinga.de.jongh@gmail.com
@nellis_eketorp

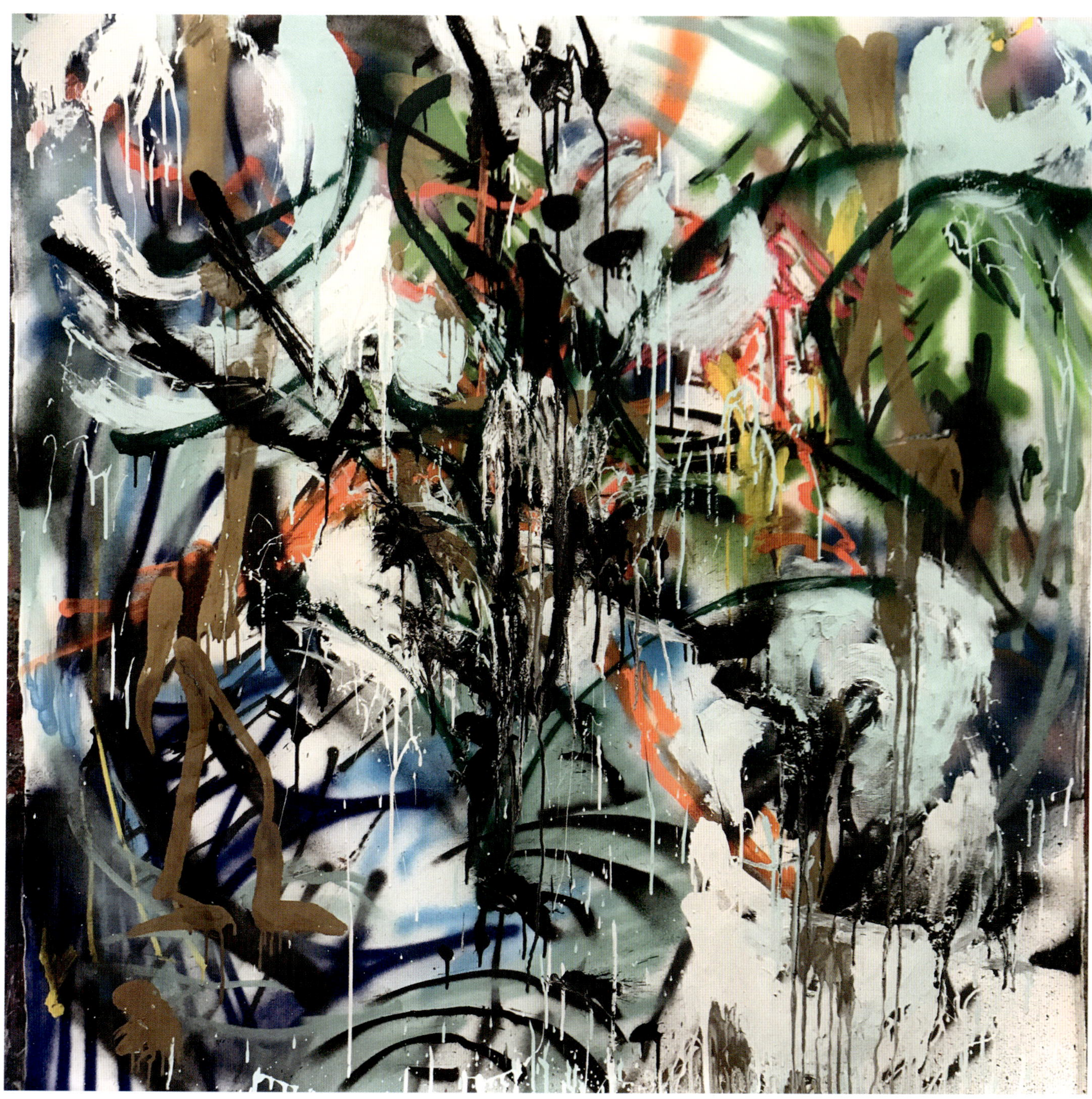

Aristotelis Deligiannidis
"My work is the 'confession' of my soul," says Aristotelis Deligiannidis. Deligiannidis's painting gestures seem to abut the tradition of Abstract Expressionism, even from afar. However, his painterly expression, using strong gestures, also refers to the Figuration Libre movement and graffiti. On transparent or nontransparent underlayer, with feverish, laborious gestures, the artist repeats a process of imprinting his mark, similar to a game of free-drawing patterns or a mechanism using energy toward the conquest and organization of space. A painting of action. A swiftly executed activity. A bodily achievement. But also, a dispersion, continuous maneuvers, and reciprocations that bring forward an ethic and aesthetic attitude toward the permanent and the ephemeral, remembrance and oblivion, affirmation to life, and the compelling need to find an instruction manual to go with it.

Untitled
Mixed media on canvas
54 x 50 in.

deligiannidis.aristotelis@gmail.com
aristotelisd.com
@deligiannidis.aristotelis

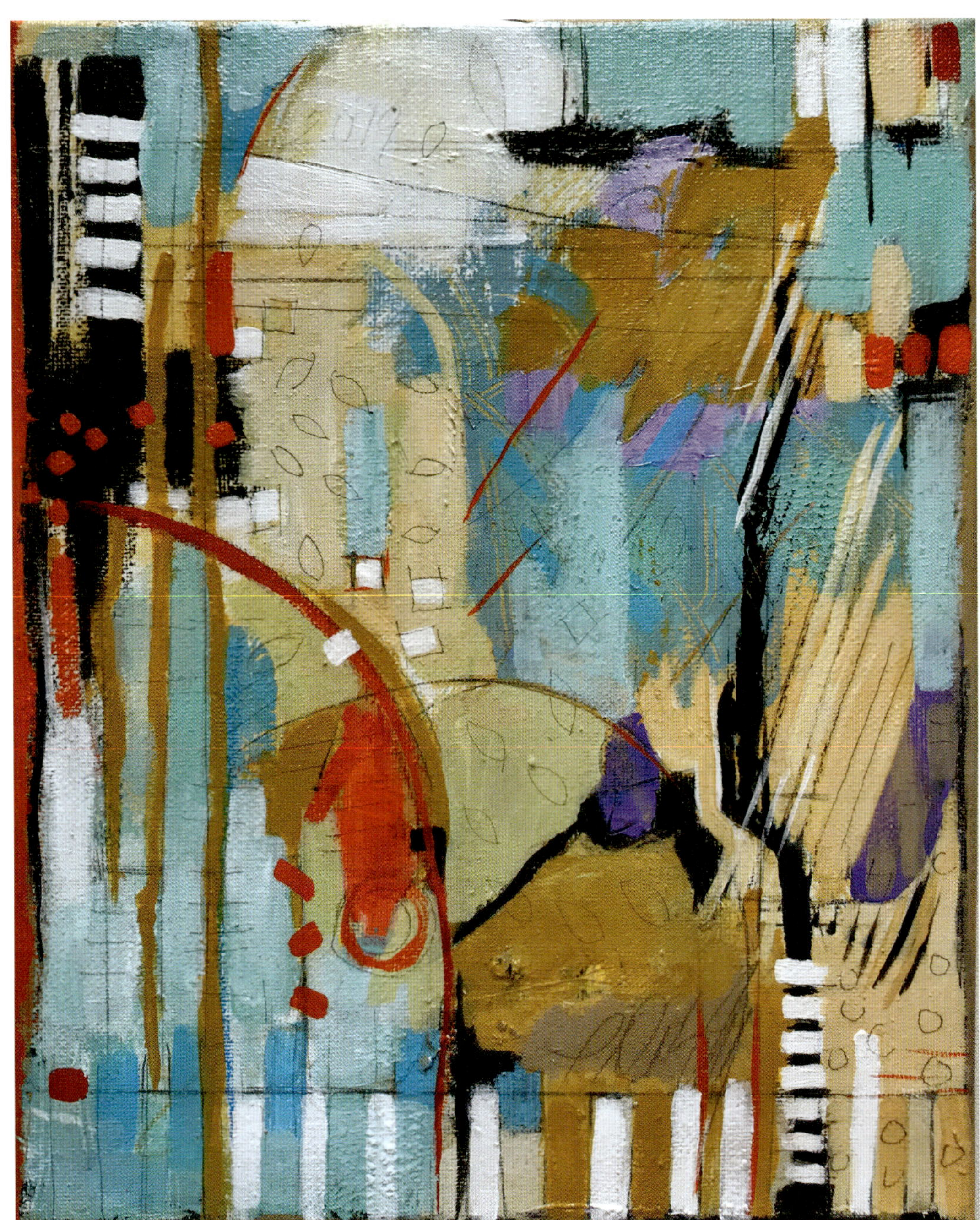

Paula DeStefanis

"I love the physical process of applying paint to canvas and the real sense of freedom I get in allowing a spontaneous application of color and line to the prepared surface. The unpredictability and potential sense of discovery are very exciting and one of the main reasons I do what I do," Paula DeStefanis says.

DeStefanis has always subscribed to the theory of "paint for paint's sake" by celebrating the qualities of the medium while including the images and textures that move her. She believes that each medium renders a unique response. In acrylic, she tends to draw from her daily experiences, beginning each canvas as a written journal, resulting in multilayered and often very geometrical works. In oils, she tends to be drawn to the patina and decay of aged surfaces.

"My goal is to create work that will engage the viewer and foster a dialogue that is invigorating, educational, and rewarding," she says.

September II
Acrylic
10 x 8 in.

paulaspalettestudio@
gmail.com
pauladestefanis.com
@pauladestefanis

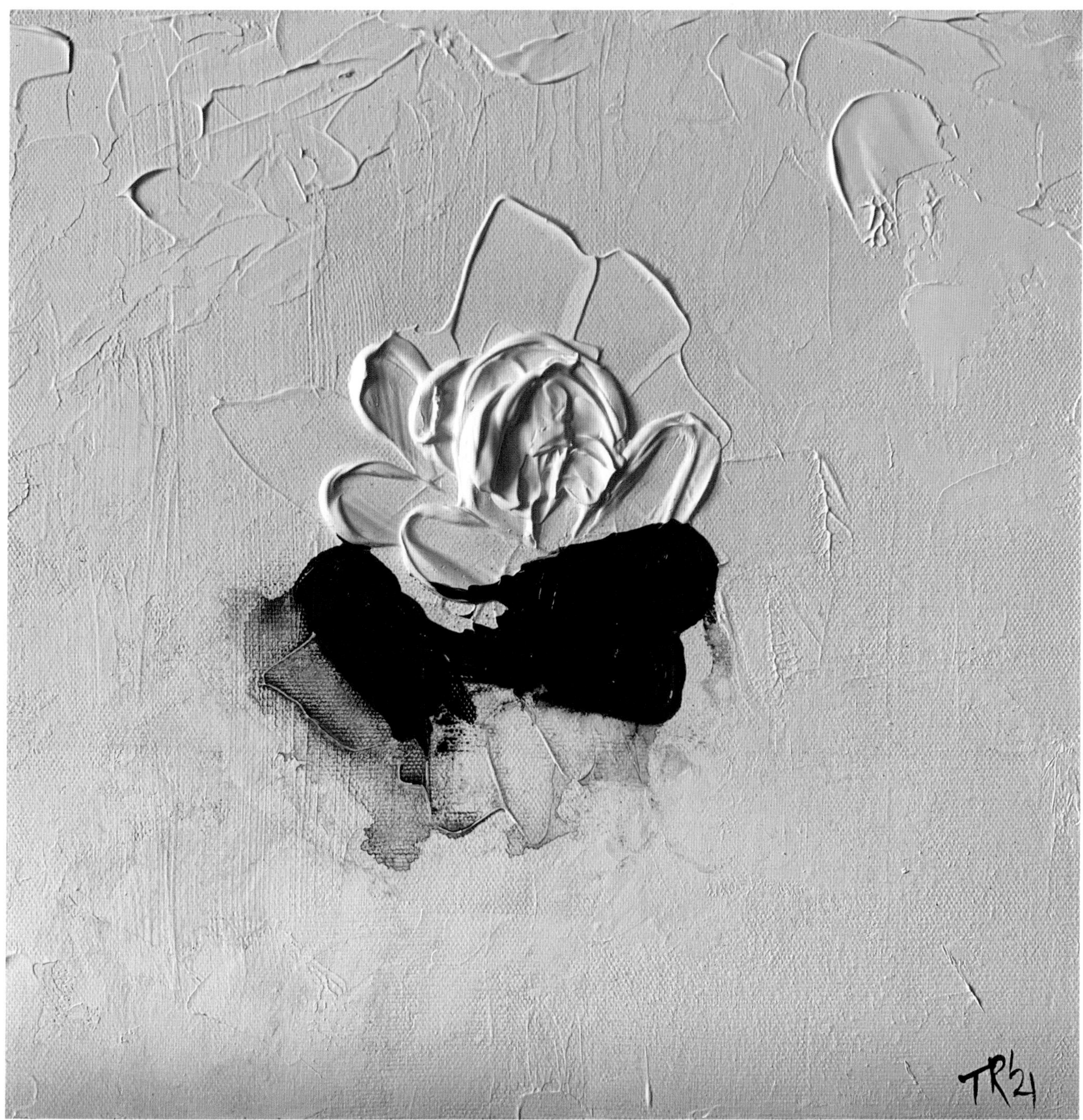

Trisha Dullu

Trisha Dullu is a self-taught visual artist focusing on modern abstracts and contemporary impressionistic landscapes and seascapes. She works predominantly with acrylic paints. She also likes to incorporate other mediums, like oil, charcoal, and ink, in her works. Dullu is inclined toward textured art. You can see the heaviness of texture in almost all her works. She loves to experiment with different mediums to bring about a variety and depth in her works.

Dullu has always been fascinated by the polarity of light and dark and competing, opposite forces. She instantly feels a connection to any such dichotomy. It is intriguing to realize that, more often than not, she has an emotional response to such surroundings and ideas. Her abstract works are a representational outcome of such duplicities.

Sugar Magnolia
Acrylic
12 x 12 in.

trisha.rajdullu@gmail
.com
@freespirit_trishadullu

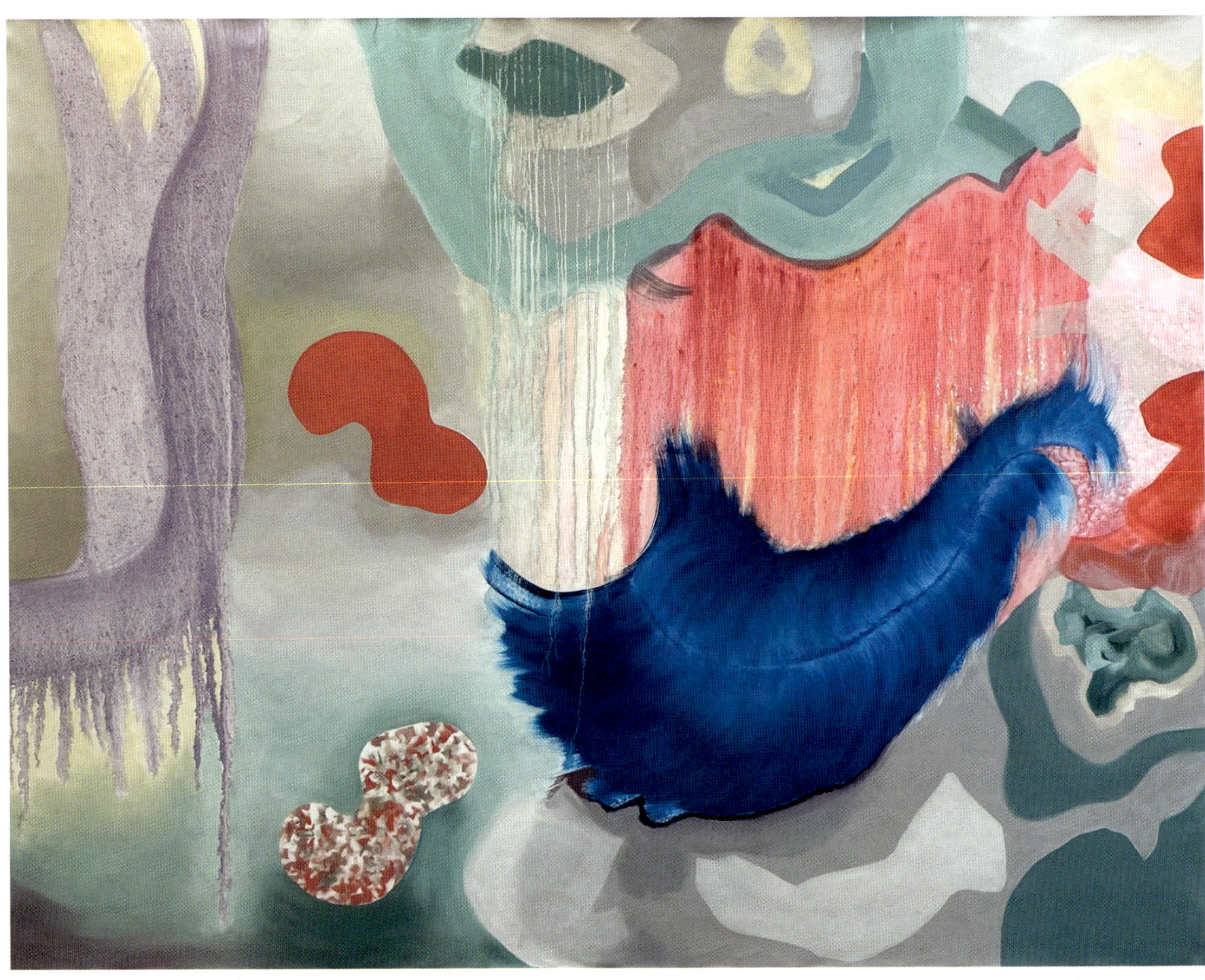

Karen Ebbs

Karen Ebbs is an abstract painter/visual artist. Through her work, she explores the phenomena of perception, how visual perception occurs, and investigates the many collaborating factors that are involved. Ebbs's practice is underpinned by research. She draws from rich contemporary wells: art, cognitive science, neuroscience, philosophy of mind, and all that feeds her spirit.

Recurring visual elements appear in all works—winding, gestural, ambiguous, unpredictable shapes, and motifs. Color, as a vibratory language, is an important element.

Ebbs's work imitates how visual perception occurs and the many possible interpretations. The lens through which we see the world is formed by all of our accumulated experiences, and we are, therefore, primed to see the world as we do.

Field Of Potentialities
Oils and mixed media
on primed canvas
63 X 78.75 in.

karenebbs@gmail.com
karenebbs.com
@karen.ebbs

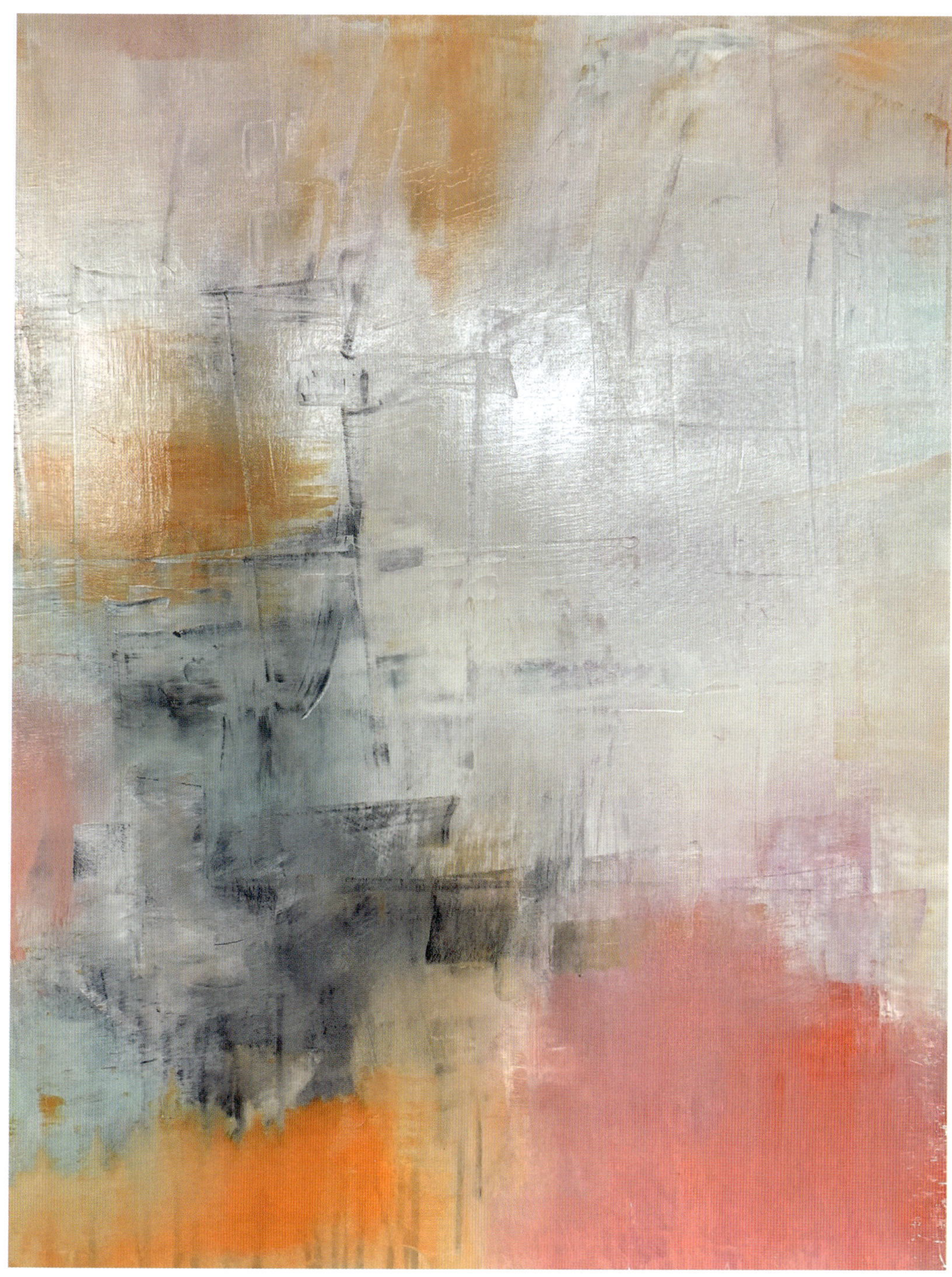

Luise Ellerbrock

The artwork *Unspoken* was created in 2021. The strong and delicate colors, which were created with a palette knife and brushstrokes in several layers on the canvas, do not merge in this work, as is typical in Luise Ellerbrock's works, but remain in their place. They meet each other but keep their boundaries. Only now and then a contrary color places itself in a foreign field.

"This artwork is meant to express different thoughts that can haunt you but you don't want to or can't express," Ellerbrock says. "Accepting that these thoughts are allowed to coexist is a challenging task. Letting go of these thoughts always allows us to change perspective, grow from them, and heal. Through my work, I want to give voice to my unspoken thoughts and welcome them onto my canvas."

It is easy for Ellerbrock to express the beauty of the world in strong and positive colors because she feels there is so much to discover and admire.

Unspoken
Acrylic on canvas
80 x 60 in.

luise_e86@yahoo.de
@colors_by_lu

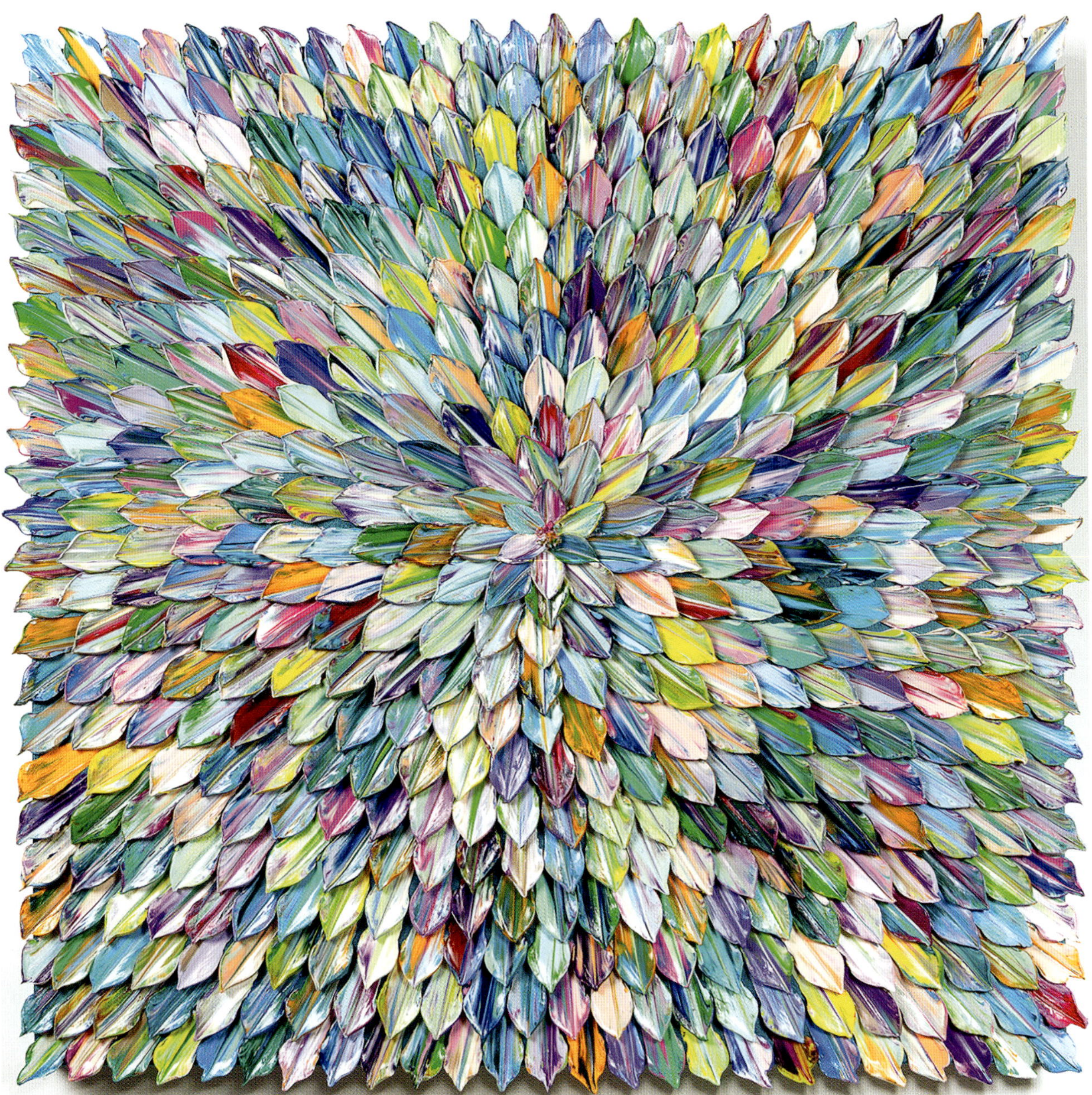

Melissa Ellis

Native Texan and Dallas resident Melissa Ellis is a palette knife painter specializing in sculptural oil paintings on canvas. Her bold use of color is apparent in all of her work, from her large-scale, multicolored pattern work to her stark black-and-white pieces. She has developed a unique style of painting by using palette knives to create beautifully distinct patterns, shapes, and designs with thick textural oil paint. This original and imaginative technique that she developed instantly became her signature style. Often described as "organized chaos," Ellis's work is a dichotomous celebration of spontaneity through the highly calculated and meticulous methods she uses to create organic motion, shadows, patterns, texture, and depth in all of her paintings. Her palette knife skills turn simple oil paint into wild and incredible shapes and patterns. Constantly pushing the boundaries to see how the paint will mix, mold, and sculpt, she creates new forms of motion and texture in each of her pieces, all while playing with unending combinations of color.

Let Your Soul Shine
oil on canvas
40 x 40 in.

melissa@melissaellisart
.com
melissaellisart.com
@melissaellisart

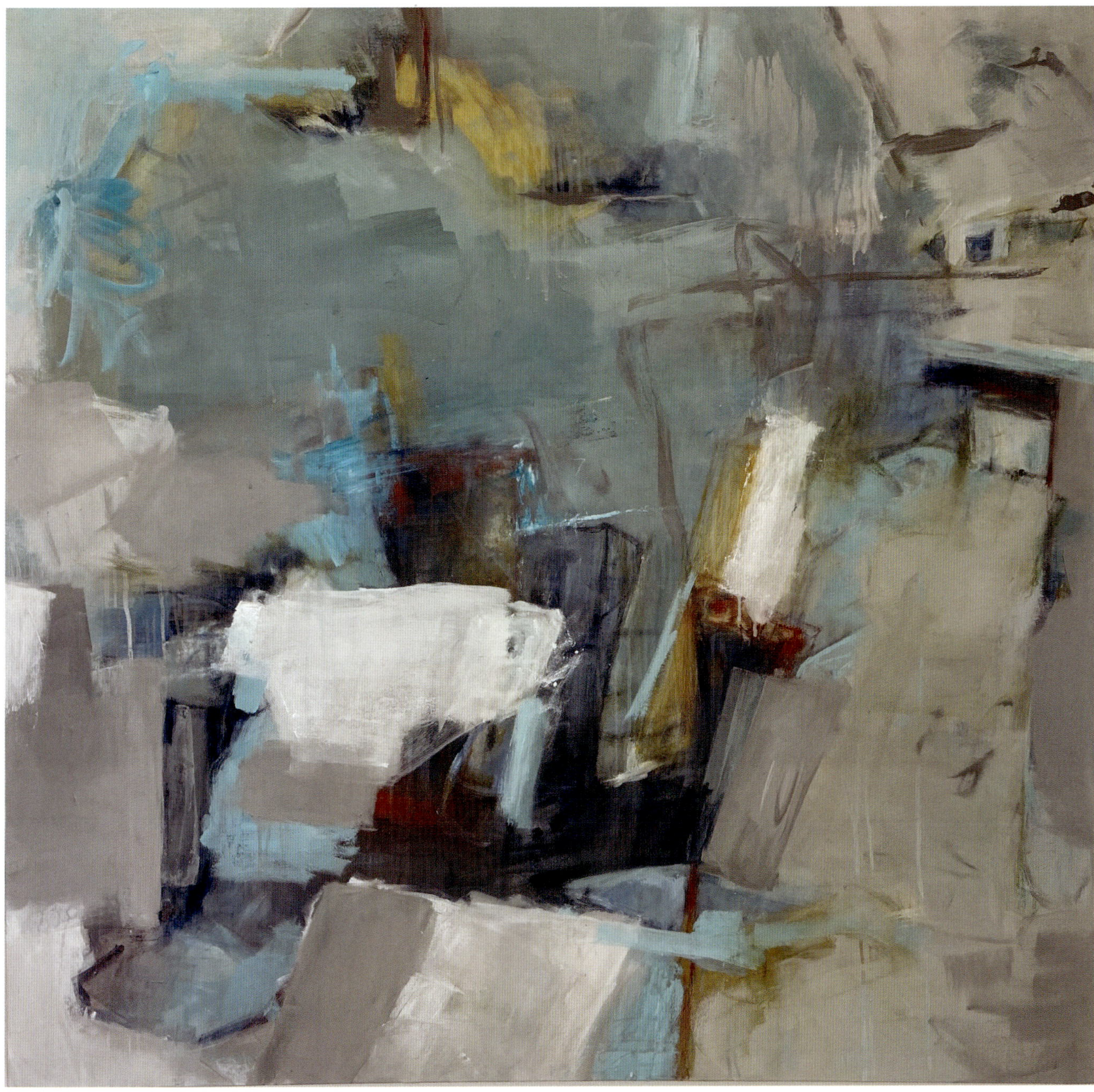

Debbie Ezell

The process of creating art is a meditative experience for Debbie Ezell. Referencing years of life drawing, the shapes and marks, now considered her nonobjective visual language, create the illusion of space and depth. A spontaneous conversation begins, and a visual order is established through the division of space, gestural marks, and blind contour drawing. Arranging forms dynamically within the canvas allows shapes to emerge, dissolve, and change. Negative spaces begin a new life. Each mark and brushstroke becomes a voice in the painting dialogue. Compositions develop through a series of decisions that are both conscious and unconscious.

"I tend to focus on particular palettes, shapes, or compositions for long periods of time, resulting in a series of closely related paintings. The paintings are an ongoing process of emergence and dissipation until elements on the canvas coexist with intensity and depth. Each work maintains authentic energy that resolves when the shapes, lines, and passages of color are in harmony with each other," Ezell says.

Here Comes the Sun
Oil, acrylic and mixed media
48 x 48 in.

dpezell@bellsouth.net
debbieezell.com
@debbieezellart

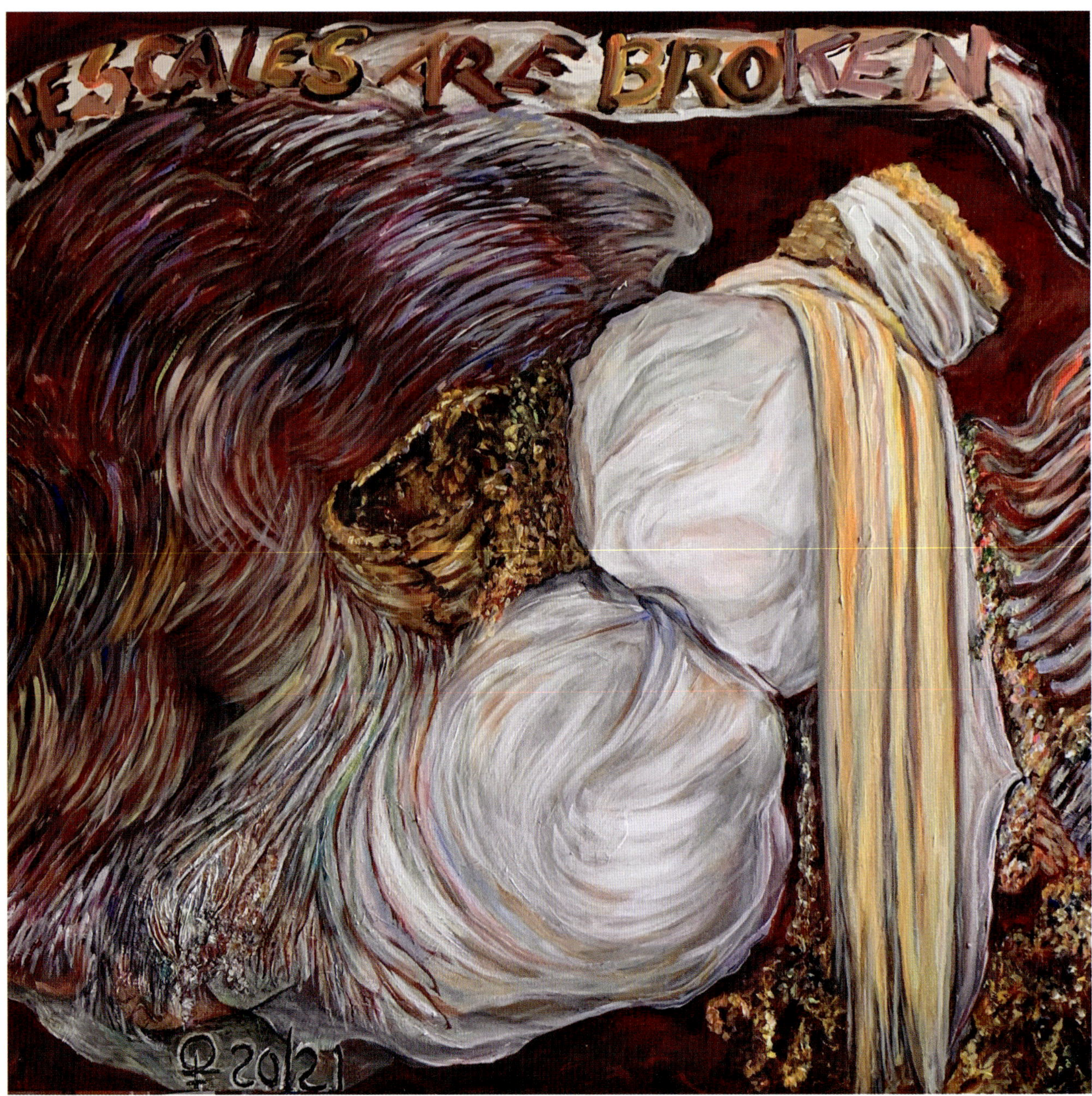

Pat Fallon

Pat Fallon has the benefit of a rich cultural education, one that mixes the magic realism of Cervantes and Gabriel García Márquez with the French, Irish, Italian, and Spanish storytellers in her family. It's that heritage that marks her style and palette and allows her work to be referred to as abstract magic realism. Magic realism is about the appearance and disappearance of things. In the visual arts, it is called surrealism. Fallon calls it magic realism and believes it is rampant in all the arts today.

Her work can be characterized as an exploitation of the possibilities that result from scientific exploration. "I am fascinated by the concept of a universe full of the movement of particles that we know exist because they leave traces of their shadows in a cloud chamber," Fallon says.

Fallon believes her work is needed in today's world because she abstracts what is seen and perceived to provide images for the contemporary viewer who wants to see where we are and where we are going.

Blind Justice of The Americas 2020-21
Acrylic on canvas
36 x 36 in.

patfallon10@gmail.com
patfallon.com
@falloncodazzi

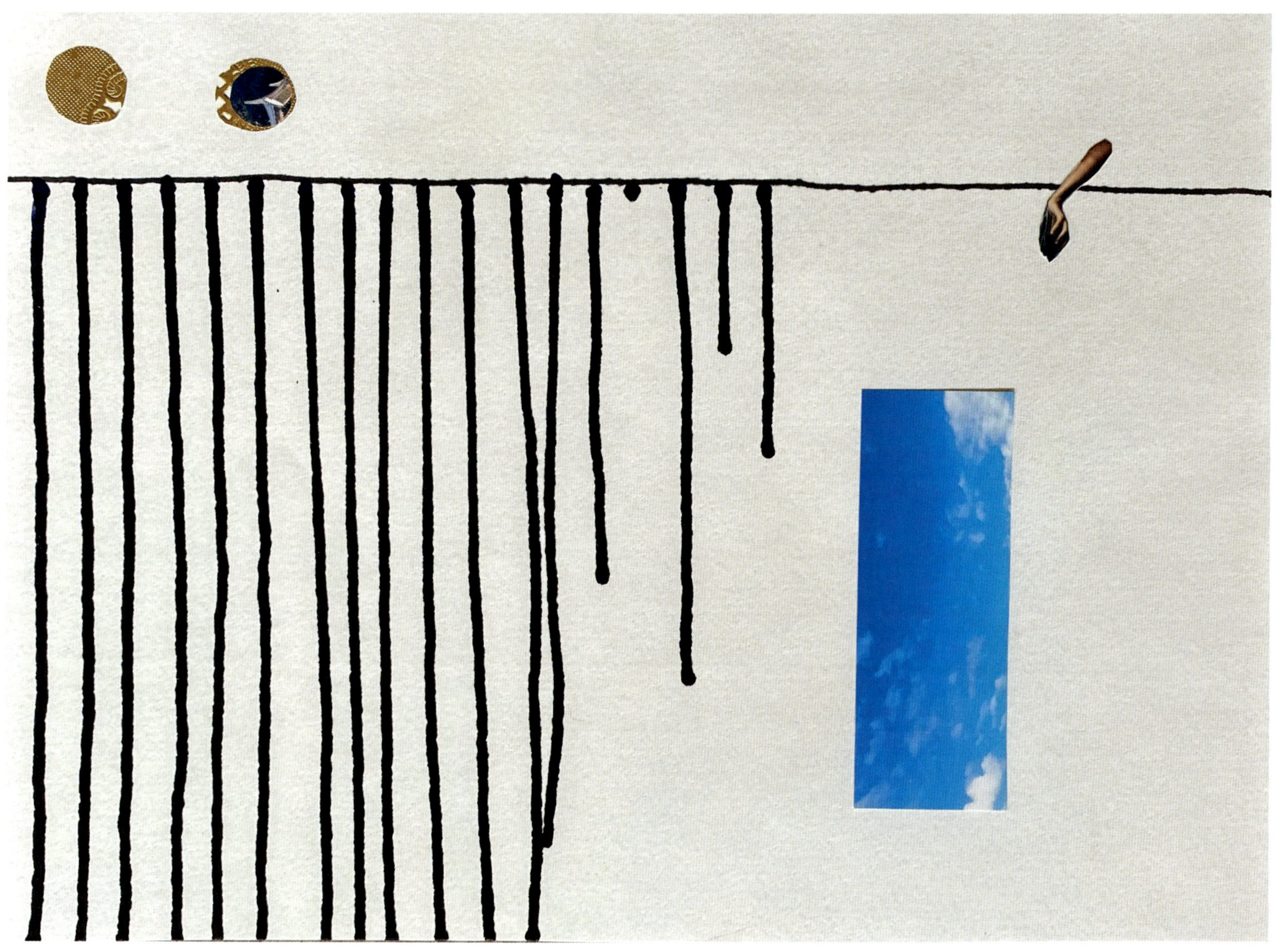

Alexandra Farber
Alexandra Farber has always used visual art as a conduit for expression and took this a step further by becoming the visual art. She began training in classical ballet at only three years old. Dance is the largest influence on her work, and she still performs to this day alongside her art creation. Dance is her nature, and it is through that intuition that her visual art narrative originates. Lines, colors, and tone often mimic the patterns she trained into her body with dance; repetition, absence, and organic materials represent their dance counterparts as well, symbolizing dedication, frustration, and the natural instrument that is the body. Farber seeks to create work that reflects the moods around all of us every day, big and small, using evocative composition. While every small detail in a piece may have a unique meaning to the artist, it is the interpretation of the audience that fascinates her the most. She aims to bring an interesting approach to the stories of daily life, causing people to question their worldviews meaningfully.

Shoulder to Cry on I
Acrylic and collage on paper
9 x 12 in.

afarber123@gmail.com
alexandrafarber.com
@alexandrafarber.art

PAINTING: TRADITIONAL/ABSTRACT

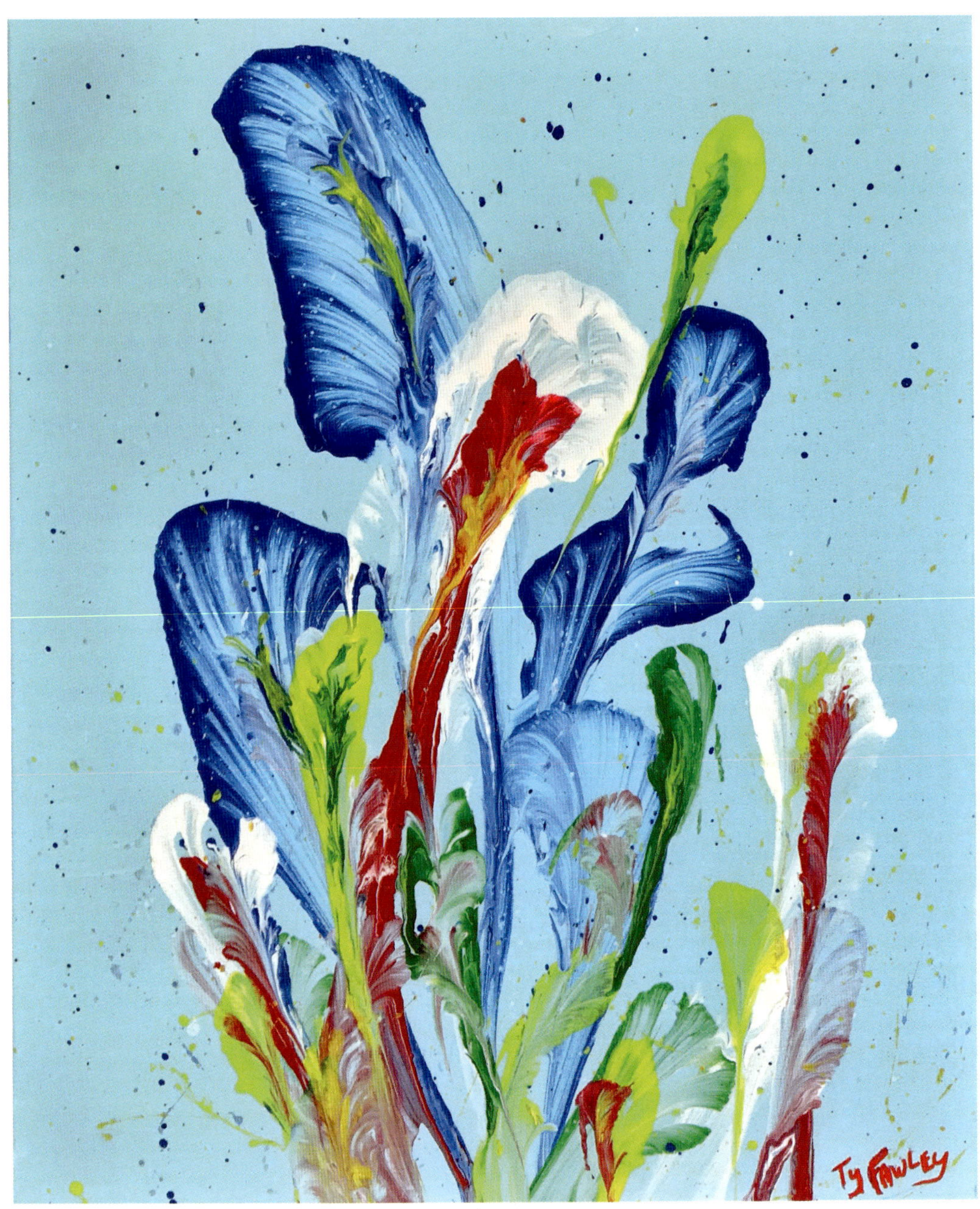

James Fawley

"Painting is my alter ego. It is the 'me' zone," says James Fawley. "Within this zone, I perceive not only the subject matter of the painting but survey the surroundings, light, color, and atmosphere around me. Painting is a progress of creativity, limited within the painting I am forming."

Fawley finds beauty in nature and seeks to respect that visualization onto his canvas. Creativity is ingrained in those that are consumed by it. He views the world and the gifts it offers and endeavors to create through brush and canvas the view that he witnesses. Color, shape, and form are gifts given to all of us, and the tones and hues are to be revealed via the frame of the world seen. Fawley is not attempting to paint precisely what he sees, but endeavors to craft his impression enthusiastically on the canvas.

"Color is everywhere, even where you may not see it. My energy is to bring those colors to the eye, and the mind's eye. I seek to generate emotion and endeavor to spark an inspired creative dialogue with the viewer as a participant within the painting. Plus, frankly, I have fun!" Fawley says.

Color Burst
Acrylic
16 x 11 in.

jlfthree@gmail.com
tyfawleyart.com
@tyfawleyart

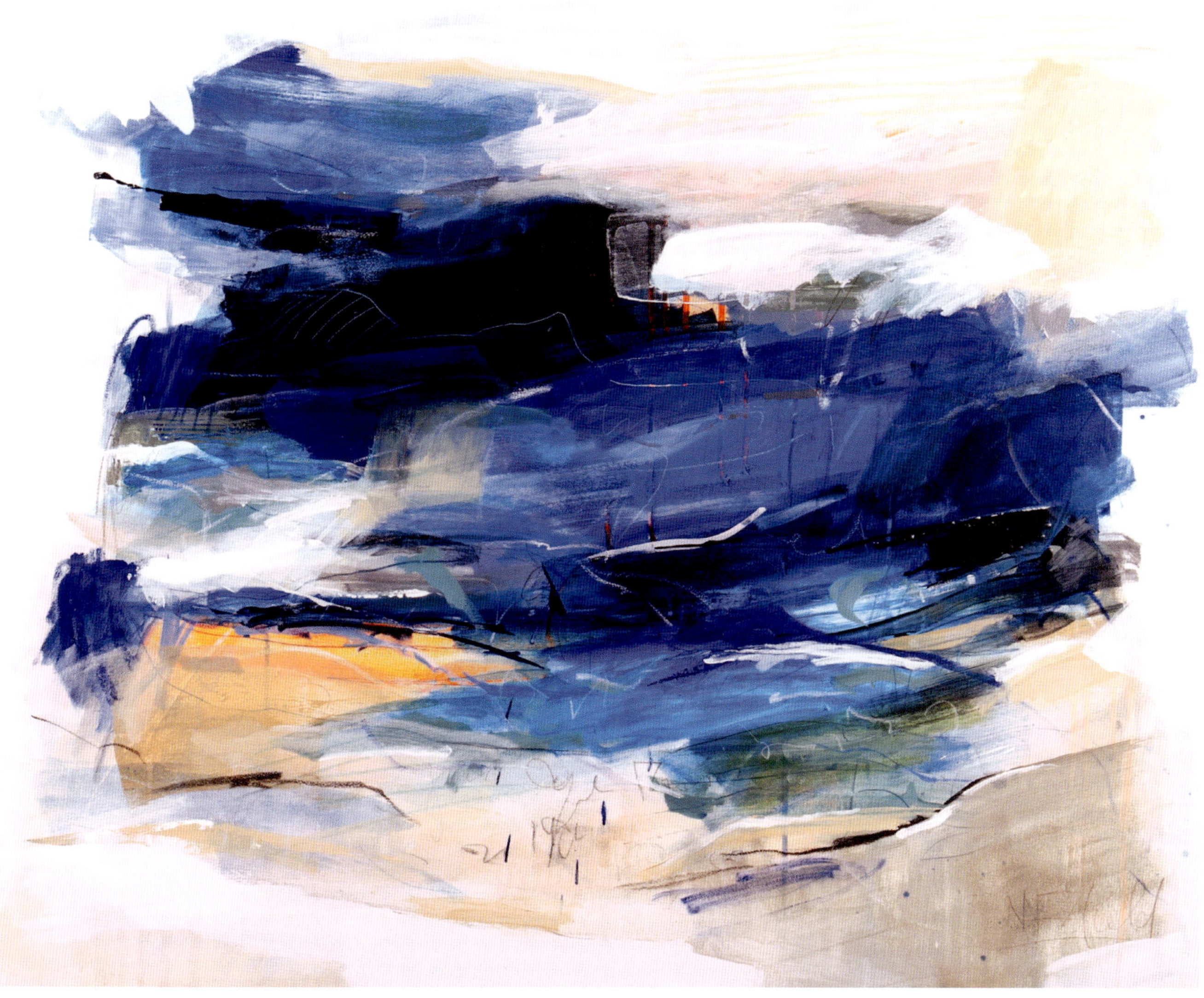

Nicole Fearfield

Raised on an island, a substantial part of Nicole Fearfield's formative years were spent floating about in the water, absorbed in some imaginary, underwater wonderland or staring hypnotized at far horizons, dreaming of adventures to be had.

Now a contemporary artist, Fearfield recognizes this was a form of youthful meditation, and she delights in tapping into a similar state of flow, immersing herself in a space of being open and still, allowing ideas and creative expression to form and move through her.

Fearfield's abstract paintings are dynamic, playful representations of life, expressed through color, metaphor, text, and humor. Indulging her adventurous side, Fearfield loves to explore the connection to others through joyful memories of fun experiences. As she begins to paint, these feelings and memories float in and out of her conscious thoughts, waiting to be made solid, captured energetically on canvas for others to see, to relate to.

Waterways, Happy Days
Mixed media on canvas
40 x 40 in.

nicolefearfield@icloud
.com
nicolefearfield.com
@nicolefearfield

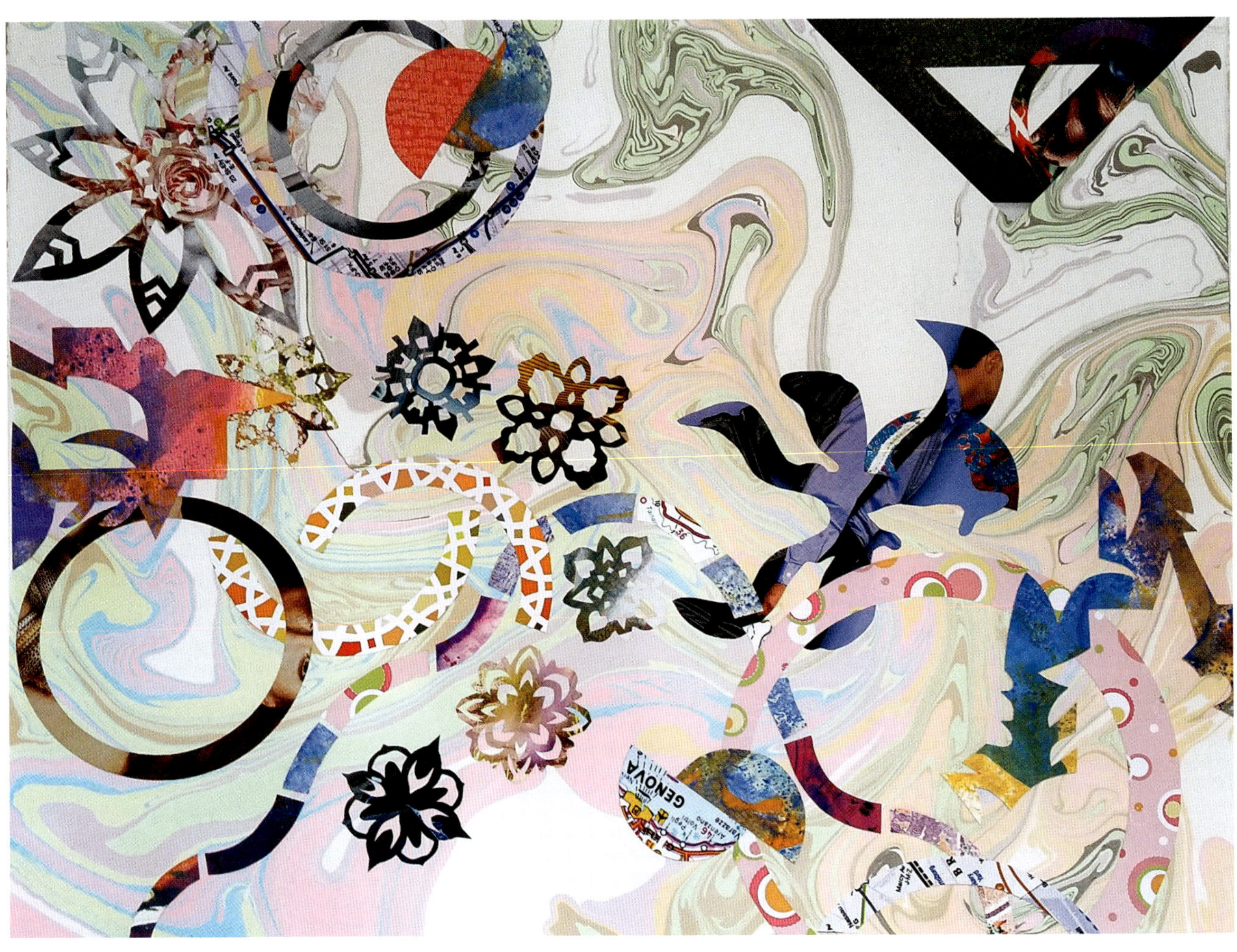

Cecelia Feld

Art can't save the world, but Cecelia Feld thinks it can make the world a better place by illuminating, provoking, persuading, and inspiring. Her work, in printmaking, painting, and collage, is about exploring the relationships of shapes, colors, lines, and textures through abstraction. The relationship of visual components in her work is like the themes and variations and improvisation in jazz. The results are unexpected. Her collagraph and monotype prints, often cut up, and her photographs and found paper build the collage.

An ongoing project is the construction of collages on marbled paper, which Feld makes using the Japanese suminagashi (ink floated on water) marbling technique. A series on suminagashi marbled paper incorporates haiku, a Japanese poetry style, created by friends for the project.

Travel fuels her imagination. Sights, sounds, order, and chaos find their way into her art. Serendipity is the hallmark of Feld's work.

Suminagashi Suite 3
Mix media and collage
22 x 30 in.

cecelia@feld.com
studio7310.com

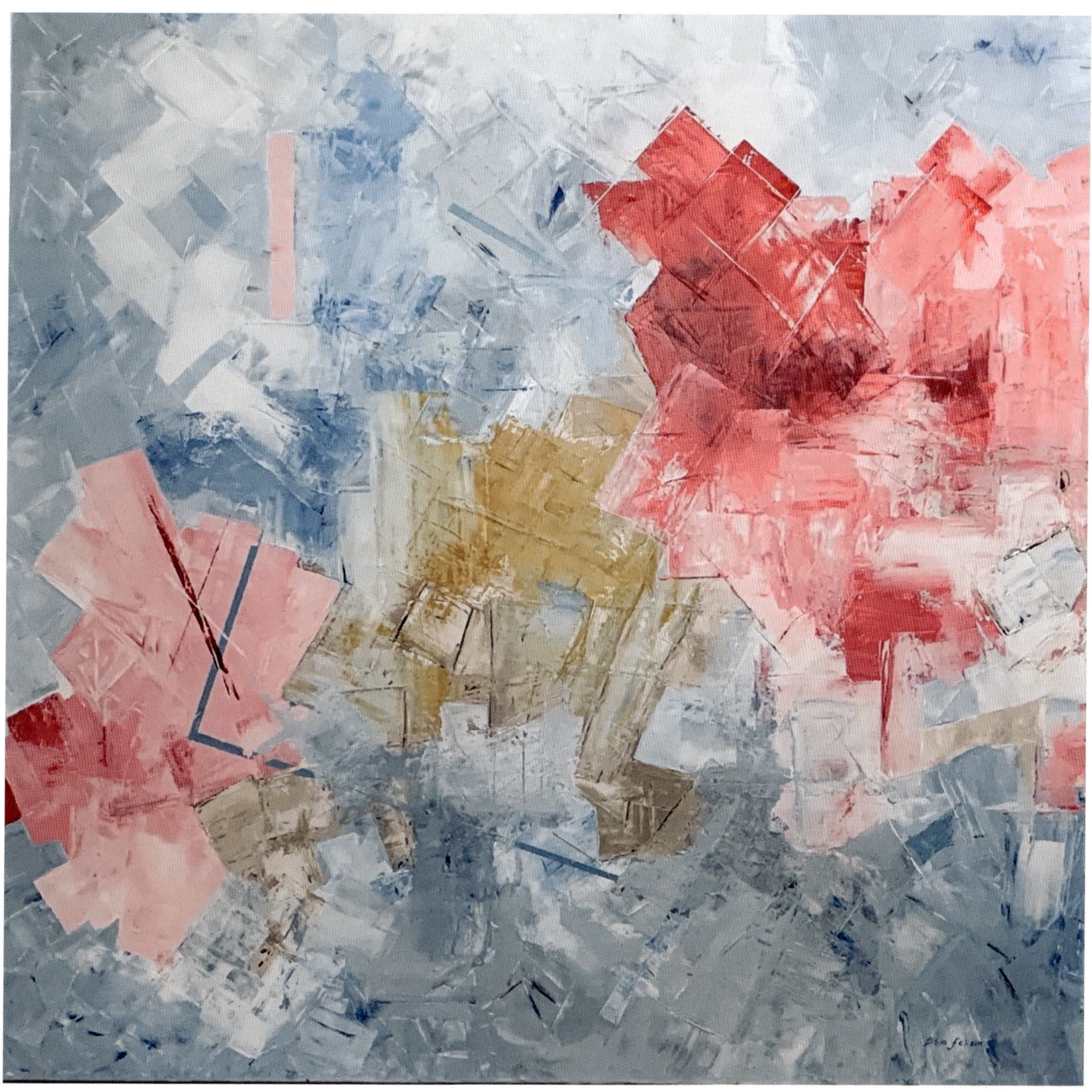

Silvia Felizia

Silvia Felizia is an Argentine artist based in the United States. Her work is a journey; a dialogue of memories, beliefs, and experiences; a place where the past overlaps and intersects with the present, traveling the emotional landscapes of her life in The Americas, Asia, and Europe.

Abstract, emotive, strong, and vulnerable, Felizia's paintings are drawn from her story and the story of her surroundings with a mixture of feelings of nostalgia. On her canvases, movement, stillness, silence, and noise feed into each other, creating interactions between color and texture. She builds layers over layers to give birth to a unified whole and to reflect the continuous search for equilibrium between the push and pull from the multiple cultures to which she has been exposed while remaining loyal to her Latinx origin. Felizia believes that a work of art—like life—has its unique rhythm and can always continue to evolve and change.

A Door in the Sky
Acrylic and modeling paste on canvas
36 x 36 in.

silviafelizia.art@gmail
.com
silviafelizia.com
@silviafelizia

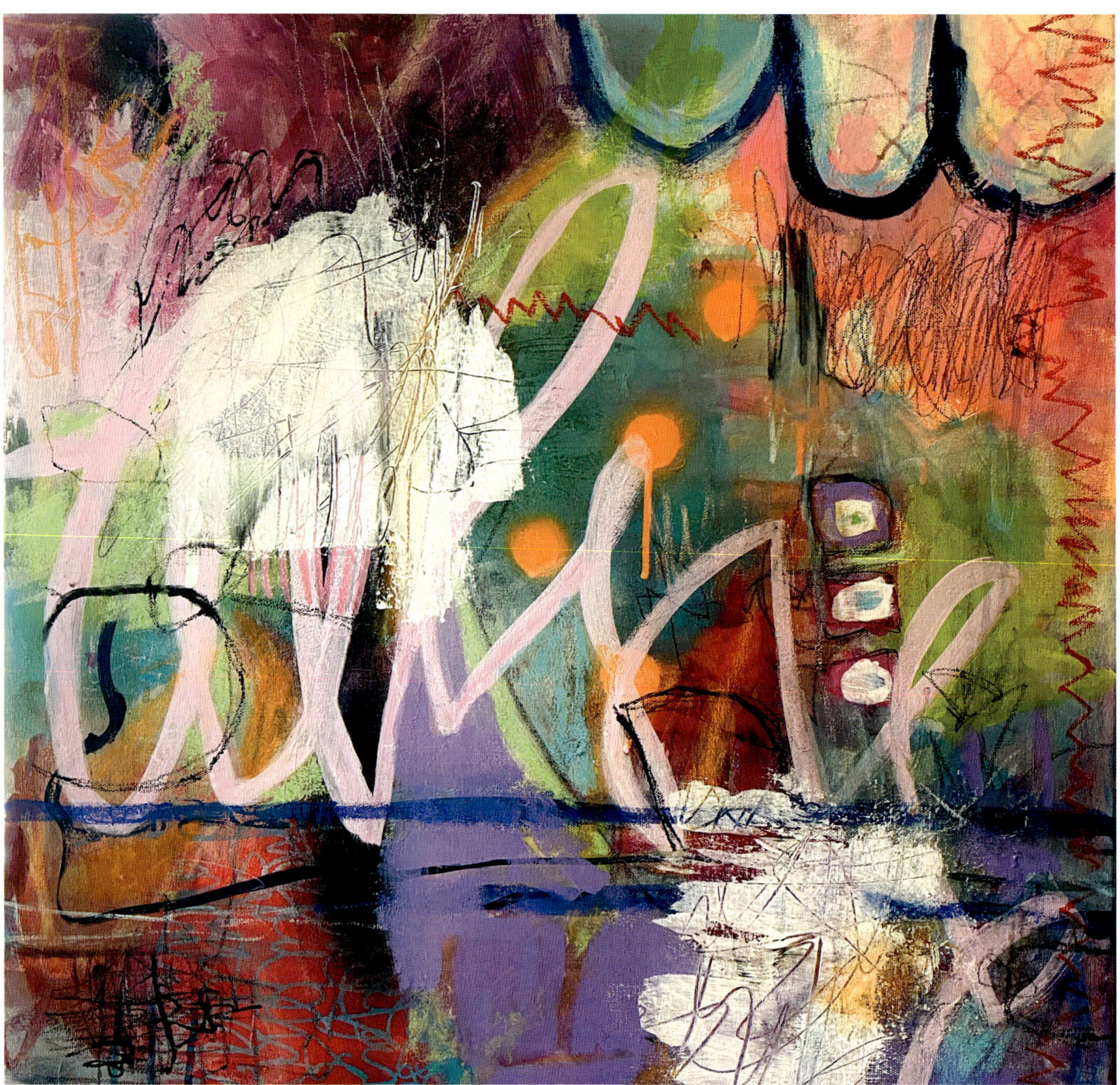

Lisa Fisher

Lisa Fisher has been painting on and off for over twenty years, but only in the last couple of years has she become a full-time artist. With her love of color at the forefront of every piece, you'll rarely see a monochromatic painting from her (although she has done some). In her abstracts, she paints intuitively, using gestural expressionism and letting the painting speak to her. She doesn't stick to abstracts only. For her "collections" of subjects, whether it be floral, animal, landscape, faces, or something else, she enjoys using creative, chaotic lines in the process. She will use a multitude of media in just one painting to get the look and liveliness she is working for. This energy in her artwork, along with her bold, bright colors, is her signature style. When she's not painting, she waits to hear from the person who sees a piece that resonates with them and makes that connection artistically and personally.

My Strawberry Milkshake
Acrylic and mixed media
24 x 24 in.

lisa@lisafisherart.com
lisafisherart.com
@lisafisherart

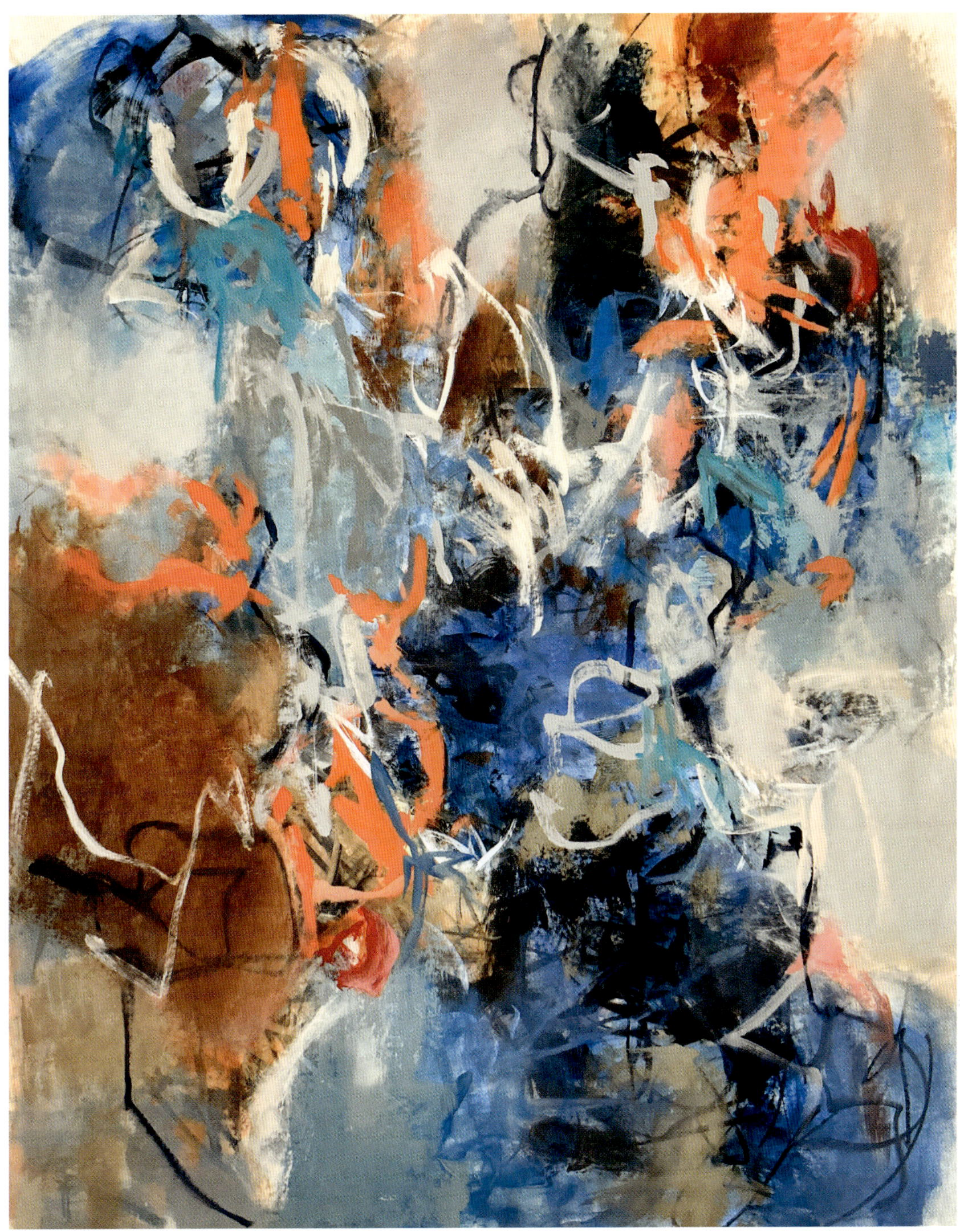

Susan Foley

A primarily self-taught artist whose world travel helped shape her unique style, artist Susan Foley creates large-scale, contemporary abstract expressionist works that teem with movement and emotional vigor. Driven by the rigors of moving paint across giant canvases, Foley's active, emotive paintings offer texture and depth in large doses. Many of her works are embellished with idiosyncratic scribbles, a feature that conjures both careful calligraphy and illegible handwriting as if meant to conceal and reveal their secrets simultaneously.

Although she never has a result in mind, she often discovers traces of past homes or fragments of locales she's visited tucked away in the features of a painting after it is completed. In this way, Foley feels she is translating her experiences of the world through paint, replicating her feelings in the depths of abstract designs and conjuring lapsed elements of her life subconsciously.

Make A Wish
Acrylic
48 x 38 in.

susanfoleyart@gmail
.com
foleyartstudios.com
@susanfoleyart

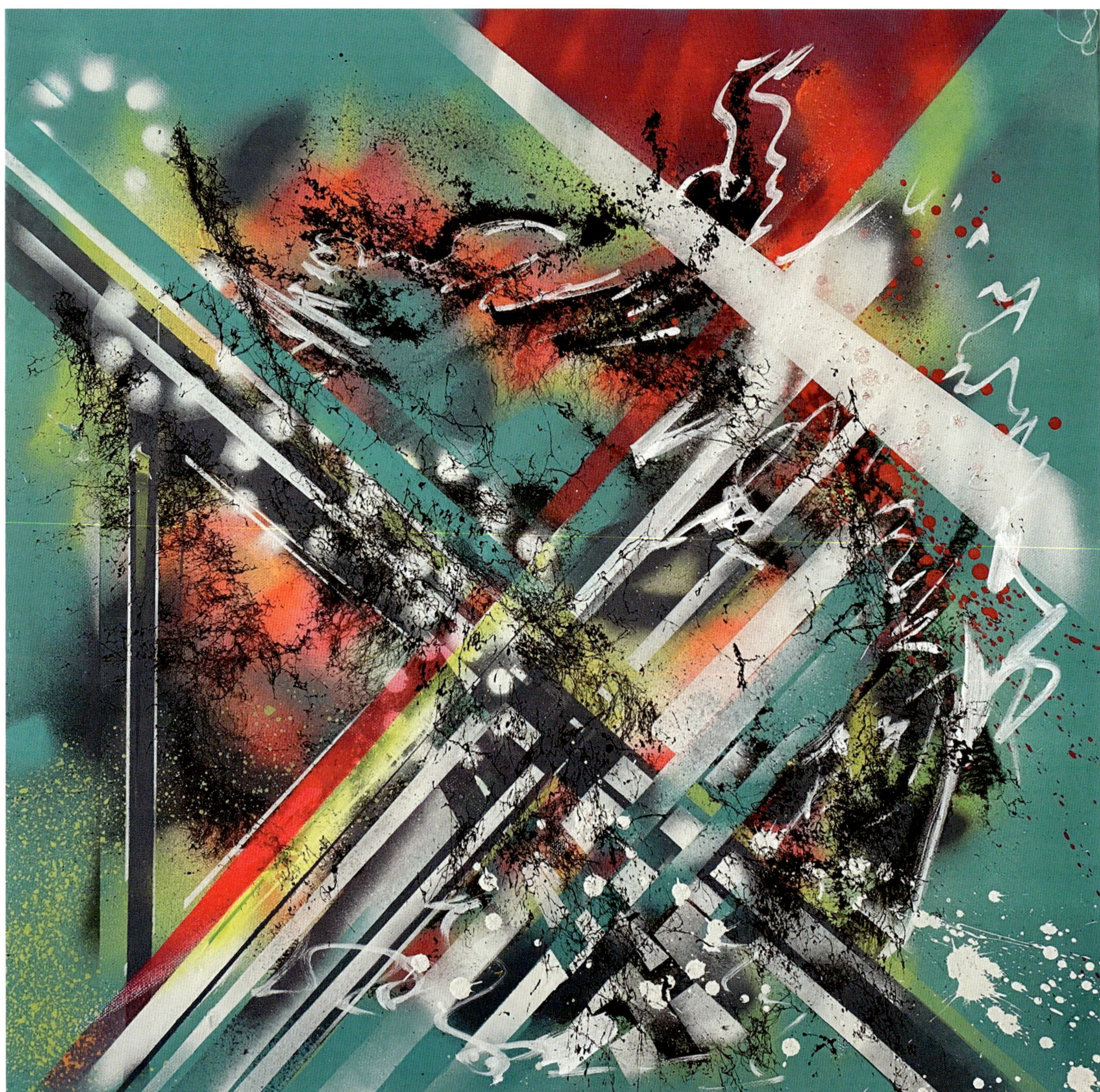

Roel Funcken

Roel Funcken is a contemporary abstract expressionist painter whose work is recognizable for its unique style that is rich in textures, colors, and shapes.

A musician and a painter, the overarching process between making music and painting fascinates the artist, and both mediums complement the other on how to approach certain elements in the creative process.

The artist constantly tries to think of new ways to apply the paint onto the canvas. His paintings are created through intuitive responses while engaged with the work. As a kid, Funcken saw abstract shapes everywhere he looked, which intrigued him. Despite being color-blind, he is addicted to colors and the contrast between them. His work is informed by color and forms found in nature and influenced by the work of painters such as Kandinsky and Pollock.

Vesper Tine
Spray paint and acrylic
on canvas
23.6 X 23.6 in.

booking@moicflo.com
roelfuncken.com
@roelfunckenpaintings

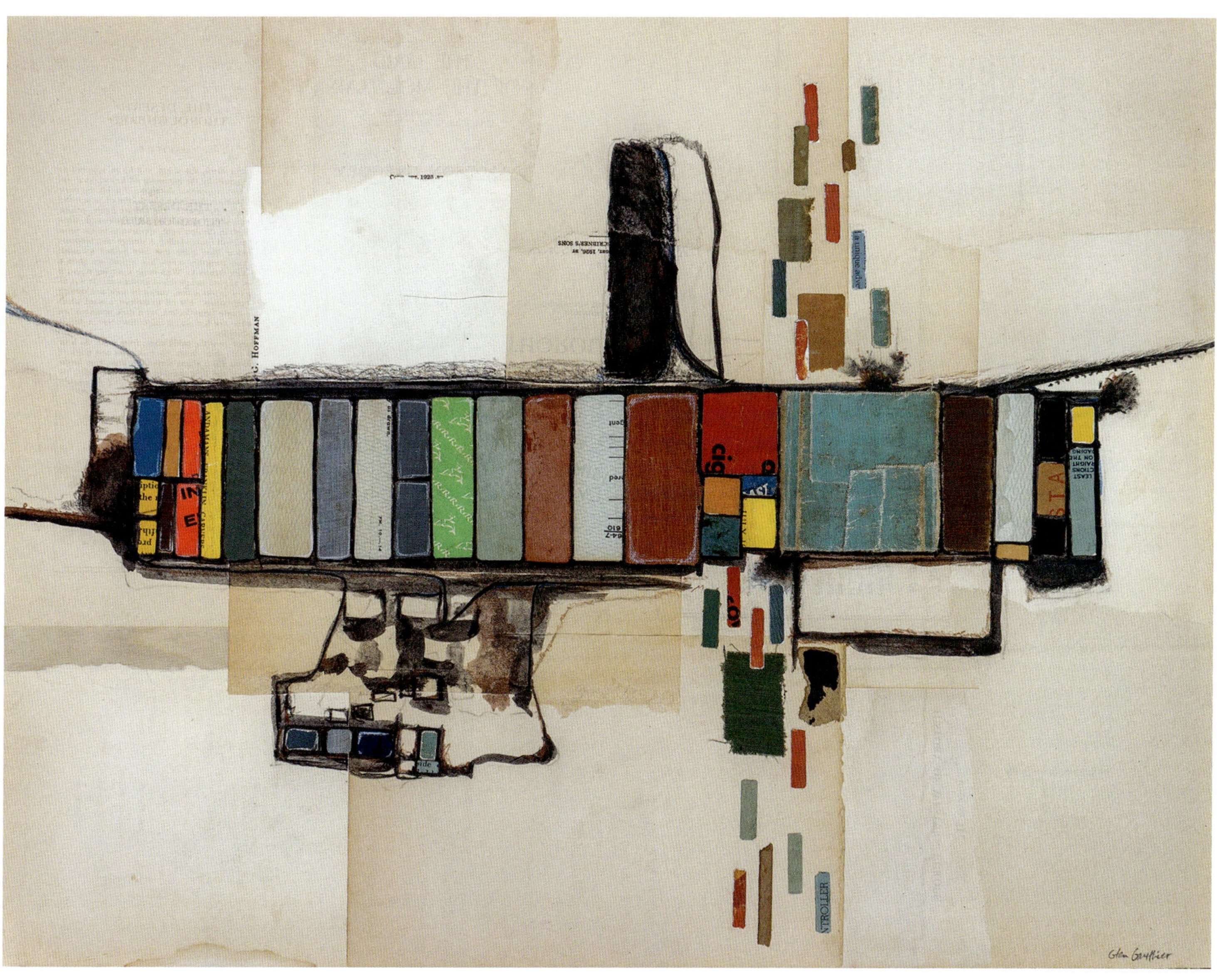

Glen Gauthier

Glen Gauthier's medium is collage, utilizing printed ephemera to serve as a kind of time machine. Things with a history have fascinated the artist since childhood. He is drawn to older homes and neighborhoods, factories, and office buildings, and especially the printed ephemera from the past. The drama of the Cold War and military conflict; the draw of the golden age of travel with its imagery and typography; the dusty, yellowed pages of old books, brochures, and documents—all these are fascinating to Gauthier and help to inform his work with a visual language that only time and imagination can bring. The themes that the artist explores include military defense, America's shifting position on the global stage, consumerism, the beauty of the ordinary, and the human connection.

"Now more than ever, my artwork is a means of communication for me, a two-way radio that speaks through time: past, present, and an imagined future. It's communication with different versions of myself and the viewer, though I don't force them to see only my story," Gauthier says.

Cellular
Collage on wood panel
16 x 20 in.

glen@streetfairstudios
.com
glengauthier.com
@glengauthier

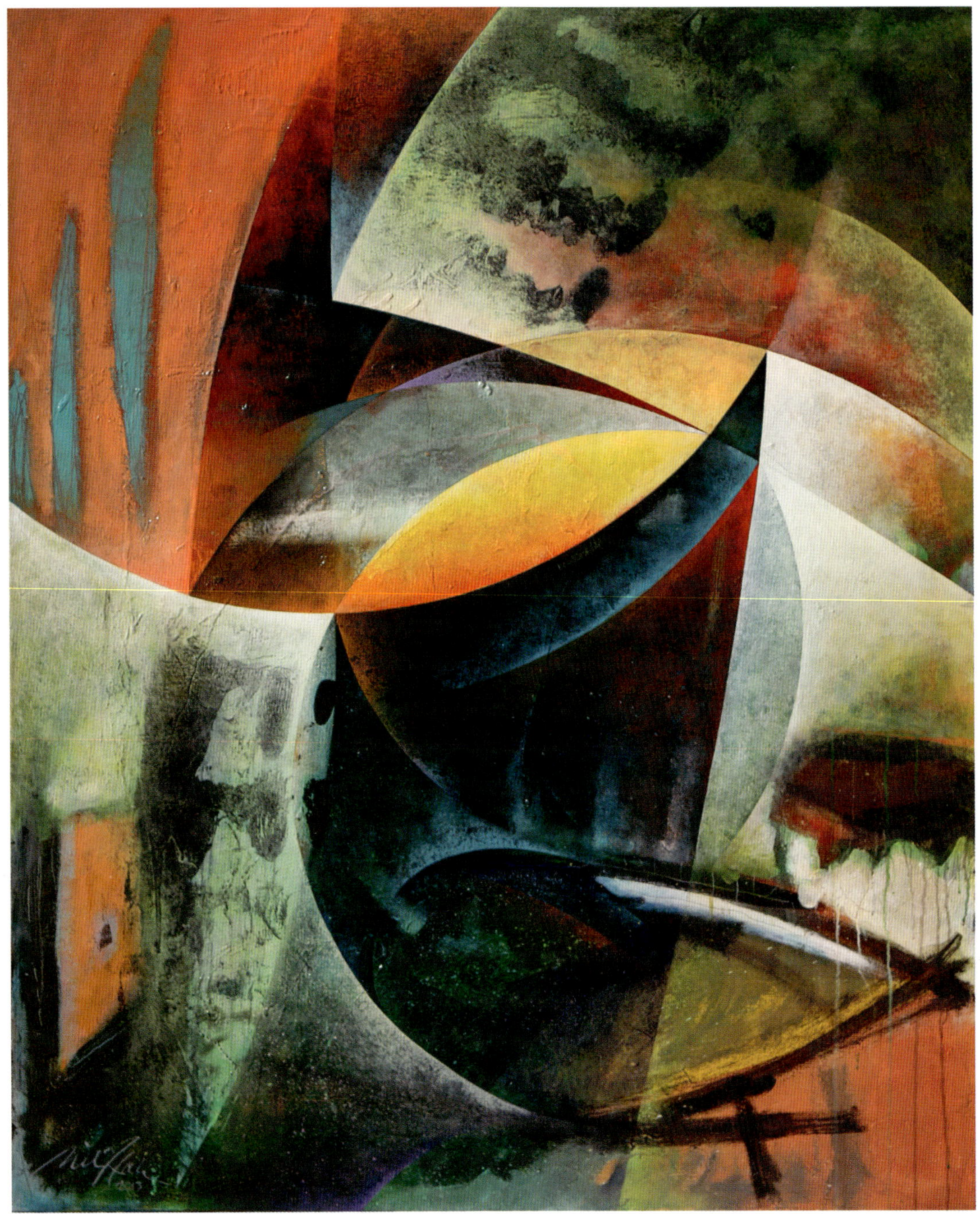

Mike Hale

Mike Hale's work embodies a unique artistic irony: "Beauty through destruction." Through a refined process, Hale pushes the boundary of each piece. The underpainting begins on a hard, flat surface, enabling him to be more physical and spontaneous. Transitioning to a vertical position, the painting is rotated frequently, challenging creative thought, limiting fixation on one area, and providing a better field of vision. By exposing previous stages—hidden layers of color, accidents, and tactile relief resurface to the foreground, becoming an integral part of the composition.

Sweeping curves, bold colors, and tectonic shapes comprise many of Hale's paintings. Resonating echoes of underlying patterns create a temporal pulse, an expression of time and movement. Complex in nature and technique, each piece is approached with passion and conviction.

In Your Long Arms
Acrylic on canvas
60 x 40 in.

mikehale@dejazzd.com

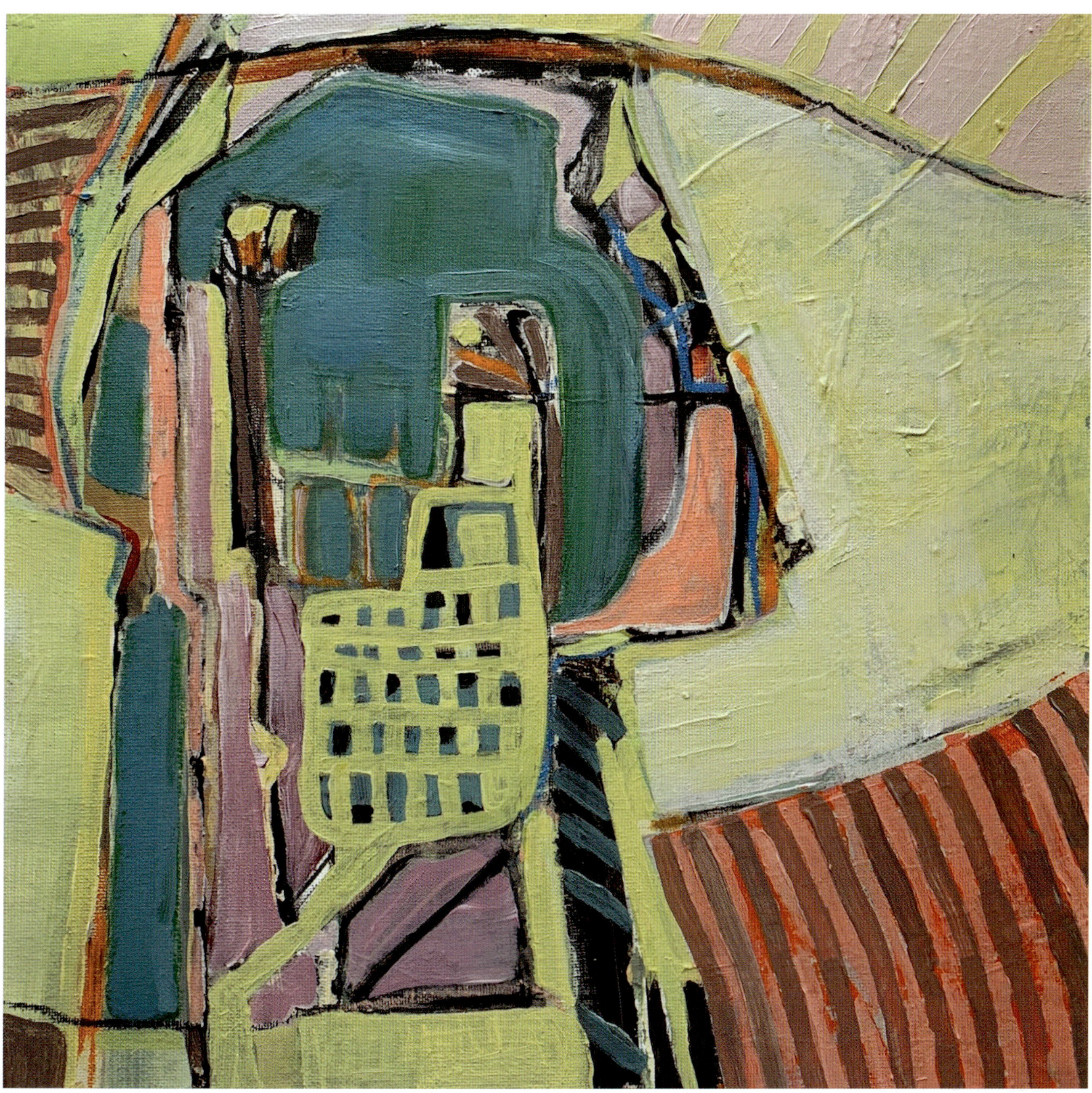

Carla Harder

Carla Harder works in acrylic mixed media and collage on paper, panel, and canvas. The use of line, pattern, and graphic elements appear frequently in her multilayered work. Her use of swift, full-body automatic drawing provides an energetic framework to explore spaces both real and imagined. Bold and sometimes fine graphic marks riddle the surfaces of her work, disappearing and reemerging randomly but always conveying physical and calligraphic energy.

Inspired by nature, these gestural and abstract images are fanciful, alluding to the fresh and innocent worlds of childhood. The immediacy of the work is conveyed through the use of unconventional tools. The artist rarely uses brushes but instead opts for trowels, spatulas, and studio-made implements to hang paint on the scaffolding of charcoal and pencil marks. The resulting layered work puzzles together shapes that speak to mile-high views of landscapes or zoom into microworlds. Harder's work feels as though it was created from the inside out, tapping into emotions and energy that are subtle and subterranean.

Sweet Chaos
Acrylic and mixed media
on panel
12 x 12 in.

Carlaharderartstudio@
gmail.com
@carlaeharder

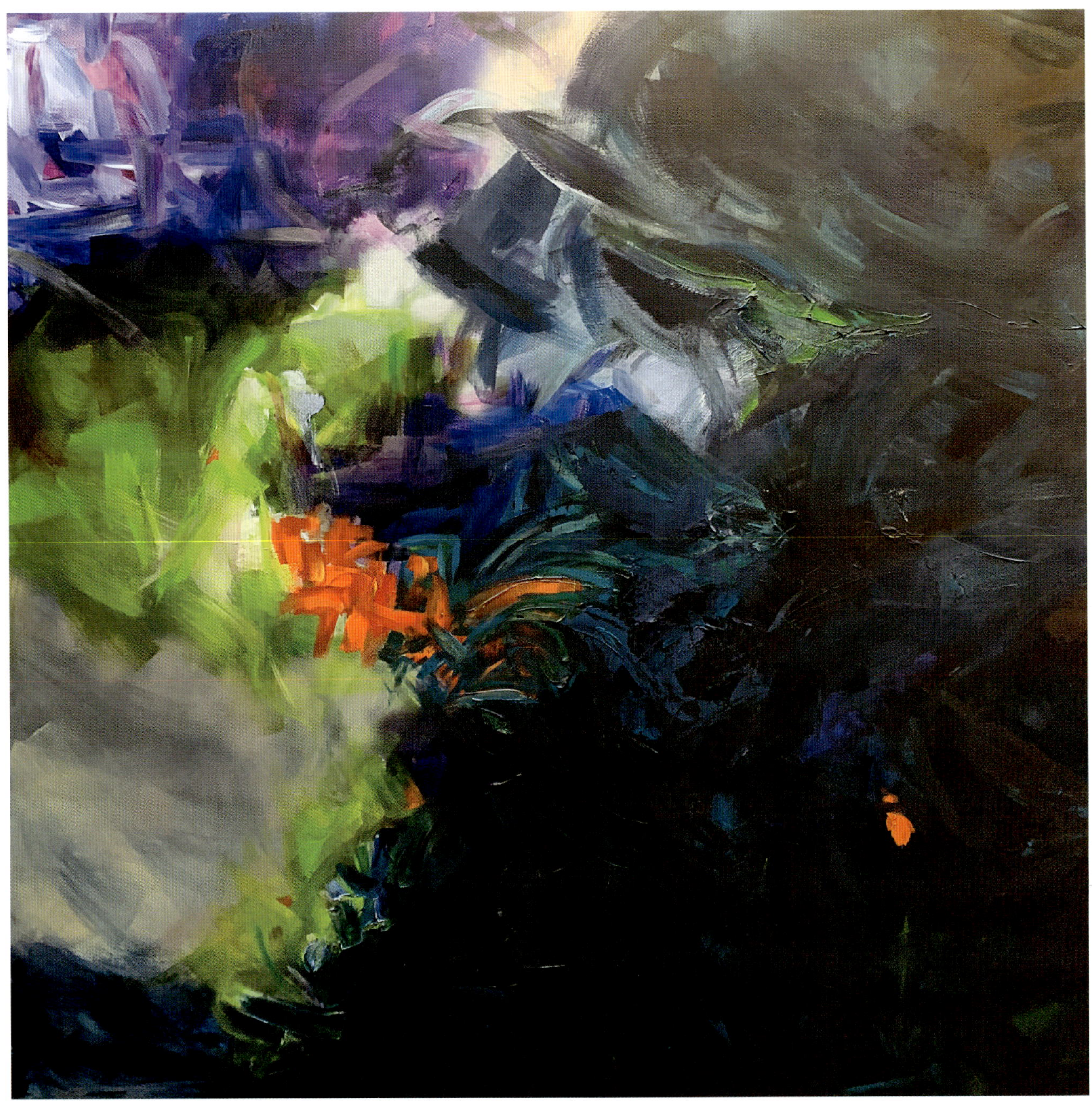

Deborah Hartigan Viestenz

For as long as she can remember, Deborah Hartigan Viestenz (DHV) has been fascinated by nature—the ebb and flow of the world around her. "I spent countless hours watching how the movement of water could transform everything, including rocks, wearing away the outer shells to reveal their inner beauty," she says.

After a creative hiatus followed by experimental works in various mediums and styles, DHV started the highly personal collection of paintings *Coming Home*, offering insight into the artist's present frame of mind. The paintings each use lessons and techniques learned as a young artist. One of DHV's most beloved movies is *The Wizard of Oz*. As a child, she was intrigued with the fanciful beauty while also feeling the fear, excitement, and longing for home.

This series documents her growth over fifty years of painting and allows the viewer to see her now through her work.

OZ-Behind the Curtain
Acrylic
72 x 72 in.

deborah@dhvartworks
.com
dhvartworks.com
@dhv_artworks

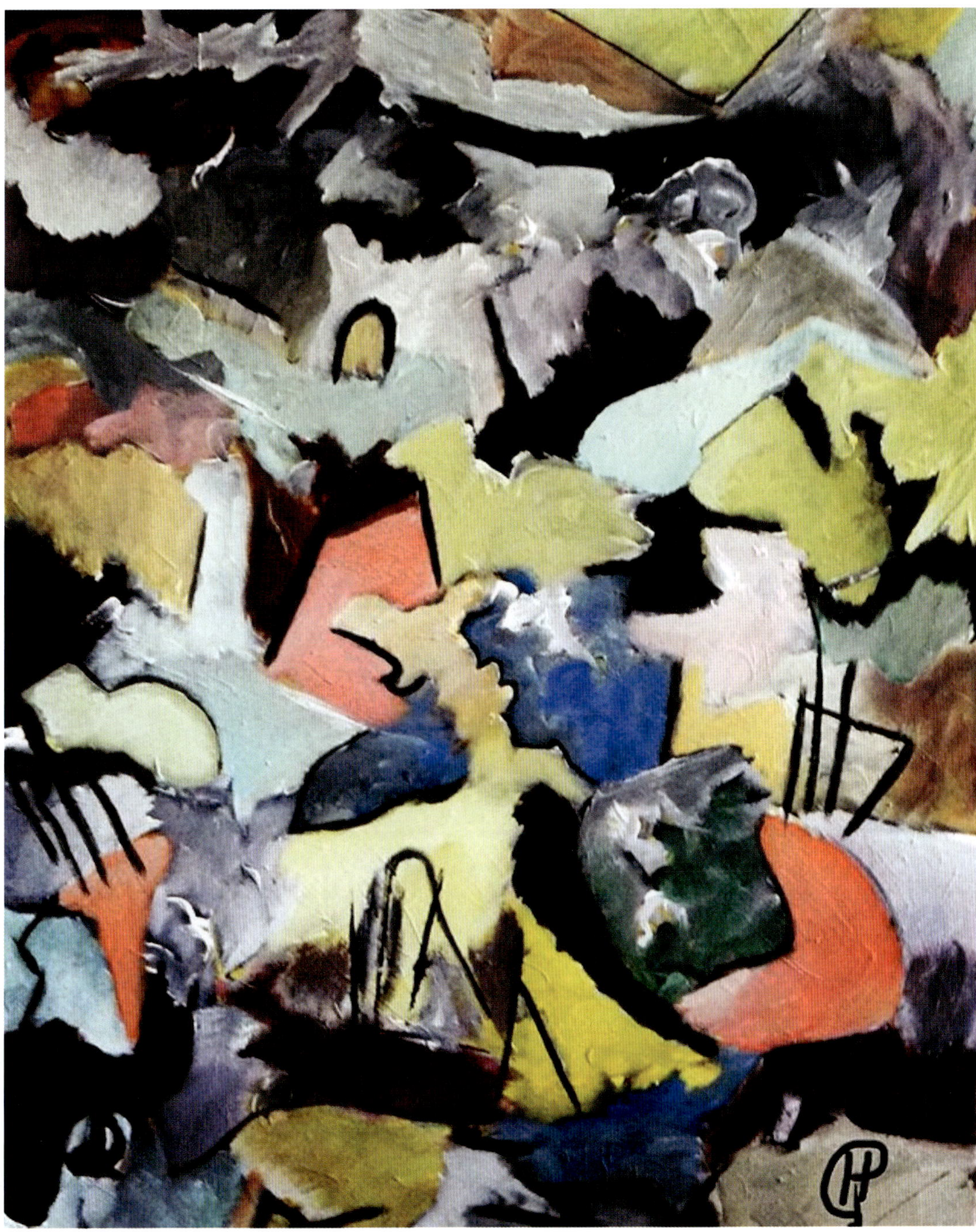

Richard Heiens

Through his artwork, Richard Heiens tries to bring color to life. No two paintings are the same and each work often consists of different styles and themes. Heiens' work is spontaneous, with shapes and objects brought out in the painting through different colors. Most of the paintings are abstract but they all have one thing in common: the use of color to make them interesting. "My interests and thoughts give life to shapes, color, and arrangement. Every finished work is meant to inspire the viewer to feel and see what they want, even if it is not what was intended to be there. It's what makes one feel good that counts," Heiens says.

Composition #10
Acrylic
24 x 18 in.

docheiens@gmail.com
dochartist.com
@dochartist

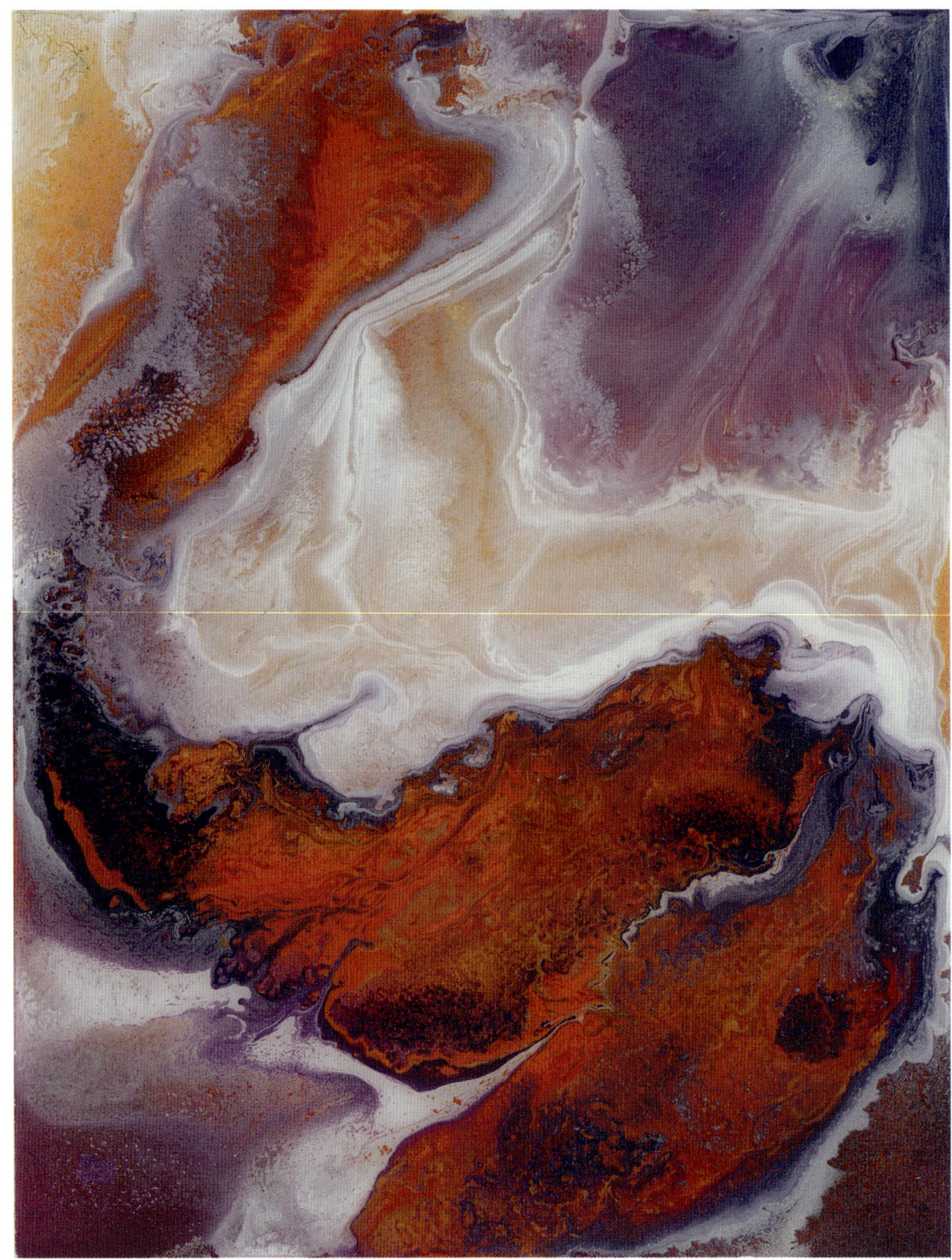

Tonda Howard

For as long as Tonda Howard can remember, creativity has been central in her life. Many of her childhood memories are of some kind of artistic endeavor, some of which got her in big trouble! Howard's parents put her in art classes, and she continued studying art through college.

As the years have gone by, Howard's methods and techniques have evolved from the traditional, classic ways of creating to the novel and experimental. The freedom of abstract expressionism provides a canvas for her creativity to grow and thrive.

"I love to explore and discover new media," Howard says. "I work intuitively from a very quiet and meditative state of mind. I try to capture fleeting beauty, freezing it in time. This process is unpredictable and uncontrollable, and I find the experience to be exhilarating. Creating art calms my mind, heals my spirit, and fills my heart, and I hope my work brings joy to others."

Celestial
Mixed media
36 x 24 in.

tondahoward59@gmail.com
tondahowardart.com
@tonda_howard_art

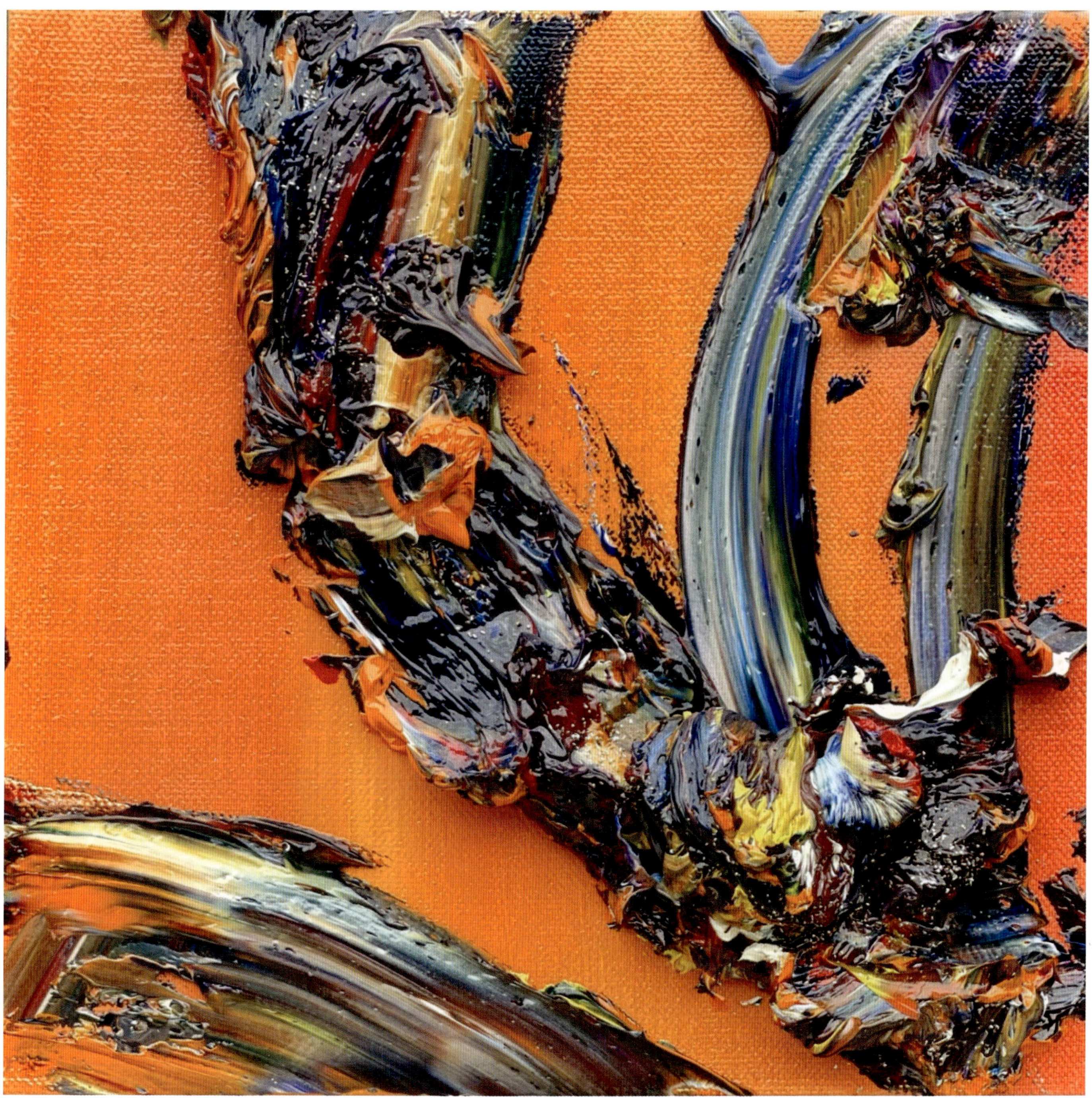

Kelly Steller Hrad

Kelly Steller Hrad is a contemporary abstract painter who expresses her thoughts on canvas through multiple mediums, from acrylic to three-dimensional oil and beyond. Her artwork is an expression of life through color and line and captivates the eye with rich, vivid layers. Her distinctive style exudes joy and peace and expresses a vibrant spirit that emanates off the canvas.

For Hrad, art is a lifelong journey. She has always loved color, and creating, imagining, and exploring the arts. Growing up, there were countless road trips that offered the time to appreciate the art of nature, architecture, museums, and galleries. As the miles rolled by, from sunrise to sunset, Hrad took in the mountains, valleys, canyons, and prairies, stashing these stunning visuals away in her memory. Decades later, she now draws on those memories to inspire her work.

Delicious
Three-Dimensional oil
8 x 8 in.

kelly@kellystellerhrad
.com
kellystellerhrad.com
@kellystellerhrad

Tina Hunt

Tina Hunt's work is a collection of atmospheric abstracts that are organic and earthy with an element of wear. Her inspiration often comes from the neutrality of nature and the weathered patina that the seasons bring forth. She tries to create a sense of age and evoke calm and reflection, often with an element of strong control.

"My process involves light gel textures with many layers of acrylic rubbed back and often finished with soft washes of white, charcoal, and pastel to create an ethereal and gentle effect," Hunt says. "My transitional textures and colors come together to produce work that is timeless and introspective, with a natural presence that is implied and yet void within the images that emerge from the surface."

Hunt's work seeks to evoke moods ranging from tranquility and solace to turbulence and chaos. Her work is reflective, often inducing a feeling of a distant memory or lost experience.

*Sometimes We Find
Somebody*
Mixed media
48 x 30 in.

tinahunt1@outlook.com
tinahuntart.com
@artbytinahunt

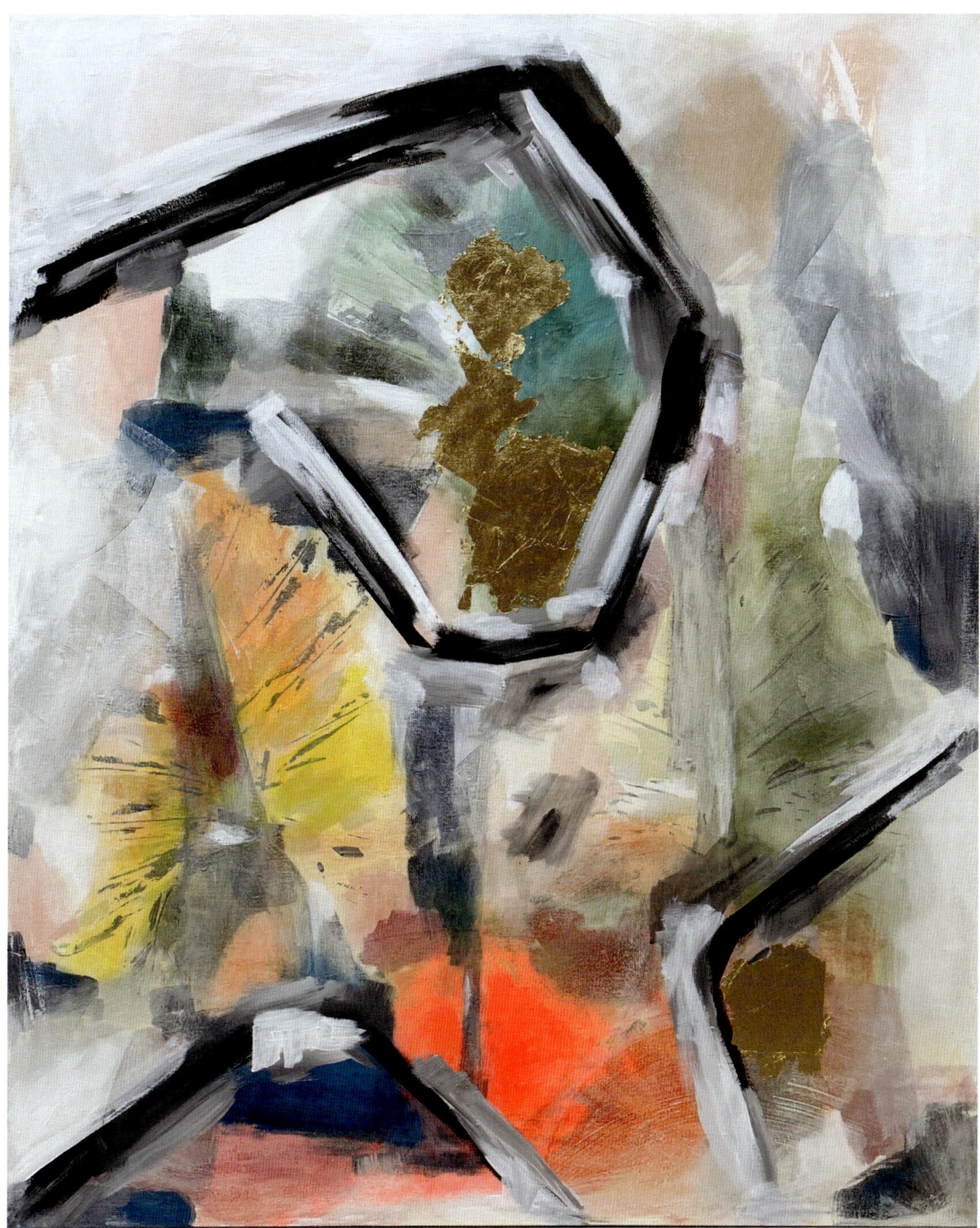

Odilia Iaccarino

Odilia Iaccarino's work involves mixed media in an abstract and contemporary style with a raw modern movement. She merges the style and technique in her artwork with raw brushstrokes and abstraction into one subject. Organic objects, like ground stone, diamond dust, and gold leaf, are just some mediums that she layers spontaneously to create a harmonious scenery on the canvas.

The process of these works involves three phases. In the first phase, she paints soft neutral colors. In the second phase, she uses bold, vibrant patterns to create secondary effects, and in the final phase, the artist begins an overlaying process to explore combinations in contrasting depth.

"My abstract works reflect a stylized approach that features bold formations and organic compositions to reveal serenity in a dramatic setting," Iaccarino says. "I find profound inspiration in everyday scenarios and design trends of our changing world."

Vislumbre
Acrylic
60 x 48 in.

odiliai@yahoo.com
odiliaiaccarinoart.com
@odiliaiaccarinoart

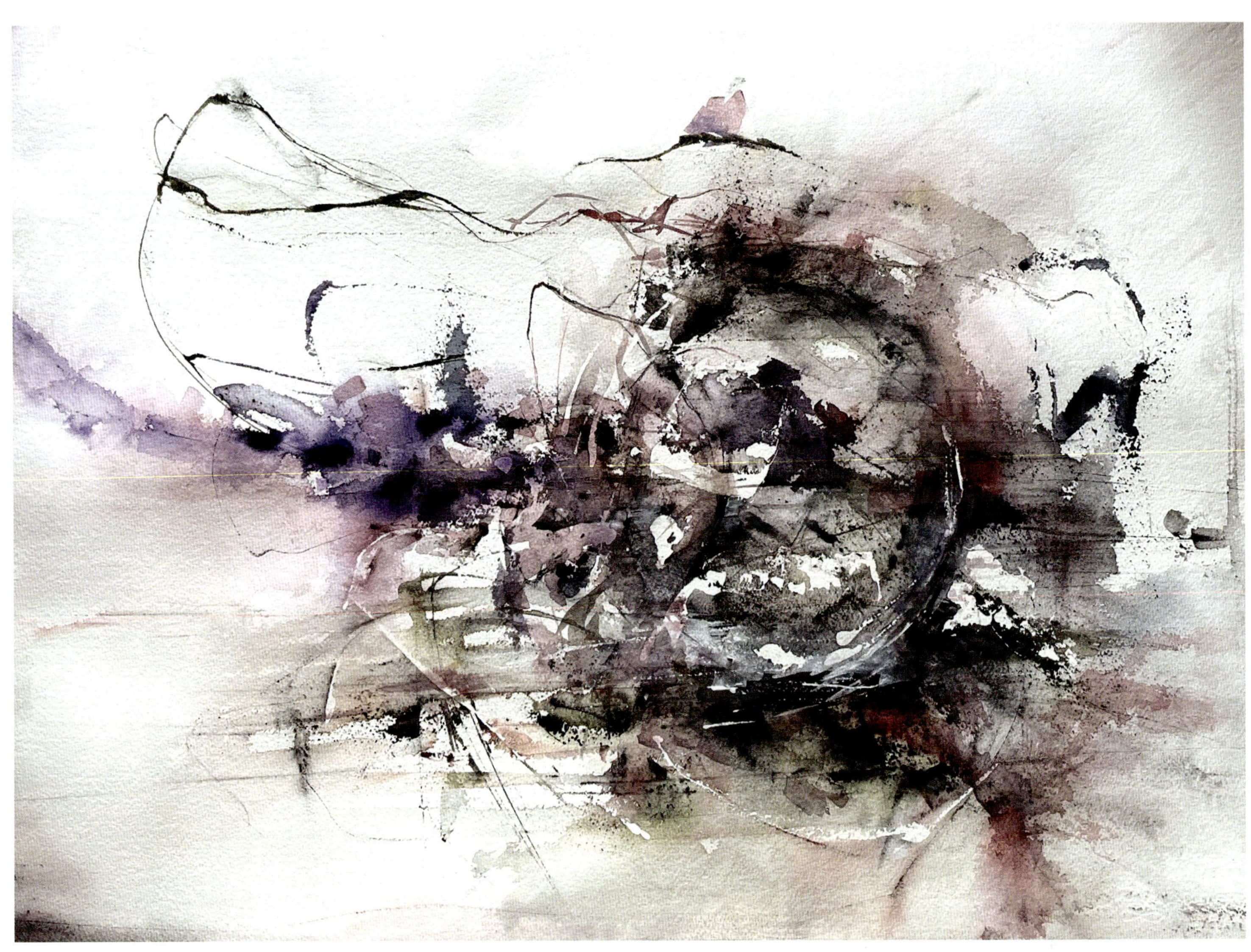

Dana Ingesson

"I see my art as my story, with colors and shapes being words," Dana Ingesson says.

Ingesson's paintings are an expression of her feelings, life experiences, and emotional maturation. Working primarily in watercolor, Ingesson creates dreamy compositions that blend the figurative and the abstracted. Her choice of color palette and gestural brushstrokes begin a conversation with her audience, drawing from her intellect, emotion, and intuition, Ingesson wants to inspire the viewer to acknowledge and engage with their own beliefs, emotions, and subconscious.

Ingesson's painting *Lines of Life* is like a little seed that will grow with the viewer's eyes, inviting the creation of their own emotions. The artist wants the viewer to be able to rest in her paintings and live in a world where the boundaries between the abstract and the imaginary have been blurred. She strives to create a meditative and cathartic experience for the viewer through her expressive, creatively filled abstract works.

Lines of Life
Watercolor
22 x 30 in.

dana-ingesson@hotmail.com
danaingesson.se
@dana_ingesson

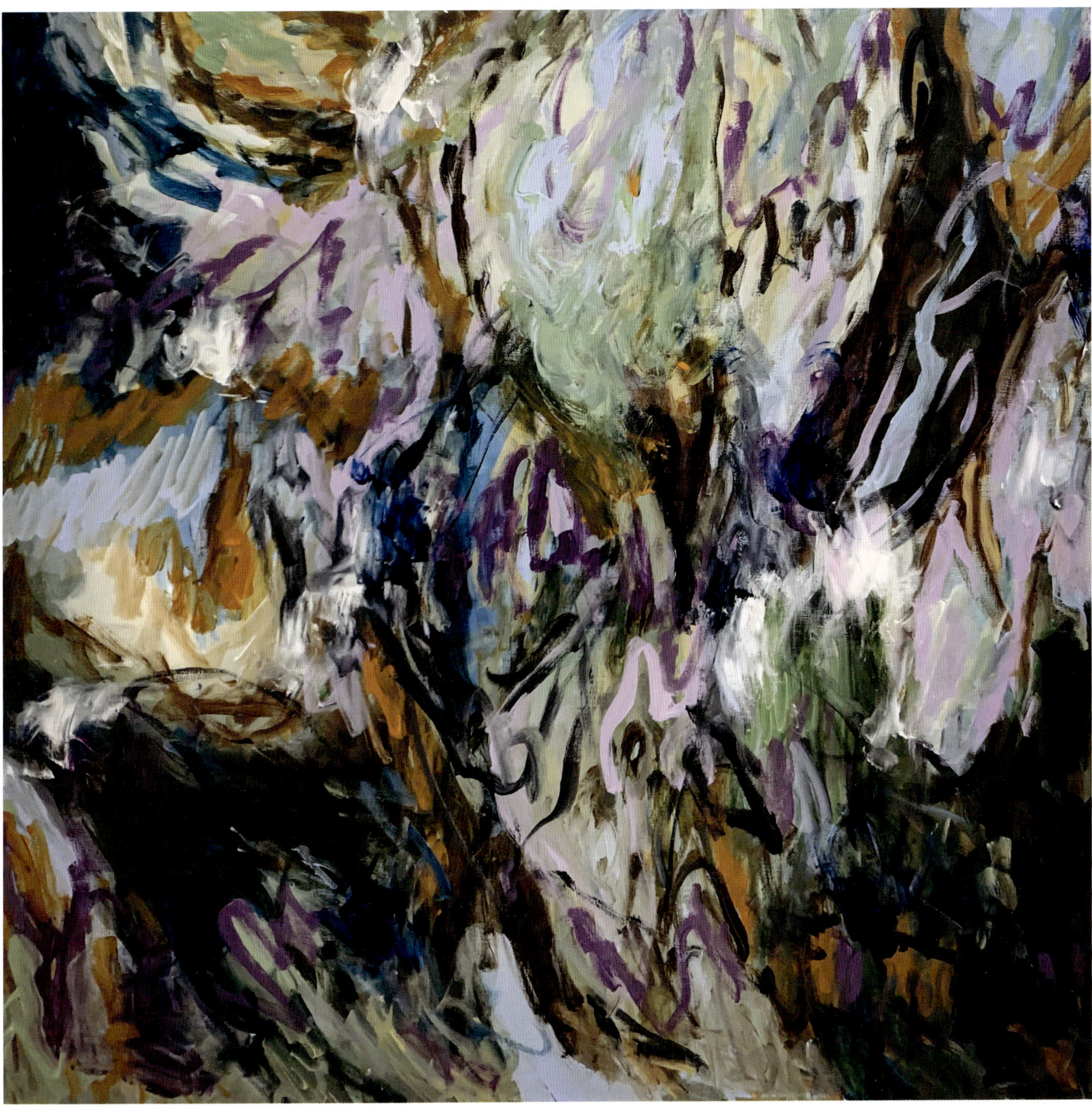

Jiwon Jang

Jiwon Jang has lived in Seoul, Korea, all of her life. She sometimes escapes from the city to be emotionally and spiritually replenished by nature. She loves taking pictures and has been working as a photographer for fifteen years.

Due to the outbreak of COVID-19, everyone had to stay at home, so Jang took this opportunity to begin painting.

Jang's inspiration is different every day. South Korea is a country where the four seasons are very distinct. The change of colors with each season of the year produced in her a flurry of emotions. She does not paint the flower as it is. Jang has never observed blooms with real care. The artist does not question herself when she produces. She just thinks the flower is pretty. That is why the flower she remembers while painting is not the form but the emotion she feels.

No.575 "Untitled"
Acrylic on linen
31.5 31.5 in.

jam0115w@naver.com
@jiwonjangart

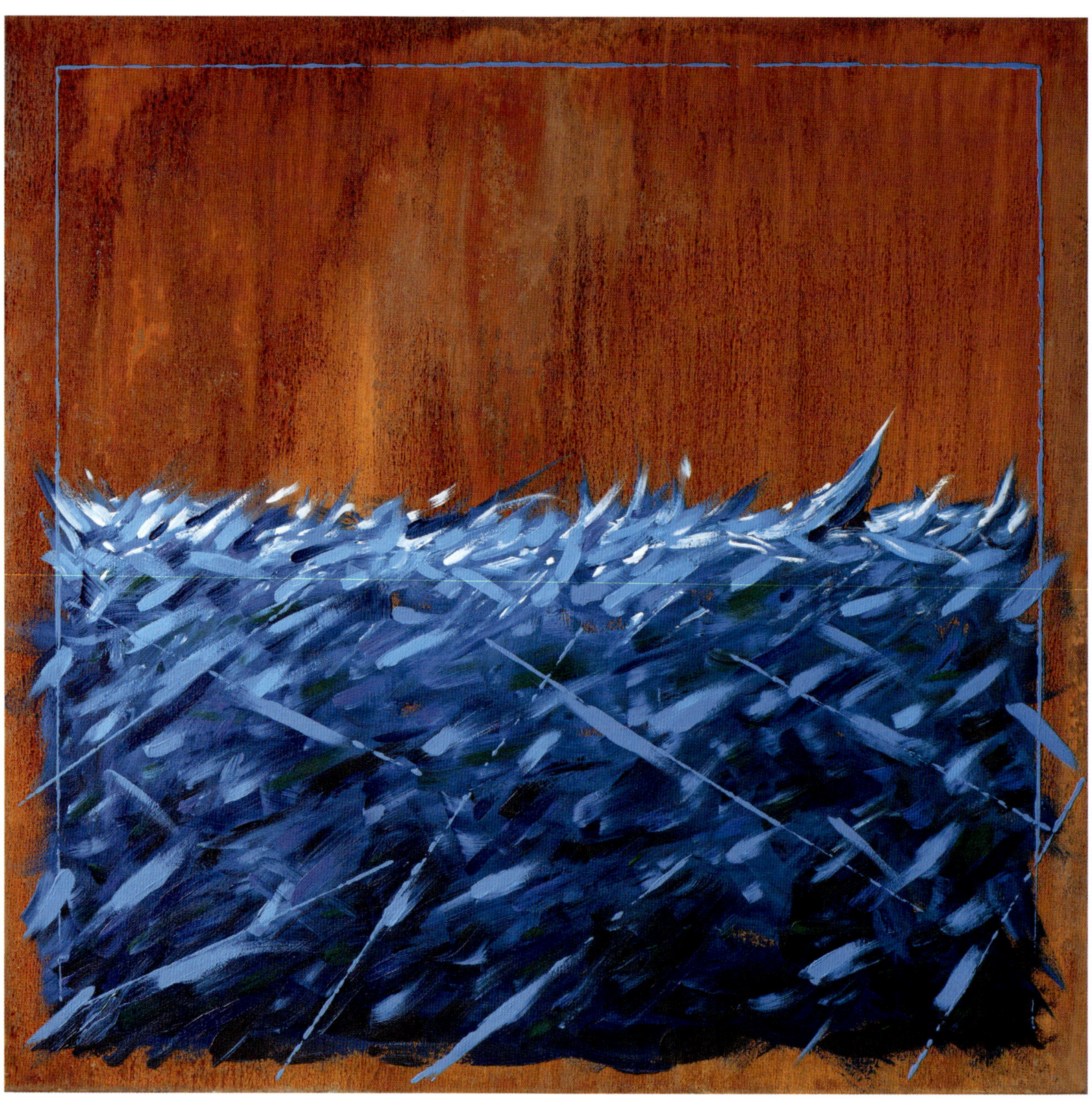

Ulfert Janssen

Ulfert Janssen first discovered the beauty of rust when he experimented with acrylic painting on weathering steel as a canvas. Since then, he has become fascinated by the elusive possibility of rust as an art medium, and he developed his special techniques to make his own rusted plates to create one-of-a-kind backgrounds for his paintings. Rust is a special medium and requires a lengthy preparatory process that takes several months before the panels are ready to be painted on. Rust is like wine and needs a ripening process until it has a certain depth, texture, and color. Janssen uses special oxidation techniques to apply different colors and patterns to the panels. The rust plates with texture and color are carefully selected and prepared for the corresponding painting over a longer period of time. The oxidized plates not only work as a canvas or background but become part of the painting. Janssen combines two very different worlds, capturing in high-contrast paintings with intense and lively acrylic colors on rusted metal plates.

Rough Sea 01
Acrylic on oxidized metal
39 x 39 in.

ulfertjanssen@gmail.com
ulfertjanssen.com
@ulfert.janssen

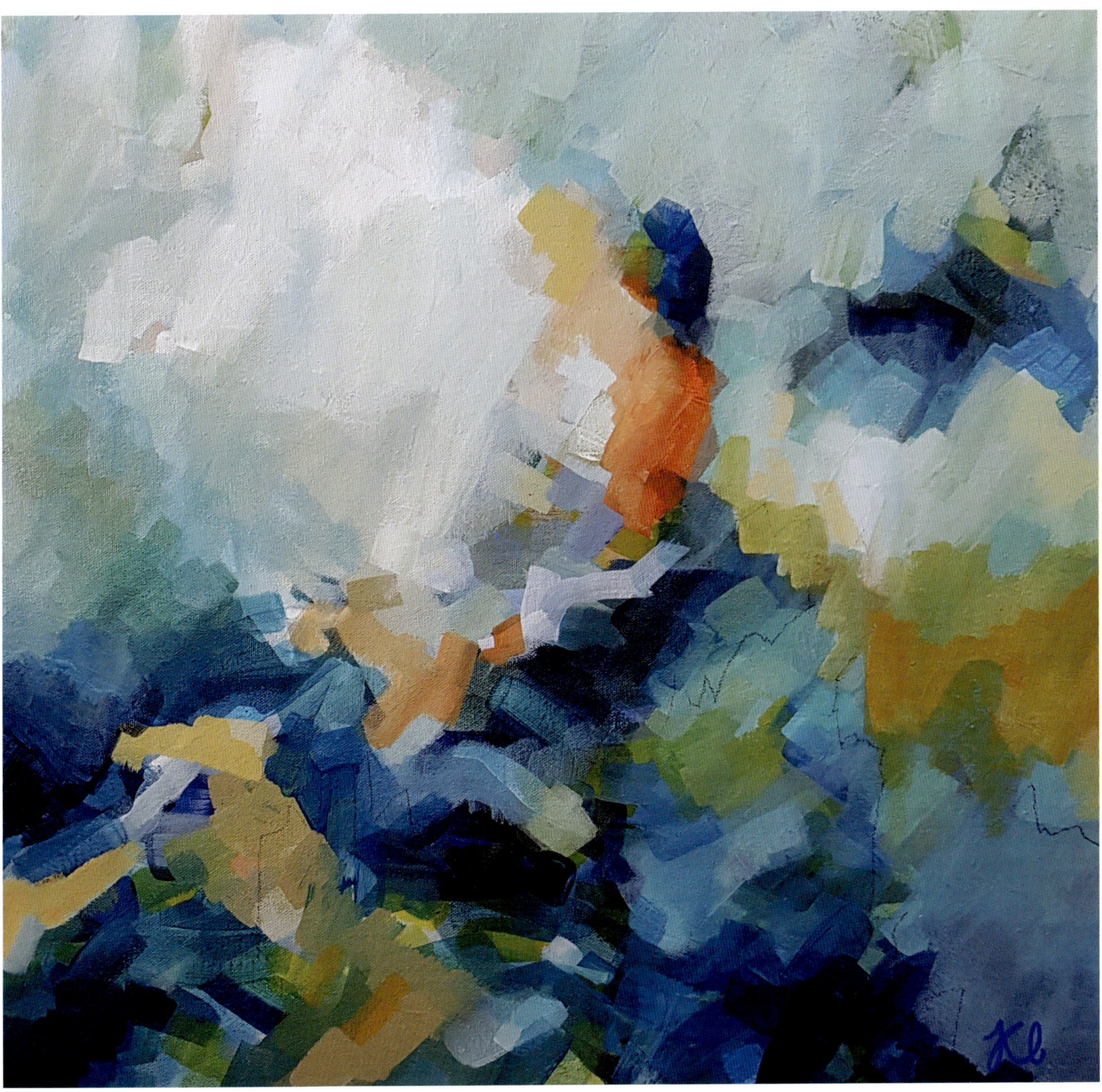

Jennifer Keeney-Bleeg

Jennifer Keeney-Bleeg has always had a visceral response to color. Her first and most vivid memories stand out in her mind largely because of the colors within them. This year, as so many parts of the world have faced hurricanes, floods, and wildfires of increasing severity, the artist has found herself thinking a lot about the environment and our relationship to it and then processing those thoughts through a lens of color.

"I kept returning to the idea of conflict and contrast. For so much of my life, I considered the environment a place of calm, solace, and renewal. While I still see it this way, there are now many more tumultuous threads woven through it," Keeney-Bleeg says. She has tried to capture this push and pull in her paintings, using layers of translucent, complementary color to convey the evolving drama and complexity of the environment and our place within it.

Uncharted
Acrylic
20 x 20 in.

jennifer@jkbleeg.com
www.jkbleeg.com
@jkbleeg

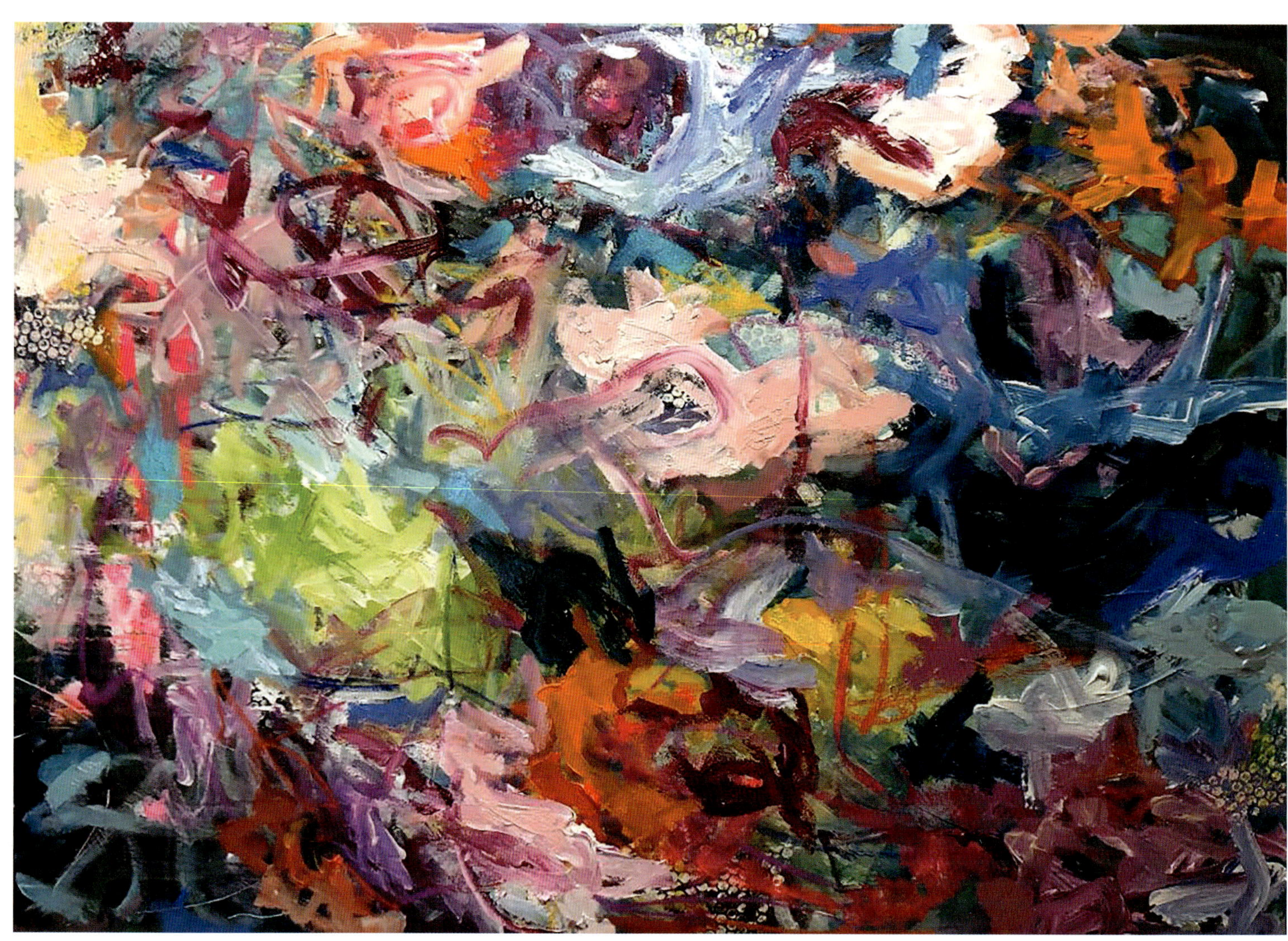

Isabelle Lopez Kotara

Isabelle Lopez Kotara has painted for her personal pleasure all her adult life. It has always been a form of expression and a way to capture her thoughts and perceptions of the world around her. In the last three years, she has begun seriously pursuing a career in art.

Kotara's current pieces isolate movements of nature, time, and our own vulnerabilities. She intentionally tries not to reference a recognizable form but more the concept to allow for many different interpretations.

By applying abstraction to the subject, Kotara can create an intensely personal moment, luring the viewer into personal interpretations of her work. These moments are revisualized through the abstraction, forged into new imagery where interpretation becomes multifaceted for the viewer. In this way, Kotara allows the viewer to submerge themselves into a new relationship between color, light, nature, and emotion.

C'est La Vie
Acrylic and pastels
36 x 48 in.

imlopez458@yahoo.com
isabellelopezkotaraart
.com
@isabellelopezkotara_
art

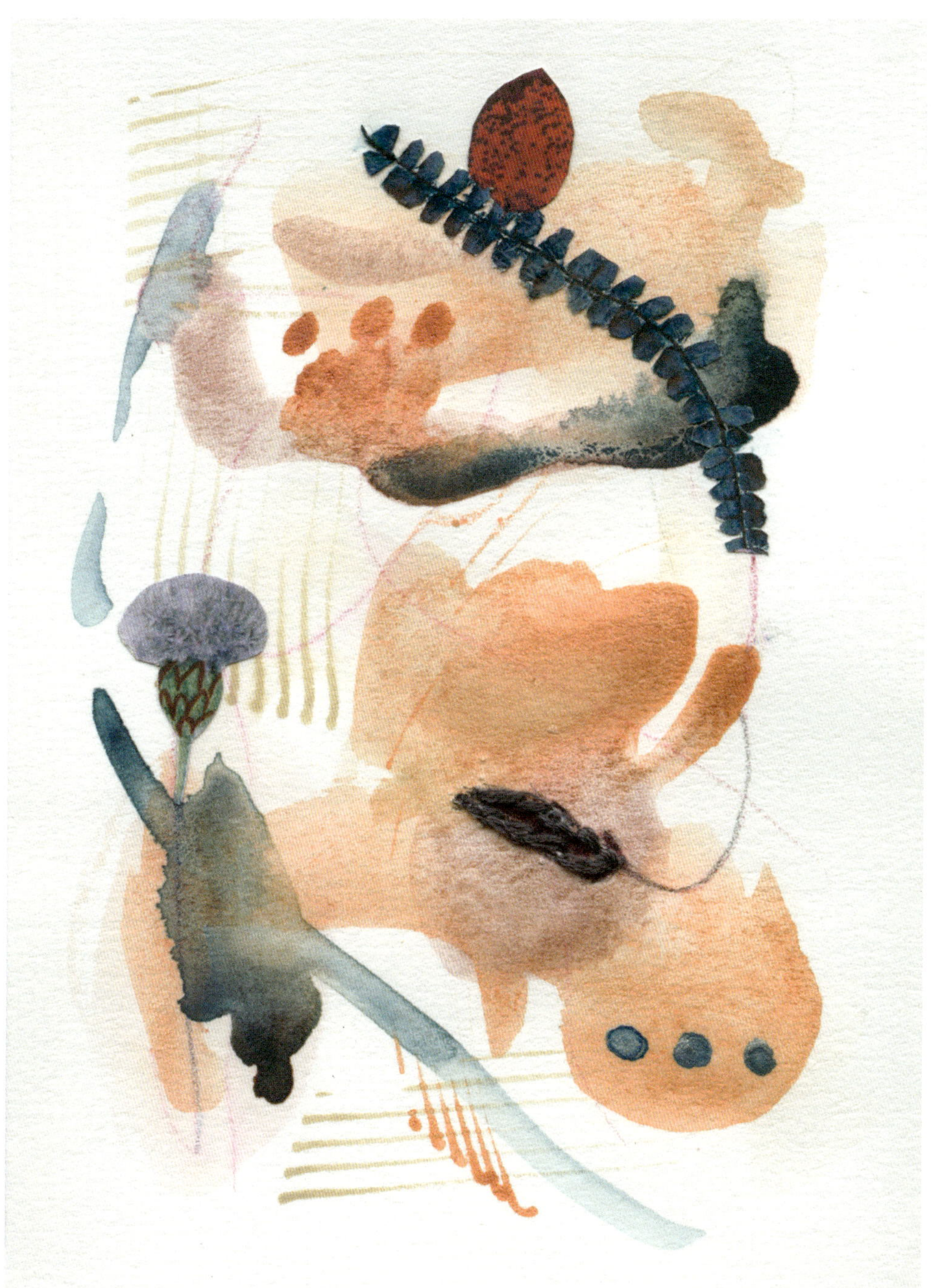

Andrea Lamarsaude

Andrea Lamarsaude is a mixed-media artist who enjoys using a variety of mediums in her art including acrylics, oil pastels, watercolor, alcohol and India inks, hand-painted papers, collage elements, image transfers, and mark-making tools.

"I love combining and contrasting fluid, free-flowing layers of watercolor with hand-painted papers or collage elements to create intuitive and expressive nature-inspired works. My imagination, emotion, and life experience guide me in my process to paint memorable creations that reflect joy," Lamarsaude says. "I strive to emulate the beauty, splendor, and exquisiteness of our world and the sense of happiness it can bring us."

Lamarsaude's desire is to visually tell stories with her art and create paintings that reflect the moments that touch her life. She hopes that her work encourages conversations and brings positive, creative energy into the world.

"Trusting my intuition and following my heart has always been the best way to create not only my art but also my life," the artist says.

Flora I
Mixed media
7 x 5 in.

alamarsaude@gmail
.com
andrealamarsaude.com
@andrealamarsaude

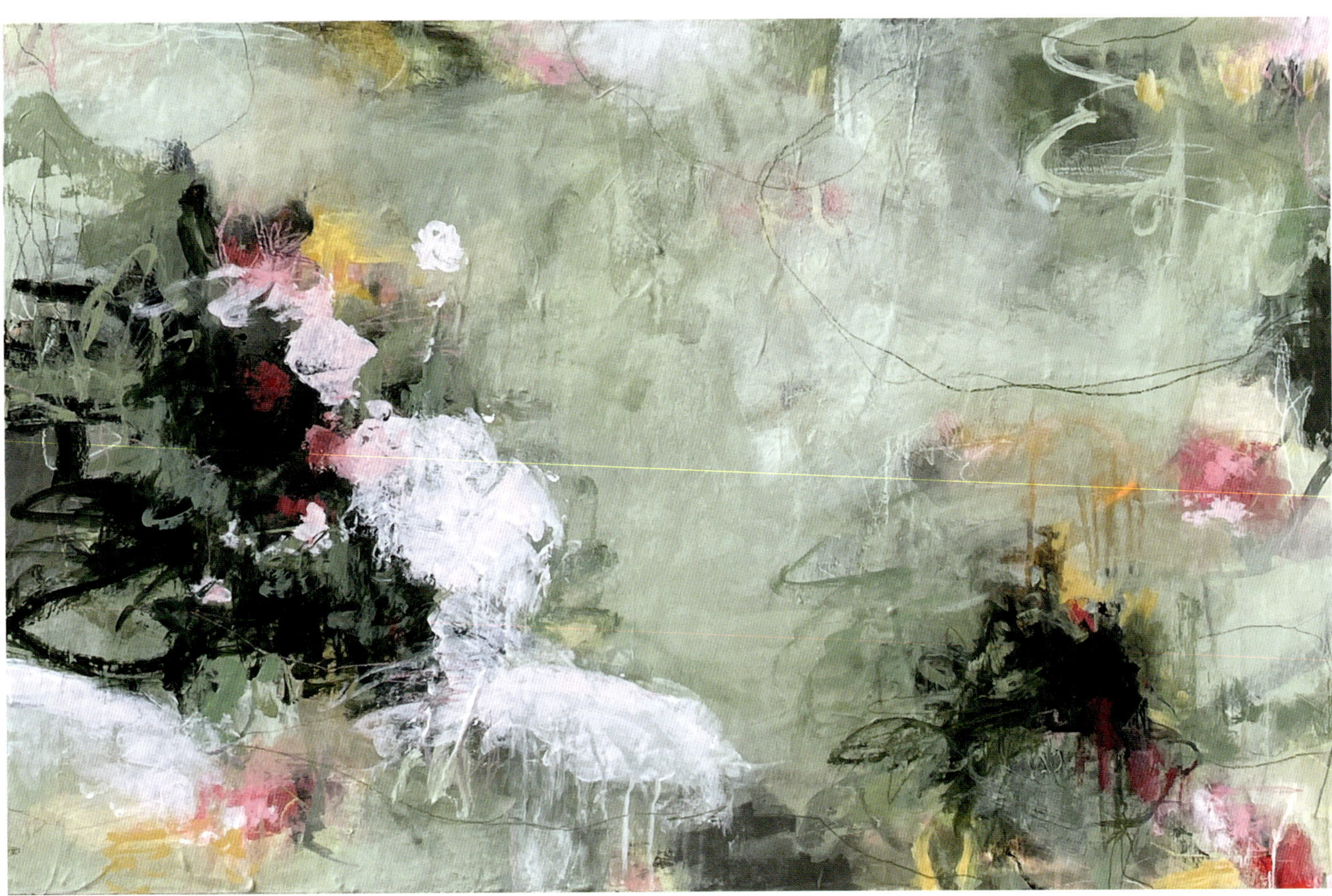

Patricia Langevin

Patricia Langevin creates colorful abstract paintings that seek to reconnect with a sense of play and embrace the unexpected. Her acrylic paintings are expressionist in style and characterized by bold and dynamic brushstrokes along with mark-making that create pathways for the eyes and mind to wander.

To convey emotions and a sense of play, Langevin begins each painting with spontaneous drawings, using graphite or wax crayon without a preconceived plan. She continues by adding translucent layers and scraping through the paint to reveal layers underneath, then adding marks with various tools. As the layers build and a composition starts to emerge, her brushstrokes become more intentional until the painting has achieved a balance between spontaneity and control.

Through her artwork, Langevin hopes to infuse a sense of wonder and bring a joyful experience to the viewer.

Sounds of Spring
Acrylic, graphite, pastel and pencil on wood panel
24 x 36 in.

langevin.patricia@gmail.com
patricialangevin.com
@patricialangevinart

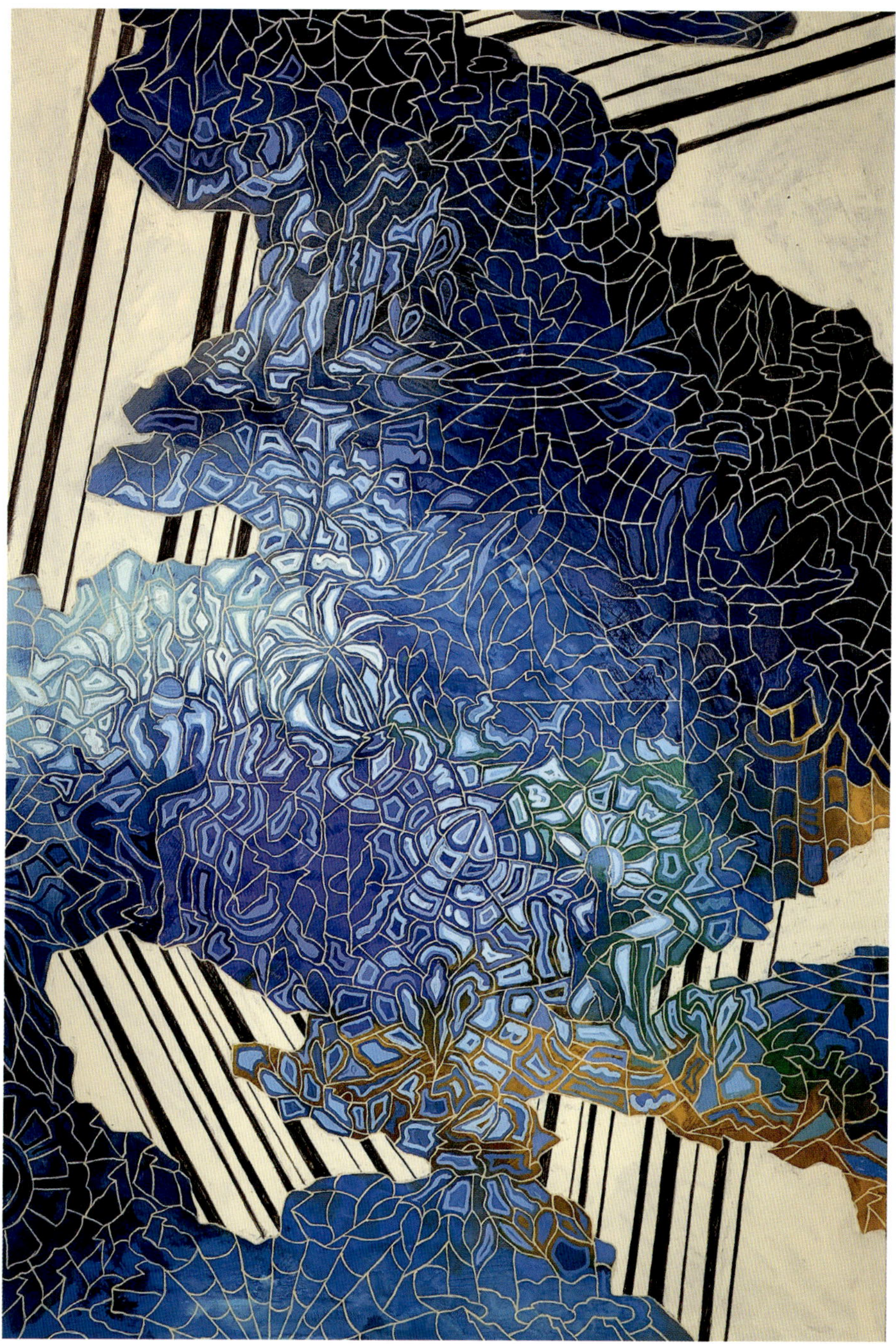

Peggy Lee

Peggy Lee believes that human connection is about being of a selfless nature. "Over the years, technological advances have surpassed our expectations and have left both a positive and negative imprint on our lives. In the past, communication was necessary and vital. Today, slowly our ability to look at the world and issues in our relationships seem adversely affected," Lee says.

So, indirectly, her paintings reflect the need for more unity, togetherness, and equilibrium. Returning to a certain level of personable relationships and having an understanding of what tradition truly means is the primary message of her art. Another concept found in her work is for humans to reach out and use our naturally given senses to make a difference in humanity.

"My works can be seen as a huge cobweb in its entirety, which ironically mirrors how technology works. It represents our obsession with networking and the need to return to morality, respect, and a love for humanity."

Ordinary Days III
Acrylic on canvas
36 x 24 in.

peggy3art8@gmail.com
peggyhlart.com
@haeggy5

PAINTING: TRADITIONAL/ABSTRACT

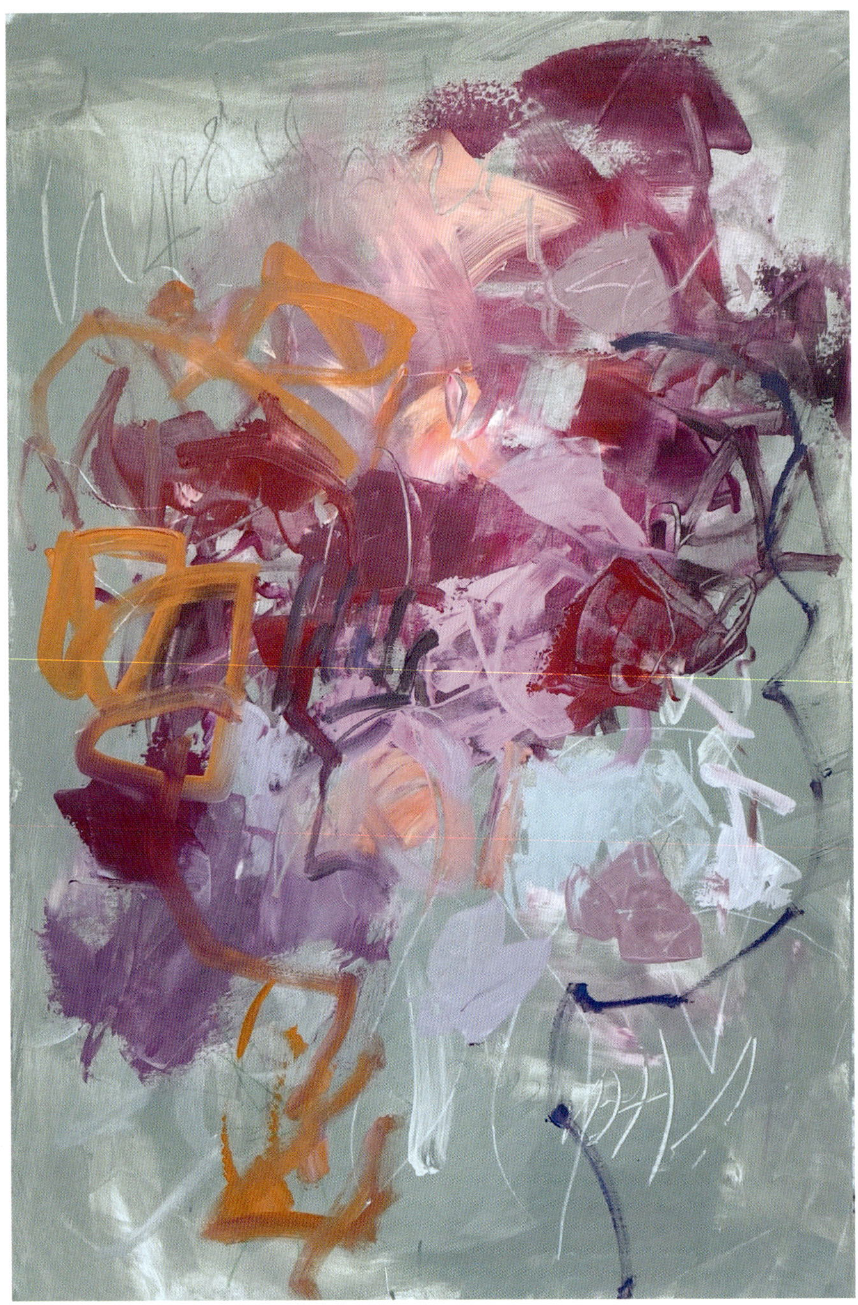

Michelle Marra

American abstract painter Michelle Marra describes herself as a "spirited colorist," a perfect expression of the high level of emotion, energy, and luminosity she imbues into her paintings. In some of her series, such as *Bold and Beautiful* and *Abstracted Blooms*, she layers her acrylic paint into thick impasto surfaces, which contrast beautifully with her lyrical, gestural brush marks, creating an interplay of seriousness and whimsy. The biomorphic forms and lush color relationships in these paintings are grounded in the natural world, evoking images of wildflower gardens and tangled jungle landscapes. Other series, such as *Crossroads*, suggest the artist's penchant for pure abstraction, demonstrating her instincts for capturing the interplay of light and shadow, and her clear love for painting.

Marra paints daily and feels that creating joy and happiness in her paintings is a blessing she is very lucky to share with others.

Intermingle
Acrylic on canvas
48 x 30 in.

michellemarra@
comcast.net
michellemarrastudio
.com
@michellemarrastudio

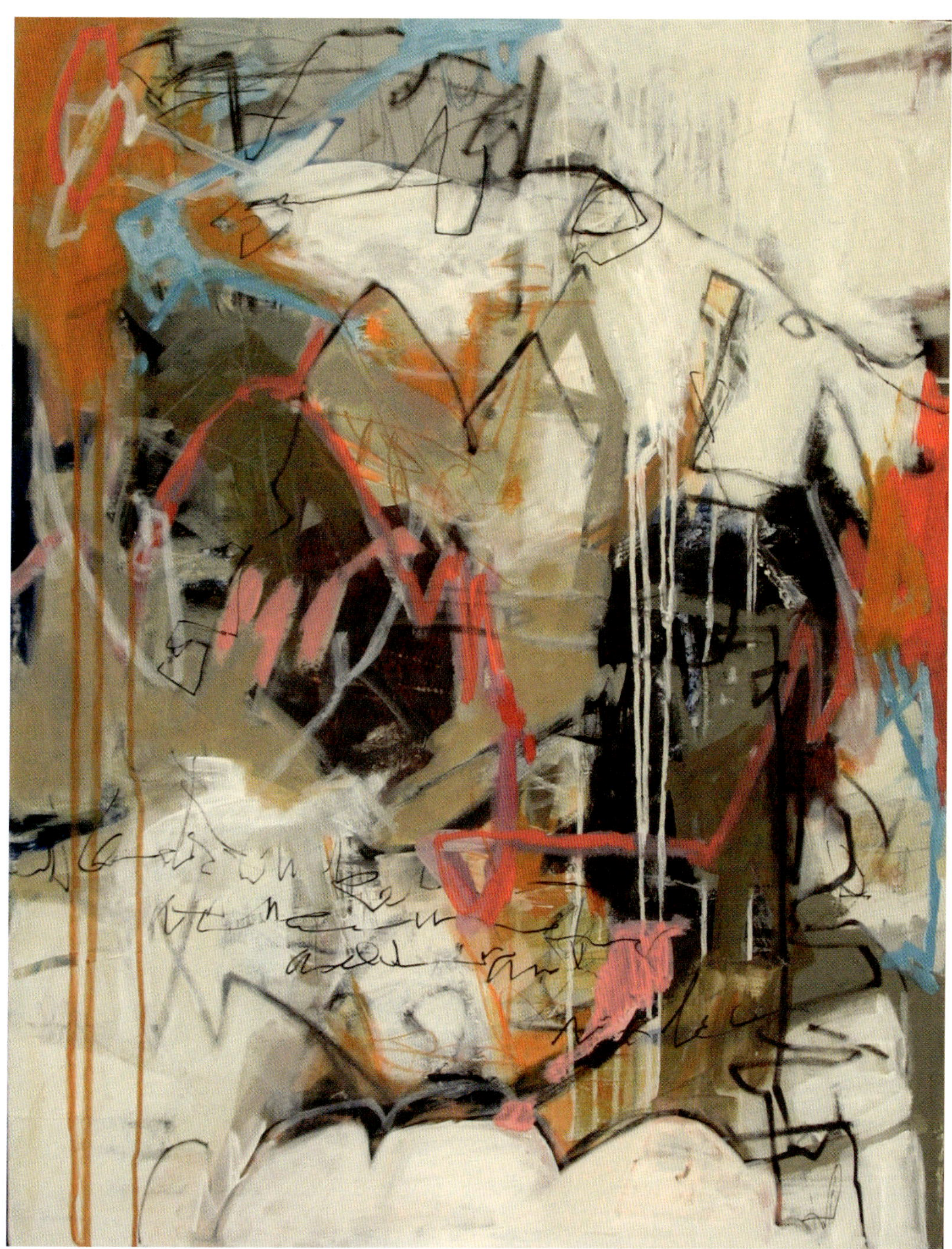

Jinnie May

With a spontaneous, intuitive painting as her objective, there is no preconceived concept or preplanning in Jinnie May's art, the composition evolves as she paints. She begins by creating an underpainting consisting of marks, lines, and shapes that creates the structure of the acrylic painting. May then adds layers upon layers of color, plus black-and-white paint, adding and subtracting, letting some of the underlayers peek through. Scratching into the wet paint with a variety of rubber scrapers and tools reveals previous layers and adds interest to the work. She next adds text or illegible words, marks, splatters, and drips to pull the composition together. To complete the painting, the elements of design are considered to create a pleasing yet stimulating painting.

Titles are an important part of May's process. *Are We There Yet? II*, painted in late 2020, is a worrisome question that anticipates the coming of a new year, begging for it to please be better than 2020.

Are We there Yet? II
Acrylic
40 x 30 in.

jinnielou@aol.com
jinniemay.com
@jinnie_may_art

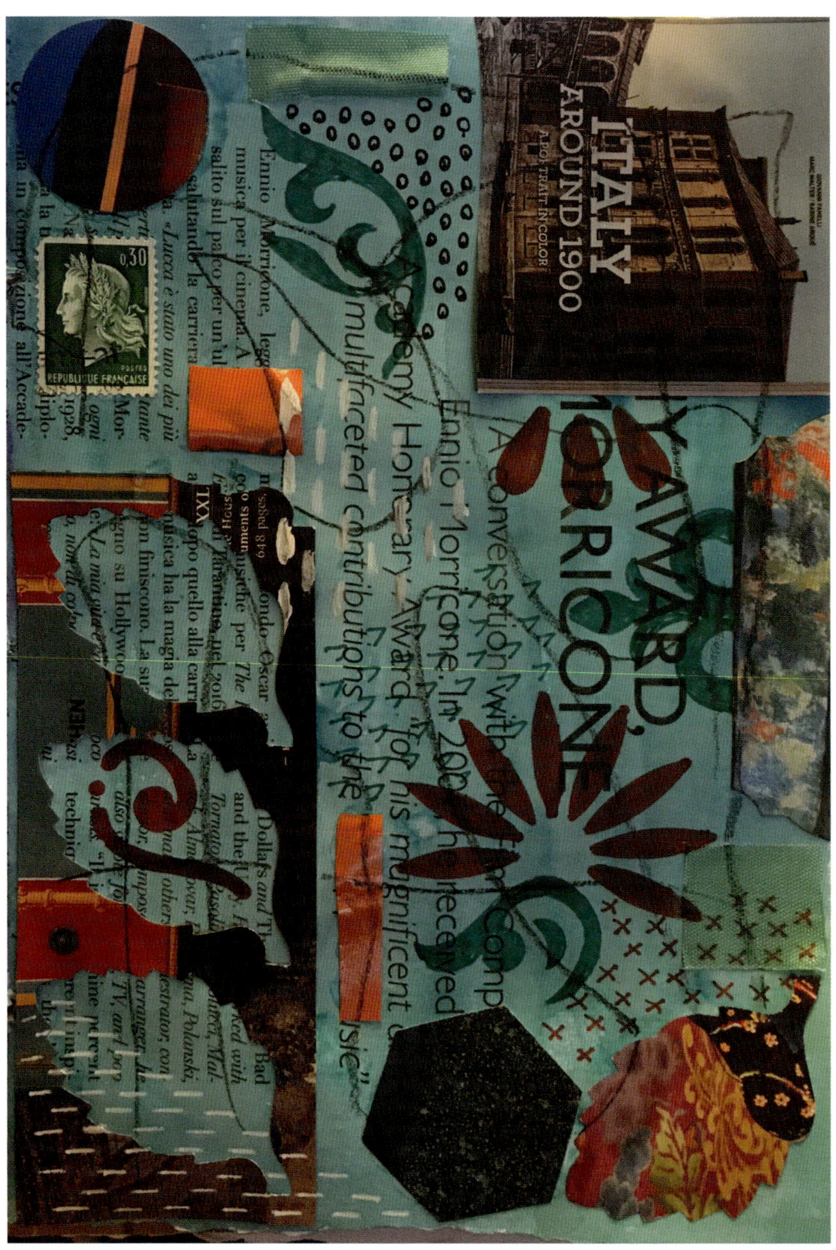

Beth McCoy

Beth McCoy has been influenced by many artists. This series combines components from her favorites. She employs the iconography of Jasper Johns and Claes Oldenburg. Her base elements evoke both Robert Rauschenberg and James Rosenquist because she loves their visual textures. The pigment technique reflects both the color exploration and streamlining of Andy Warhol, and the random precision of Helen Frankenthaler. The geometric elements borrow from Frank Stella and Larry Poons and explore their aspects of graphic representation. She uses mark-making like Willem de Kooning, Jackson Pollock and Jean Dubuffet, and the pigment disruption effects of Cy Twombly. The textural details reflect her interest in the work of Louise Bourgeois and Poons. The storytelling features hearken to the magic of Faith Ringgold and Marc Chagall. She exploits the spirit of graffiti to represent a tone of vague defiance, like Banksy, Mark Wallinger, Blek le Rat, Jean-Michel Basquiat, and Keith Haring, but with an overlap between street art and graffiti, where the message is more important than technique.

Vibrant
Mixed media
10 x 7 in.

lenabethe@gmail.com
lenabethe.com
@lenabethe

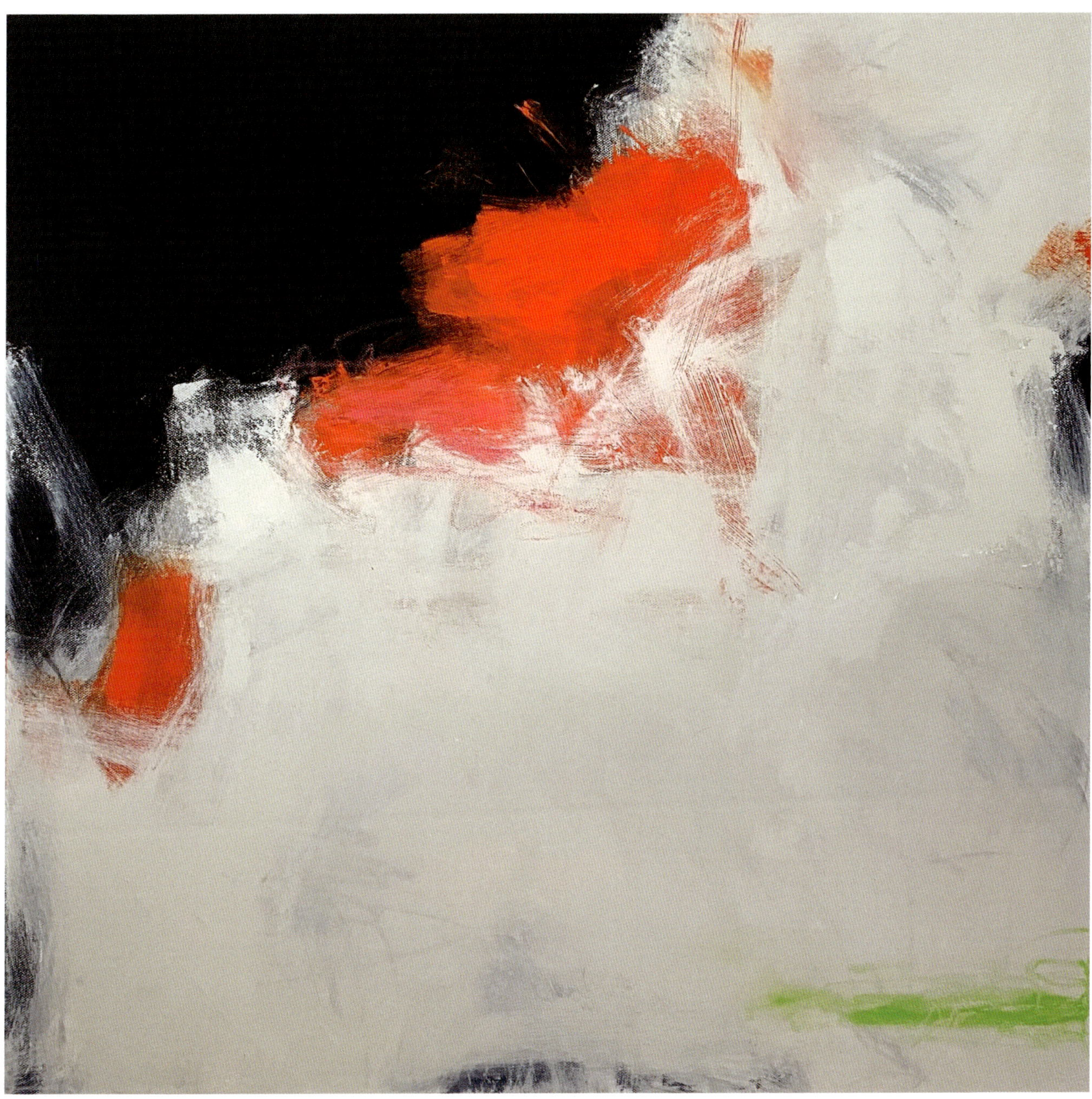

C.S. McIntire

C.S. McIntire is both thankful for and frustrated by his extremely vivid imagination. He has always been a visual person. "I like to look at things. I look at colors. I look at shapes. I look at how color and shape change in different light or while in motion," the artist says.

Nature always centers McIntire. A simple hike sparks creativity and inspires his palette. For him, creating is all about connection. The deeper he gets into creating, the deeper he drops into and connects with his own open and authentic space. Be it a pairing of intense colors, bold brushstrokes, or subtle mark-making, McIntire wants to convey the energy and emotion that he feels in that moment and to connect with the viewer. He draws inspiration from great artists such as Willem de Kooning, Jackson Pollock, Richard Diebenkorn, Gerhard Richter, and Vincent van Gogh, as well as from colors and forms found in nature.

Congruence
Acrylic, graphite, oil pastel on canvas
24 x 24 in.

craigmcintire@hotmail.com
csmcintire.com
@c.s.mcintire

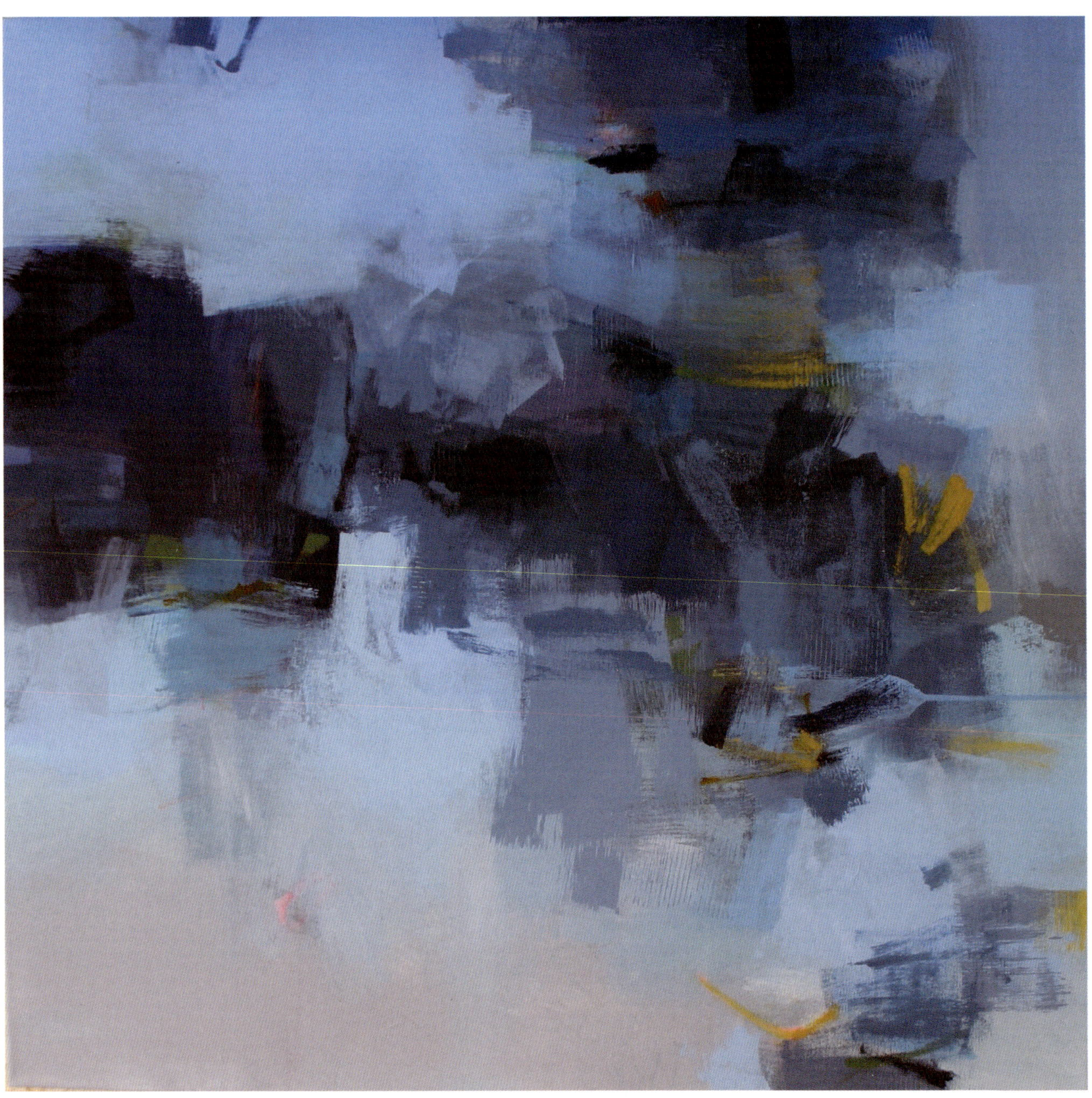

Valerie McMullen
Arizona artist Valerie McMullen's love of color translates to the canvas with her bold use of striking color palettes. Her mixed-media paintings are an exploration of imagination and wonder. As an intuitive painter, she combines random mark-making, lines, and texture to help guide the forms and shapes that develop. The visual story that emerges is often a relationship between geometric and organic shapes combined with patterns.

Utilizing various tools to create texture and apply the paint, McMullen's colors form relationships that dance across the canvas. This celebration of movement and color leads the viewer on a visual path of discovery. Engaging the viewer to take a closer look plays a vital role in her painting process. Each mark creates a history and contributes to telling the overall story. Her mission is to explore new ideas and have never-ending conversations with color.

Rhythm And Blues
Mixed media
30 x 30 in.

vmcmullen14@gmail.com
valeriemcmullen.com
@valeriemcmullenart

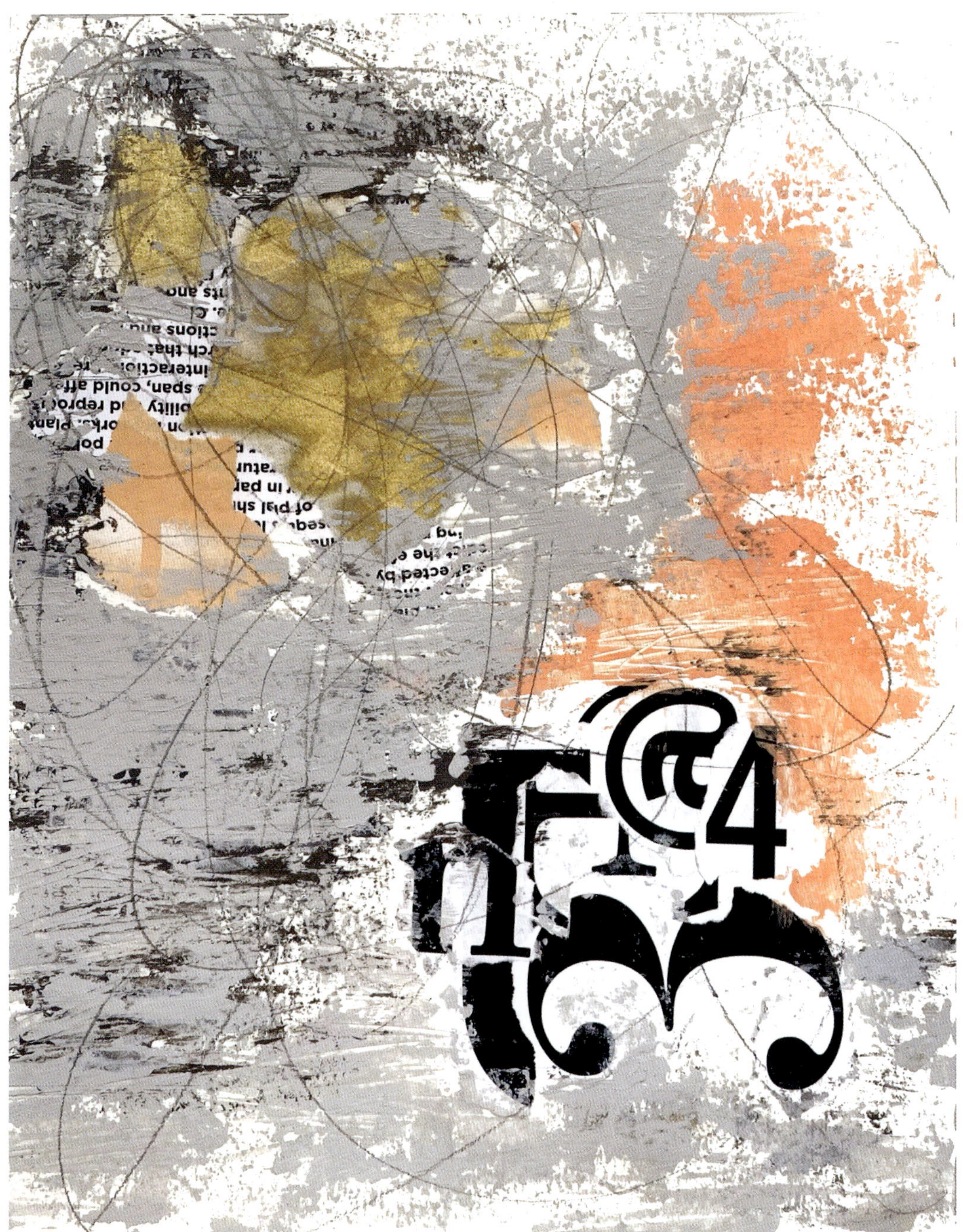

Fran McNamara

Fran McNamara's work draws inspiration from the idea that everything in nature is connected to everything else.

Using carefully chosen materials and mediums, the artist's compositions begin to encompass a journey through a multitude of layers that combine with unconventional methods, gradually revealing a history of spatial interpretations. McNamara explores space and form by mapping out the underlying paint layers, with collage and drawing leading to the intersection of abstraction and the natural world. While some of her process is predetermined, other aspects arrive organically through subtracting and adding, carving, and peeling away paper and paint to reveal earlier parts of the work.

McNamara's resulting multilayered, two-dimensional and repurposed three-dimensional works are metaphors for survival and hope. They serve as windows into natural landscapes and urban spaces, with pollution and consumerism hanging at the edges.

Three's A Crowd
Acrylic, collage, spray paint, graphite on paper
12 x 9 in.

frannymack1@gmail.com
franmcnamara.com
@franmcnamara

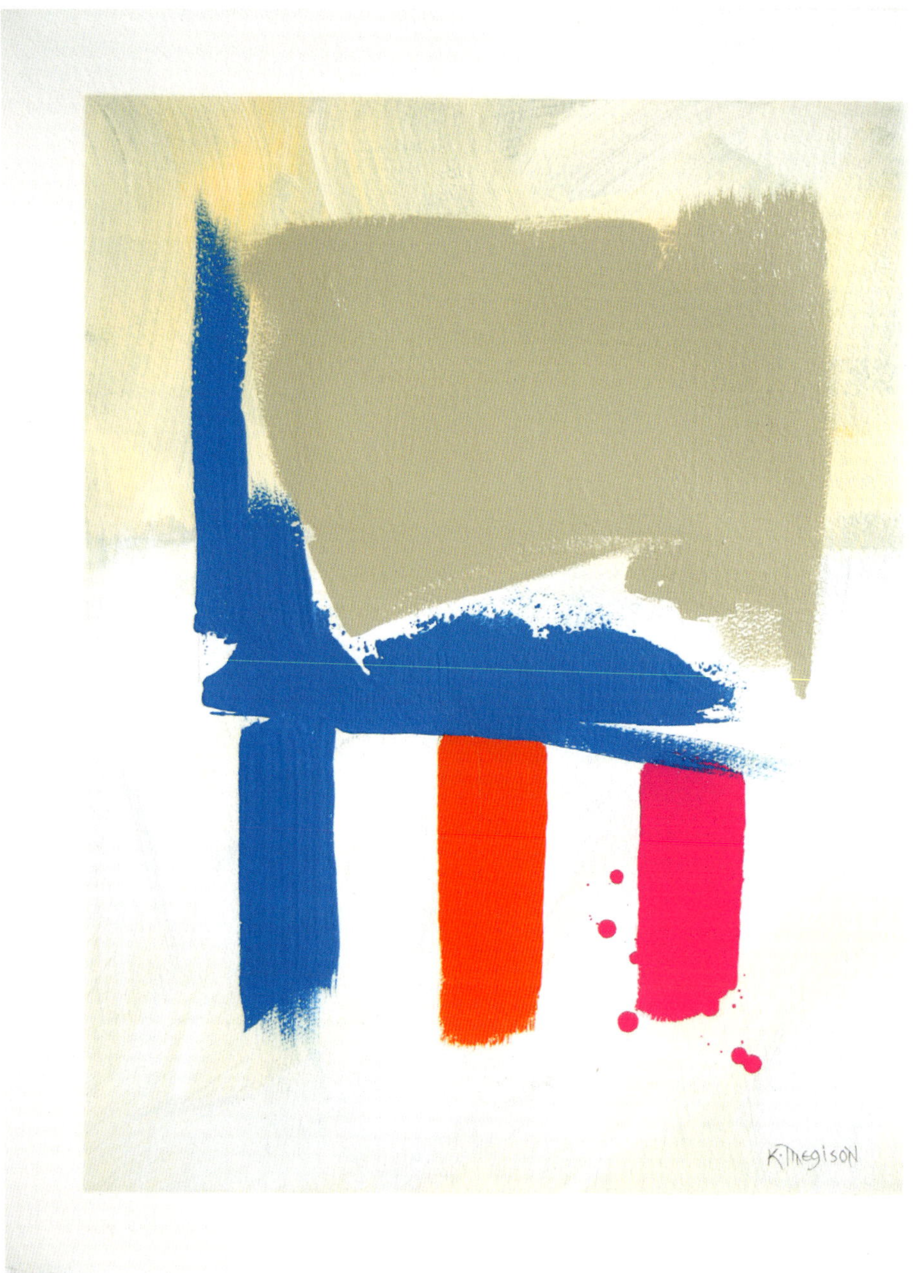

Kevin Megison

Kevin Megison's art is evolving and expanding. His goal of moving forward requires a path of exploration and discovery. He prefers working on large-format canvases, although lately, he has been exploring the effects of working with acrylic on paper.

Megison has a graphic design background, which in some instances intuitively influences his painting compositions. Geometric shapes and repeated patterns emerge as though to provide elements of infrastructure to his abstract creations. He prefers the use of unconventional tools to generate desired effects: wooden trowels, broad blade palette knives, the dovetail end of a wooden plank, as well as some tools he has crafted himself.

Megison's work is often bold, vibrant, textured, and engaging. His philosophy is to provide the viewer with an art experience that is unexpected and thought-provoking with an emphasis on color. The takeaway experience is hopefully one of art appreciation and enrichment.

Triad 01
Acrylic on paper
28 x 22 in.

kevinmegison@att.net
kevinmegisonart.com
@kevinmegisonart

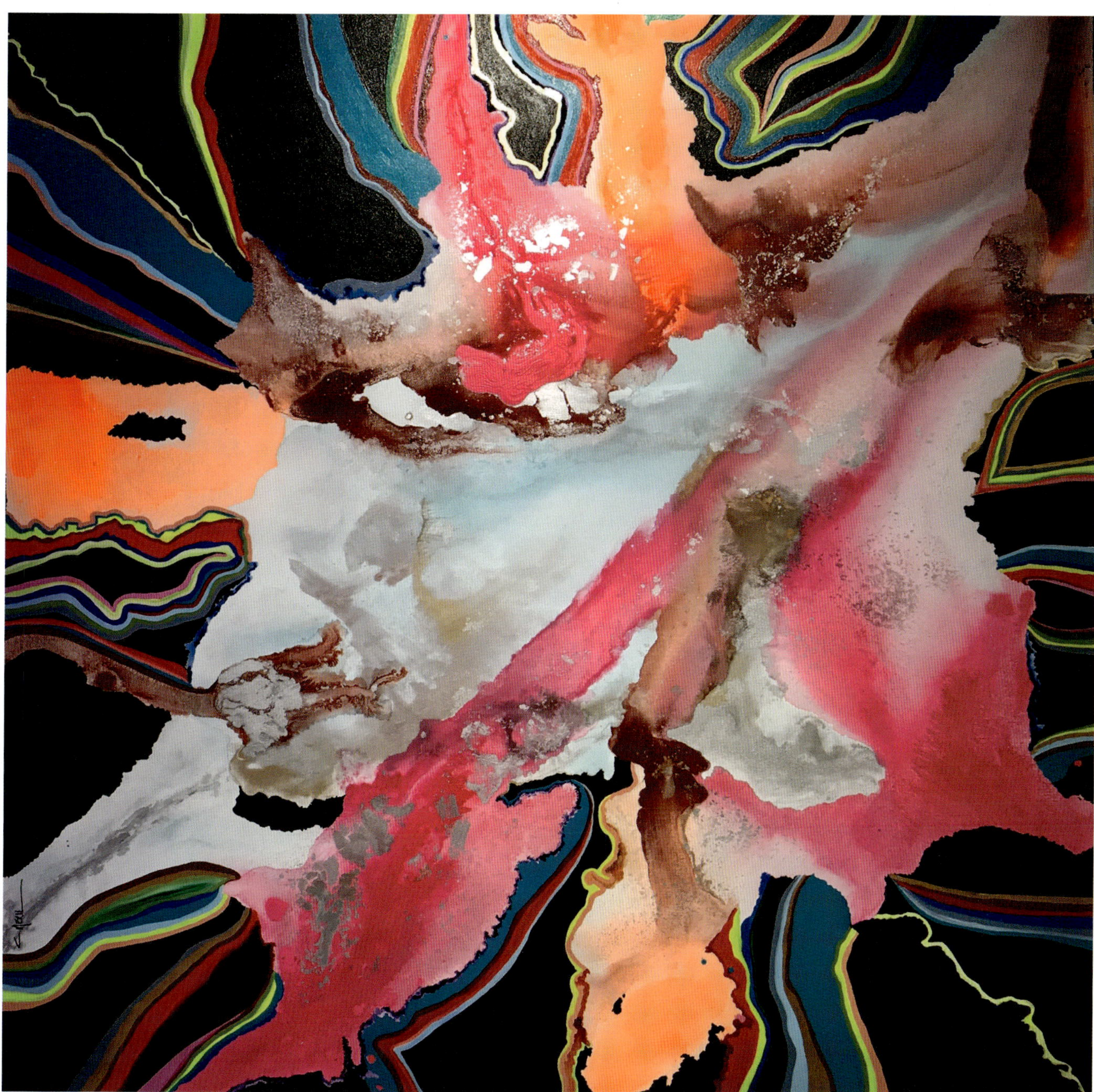

Christi Meril

Set Your Soul Free was created by artist Christi Meril to express the mystery of life's journey. She believes each life has purpose and meaning. The power of a soul living their life motivated by love is especially beautiful and impactful in countless ways that ripple throughout eternity. The artist hopes that this painting will convey the courage, passion, grace, deep love, and joy of the individual and the collective path we walk on life's course.

Meril accomplishes her expressionistic style, often filled with bold color and texture, by combining mediums such as oil, acrylic, pastel, ink, paper, and custom neon light on canvas and wood.

"Emotion and message dominate my creativity, which pushes me into the world of expressionism. Each piece reveals itself organically as I create," Meril says. "I often use layers of color and texture to tell a story rooted in my love of people, skyscrapers, and the Rocky Mountains. Intertwining modern ideas with nature takes me down a beautiful path where the possibilities of exprcssion are endless and bring me great joy."

Set Your Soul Free
Oil, acrylic, pastel, ink, watercolor on canvas
72 x 72 in.

christimerilart@gmail.com
christimerilart.com
@christimerilart

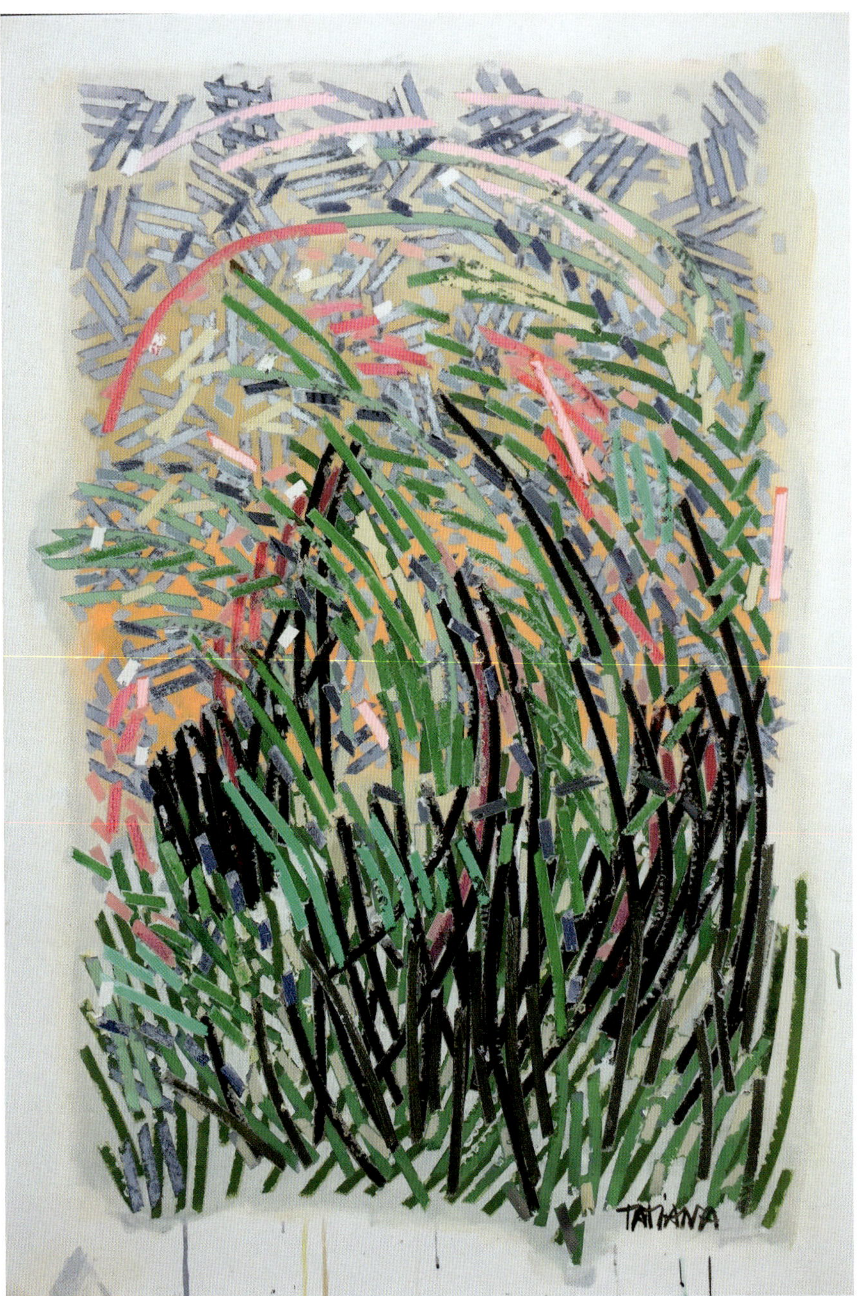

Tatiana Moya

There are two main themes Tatiana Moya explores in her art: nature as inspiration and the way of the materials. Dynamism and strength lie in the rhythm and color that commune in each piece.

Moya's work results from the superposition of elements that entangle on multiple levels into an intricate design. The artist is never certain what the final result will be because she has no control over the behavior of each material. She prefers to let the material react naturally as this increases the possibilities of expression and converts each piece into an irreplicable object.

Sauce
Acrylic on canvas
47 x 35 in.

tatianamoyao@gmail.com
@tatiana_moya_o

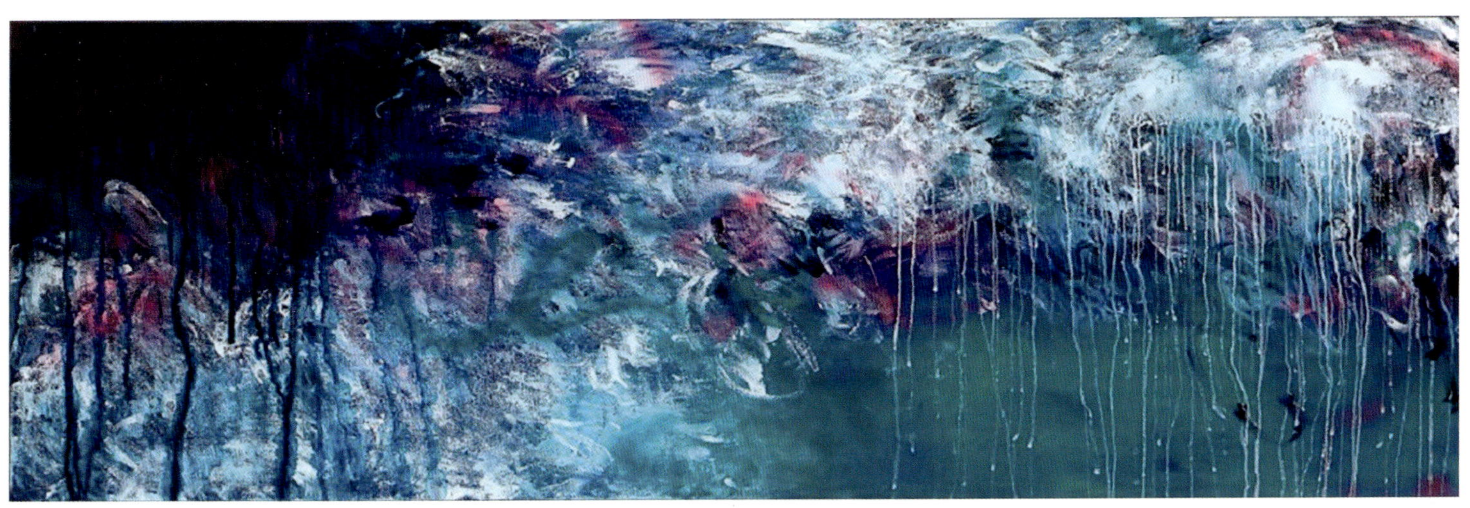

Belinda Nadwie

When observing Belinda Nadwie's art, it becomes very clear that Mother Nature's gifts are the artist's inspiration. Her deep connection to nature and the spirit of the land Australians commune on is projected as abstract expressionism onto the canvas. She works primarily with acrylic, oil, and spray paint.

Nadwie's artwork takes many avenues, inspired by the ocean, native flora, and the spirit of the land, as she prolifically captures the true essence of all that Australia and its surroundings have to offer. Her artistic expression not only encapsulates what she feels and senses within, but she has the ability to convey her soul to such a degree that others share in her vision.

Remember Your Place was inspired by the Xavier Rudd song *Follow the Sun*. One of his lyrics is "If life is coming down on you like a heavyweight / Take yourself to the nearest water's edge / Remember your place."

Remember
Oil, acrylic and spray paint
35 x 106 in.

julie@belindanadwie
.com
belindanadwie.com
@belindanadwieart

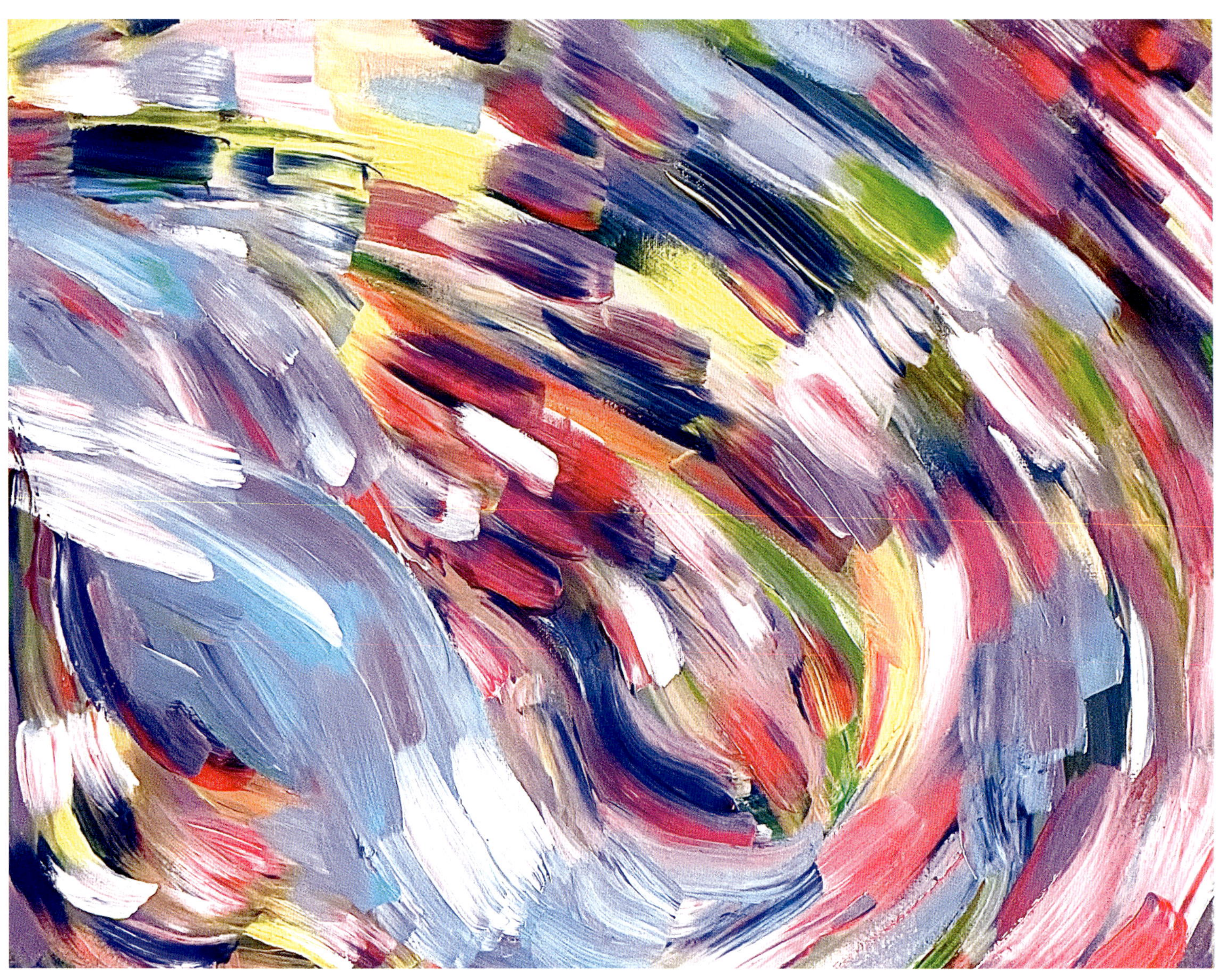

Katherine Noone

Katherine Noone lets her free-spirited, independent nature guide her, with her intuition and emotions leading the way as she paints. She loves painting because of what a freeing experience it is, and how beautiful the different color combinations and textures are within a piece. Painting is truly an invigorating experience for her; Noone loves the way the colors make her feel. Painting allows her to release anxiety, emotions, and even pain, and she sees it as an amazing outlet. She hopes that her abstract paintings allow others to feel different emotions and feelings while connecting to a deeper place within themselves. Noone's paintings have a flow and fluidity to each one, and she hopes her paintings have a healing effect on others. She wants viewers to feel a connection with her paintings and that this connection opens a deeper part of themselves, providing them with a deep sense of comfort.

Euphoric Journey
Acrylic on canvas
16 x 20 in.

katienoone223@gmail
.com
@pink_tea_roses_art

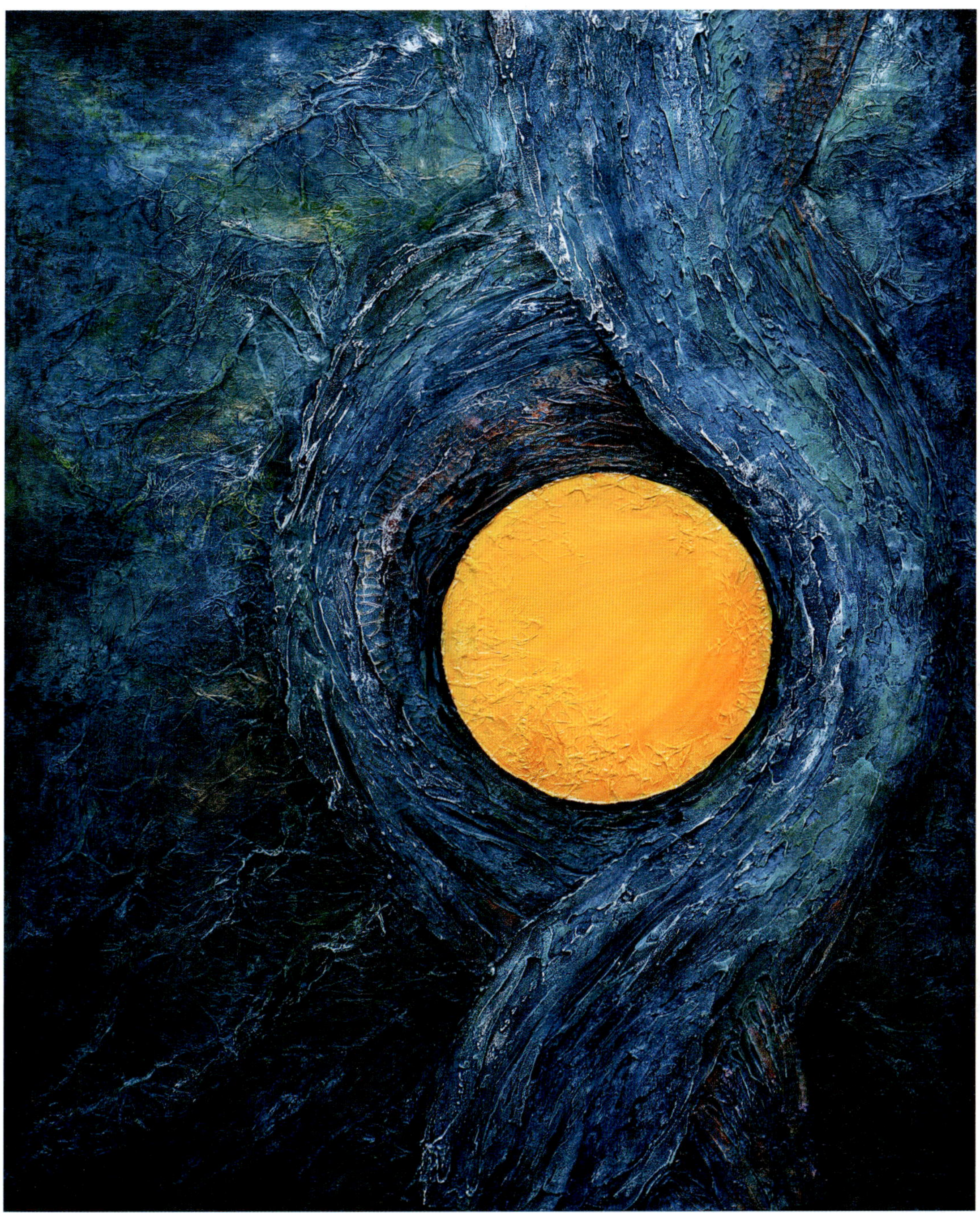

Siobain O'Brien

Siobain O'Brien's inspiration for her abstract paintings comes from the power of the natural world, which is so rich and varied in County Clare, Ireland, where she lives.

The artist's love of clay and tactile materials has led her to favor heavy texture in her art, incorporating rich layers and depth. When she begins a piece, she doesn't think about paint, instead she uses a texture medium to create a form.

When she begins a piece, O'Brien may have a loose idea of what she wants to create, but it's an organic process and she allows herself to go where the journey and the palette knife takes her. Sometimes it's slow and hesitant; other times it's a glorious frenzy of creativity. Her next step is to add acrylic paint, using brushes and her fingers. The artist loves saturated color in intense, vibrant hues, contrasting light and dark, and a vivid interplay of hard edges and soft blends. She uses neutral colors to create balance while introducing blues and greens to calm the chaos of the energy she is harnessing.

Danica
Acrylic
39 x 31 in.

siobainobrienart@gmail
.com
siobainobrienart.com
@siobainobrien.art

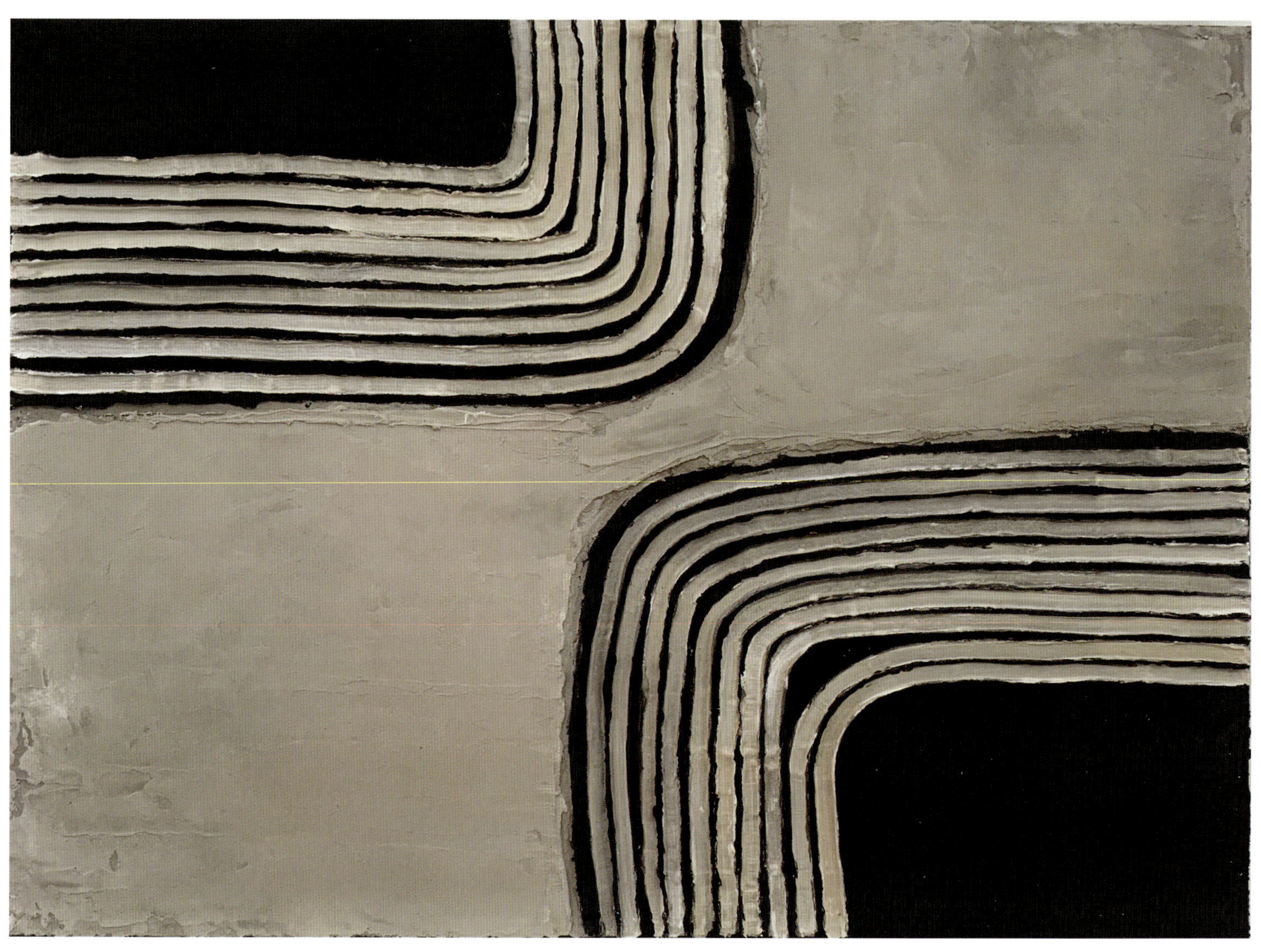

Brenna Lee Olsen

Brenna Lee Olsen is an abstract painter from Minnesota whose works are inspired by the perfectly imperfect—handmade items, rocks molded by the sea, old walls with layers of history. Her paintings are based in concrete and juxtaposed with watercolor acrylic effects. The texture she is known for is achieved through layers of concrete, hand-drawn palette knife groves, and spalling. Olsen aims to blur the lines between the two-dimensional and three-dimensional, urging the viewer to walk around and even touch the piece as you would a sculpture. Her objective is to capture and entice as many senses as possible, to bring a feeling of calm and escape to the viewer, and for them to feel like they almost hear something.

The Sound Of aims to capture what a piece of a song might look like with a background inspired by an old European wall. As the viewer walks around the piece, they will see movement and depth in the different tones of color.

The Sound Of
Concrete and acrylic
30 x 40 in.

brennaleeolsenart@
icloud.com
@brennaleeolsen

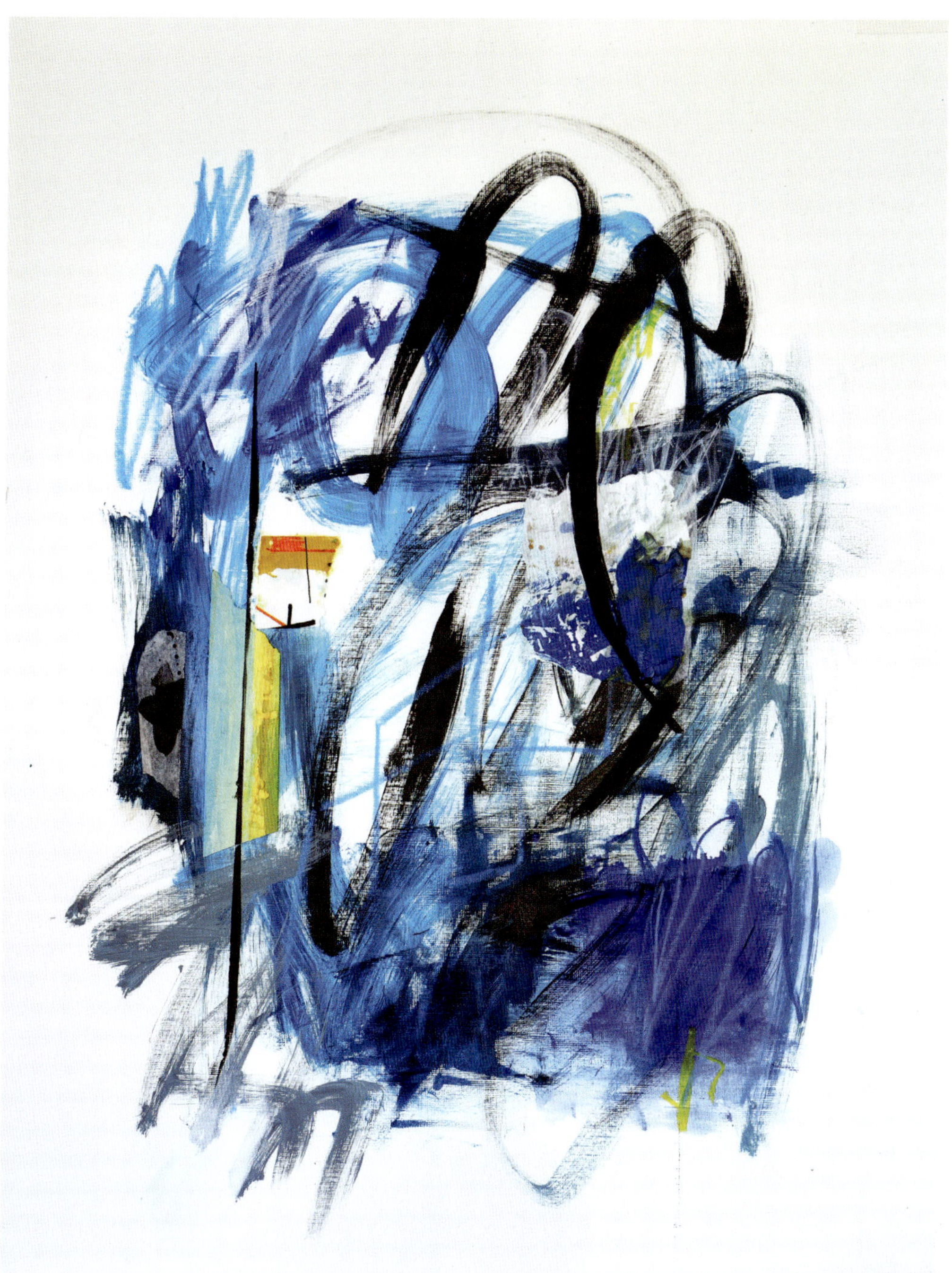

Linda O'Neill

Linda O'Neill's abstracts are intuitive and expressive, and they communicate her deepest emotions with color, movement, and form. Being surrounded by nature has always been a source of inspiration for her. Abstracted bits of beautiful skies, mountains, and oceans can be seen in her paintings in various ways.

After experimenting for many years with other mediums, she now prefers to paint with acrylics on canvas and paper. She enjoys working briskly and purposefully so that she can bring authentic emotions to the surface. She often incorporates other mixed media, such as collage, paint pen, oil pencil, Caran d'Ache pens, and ink.

"My goal is to let go of critical thinking, preferring to let my subconscious run the paintbrush," she says. The artist has lived with OCD and migraines most of her life, so elements of that experience also weave their way into her work. "I want to create an emotional journey for the viewer, highlighting redemption, healing, hope, and joy. Art has been very therapeutic and restorative for me," O'Neill says.

Free To Be True
Acrylic on paper
24 x 18 in.

linda@
abbycreekstudios.com
abbycreekstudios.com
@abbycreekstudios

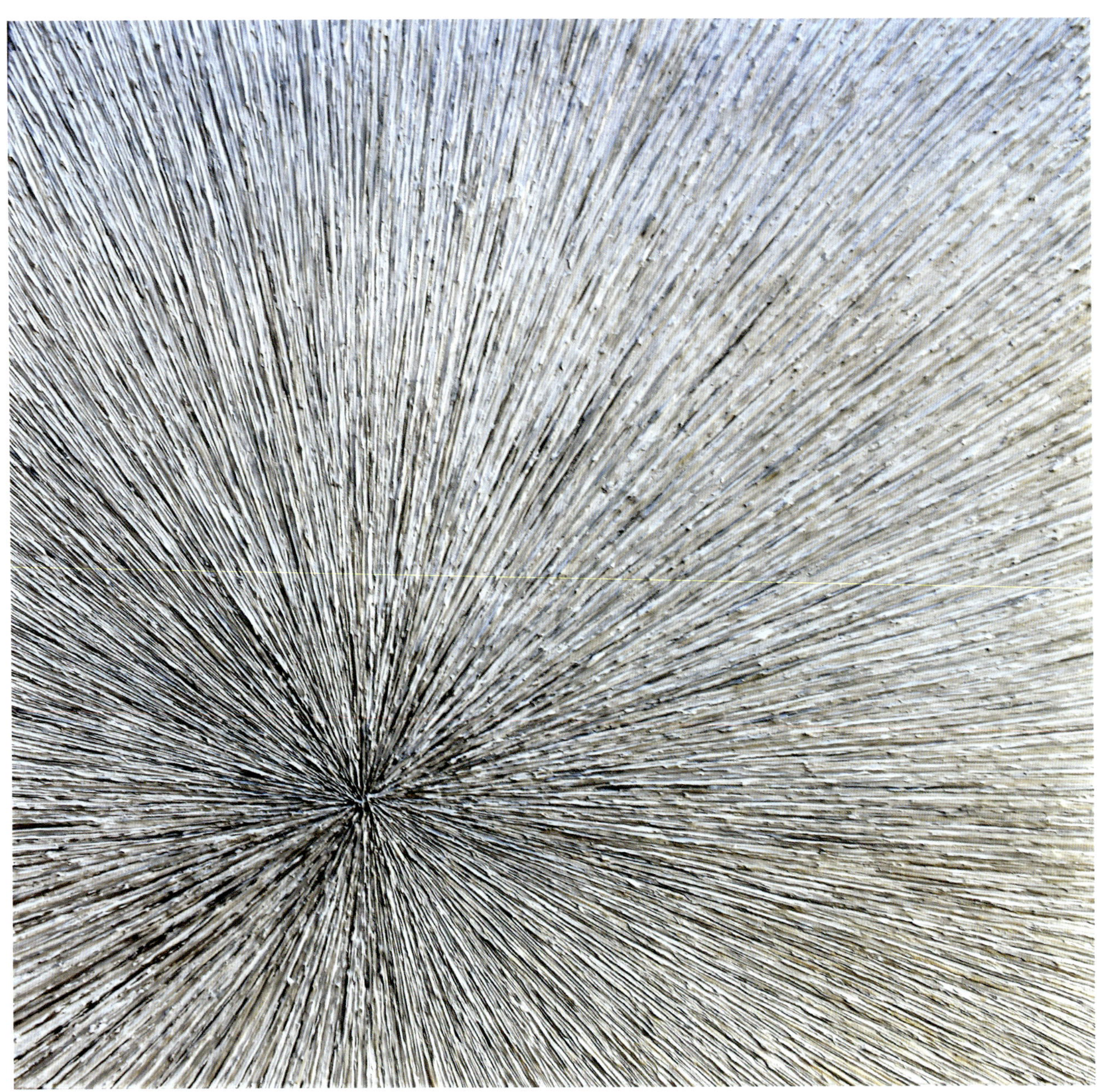

Daniela Pasqualini

"My paintings convey years of travel seeking stories of all kinds, experiences involving nature, places, people, and sounds that are woven into the relationship with vibrant colors, texture, and lines. It is a sculptural interpretation of the images and emotions accumulated from my travels," explains Daniela Pasqualini.

The artist's use of acrylic paint with gel allows her paintings to jump off the canvas and come alive, resulting in a sculptural, three-dimensional appearance. Pasqualini's feelings and moods will guide the mix of colors and the temperament of the paintings. The intention is to give the viewer a unique and emotional axperience, allowing for a connection to be made between the artwork and their own emotions.

"I hope that through my paintings, where all the elements of an experience come together, I am able to communicate the essence of my surroundings," Pasqualini says.

Emergence XII
Mixed media
36 x 36 in.

daniela.pasqualini@
gmail.com
danielapasqualini.com
@art_by_dany

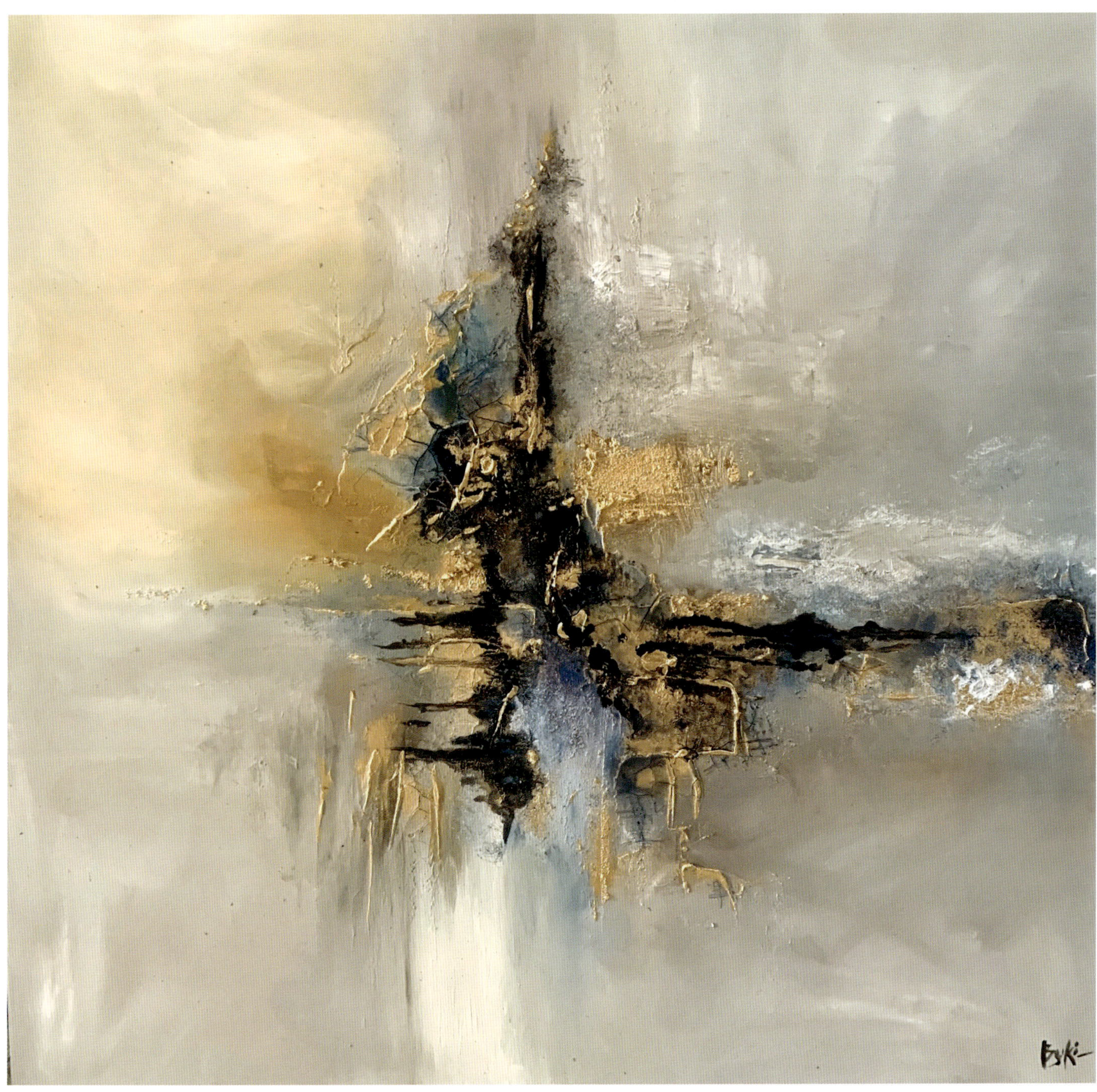

Sumali Piyatissa

Sumali Piyatissa's art takes on an abstract interpretation of her inspirations and observations. "As I engage with my surroundings and the ambiance, I allow myself to be present in all of my artwork. Each piece reflects my emotions, and the choice of color palette and technique I use differs as per my mood and surroundings," Piyatissa says.

"I believe life is like a blank canvas that we paint our picture on. It doesn't transform into a beautiful painting from the moment you pick up that brush. It takes time, it takes stages, it takes waiting, it takes fixing and maybe starting all over, but through it all, a beautiful picture transforms out of it," Piyatissa says.

Buki', the name the artist signs on her work, is an expression of love for her parents, especially her father, as it was his desire to see Piyatissa pursue her dreams and become the artist that she is today.

Old is Gold
Mixed media on canvas
34 x 34 in.

sumali.piyatissa1@
gmail.com
bukiarts.com
@bukicreations

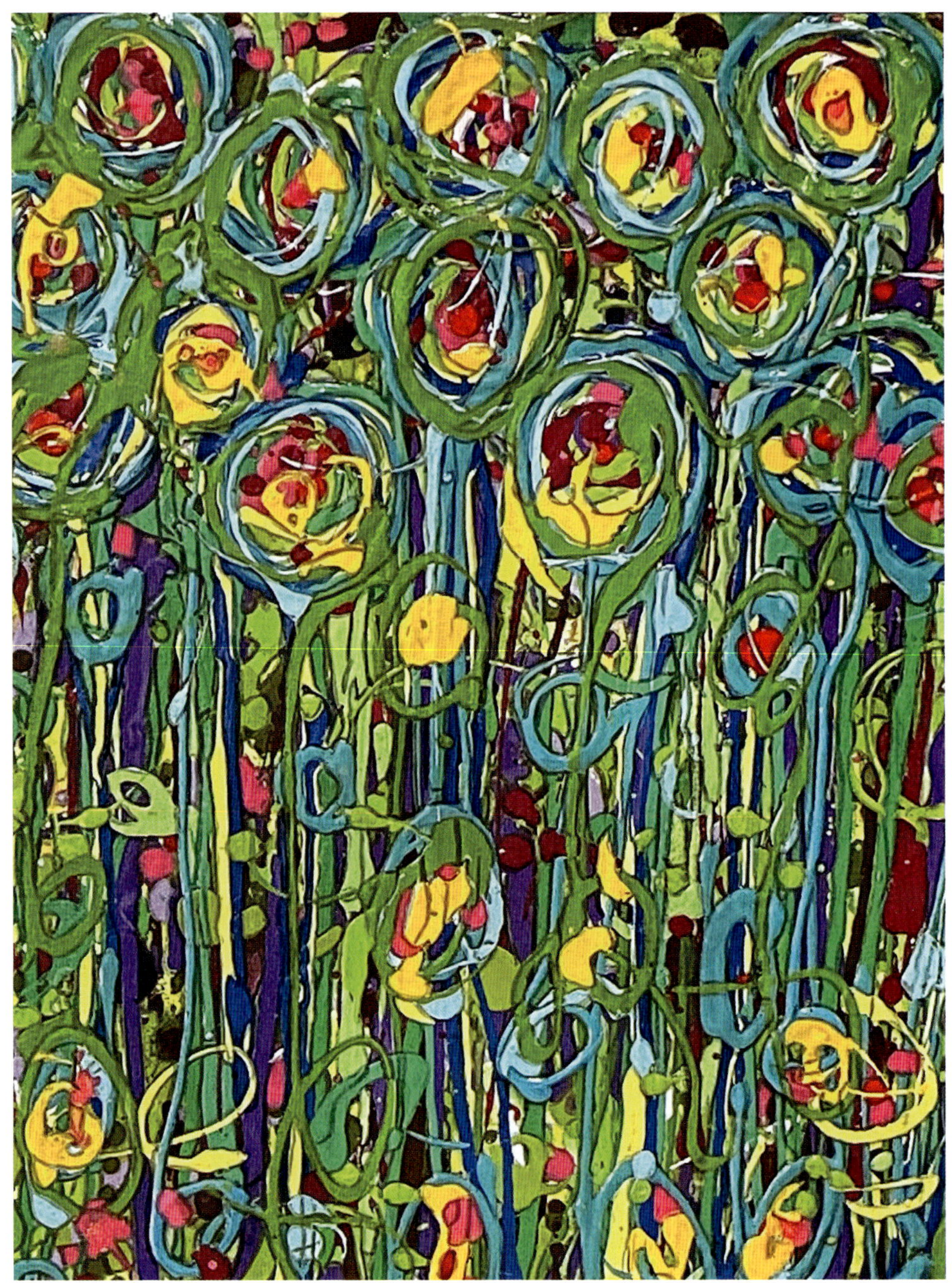

Margaret Rehwinkel
Margaret Rehwinkel has been on a creative path most of her life. She thoroughly enjoys creating and innovating through any platform—whether painting, designing an interior, creating a beautiful garden, or just choosing a wall paint color. "I have taken this knack for creativity and made a career of it, focusing on commercial art and interior design," she says. "These decades of experience now fuel how I approach painting."

Like many artists, nature and the natural world inspire her artwork. Her collection of paintings focuses on organic subjects, textiles, and shapes, often featuring bold colors and designs. Rehwinkel's work spans different styles.

Unique shapes and colors characterize her abstract art, while nature and organic matter strongly influence her *Meadows* series. Strong attention to detail shapes all her work.

Natures Way 1
Acrylic/ink on canvas
22 x 22 in.

shoe1955@aol.com
@margaretschumacher-rehwinkel

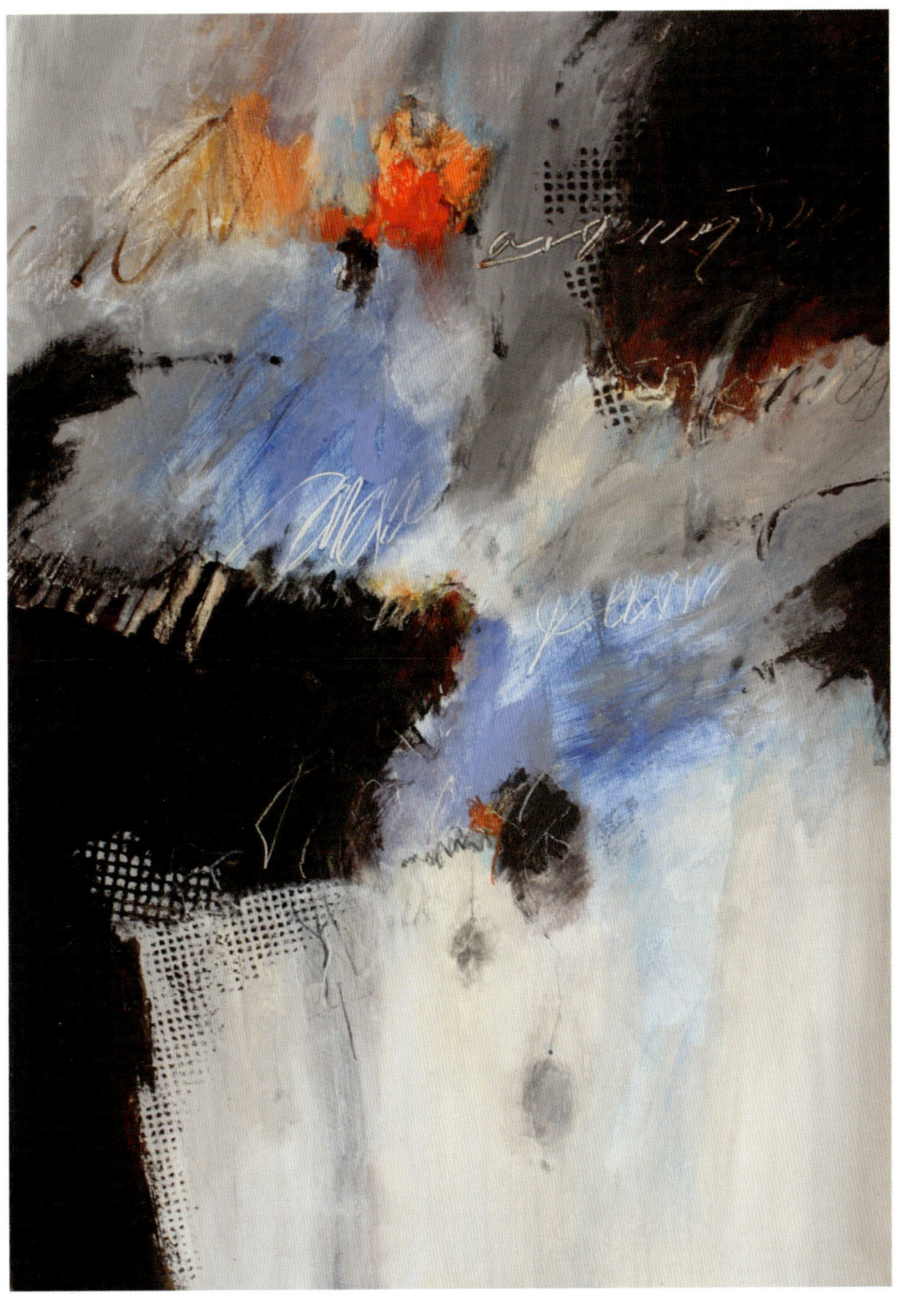

Doreen Renner

Doreen Renner is an abstract artist. After many years of being a watercolor artist, where her subject matter included traditional landscapes, still life, and florals in a very typical representational style, Renner decided to explore abstract work using acrylic paint. Painting abstractly was a more challenging and complex style, but it has allowed her to evolve as an artist and create a more personal form of artistic expression. Her images explore interpretations of everyday events and are inspired by an internal response to an emotion, a memory, or a life experience. Her paintings are unique and compelling, some deep and mysterious while others are light and whimsical. She is very much an intuitive painter, allowing the images to dictate the direction they choose to evolve by using multiple layers of acrylic medium infused with richness in value contrast, embellished with gestural calligraphy, and designed to engage the viewer and encourage closer observation and personal interpretation.

The Abyss
Acrylic
22 x 15 in.

doreenrenner@rogers
.com
doreenrenner.com
@doreen_renner

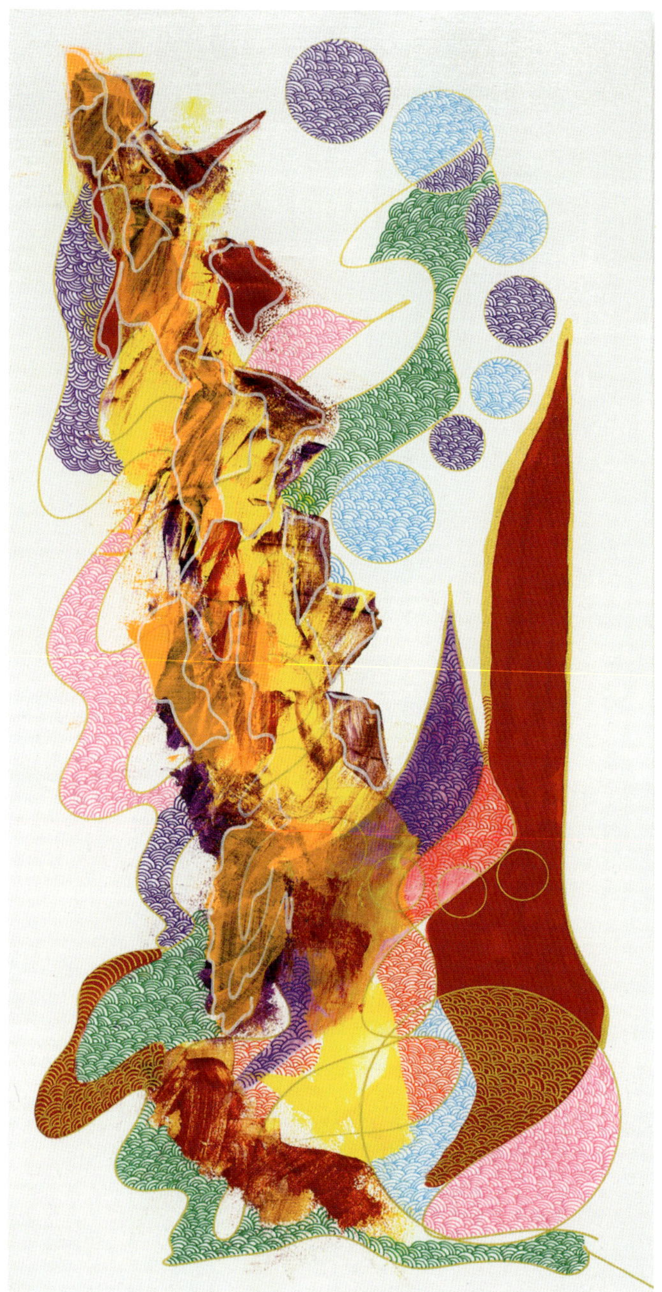

Carole-Yvonne Richard
Carole-Yvonne Richard paints from her daily life—the encounters and events of ordinary, extraordinary, and common life. She paints a human landscape woven with encounters, friendships, and events of all kinds. Her work focuses on the emotions and feelings associated with certain life experiences that we all face at one time or another in our human journey.

To her paintings, she adds elements of collage, photos, words, and symbolic objects that she staples, knots, ties, wraps, or glues to a work. She also works by accumulation of pictorial elements, assembling several pieces to form a larger artwork that she calls a mosaic. Her paintings develop from spontaneous and constructed gestures. The spot, the line, the repetition, and the shape become her guides. By suggesting landscapes, portraits, and abstractions, her work evokes different styles or conventions of art history. In sum, it is her intent to capture the human presence that allows us to collectively experience the feeling of being alive.

C'est la fête!
Acrylic
12 x 24 in.

carole-yvonne@
cyrichard.com
cyrichard.com
@cyrichard

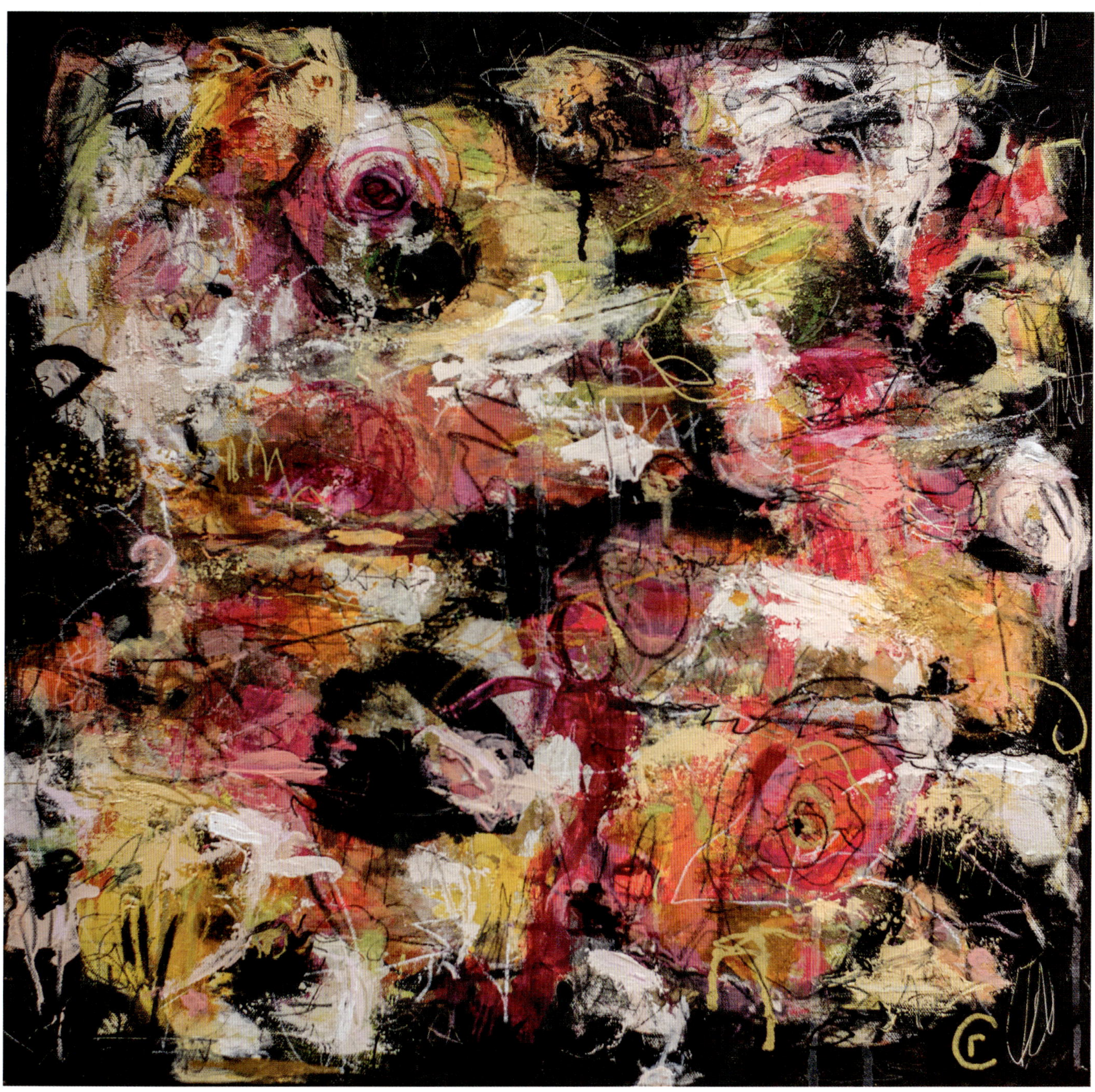

Catherine Richardson

Catherine Richardson is a Canadian artist who paints the human condition in the form of abstraction. As a person and an artist, Richardson is a dichotomy between masculine and feminine visuals, love and lies, laughter and reverence, and every other human dilemma. Juxtaposition is at the cornerstone of each piece. She looks to her daily observations of people, places, and emotions as her primary sources of inspiration.

Richardson's immersion into the land of abstract painting was prefaced by a business background, furniture design, homebuilding, activewear design, and color forecasting. While loving parts of all her escapades, it is through abstract painting that she truly came alive.

Major influences include nature, music, and jewelry design. She is surrounded by beauty in Northern Ontario, Canada, where she grew up running wild on the shores of Trout Lake. If you ask Richardson what she wants her art to say, she would reply, "My dream is for the viewer to emote and have an inner conversation."

Midnight Garden X Lovers
Acrylic
24 x 24 in.

info@
catherinerichardson.art
catherinerichardson.art
@catrichardsonabstract

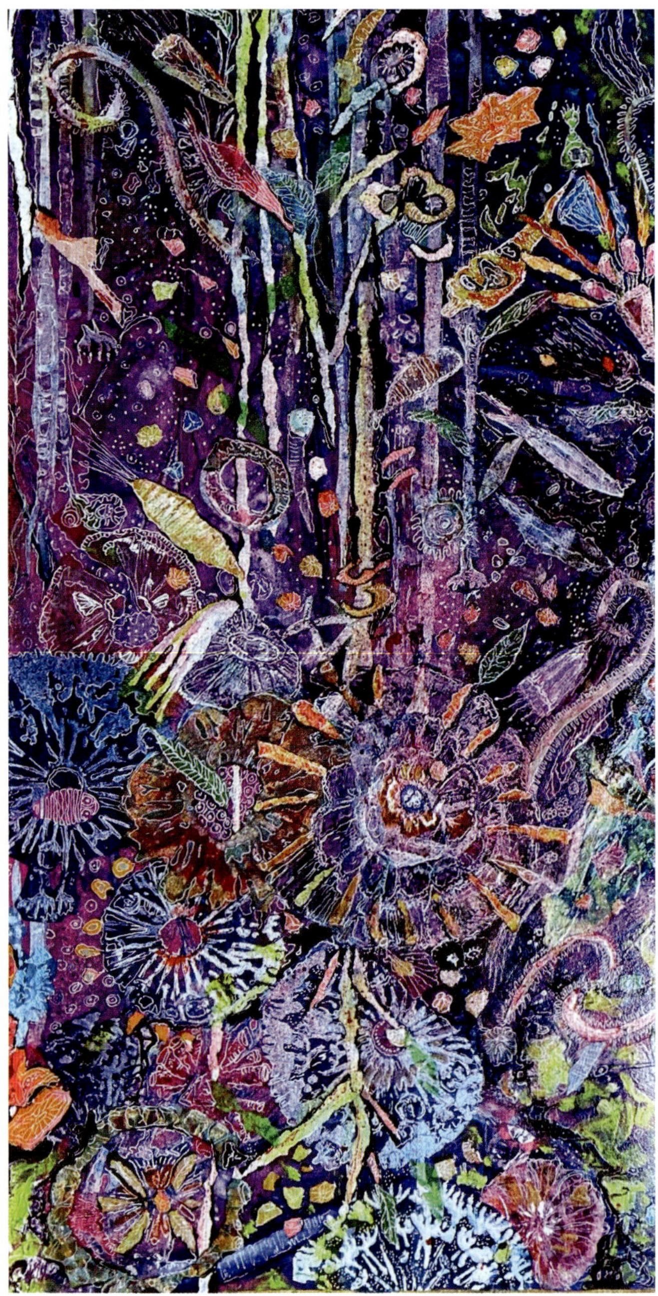

Johanna Riddle

"I am captivated by the power of the visual storyteller to arrange, rearrange, add, and layer elements to shape a narrative, feed the imagination, evoke memories and emotions," Johanna Riddle says. She began exploring this idea by developing panels that could be rearranged and interleaved. Her process has evolved to the construction, deconstruction, and reconstruction of mixed-media art to create fresh and often unexpected stories. Layers, transparencies, and connections between media and subject are vital parts of her process. Like memories, images and colors float across the canvas. The ultimate story is born in that spark of connection between an artist and a viewer.

"I tell my story," Riddle says. "The viewer makes fresh interpretations, discovers details, layers their own life experiences over the image. A richer, more meaningful message emerges. Each piece I create ultimately becomes a never-ending tale."

Things Unseen: A Teaspoon of Ocean
Mixed media
33.25 x 20 in.

johannariddle@gmail.com
johannariddle.com
@johannariddleart

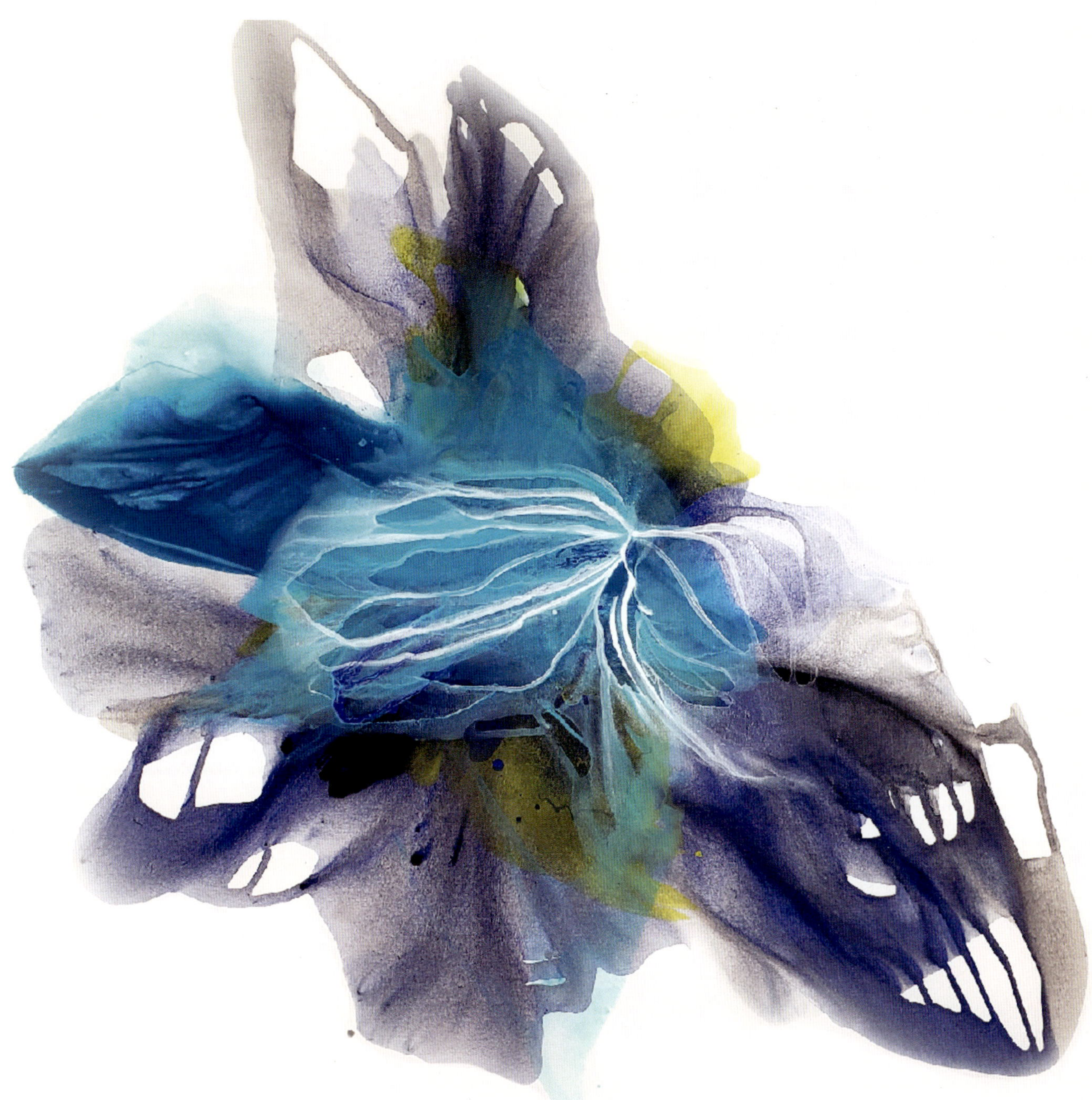

Bette Ridgeway

Bette Ridgeway is best known for her large-scale, luminous poured canvases that push the boundaries of light, color, and design. For the past two decades, the high desert light of Santa Fe, New Mexico, has fueled Ridgeway's art practice. Her three decades of mentorship by the acclaimed Abstract Expressionist Paul Jenkins set her on her lifetime journey of nonobjective painting on large canvases. She explores the interrelation and change of color in various conditions and on a variety of surfaces. Ridgeway has spent the last 30 years developing her signature technique, called "layering light," in which she uses many layers of thin, transparent acrylics on linen and canvas to produce a fluidity and viscosity similar to traditional watercolor. Delving further, Ridgeway expanded into three-dimensional work, joining paint and resin to aluminum and steel with sculptures of minimal towers. Ridgeway depicts movement in her work, sometimes kinetic and full of emotion, sometimes bold and masterful, sometimes languid and tentative.

Web of Dreams
Acrylic on canvas
52 x 52 in.

ridgeway@
artworkinternational
.com
betteridgeway.com
@ridgewaystudio

PAINTING: TRADITIONAL/ABSTRACT

Machiel Roest

Machiel Roest has always had a passion for art and philosophy, particularly that of Ludwig von Wittgenstein, Friedrich Nietzsche, and Martin Heidegger. He started drawing and painting what their philosophy meant to him, trying to find ways to bring their theories in a two-dimensional transition toward a more general understanding of what they in fact meant.

"Too many times philosophers are used for political or other purposes instead of just their thoughts," Roest says. "I realized that using language to read, to think, and to study the works of great philosophers is only a limited, one-sided form of philosophy."

The need arose for the artist to "translate" the philosopher's beliefs into his "drawn reality." He wanted to express his interpretation of philosophy through the universal language of art rather than through words. The titles of all his paintings correspond to aphorisms or expressions made by the above-mentioned philosophers.

Be careful when you cast out your demons that you don't throw away the best of yourself.
Oil on paper
39 x 27.5 in.

machiel@machielr.eu
machielr.eu
@macphi

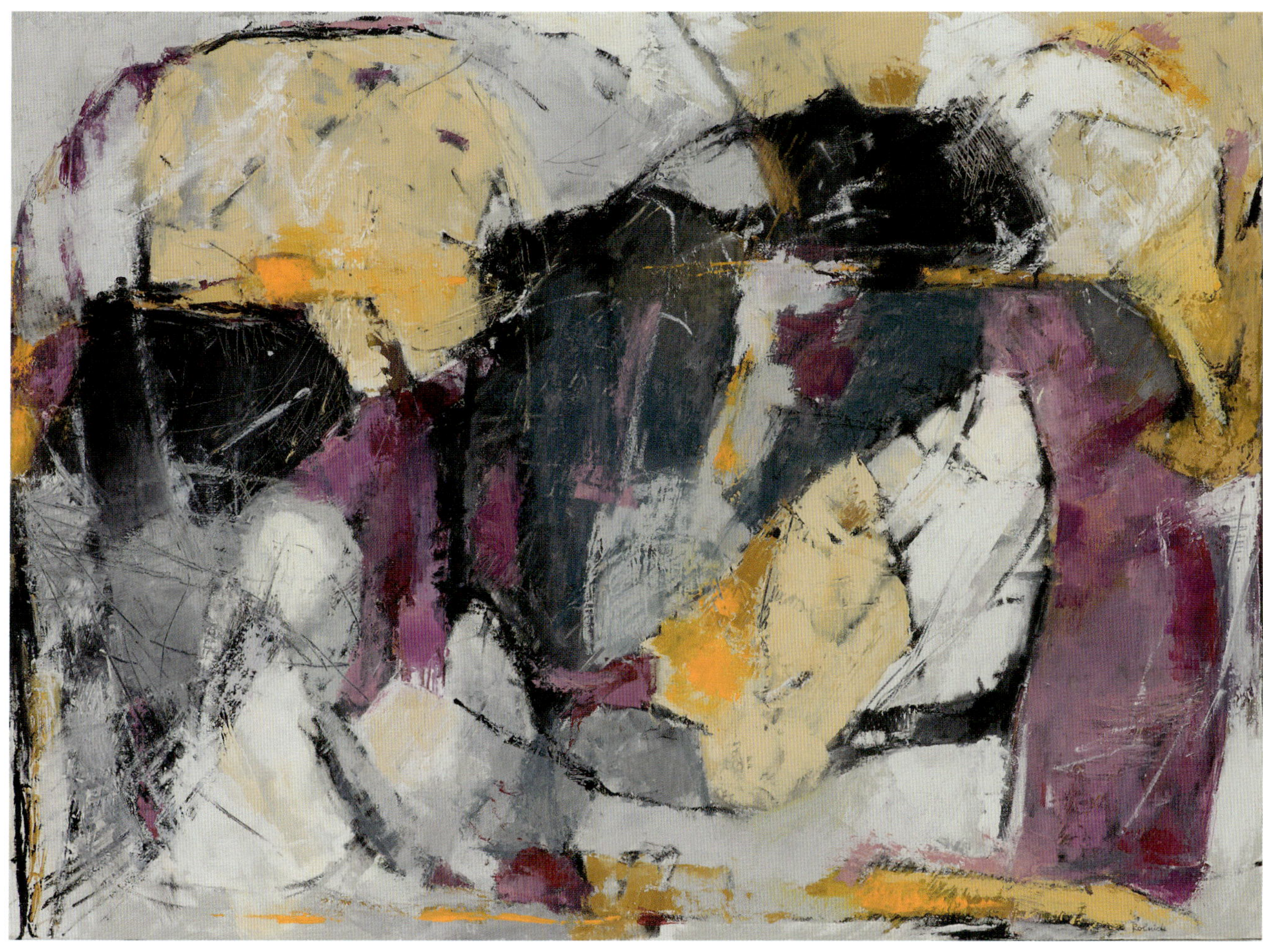

Digging Deep
Oil
30 x 40 in.

leslierolnick@gmail.com
@leslierolnick52

Leslie Rolnick

Painting is Leslie Rolnick's personal form of spirituality—the only place where time and conscious thoughts are completely suspended for her. While painting, her palette and material choices, mark-making, and creation of texture and forms, begin with no preconceived goal. Rolnick is only involved in the immediacy and problem-solving of the work, the excitement of the process. She feels a call and response between herself and the piece, alternating between conscious structure and unconscious material. Rolnick works on a piece until it feels right and she has expressed all that is needed for that particular moment in time.

Pushing paint has been an endless source of fascination her entire life. Transitioning from her classical training to abstract expressionism, Rolnick now uses stronger colors and feels freer to experiment differently, letting mood, intuition, dream imagery, travels, nature, and memories all come to the fore while working on each painting.

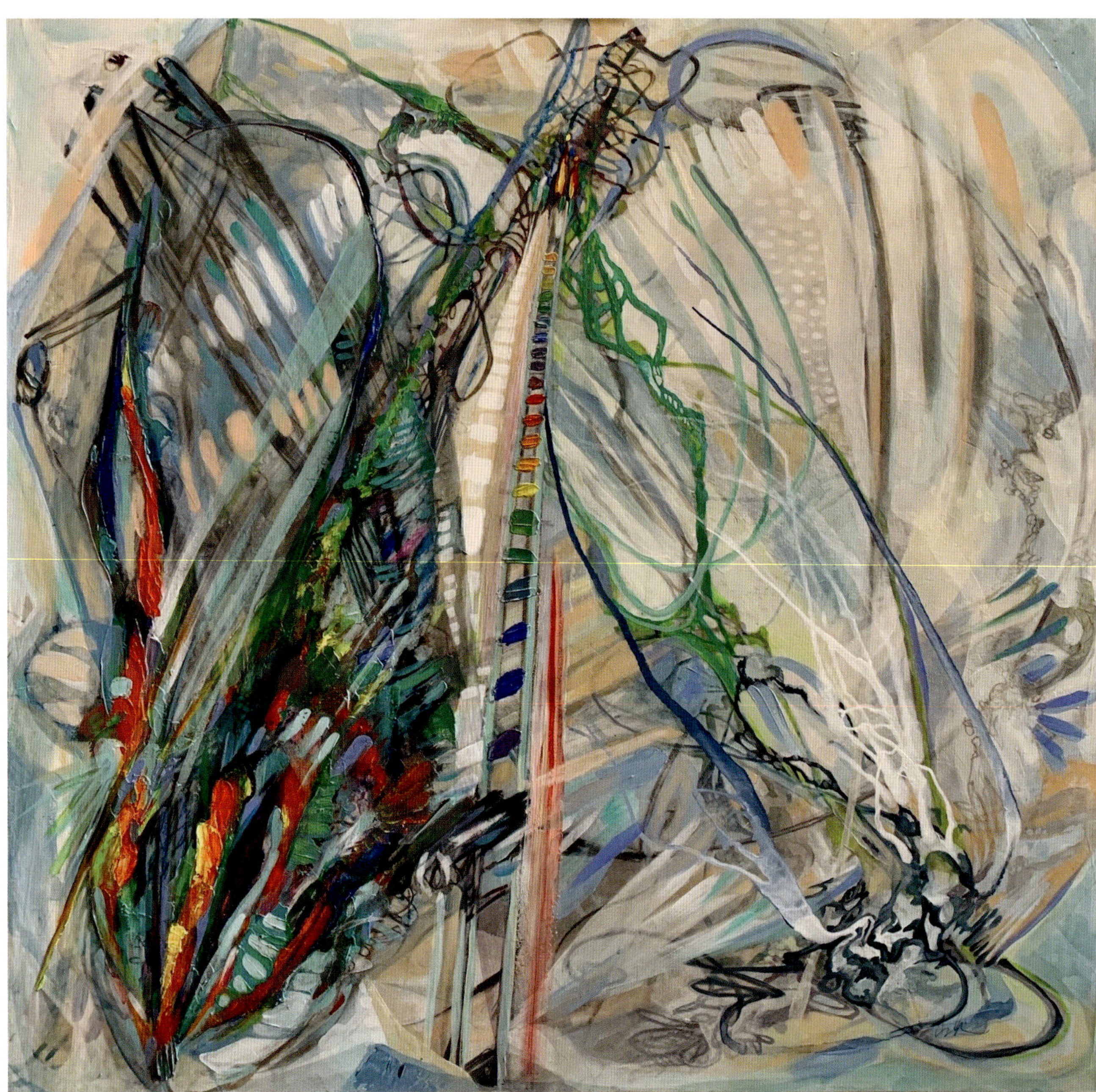

Anastacia Sadeh

Anastacia Sadeh's paintings explore metacognition and the complex nature of human emotions as they relate to mental health. She often begins the foundational layers of her works by creating various surface textures with Venetian plaster on either canvas or wood panel. Sadeh creates this foundational layer to purposely influence the subsequent layers of paint as a nod to the effects that our pasts have on our present methodologies. She then creates the next painted layers with an ironic sense of purposeful accident by allowing for her chosen color and medium to move without her immediate influence. This loosely guided composition forms the skeleton upon which the entire work is then based. This process represents that much of our circumstances and our resulting emotions cannot be chosen or controlled. Sadeh then uses these marks to begin her finished work in the same way she is learning to observe her own thoughts before she intentionally responds to them. Most recently, the artist is including figurative elements within her abstract works.

Fraction of a Moment Explored
Acrylic acrylic, India ink, graphite, and Venetian plaster on canvas
36 x 36 in.

sadehstudioarts@gmail.com
anastaciasadeh.com
@sadehstudioarts

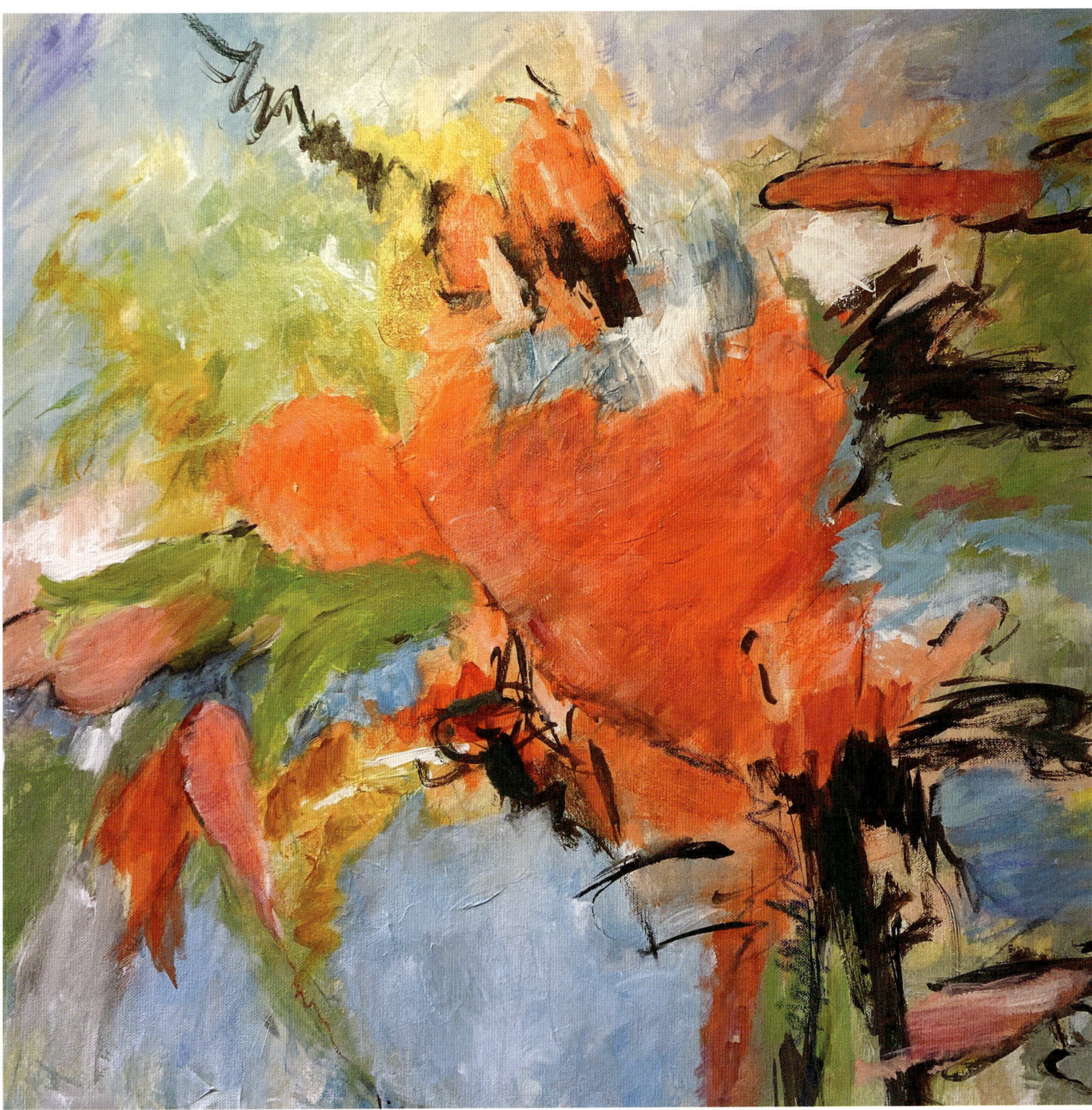

Karen H. Salup

As an abstract expressionist, Karen H. Salup concentrates on the actions involved in creating artworks rather than trying to produce images that people could recognize. Salup is searching for a kind of underlying unity that takes into account the materials on hand, a method, and a fairly clear personal point of view. Form, space, content, and especially the qualities of color and light are a part of the dance called "Action Painting." As a painting evolves, Salup makes changes that reveal and suggest other possible directions; thus, there is an ongoing shift of centers of interest.

Salup's works vibrate with color and come alive with gestural brushstrokes while images fight to appear and the references to nature seem apparent. The freshness of the gesture allows the viewer to feel the painting develop as though she is making the decisions to add, subtract, change colors, and dance with the space.

Flying Flamingo
Acrylic and mixed media
36 x 36 in.

monet12@bellsouth.net
karenhs.com
@ksalup

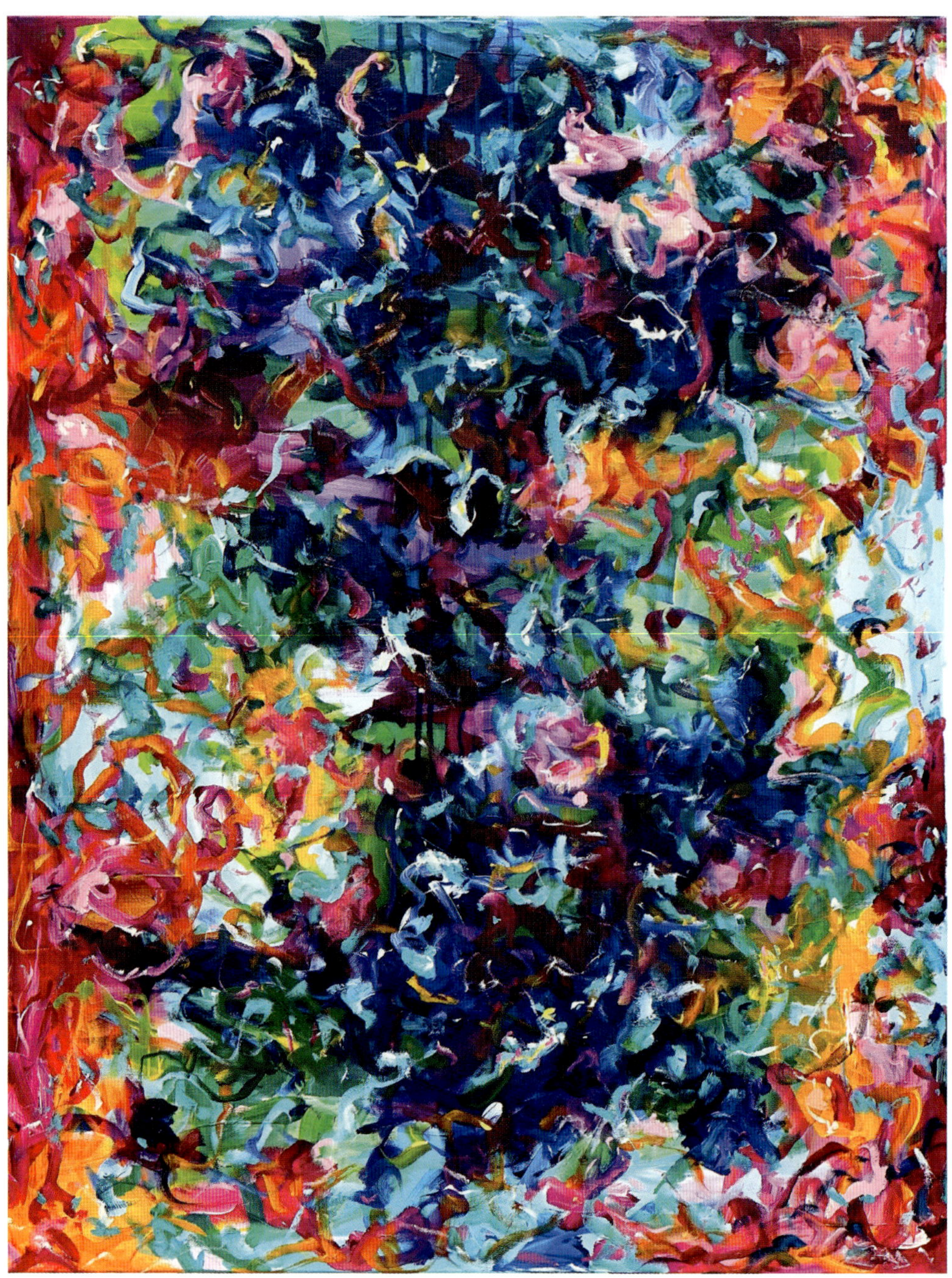

Peyton Sauer

Art has the ability to connect people to other spaces and times. Peyton Sauer's paintings are how she time travels. Her work is a mixture of feelings and memories that examine the relationship of her current self to the prior versions of herself. As a mental health advocate and an open book about trauma therapy, Sauer uses paint as a medium to work through memories long since passed and records her version of them. Letting her intuition lead the way, she twists the memories that have no place to go into the language of shape and color, enabling them to speak to countless people from all walks of life. Sauer prefers to leave her work open for interpretation rather than spelling out the meaning for the viewer. She wants the viewer to gain whatever they need from the experience and believes only they know what that is.

High Alice
Acrylic
40 x 30 in.

peyton.sauer@gmail
.com
@peytonleighart

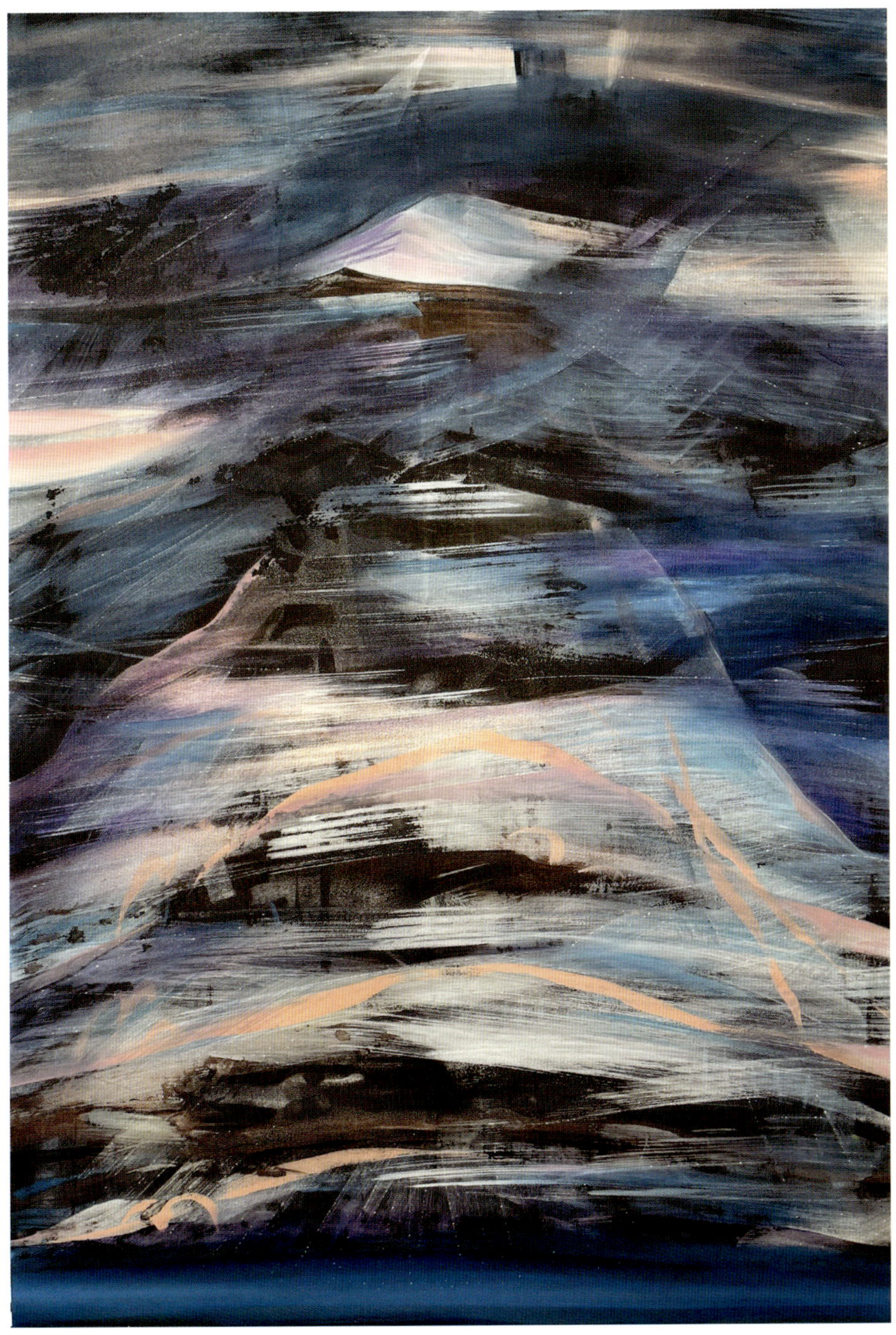

Carita Schmidt

Carita Schmidt's insights on cultural and natural landscapes have been shaped by her time living and working in Helsinki, Stockholm, Kavala, Athens, and now Berlin. The diversity of structures, merging lines, and different light qualities define her work. Schmidt has developed a mark-making technique that combines drawing, painting, and playing with gestures as a way to express movement beyond borders. The question of renegotiating the notion of borders, as a choice to communicate between different areas and nations, fascinates her.

"I am interested in a movement that does not stop or allow itself to be limited," Schmidt says.

The essence of her work is related to connectivity and movement. She accomplishes this sometimes with subtle abstract drawings, sometimes with energetic brushstrokes. She is always searching for a vibrant expression, making her work recognizable.

True North
Mixed media
47 x 35 in.

caritaschmidt@gmail
.com
caritaschmidt.com
@caritaschmidt_painter

PAINTING: TRADITIONAL/ABSTRACT

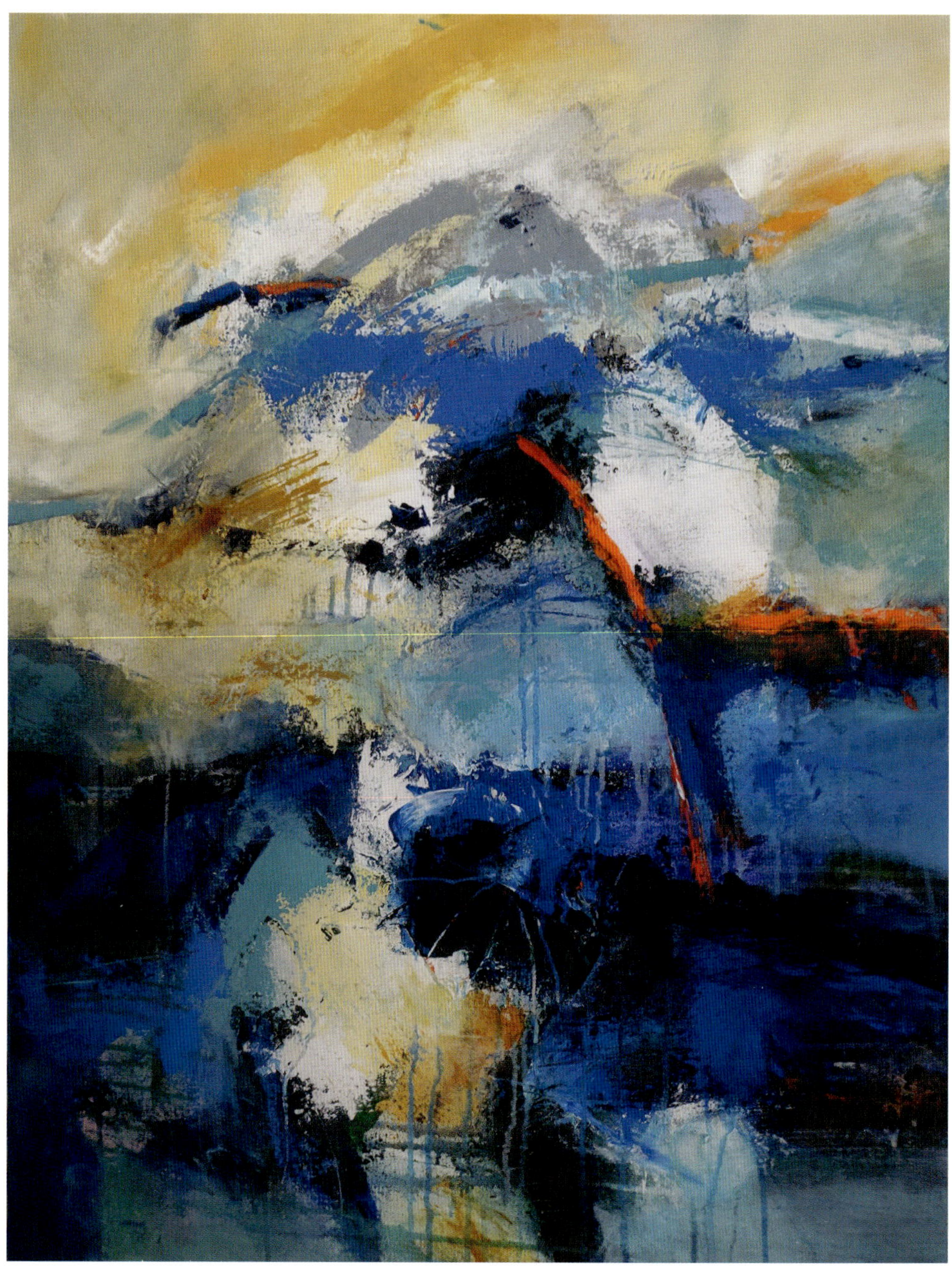

Neena Singh

Neena Singh owes her life to the act of painting and what emerged from the process. For her, the act of painting is not a choice, it is an inner compulsion. The process of creating art frees her from the relentless toll of Sisyphus by giving a purpose to her life. Art enabled her to create a new world beyond intellect, rationality, and expediency. Through her luminous paintings, she creates meaning in an otherwise absurd existence. For her, the process of painting creates a "Twilight Zone" that bridges the gap between the known and what lies beyond the obvious. This world is filled with luminosity and infinite possibilities. Painting helped her to truly see the world, relieved her of ennui. The impetus to grow and live intensely is a very powerful urge in her and with each painting, she experiences the expansion of her limited being.

Searching for Totality
Acrylic on canvas
40 x 30 in.

neena.art.singh@gmail.com
neenasingh.com
@neenasinghart

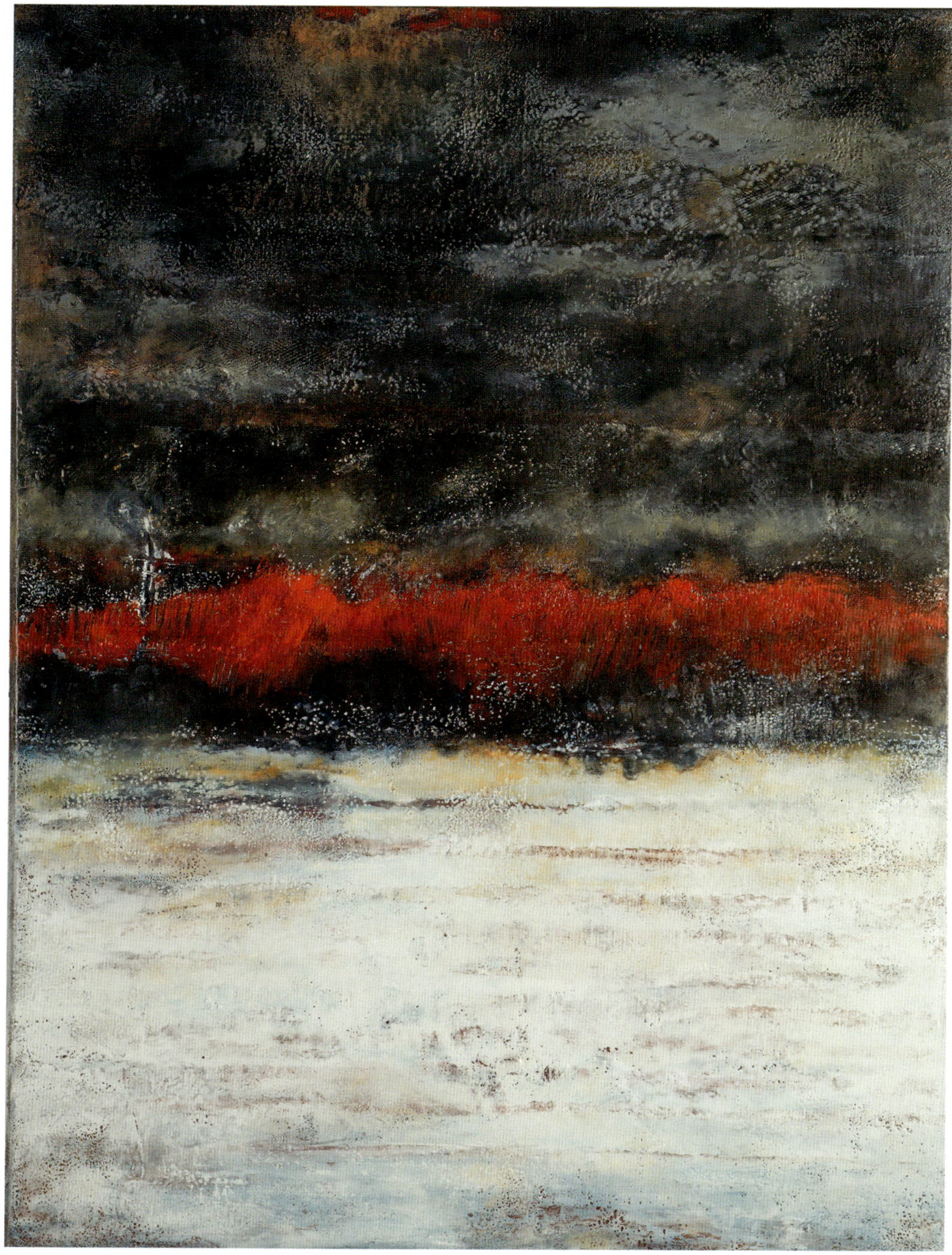

Catherine Eaton Skinner

As a multidisciplinary artist committed to learning, Catherine Eaton Skinner divides her time between studios in Seattle, Washington, and Santa Fe, New Mexico. She works in beeswax, resin, and oil, often incorporating stones, found objects, lead sheeting, precious metals, textiles, papers, glass, and bronze. A constant thread in her work is the elemental archetypes of the physical and cosmic world: water; fire; woods, mountains, and earth; air and wind; space and ether.

Horizontal lines offer visual boundaries: sky and ocean with the simplicity of shadows and light; strata of earth walls with subtle seeps of water; pathways in quiet snow. The work vibrates between opposites: marks of delicate tracery against heavy incising; smooth melted wax confronted by textured oil stick; reversal of colors with reflections of metal leaf.

"My work hopes to link us to the anima and earth: seeing with open eyes and cherishing the waters that ensure our survival," Skinner says.

Between the Gates XVI
Encaustic and oil stick on panel
40 x 30 in.

ceskinner@
artworkinternational.com
ceskinner.com
@ceskinner

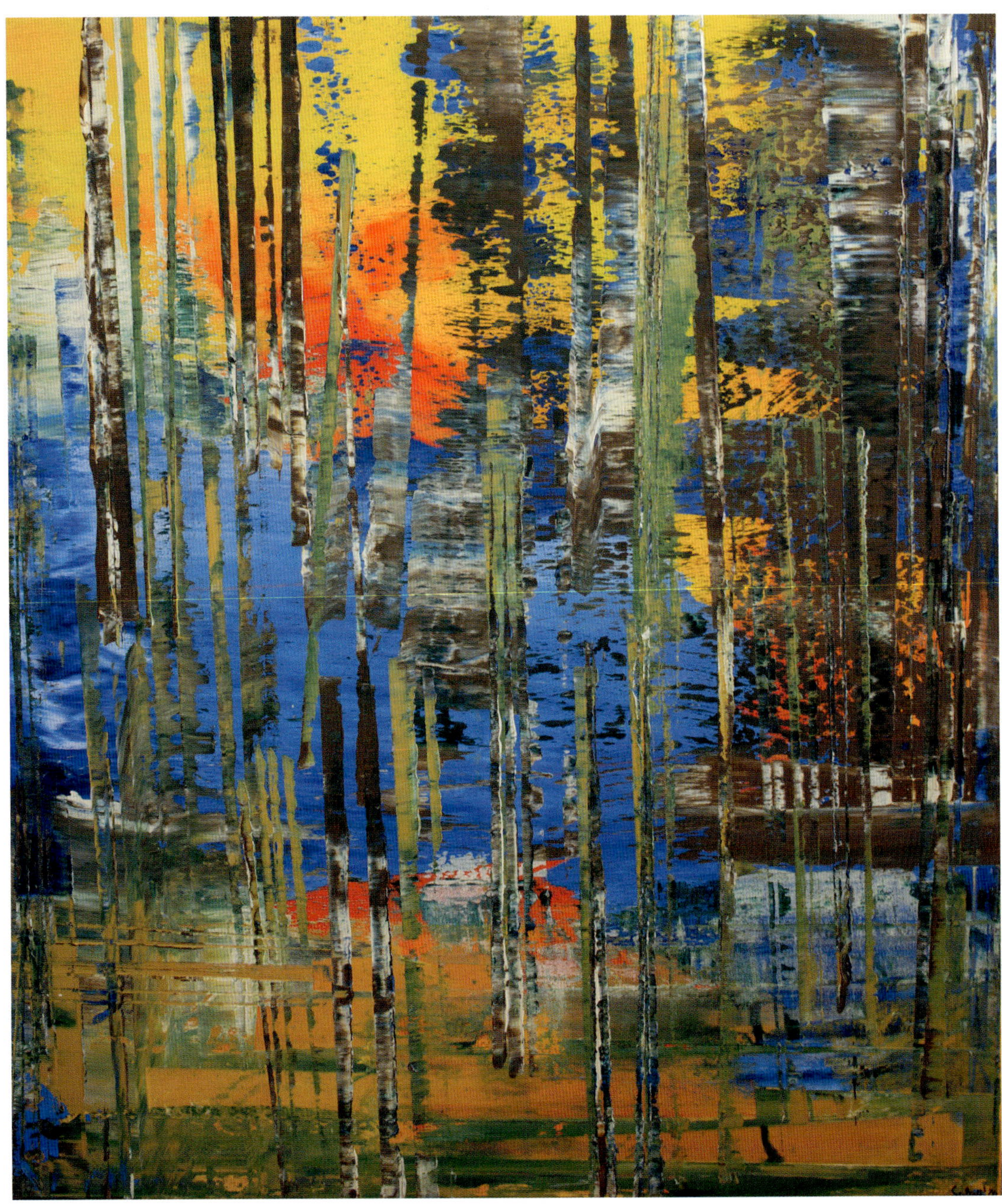

Kerstin Sokoll

Art as an emotion of the unique. This is the message that Kerstin Sokoll wants to convey with her art. Using expressive color in combination with energetic completion, her artwork touches people from within. Her work is an expression of explosive determination and complex calculation. She cites the emotional-creative process as being at the center of her works, whereby the expressive complexity is both intention and effect. In Sokoll's abstractions, the experimental interaction of color and structure plays a vital role, resulting in an emotive optical eruption.

Sokoll works with classic means of painting, using acrylic on canvas. Making use of the mixed-media technique, she creates two-dimensional sculptures. The cellular structure of the surface of her paintings plays an important part. In this way, she creates beguiling underwater worlds, exotic landscapes, or fantasy worlds that remind the beholder of oscillating galaxies.

Forest Bathing
Acrylic on canvas
47 x 39 in.

info@kerstin-sokoll.de
kerstin-sokoll.de
@arts_by_sokoll

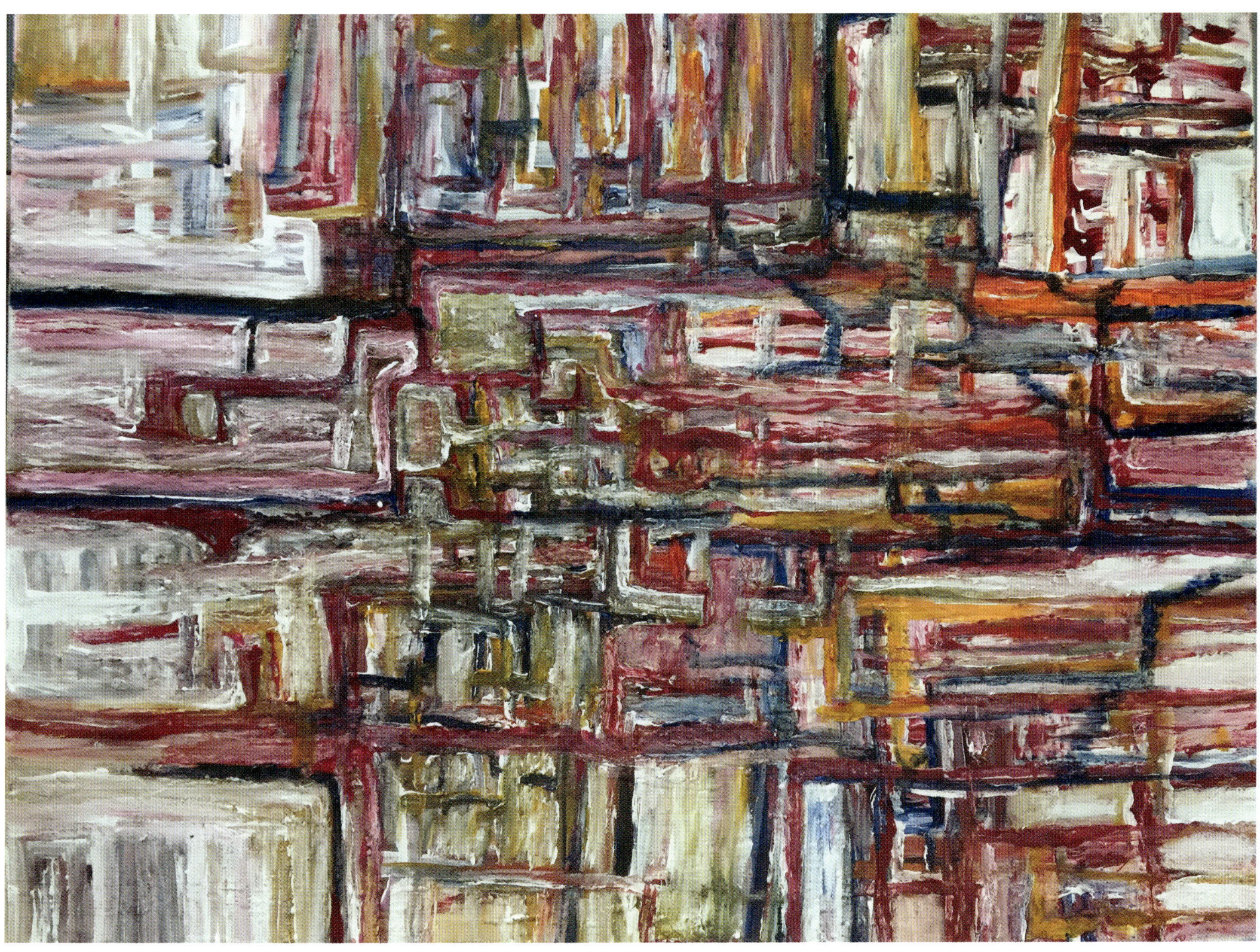

Patricia Spoon

Patricia Spoon expresses self-individualism through her art, using lines, angles, and geometric patterns. Colors both bold and soft are included in the composition of the geometric patterns and set the mood and tone of her work. Motion is an expressed component of individuality in her art. The interpretation of movement and self-individuality is significant in her paintings. "I covey passion for self-individuality in my art," Spoon says. "I paint to display how lines and angles can be used to express mood, tone, and individuality." Spoon's art is a display, on a canvas, of how self-individuality is an orchestra.

Cubed
Oil
18 x 24 in.

spoonpatricia2@gmail.com
@Patriciaspoonartworks

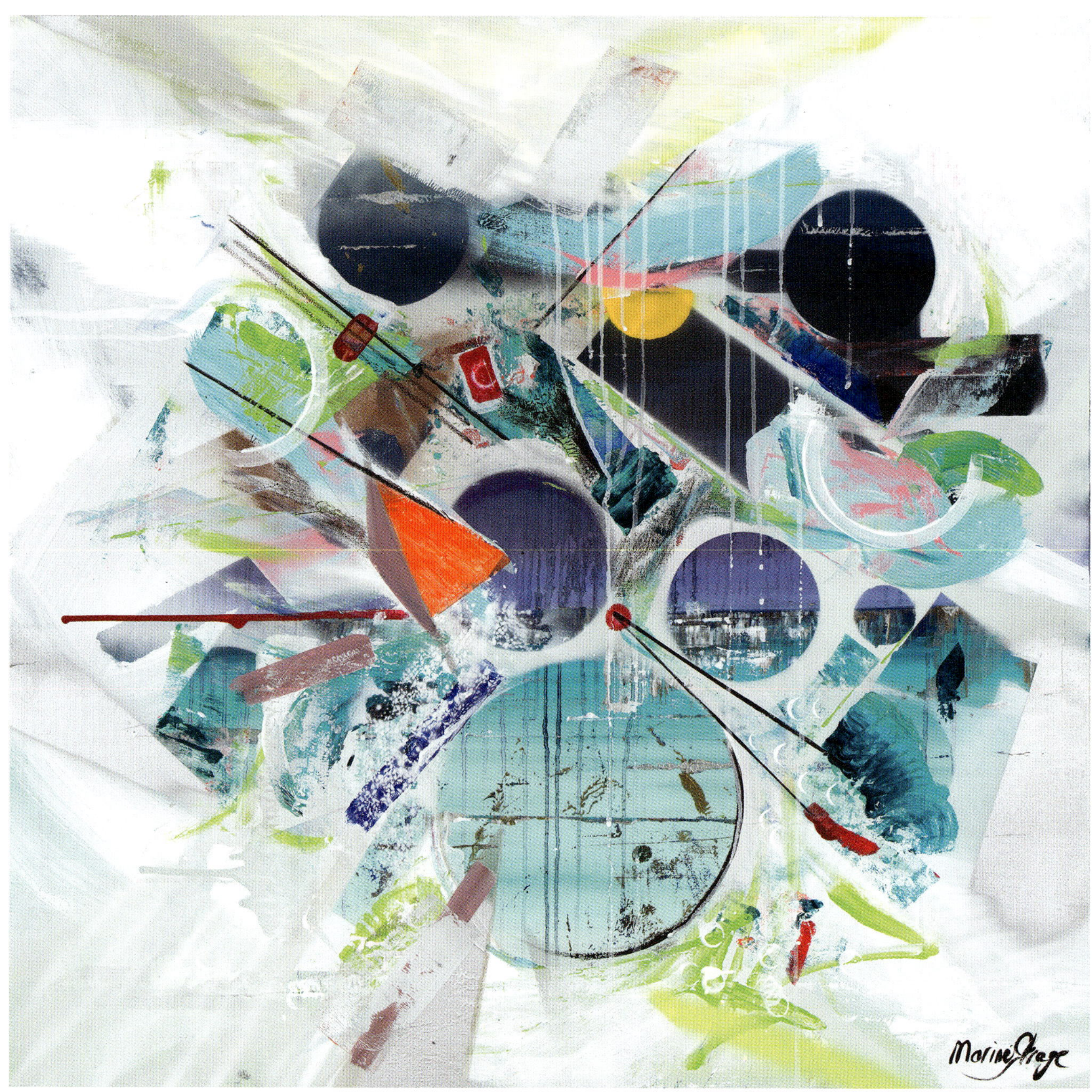

Marine Strage

Marine Strage's art explores the relationship between what she observes and what she experiences internally. It is about translating perceptual states into visual language. "I am particularly interested in creating atmospheres that awake our sense of wholeness and evoke energy and interconnectivity," she says.

This particular painting series explores the abstraction of shapes inspired by the traditional costumes and fabrics of Brittany. The artist's memories of the beach atmosphere, the seaweed, and the seashells she collected entwine with the imprint of embroideries and lacework from her childhood.

Strage's process involves collecting imageries, drawing, and painting with a range of media. She navigates between pouring, dripping, veiling, glazing, pushing, and pulling forms while playing with a variety of expressive brushstrokes. "With my art, I aim to spark a connection between our inner lives and the outside world to create further awareness of our nature," Strage says.

Bubblegum (Des ronds dans l 'eau)
Acrylic on canvas
40 x 40 in.

marinestrage@gmail
.com
marinestrage.com
@marinestrage

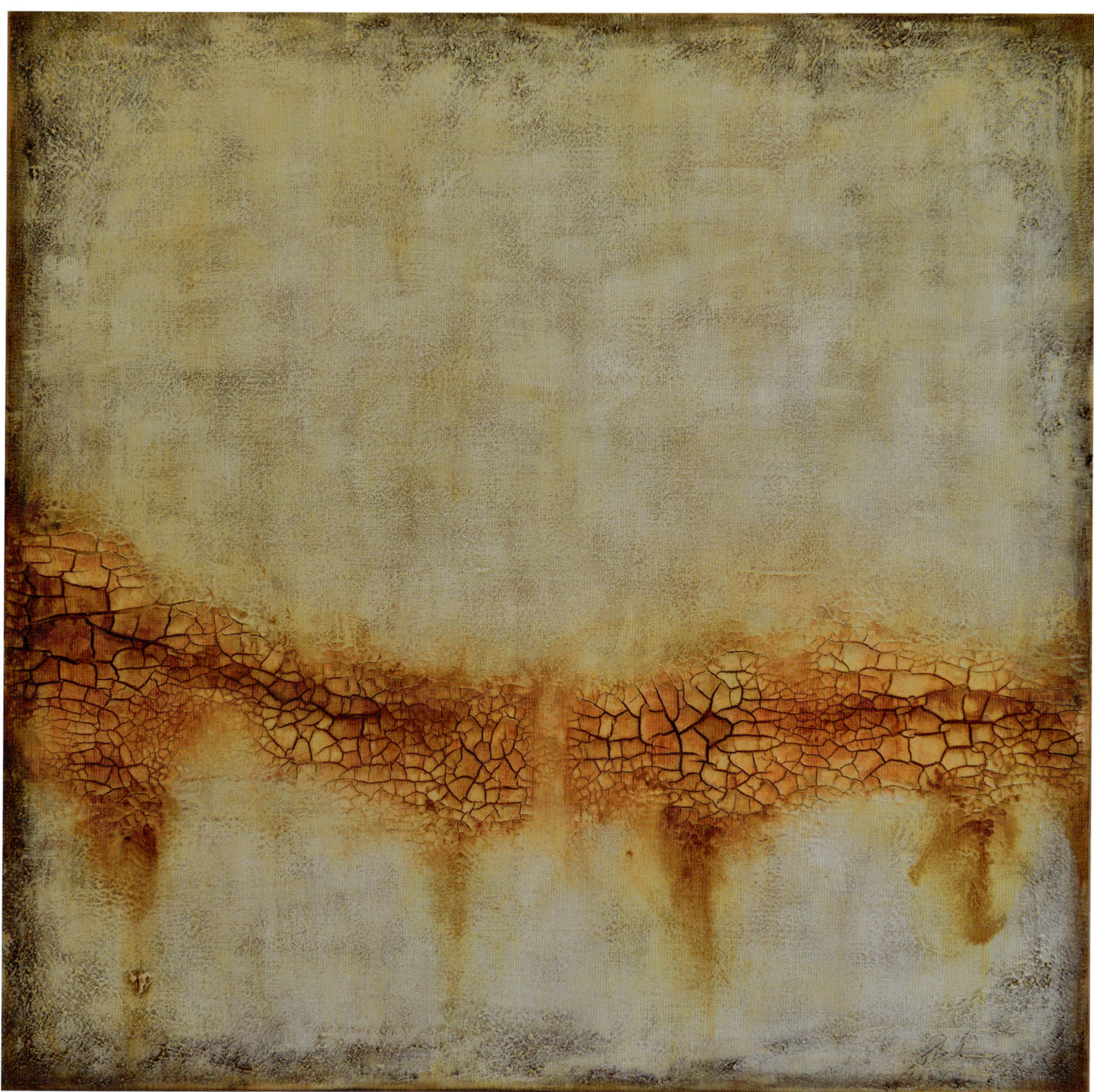

Barbara Stratmann

Barbara Stratmann is a German abstract artist known for her strongly textured acrylic and mixed-media paintings.

Finding inspiration in nature, Stratmann's work is intuitively translating her ideas and emotions onto the canvas, with multiple layers of paint, ink, and rough textures at the heart of each artwork.

The essence of her work is largely inspired by the Japanese concept of *wabi-sabi*, representing a different concept of beauty—finding it in every aspect of imperfection in nature. Stratmann loves this idea of aesthetic appreciation of aging or flaws and the beauty of the effects of time and imperfections, and she embraces it by including rusty, cracked, or torn elements in her work, giving her paintings often a rough and weathered look with a strong haptic feel. Her generous use of texture almost blurs the line between painting and sculpture, inviting the viewer to touch and add a tactile experience to the purely visual one.

In the Line of Fire
Acrylics and mixed media on canvas
39 x 39 in.

barbara_stratmann@gmx.de
barbarastratmann.art
@barbarastratmann.art

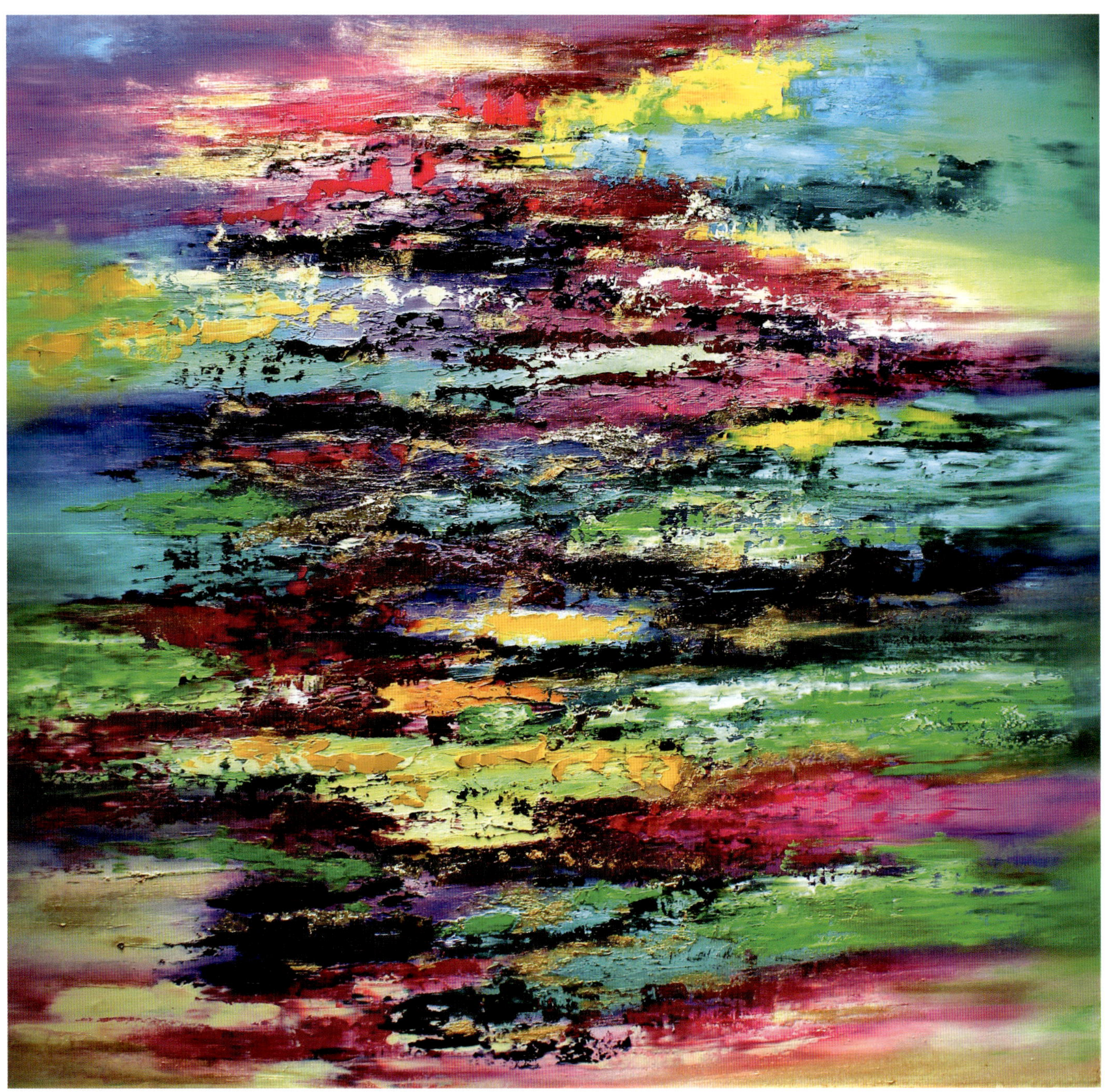

Hanna Supetran

Mainly abstract in style, all of Hanna Supetran's artworks are painted intuitively using oil. Every stroke heightens the anticipation. Every scrape fuels the excitement. Every color mixed suspends time. Each creation is an exhilarating ride, making the once invisible visible, giving the once intangible a tangible form.

"There is nothing like transforming a blank canvas into a timeless art piece," Supetran says. "Art is a fulfilling and rewarding creative expression that adds beauty and quality to life—the very reason why I paint."

Each of Supetran's paintings reflects the vibrancy of life, a balance of intense texture and soft movements, between dark and light, cold and warm. Each pulls the viewer toward self-reflection, toward an inward journey, toward an adventure of the soul. It can emotionally evoke or mentally provoke. Either way, it communicates to the soul in a manner that is only known to the one viewing it.

Tranquility
Oil on canvas
48 x 48 in.

hanna@
hannaintuitiveartist.com
hannasupetranartgallery
.com
@h_supetran

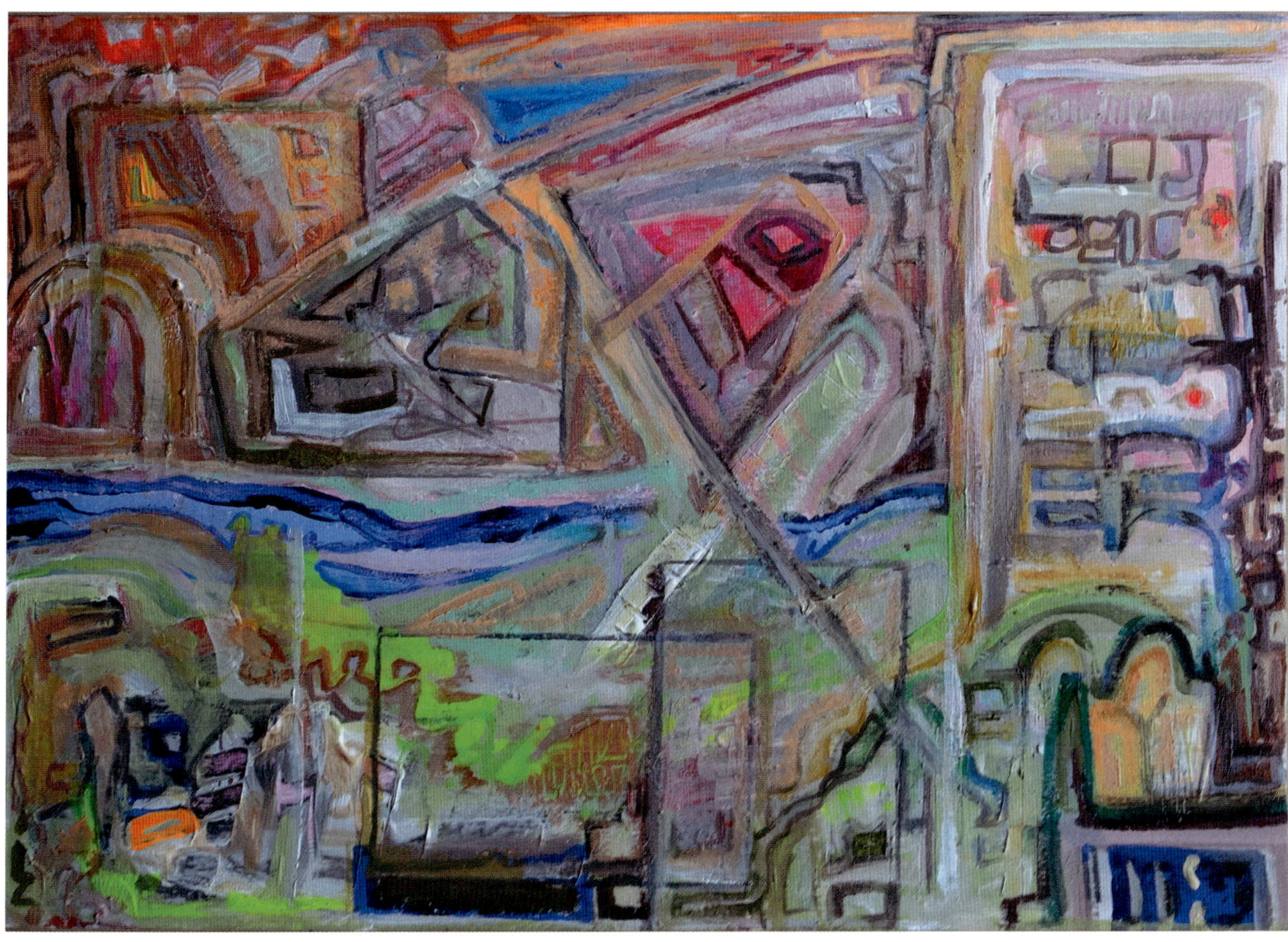

Shereen Tabet

Shereen Tabet is a Scottish Lebanese abstract expressionist artist. Mostly self-taught, her work is inspired by Action painters. Tabet's practice explores an obsession with color, light, texture, and layering through mixed-media painting. Acrylic, oil, graphite, and pastels are applied using brushes, palette knives, and adapted household tools. Her abstract work incorporates textured brushstrokes and subtle suggestions of shape, juxtaposed with fragments of bold mark-making and sometimes the inclusion of hidden figures, inviting the viewer to look closer.

With recurring themes of heritage, motherlands, femininity, and relationships, Tabet has an interest in how our memory interprets past experiences, people, and places, often including locations she feels deeply connected to through family ties and love. Her paintings reflect the nature of our memories: vague, fleeting, at times interspersed with moments of clarity and lucidity.

Zaitunay Bay
Mixed media
8 x 11.5 in.

shereentabetart@yahoo
.com
shereentabet.com
@tangereenart

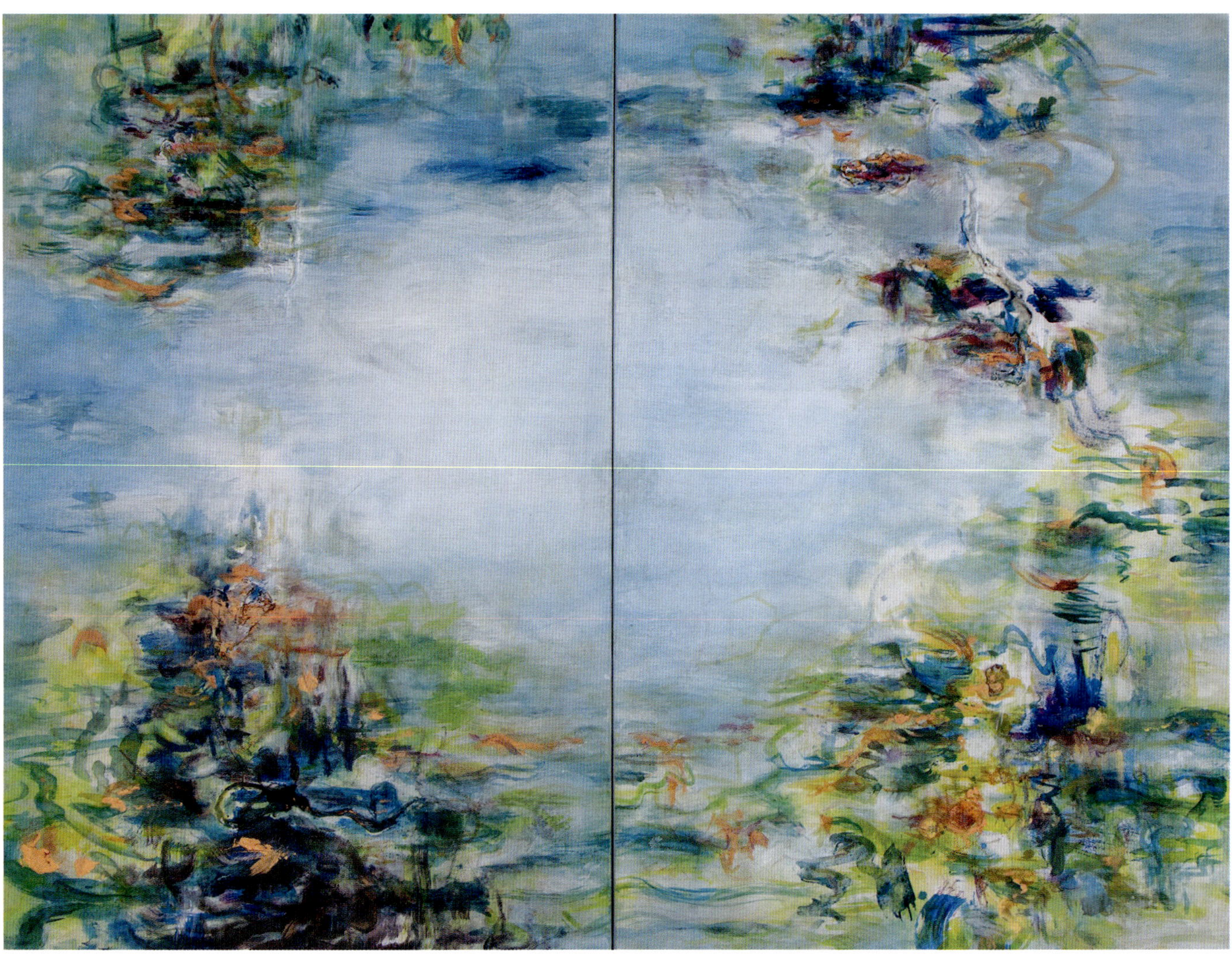

Roberta Tetzner

Roberta Tetzner seeks to capture the powerful feelings inspired by the beauty of the natural world and translate that experience into a visual record that is both sensual and intellectual. Working from her garden studio in Oxfordshire, in the United Kingdom, Tetzner is inspired by her surroundings and travels. Oftentimes, this involves the allure of water within the landscape, as she lives close to the Thames River. She seeks to create an opportunity for the onlooker to pause, reflect, and feel uplifted, allowing for a moment of tranquility in our busy lives. Striking a balance between abstraction and realism, her work facilitates an intense description of the truth of a moment recalled. Color plays an intrinsic part as does texture, with the inclusion of domestic waste material. While the striking color combinations in her work produce the initial interest, the added textures help layer and wholly capture powerful emotions in the viewer.

Water Jazz 1 & 2
Mixed media on canvas
30 x 40 in.

roberta@tetzner.com
robertatetzner.com
@robertatetzner

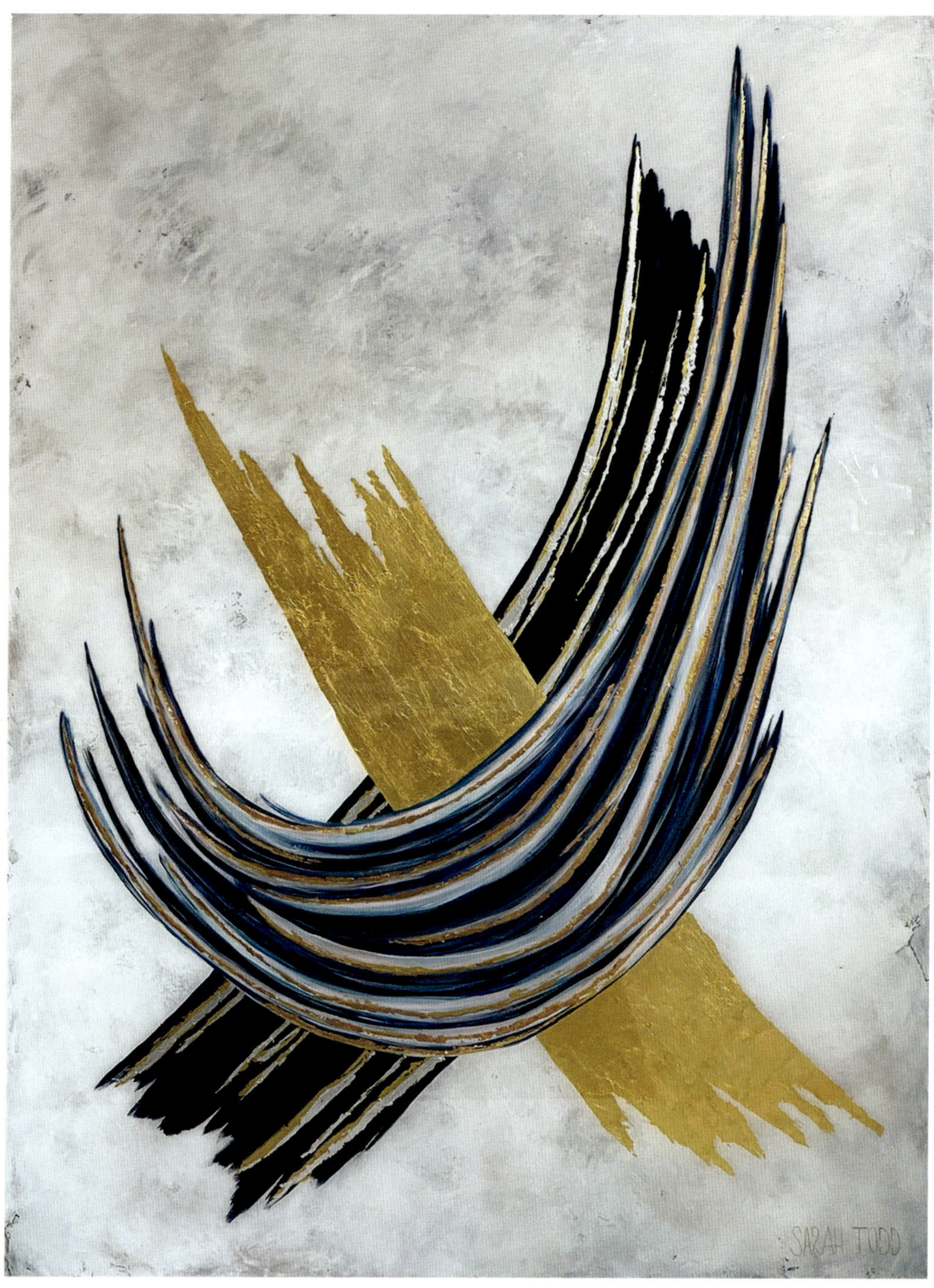

Sarah Todd

"I am so blessed to use my skills to create art that is reflective of this world yet exists in its own realm," says Sarah Todd, whose work is inspired by her travels, organic formations, and light reflecting on surfaces. In her work, the contrast of the twenty-four-karat gold leaf and vibrant paint mimic the way the warmth of the sun and the coolness of the water interact with each other. The vertical and organic movement in her paintings, along with resin, emphasize the natural beauty of water. The contrast of the metallic gold and bold colors do not compete but rather complement each other to create harmonious visions.

"My desire for the viewer is to evoke a sense of wonder and peace as they engage with my art and use their imagination to discover what the painting means to them. It is my honor to leave my mark on this world through my brushstrokes," Todd says.

Once in a Blue Moon
Mixed media
78 x 48 in.

sarah@sarahtoddart
.com
sarahtoddart.com
@sarahtoddart

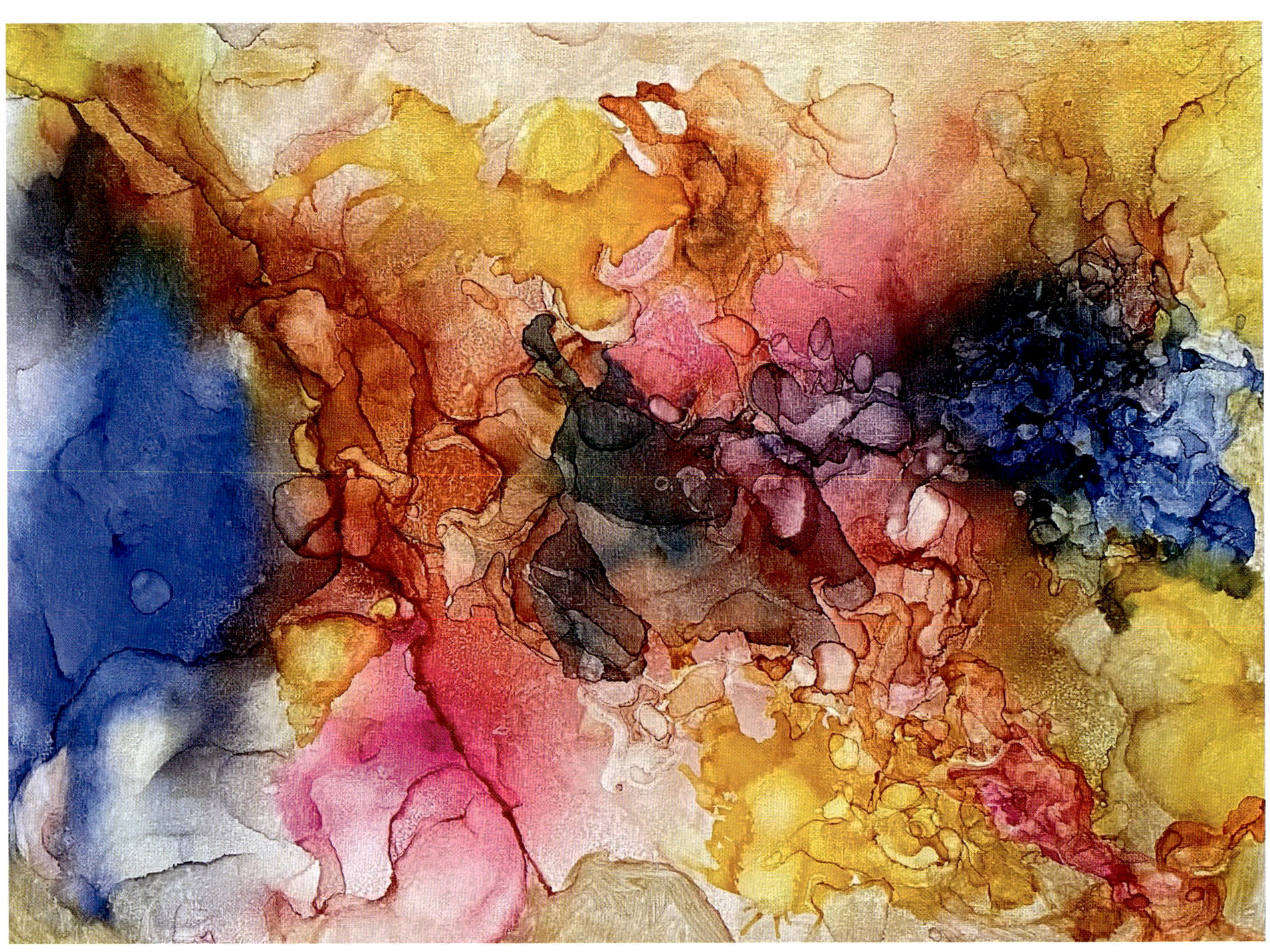

Edith Torres

Edith Torres' creations are essentially an extension of her personality emerging from her interior. The gestural and vigorous brushstrokes transmit the joy, color, and sensuality of the implicit forms. Her intense, bright colors radiate the energy, the love, the passion with which she creates her work. She manifests in them her fiery personality, where color is the structural element. The geometric element is bathed by bright, hot colors that seem to burst a few times and attenuate others. Lines, shapes, and textures combine with color and light to play a leading role. Torres uses brushes, spatulas, pencils, cardboard, wood, ink, plastic, encaustic, ebrú marbling, and anything that allows her to transmit her feelings in the creation process.

"I hope the viewer enters my world through my playful images and comes out with the same feelings of joy and emotion that I used to create them," Torres says.

Be Reborn
Ink on canvas
16 x 20 in.

edith@ebecolor.com
edithtorresfineart
@edith Torres Fine Art

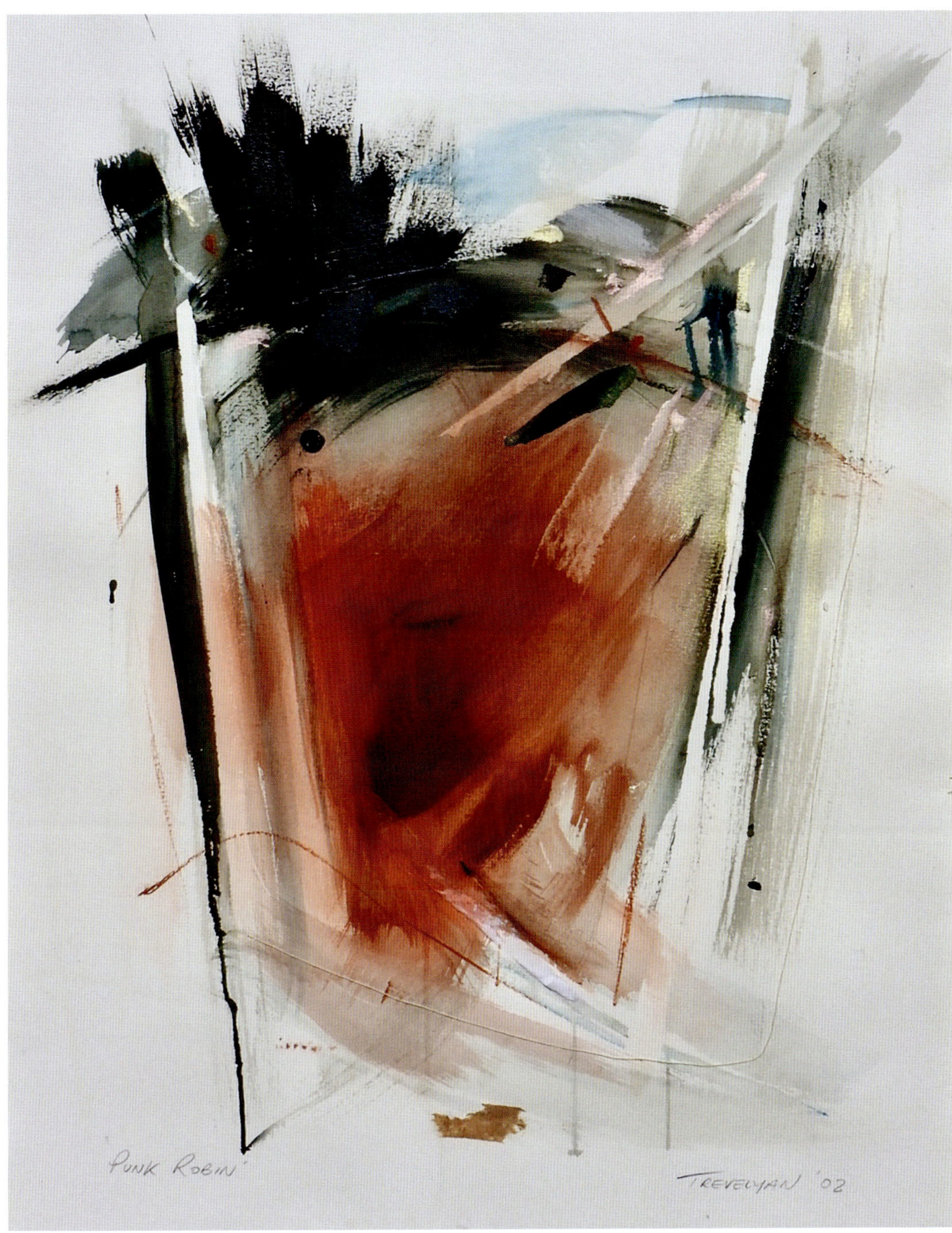

James Trevelyan

James Trevelyan calls himself a creative naturalist. This designation allows him to interact and reflect upon the powerful physical world that he is surrounded by, through the language and forms of his other great love, the world of abstract art. His work has been shaped by diverse influences, from Chinese calligraphy to gestural and color-field abstraction to Dada (mixed-media found-object collage). Another influence in his work has been that of Idealist philosophy, from the romantic naturalism of Goethe to phenomenology (Edmund Husserl and Gaston Bachelard).

Trevelyan uses abstraction to achieve a greater sense of reality and as a way to link the physical with the metaphysical, or, as Benedetto Croce put it, "Art as a longing enclosed within the circumference of an image."

Punk Robin
Mixed media
30 x 22 in.

j.trevelyan@shaw.ca
jtrevelyan.com
@j.trevelyan2018

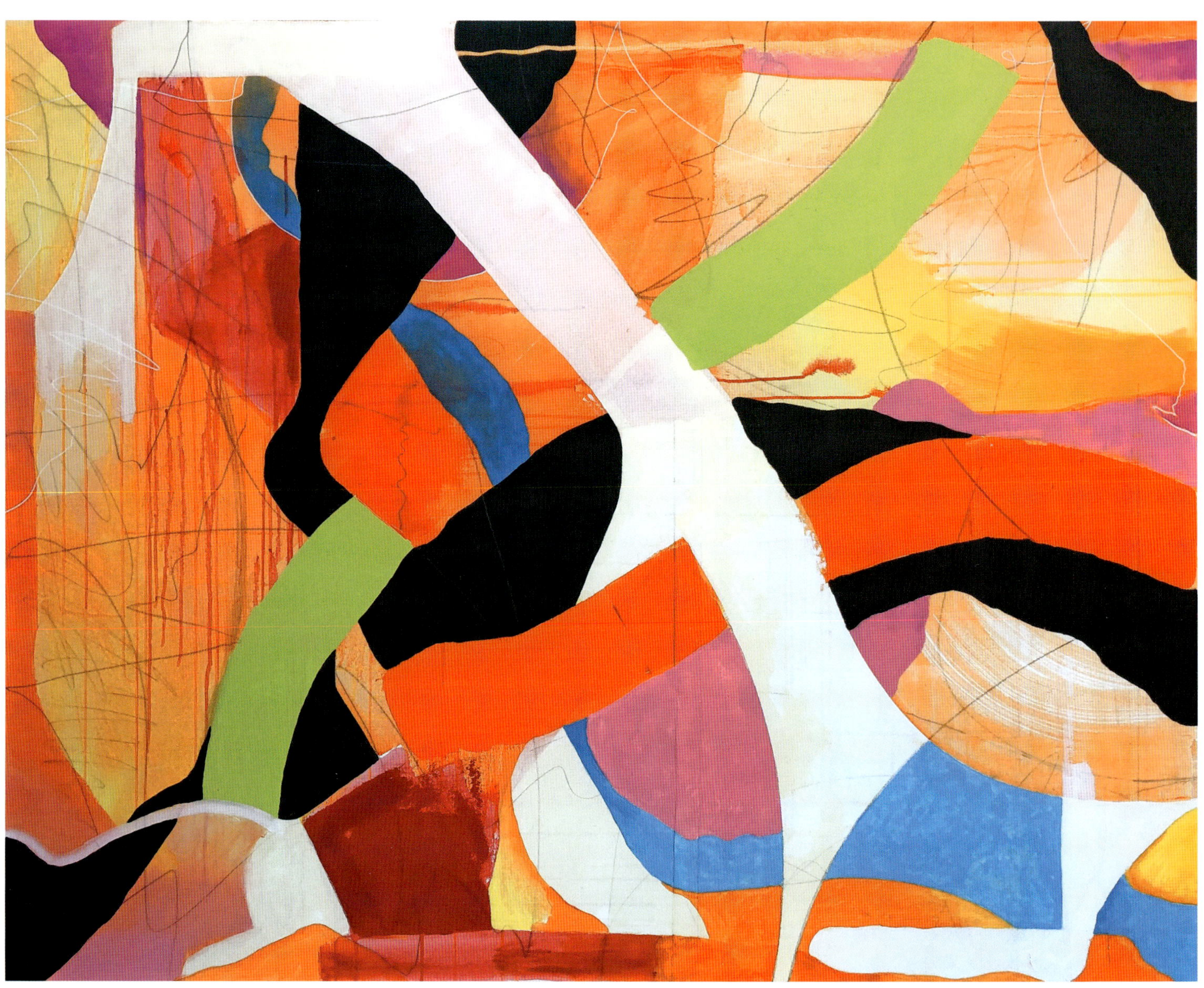

Chris Turner

Chris Turner is a painter best known for layered compositions of bold colors inspired by landscapes of the American West. His paintings are an invitation to explore our own inner landscapes as seen through color, composition, and texture. He works primarily in acrylic and mixed media on canvas and on paper.

"My creative process is rooted in my extensive travel and the artistic expressions and impressions of the people and cultures that I encountered. It is also a product of my experimentation, so my work is continually evolving," Turner says.

His compositions contain loose organic layers, shapes, and scribbles along with defined linear elements of color or texture. These two means of expression are a continuous thread in his work and represent his attempts to explore the intersections and contradictions between the worlds of logic and emotion, reason and faith, and the natural and supernatural.

Into The West
Acrylic on canvas
48 x 60 in.

chris@christurnerartist
.com
christurnerartist.com
@christurnerartist

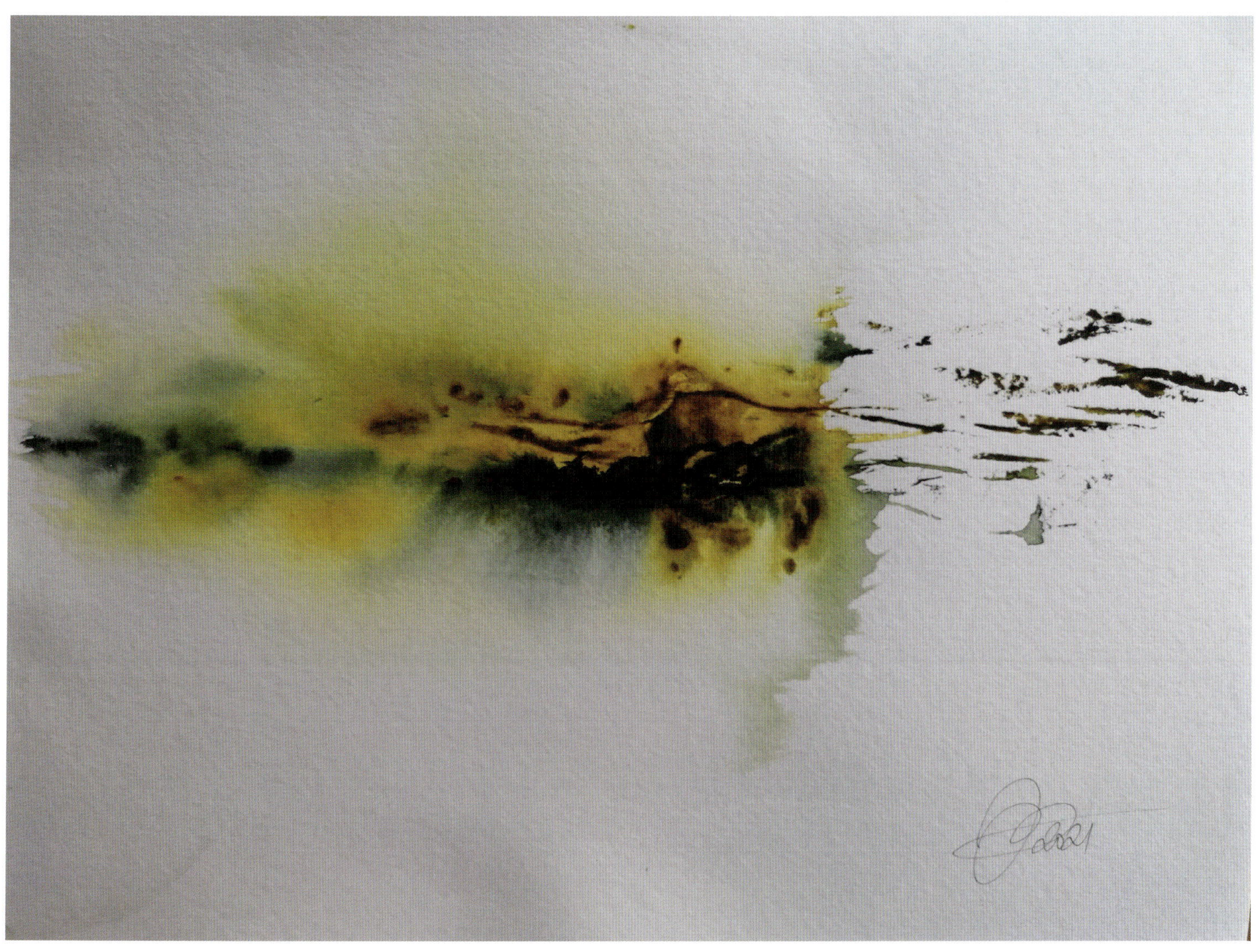

Jasmina van Doorn

Jasmina van Doorn is a self-taught Dutch artist, currently based in Luxembourg, with Croatian roots. Seeing her children develop as creative individuals, she was reminded of how much she enjoyed being creative herself. This sparked her passion to explore and reignited something that was concealed within, and she began refining her art skills over the last few years.

Watercolors add life into her contemporary abstract paintings, inspired by nature and its beauty. Over the years, her style developed from illustrative to abstract. Her paintings aren't planned; they develop naturally through the use of water and manipulation with palette knives. Each piece expresses her passion and emotions through the experimental use of color. Many of her works are evocative of a feeling or place, so people can read their own places into them. Lately, van Doorn has enjoyed using one color for her paintings, which inspired a monochrome collection.

Inner Peace
Watercolor
9 x 12.5 in.

jasmina.vandoorn@
gmail.com
@jasmina_artandmore

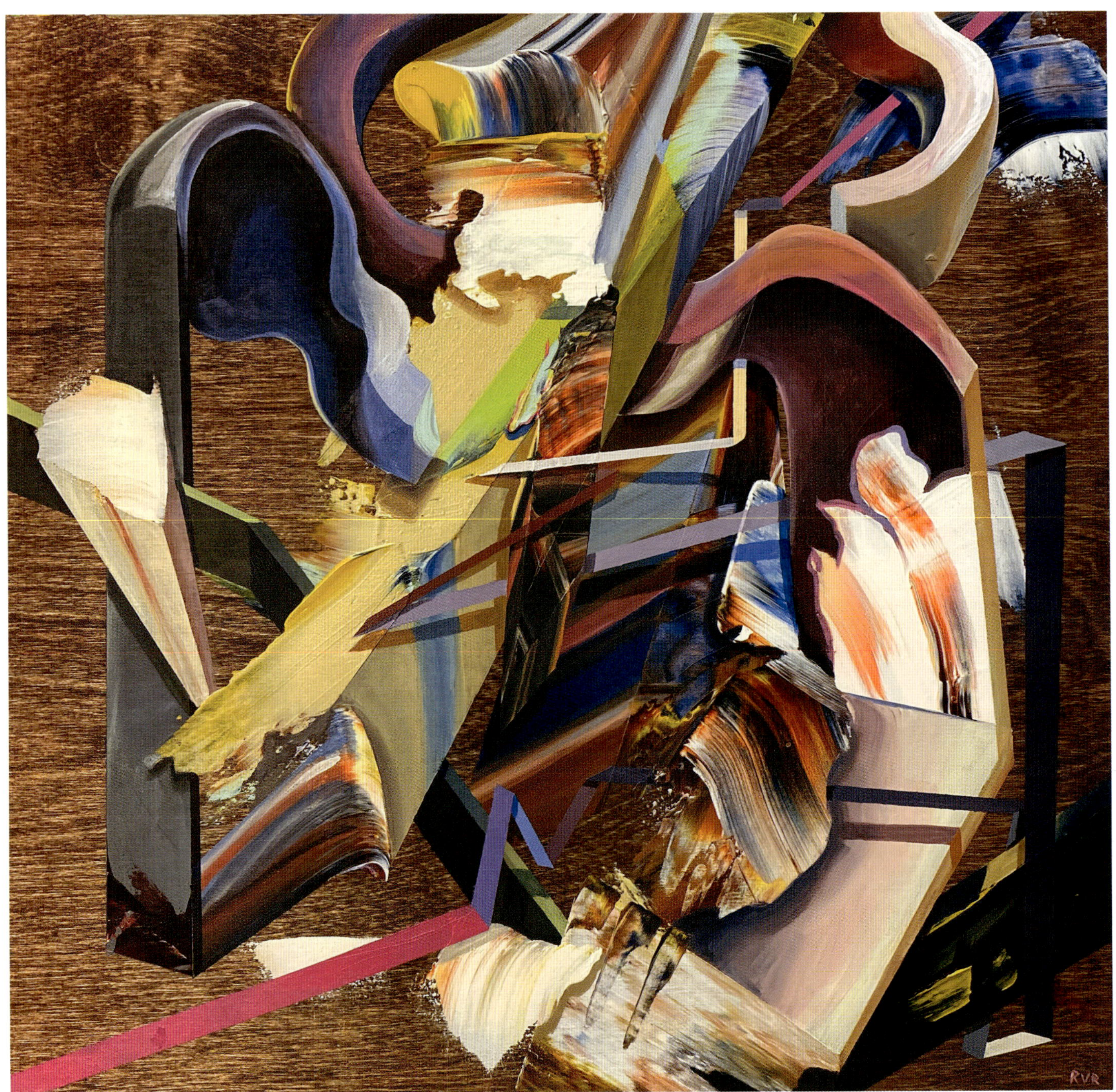

Ross von Rosenberg

Ross von Rosenberg is a painter, graphic designer, and photographer. The artist has been exploring the visual world of art since he was a child. He grew up in Austin, Texas, and graduated with a degree in design communication from Texas Tech University. He now lives with his wife in East Dallas, working as a senior art director for an ad agency while continuing to grow as an artist. He is fascinated with texture and the human figure and likes to explore these subjects by combining traditional, abstract, and modern art ideas with a graphic designer's touch. He is also fascinated with words, either in their narrative sense, poetic sense, or even in their fragmented absence. Through texture, images, and words, von Rosenberg communicates his vision to the world by encouraging people to reach out and look closer so they can see what his work says to them.

Iron Lung
Acrylic on stained wood panel
18 x 18 in.

rossvon7design@yahoo.com
rossvon7design.com
@rossvon7

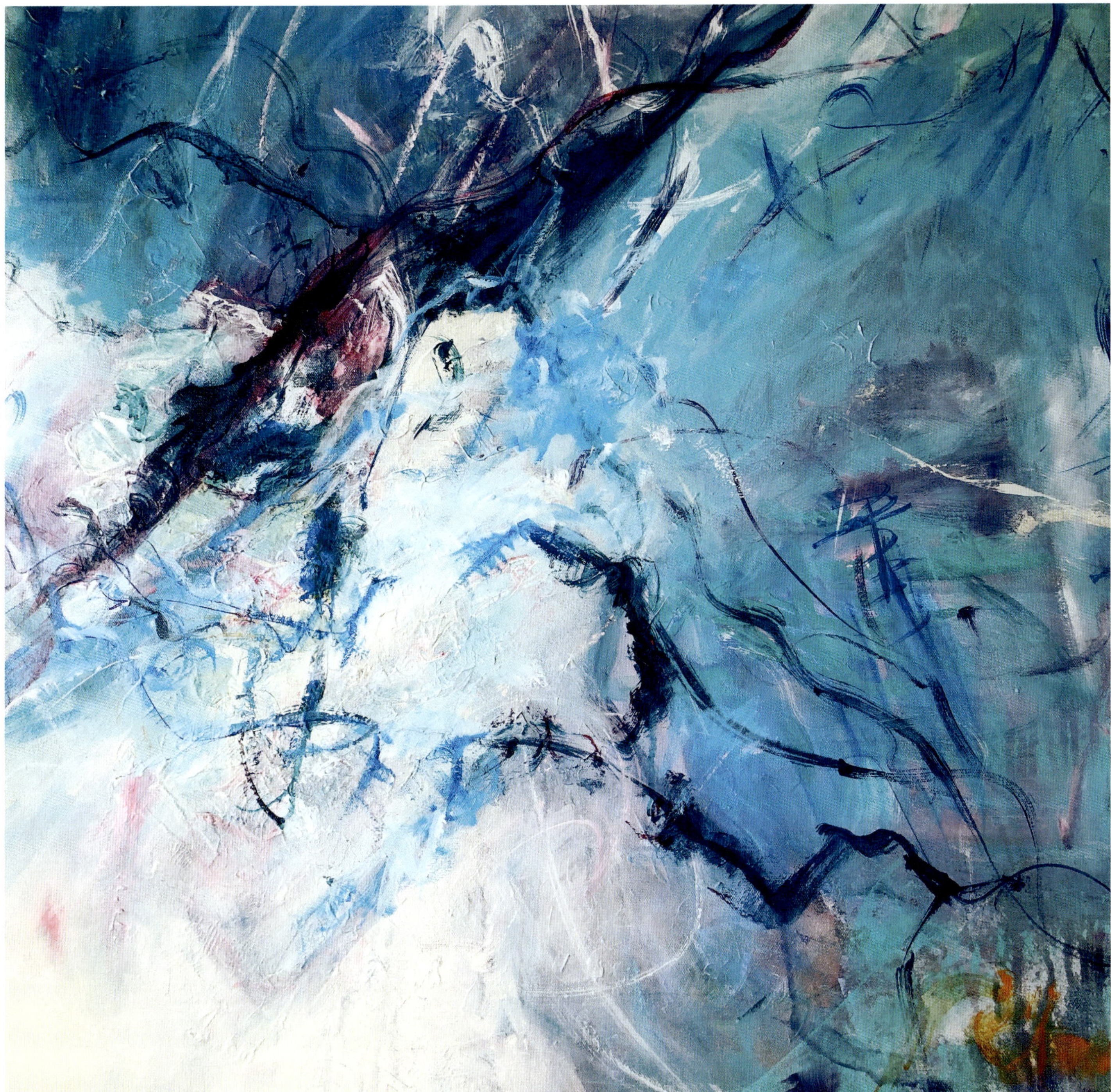

Adrienne Walker

Known for her mastery of colors, Adrienne Walker began painting late in life when she married her husband. While sculpting in stone one day, she decided that she wanted a more instantly ready birthday gift for him. Unable to complete a stone sculpture in one day, she decided to experiment with watercolor. The moment the brush touched the canvas, she fell in love with the way the colors mixed and mingled, creating new worlds for her to explore. Now, years later and after experimenting with several mediums and styles, she has embraced her dominant command of abstract expressionism. Using mark-making to enhance the movement of the paints on the canvas or substructure, the worlds she creates are full of emotion, color, and action, and her art is an expedition or a window into that universe.

Soaring into the Blues
Watercolor
36 x 36 in.

adriennew4199@gmail
.com
adriennearts.com
@adriennewalkerart
.com

PAINTING: TRADITIONAL/ABSTRACT

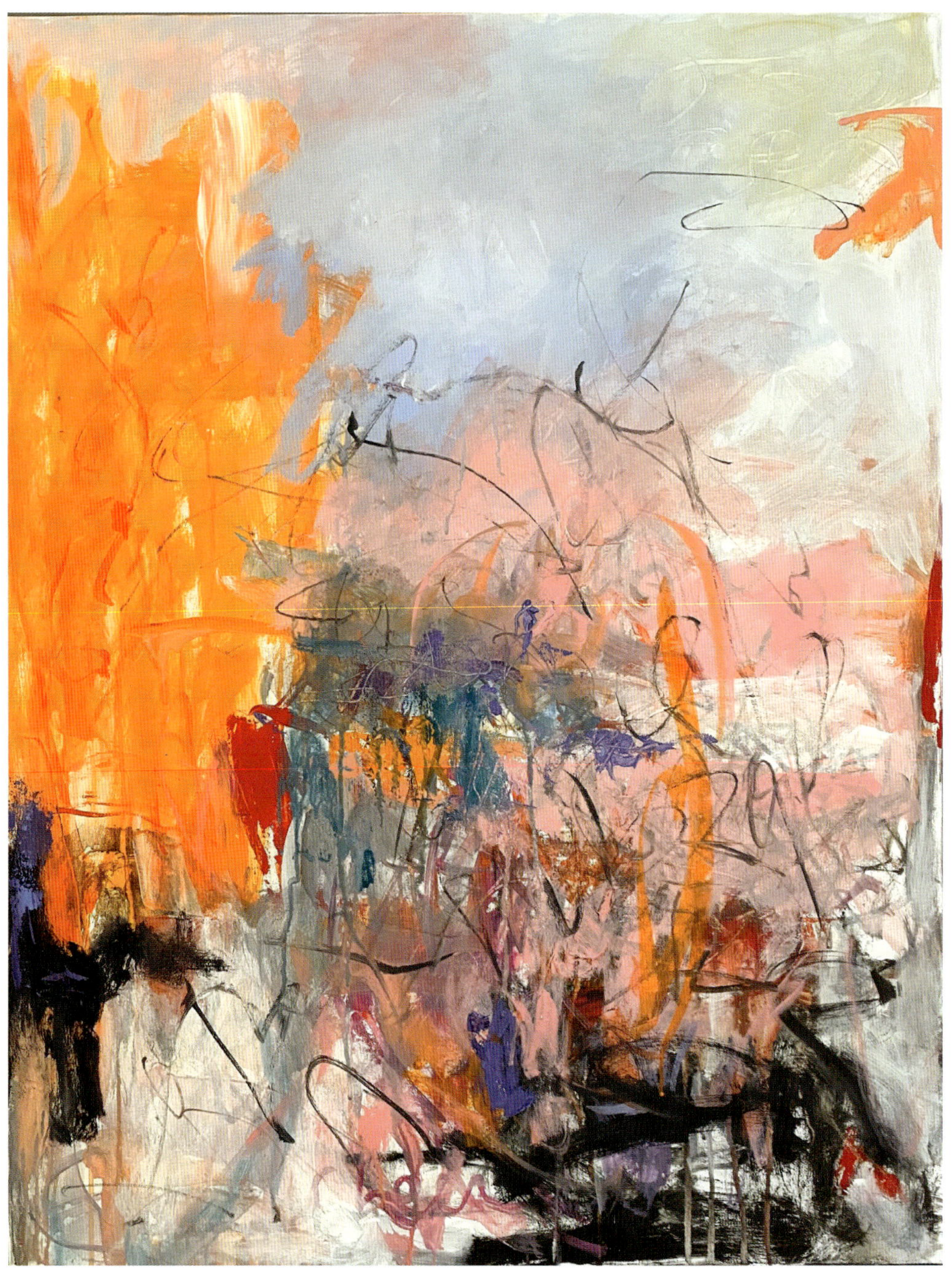

Sandy Welch

"Painting is vital to my life," says Sandy Welch. "A day doesn't go by that doesn't involve painting in some way. When I am not painting, I'm thinking about it or looking at paintings for inspiration."

Sweet coloration and sweeping, gestural brushstrokes (with fine detail and sometimes mysterious words) are what Welch's work is about. Seasonal gardens and sunny beaches influence her work. The bold innovation of Abstract Expressionist Joan Mitchell has had a powerful impact on her work, as had the work of Willem de Kooning and Henri Matisse.

Quirky shapes and intense, colorful, energetic marks applied in a feminine way are typical elements in Welch's work. One look and you may be overcome with joy, excitement, wonder, and a little bit of mystery and drama. "There is no doom and gloom on my canvas. Ever!" Welch exclaims.

Road Trip On The Paci
Acrylic on canvas
40 x 30 in.

welcho@comcast.net
sandywelch.com
@sandywelchart

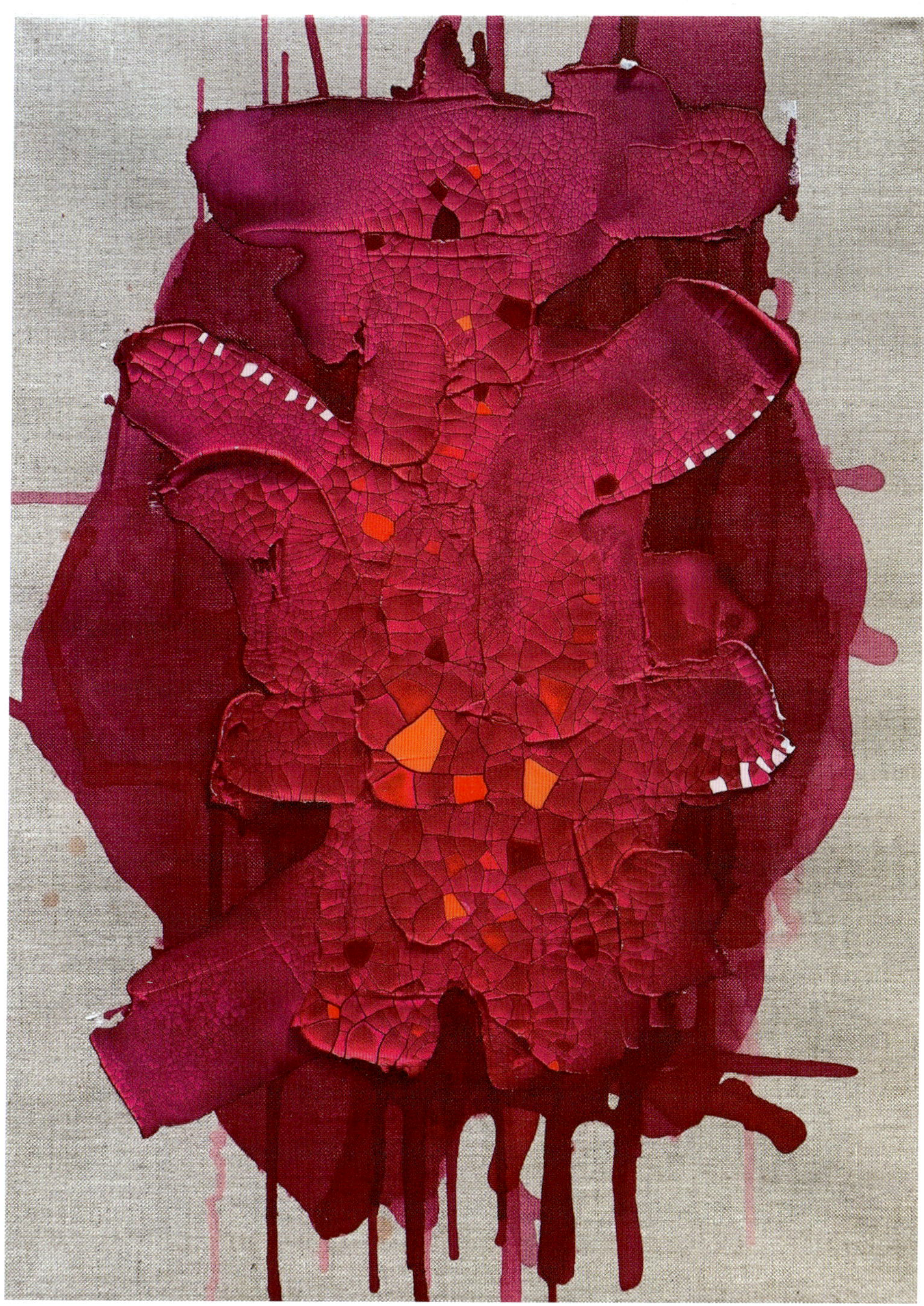

Delicious Serendipity
Mixed media
27.5 x 19.5 in.

Krista Werdelin

It is indefinable beauty that Krista Werdelin strives for in her work. She works with many mediums and explores their qualities. Combining them like an alchemist, she discovers what happens as they interact with each other and also what happens on various surfaces. Werdelin does not dwell on a particular style or movement, instead she relies to a certain extent on complete improvisation.

"I like to embrace accidents and contingencies and work with them," Werdelin says. "I am intrigued by the beauty I discover through this practice."

The pulse of her work is this constant experimentation, which she strives to perfect and create aesthetically poetic and pleasing works. For all of her work, no statement or message is forced upon the viewer, instead, all that remains is color, contrast, and balance.

krista@werdelin.dk
kristawerdelin.com
@kristawerdelin

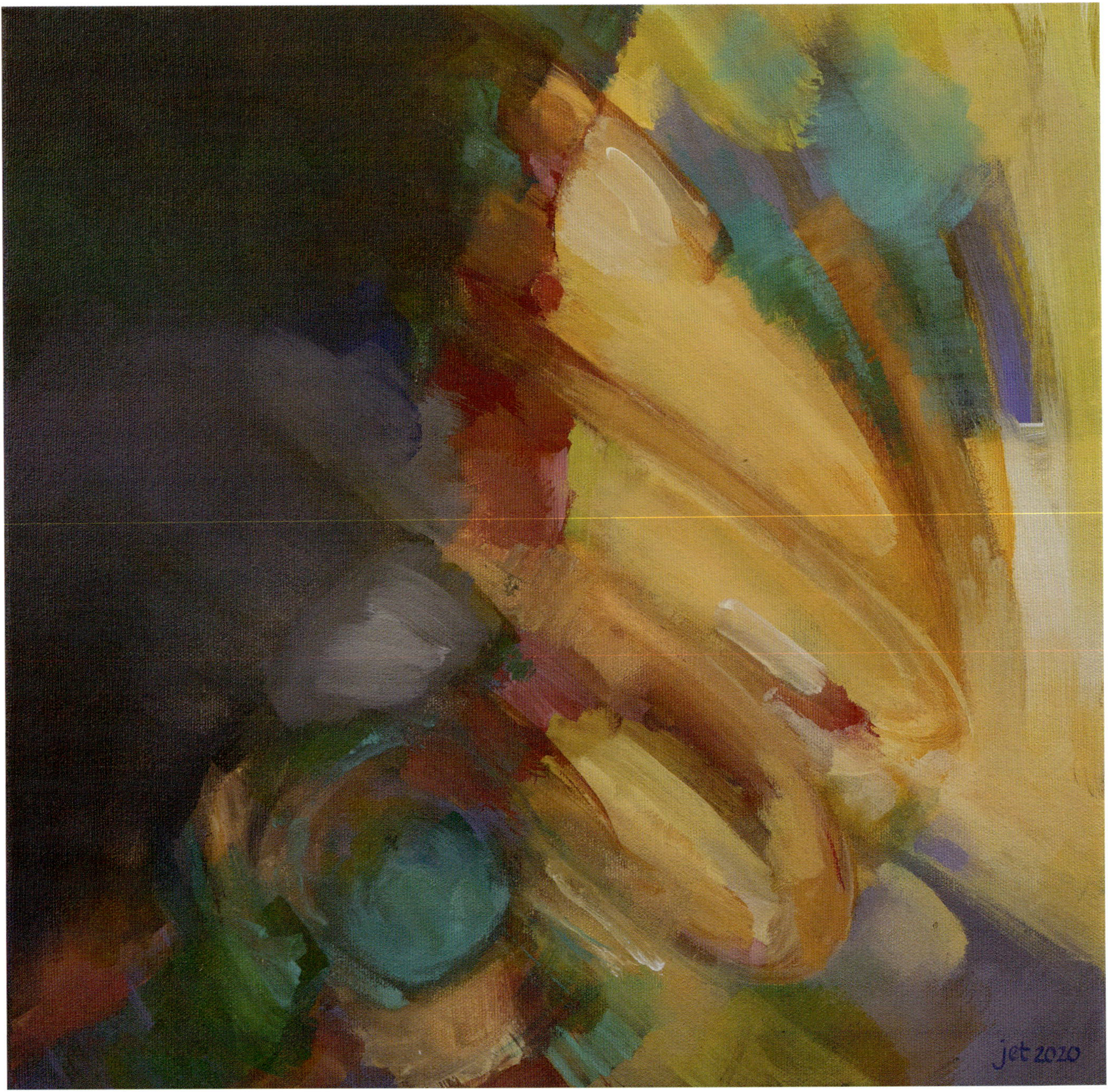

Jet Willems

The abstract and intuitive images Jet Willems creates originate from her personal mystical and spiritual experiences. The key components of her work arise from her fascination with myths, legends, the wisdom of indigenous peoples, esoteric themes, meditation, music, literature, and nature. The expression in movement, contrasts, textures, multiple layers, and the intensity of vibrant colors work together, evoking a transcendent image to the unknown, the hidden realms just beyond the veil of knowledge. Each of Willems's paintings has its own atmosphere, energy, and specific color palette.

"I believe that trusting my intuition and following my heart is the best way to create my soulful art," Willems says. "I hope my works bring joy, light, peace, and healing through the experience of viewing and feeling the images."

Light of life
Acrylic
40 x 40 in.

jet.willems@chello.nl
jetwillemsart.com
@jetwillemsart

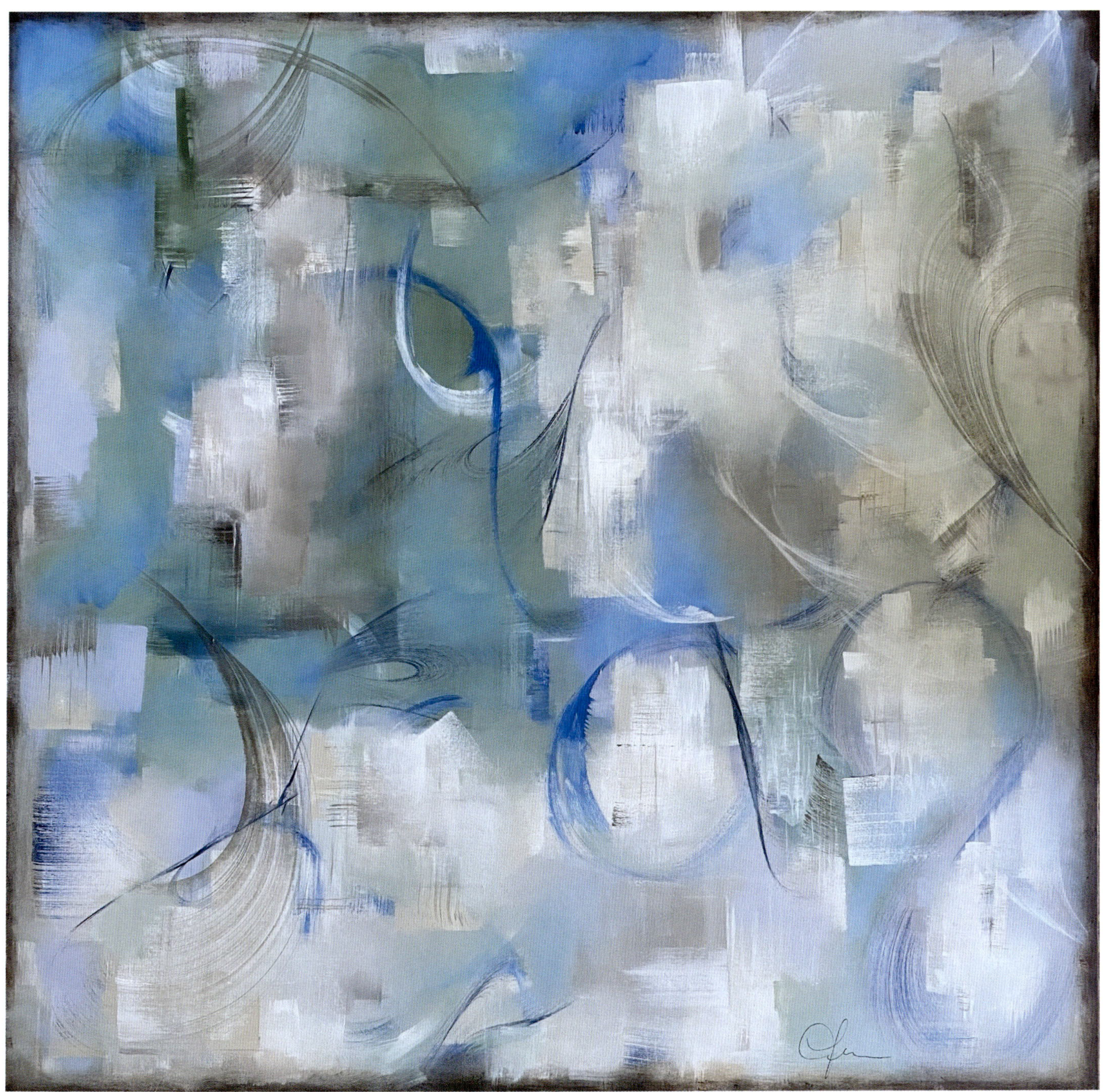

Terese M. Young

Balance and flow are always top priorities in Terese Young's work and life. Balancing stillness with movement and natural colors with bold ones are a consistent focus when she creates. Like many abstract artists, intuition plays a huge role in her creative process. She is always pushing herself to experiment and grow in her palette choices and design techniques.

Each piece tends to reflect the continually changing events in Young's life. She uses painting as a way to process the world around her. Oftentimes, working late in the evening gives her easier access to the emotions she wants to show up on the canvas.

Most of Young's work is regularly described as being both "soothing" and "exciting" at the same time. Large swooping brushstrokes sprinkled in usually add the excitement and movement she likes to emphasize. She'll then go in and carefully blend, blend, and blend some more to bring that final cohesion and flow to a piece.

In the Moment
Acrylic
48 x 48 in.

teresemyoung@icloud
.com
teresemyoung.com
@teresempaintings

Artist Index

BEST IN SHOW
Cat Tesla
Lilburn, GA
catteslaart@gmail.com
artbycat.com
@cattesla

ABSTRACT PHOTOGRPAHY
GOLD
Natalie Christensen
Santa Fe, NM
n.christensen@artworkinternational
.com
nataliechristensenphoto.com
@natalie_santafe

ABSTRACT PHOTOGRPAHY
SILVER
Jeff Corwin
Santa Fe, NM
jeffcorwin@artworkinternational.com
jeffcorwinfineart.com
@jeffcorwin_mt

Deborah Anderson
Asheville, NC
blanche6028@aol.com
ahdraart.com
@blanche6028

Petra Bernstein
Salisbury, MD
pmbernstein@comcast.net
petrabernstein.com
@petra.bernstein

Ron Evans
Atlanta, GA
ronevansphotography@ymail.com
rontheartist.com
@rontheartist

Robert Evermon
Sechelt, Canada
bob-evermon@dccnet.com
@evermon.4mg.com

April Fretwell
Greenville, SC
aprilfretwel@gmail.com
@aprilfretwellstudio

Rick Hurst
St Petersburg, FL
RickHurstArt@gmail.com
RickHurstArt.com
@rickhurstart

Barb Kreutter
Calgary, Canada
kreutter@telus.net
kreutter.zenfolio.com
@barbkreutter

Peter Toth
Prosper, TX
peter3031T@gmail.com
peterTcontemporary.com
@peterTfineart

SCULPTURAL/ DIMENSIONAL
GOLD
JR Chuo
Colchester, Suffolk, UK
jrchuo15@gmail.com
jrchuo.com
@jrchuo

SCULPTURAL/ DIMENSIONAL
SILVER
Jody West
Fort Valley, VA
jwest140@shentel.net
jwestfoundart.com
@jodywestfoundart

Christy Chor
Oakville, Ontario, Canada
christyymchor@gmail.com
@christychor.com

John Denis
Miami, FL
john@johnjosephdenis.com
johnjosephdenis.com
@johnjosephdenis

Emily Dvorin
Kentfield. CA
emily@emilydvorin.com
emilydvorin.com
@emilydvorin

Kintsugi Grace
San Antonio, TX
KintsugiGrace@gmail.com
kintsugigrace.art
@kintsugigrace

William Hall
Cedar Hill, TX
william@williamhall.com
williamhallart.com
@williamhallart

Mark Yale Harris
Santa Fe, NM
markyharris@artworkinternational.com
markyaleharris.com
@markyaleharris

Alexandra Kapogianni-Beth
Mainz, Rheinland-Pfalz, Germany
kontakt@bildhauerwerke-ak.de
bildhauerwerke-ak.de
@kapogiannibeth

Kenan Koçak
Balıkesir, Turkey
absart@outlook.com
kenank.art
@kenank_art

Keith Kriegel
Frisco, TX
the.kriegels@tx.rr.com

Denise Lion
Plano, TX
dlplano@msn.com
Deniselion.com
@dlplano

Jim Maunder
St. Catharines, Ontario, Canada
jimmaunderart@gmail.com
jimmaunder.ca
@jimmaunderartist

John Meacher
Wickford, Essex UK
johnnypapercuts@gmail.com
johnnypapercuts.com
@johnnypapercuts

Nicole Moan
Oklahoma City, OK
nicolemoan@gmail.com
nicolemoan.com
@nicolemoan

Cecelia Moseley
Meridian, MS
cecemoseley@comcast.net
cmoseleyfineart.com
@cc_art_design

Remains
Dallas, TX
Deborah@dhvartorks.com
dhvartworks.com
@dhv_artworks

Emmanuel John Santos
Caloocan City, Manila, Philippines
emansantos1@gmail.com
@emanm.santos

Joel Shapses
Naples, FL
joelshapsesstudio@gmail.com
joelshapsesstdio.com
@joelshapsesartist

Todd Sorrin
Boca Raton, FL
todd@sorrin.com
@toddsorrin

Chan Suk On
Hong Kong, Hong Kong
chansukon@gmail.com
httpschansukon.com
@sukon.chan

Will Ursprung
Gilbertsville, PA
holcombe.photo.service@gmail.com

Bernardo Vallarino
Fort Worth, TX
bernardo@bernardovallarinoart.com
bernardovallarinoart.com
@bernardovallarinoart

Gwen Waight
Peninsula, OH
gwaightee@yahoo.com
@gwaightee

Valerie Wilcox
Redondo Beach, CA
vwilcox59@gmail.com
valeriewilcox.com
@valeriewilcox_art

Silvia Zimerman
Caesarea, Israel
glassart@silvia-zimerman.com
@silvia-zimerman.com

DIGITAL GOLD
Anindita Dasgupta
Aubrey, TX
asguptaanindita11@gmail.com
artsywanderlust.com
@anindita.art.etc

DIGITAL SILVER
Richard Devonshire
Letchworth Garden City,
Hertfordshire, UK
Richard.Devonshire@yahoo.com
richard-devonshire.com
@richard_devonshire_art

Christopher Brown
Dallas, TX
chrisbrownartist@att.net
@christopherbrownstudio

Kat Evans
Colchester, Essex, UK
ktheo2010@gmail.com
katevans.art
@kat_evans_artist

Jenny Jiyoung Han
Hasselt, Belgium
jenjiyoung09@gmail.com
jenny-jiyoung-Han.format.com
@jennyjiyounghan

Pierre-Hugues Hétu
Ste-Marcelline-De-Kildare, Québec,
Canada
puguess@gmail.com
puguess.com
@puguess

Tyler N. Horton
Charleston, SC
tnhforum@gmail.com
tnhortonforum.com
@tnhortonart

Joanne Huxford
Norwalk, CT
jkhuxford@gmail.com
@jojohuxford2

Lawrence Lee
Tucson, AZ
lawrence@lawrenceleeart.com
@lawrenceleeart.com

Michael Price
Phoenix, AZ
michael@michaelpierreprice.com
michaelpierreprice.com
@mpp_digital_art

Peter Sealy
New York, NY
peter@petersealy.com
petersealy.com
@petersealystudio

Diana Whiley
Adelaide, Australia
dizwhiley@hotmail.com
dianakwhiley.weebly.com
@dizwhi

**PAINTING - TRADTIONAL/
CONTEMPORARY - GOLD**
Tracy Murrell
Atlanta, GA
tmurrellart@gmail.com
tracymurrell.com
@tracymurrellart

**PAINTING - TRADTIONAL/
CONTEMPORARY - SILVER**
Julie England
Dallas, TX
julie@julieenglandart.com
julieenglandart.com
@julieenglandart

Gaby Avila
San Luis Potosi, Mexico
gabyavila2401@gmail.com
@gabyavilasanchez

Franco Baldazzi
Sondrio, Italy
frabaldo69@gmail.com
francobaldazzi.com
@francobaldazzi

Max Boyang
Okemos, MI
boyangtwins@gmail.com
boyangtwins.com
@boyang_twins_art

Marilynne Bradley
Webster Groves, MO
mgbrad@aol.com
marilynnebradley.com

Laura Castro
Cedar Rapids, IA
Castro@LauraCastroArt.com
LauraCastroArt.com
@castrofineart

Alec DeJesus
Dallas, TX
adejesus708@gmail.com
alecdejesus.com
@Youcancallmealec

Patty DelValle
Woodstock, GA
Patty@PattyDArt.com
pattyd.art
@pattyd.art

Amylia Faizal
Bandar Seri Begawan, Brunei
amyliafaizal@gmail.com
amyliafaizal.com
@amyliafaizalart

Claudia Fischer
la Ciotat Bouches-du-Rhône, France
cldfischer12@gmail.com
@animaemela

Kathleen Frank
Santa Fe, NM
k.frank@artworkinternational.com
kathleenfrankart.com
@kathleen-frank

Kelly Gowan
Holly Lake Ranch, TX
kellygowanart@gmail.com
kellygowanart.com
@kellygowanart

Annie Griffeth
Dallas, TX
anniegriffeth@gmail.com
anniegriffeth.com
@anniegriffeth

Leticia Herrera
McKinney, TX
leticiaherrera@leticiaherreraart.com
leticiaherreraart.com
@leticiaherreraart

Jay Hodgson
Ontario, Canada
jayhodgson@mac.com
jayhodgsonart.com
@jay_hodgson_analogcollage

Deana Jackson
Columbus, OH
emtcanvas@gmail.com

Amogh Katyayan
Calgary, Alberta Canada
amogh@amogh.art
amogh.art
@amogh_art

Rebecca Katz
San Rafael, CA
rebecca@rebeccakatz.com
rebeccakatzart.com
@rebeccakatzart

Stephanie Lawhorn
Rockwall, TX
inspiredbyhimart@gmail.com
@inspiredbyhimart

Jerome Chia-Horng Lin
Taipei City, Taiwan
jeromelin2006@gmail.com
jeromelin.net
@jeromechiahorng

Vincent MacDermot
Staten Island, NY
vincemacdermot@gmail.com
vincemacdermot.com
@vincemacdermot

Gini Mallory
Henrico, VA
ginimallory@gmail.com
ginimalloryart.com
@ginimalloryart

Andrew Manocheo
Chicago, IL
andrew@notboringart.com
notboringart.com
@notboringart

Janak Narayan
McKinney, TX
janak202130@gmail.com
janaknarayan.com
@janaknarayanartist

Isabella Penner
Edmonton, Canada
isabellapenner.artist@gmail.com
isabellapennerart.com
@bellalona.studio

Vedrana Pinjo
Greenbrae, CA
vedranapinjo@gmail.com
vedranapinjo.com
@vedrana.pinjo.art

Sudie Rakusin
Carrboro, NC
info@sudierakusin.com
sudierakusin.com
@sudie.rakusin

Ramón Rivas
Ciudad Real, Spain
ramonrivas2012@yahoo.es
rivismo.com
@ramonrivas_rivismo

Stewart Russell
Irvine, Scotland, UK
russells187@gmail.com
stewartrussellart.bigcartel.com
@stewart_russell_art

Sylvia Sarzynska
East Windsor, CT
sylviasarzynska@yahoo.com
sylviasarzynska.com
@sylviasarzynska

Durand Seay
Fairhope, Al
durand@durandseay.com
durandseay.com
@durandseay

Mira Seeman
Bet Yitzhak, Israel
mirasee121@gmail.com
miraseeman.com
@Mira Seeman

Gordon Skalleberg
Santa Fe, NM
skalleberg@artworkinternational.com
gordonskalleberg.com
@gordonskalleberg

Meghan Sola
Cockeysville, MD
solameghan@gmail.com
solameghan.wixsite.com/mysite
@msolaart

Petra Stefankova
Bilkove Humence, Slovakia
petrastefankova@gmail.com
petrastefankova.com
@petrastefankova

Tricia Trinder
Wahroonga, Australia
tricia@trinder.net
triciatrinderart.com.au
@tricia.trinder

Carmen Angela Yandoc
Manila, Philippines
cara.y.duque@gmail.com
@cara_duq

**PAINTING - TRADTIONAL/
ABSTRACT - GOLD**
Nikki Hill-Smith
Kent, UK
n.hillsmith1@googlemail.com
nikkihillsmith.art
@nikkihillsmith

**PAINTING - TRADTIONAL/
ABSTRACT - SILVER**
Ai-Wen Wu Kratz
Chantilly, VA
kratz@aiwenwukratzartstudio.com
aiwenwukratzartstudio.com
@aiwenwukratz

Caren, Akers
Jensen Beach, FL
carens.art@gmail.com
caren-akers.com
@carenakers

Wendy Alber
Baden Württemberg, Germany
wendyalber@hotmail.com
wendyartworld.weebly.com
@wendy_artworld

Lynn Amsterdam
Delray Beach, FL
lynn.amsterdam@gmail.com
@lynnamsterdam.com

John Bacon
Bend, OR
johnwb67@gmail.com
@BaconModern

Françoise Barnes
Los Ranchos, NM
franswazz@gmail.com
franswazzart.com
@franswazzart

Antonio Bettuelli
Genova, Italy
art@antoniobettuelli.it
@antoniobettuelli_art

Johannes Boekhoudt
Rockwall, TX
johannesfineart@me.com
johannesboekhoudt.com
@johannesboekhoudtoficial

Alessio Bonini
Riccò del Golfo di La Spezia, Italy
alessio.bonini@hotmail.com
alessiobonini.com
@alessiobonini_artist

Cindy Brewer
Dallas, TX
cabrewer58@yahoo.com
cindybrewerfineart.com
@cindybrewer1

Debby Burk
Potomac, MD
debby@briskerburk.art
briskerburk.art
@debbybriskerburk

Lori Burke
Ridgeway, Ontario, Canada
lori.fickledesigns@gmail.com
fickledesignsartstudio.com
@Loriburke3667

Leslie Poteet Busker
Charlotte, NC
lesliebusker@gmail.com
lesliepoteetbusker.com
@lesliepoteetbuskerart

Anna Carll
Chattanooga, TN
annacarllfineart@gmail.com
annacarll.com
@annacarllart

Jessica M. Chaix
Lewisville, TX
jessica_chaix@yahoo.com.mx
jessicamchaix.com
@Jesschaixart

Lavanya Challa
Plano, TX
lavanyaschalla@gmail.com
lavanyachallaart.com
@lavanyachallaart

Elsie Chiu
Toronto, Ontario, Canada
elsiechiu12@icloud.com
elsiechiu.wixsite.com/elsiechiupaint-
ings
@elsiechiuart

Miles Chumley
Brookfield, IL
miles.chumley@gmail.com
mileschumley.com
@mileschumley

Amy Cline
Annapolis, MD
holt.cline@gmail.com
amyholtcline.com
@amy.holtclineart

Cynthia Coldren
Richardson, TX
cynthia@cynthiacoldrenfineart.com
cynthiacoldrenfineart.com
@cynthiacoldrenfineart

Stephanie Comegys
Catonsville, MD
Victoriousartworks@gmail.com
victoriousartworks.com
@s.comegys_art

Melanie Crawford
Nailsworth, Australia
art@melaniecrawford.com.au
melaniecrawford.com.au
@melaniecrawfordartist

Julia Crosara
Poulsbo, WA
juliacrosara@gmail.com
juliacrosara.com
@julia.crosara.art

Kathryn Crosby
Lafayette, LA
katcrosby@bellsouth.net
katcrosbyart.com
@katcrosbyart

Sami Davidson
Boca Raton, FL
samidavidson@gmail.com
samidavidsonart.com
@samidavidsonart

Kinga de Jongh
Utrecht, Netherlands
kinga.de.jongh@gmail.com
@nellis_eketorp

Aristotelis Deligiannidis
Kavala, Greece
deligiannidis.aristotelis@gmail.com
aristotelisd.com
@deligiannidis.aristotelis

Paula DeStefanis
Cedarburg, WI
paulaspalettestudio@gmail.com
pauladestefanis.com
@pauladestefanis

Trisha Dullu
Colombo, Sri Lanka
trisha.rajdullu@gmail.com
@freespirit_trishadullu

Karen Ebbs
Dublin, Ireland
karenebbs@gmail.com
karenebbs.com
@karen.ebbs

Luise Ellerbrock
Vechta, Germany
luise_e86@yahoo.de
@colors_by_lu

Melissa Ellis
Dallas, TX
melissa@melissaellisart.com
melissaellisart.com
@melissaellisart

Debbie Ezell
Marietta, GA
dpezell@bellsouth.net
debbieezell.com
@debbieezellart

Patricia Fallon
Shaker Heights, OH
patfallon10@gmail.com
patfallon.com
@falloncodazzi

Alexandra Farber
Fort Worth, TX
afarber123@gmail.com
alexandrafarber.com
@alexandrafarber.art

James Fawley
Aubrey, TX
jlfthree@gmail.com
tyfawleyart.com
@tyfawleyart

Nicole Fearfield
Bardon, Australia
nicolefearfield@icloud.com
nicolefearfield.com
@nicolefearfield

Cecelia Feld
Dallas, TX
cecelia@feld.com
studio7310.com

Silvia Felizia
Spring, TX
silviafelizia.art@gmail.com
silviafelizia.com
@silviafelizia

Lisa Fisher
Berryville, VA
lisa@lisafisherart.com
lisafisherart.com
@lisafisherart

Susan Foley
Dallas, TX
susanfoleyart@gmail.com
foleyartstudios.com
@susanfoleyart

Roel Funcken
Lantana, FL
booking@moicflo.com
roelfuncken.com
@roelfunckenpaintings

Glen Gauthier
Dallas, TX
glen@streetfairstudios.com
glengauthier.com
@glengauthier

Kelly Gowan
Holly Lake Ranch, TX
kellygowanart@gmail.com
kellygowanart.com
@kellygowanart

Larry Graeber
San Antonio, TX
LarryGraeber@icloud.com
larrygraeber.org
@graeberl

Mike Hale
Gilbertsville, PA
mikehale@dejazzd.com

Carla Harder
Nova Scotia, Canada
Carlaharderartstudio@gmail.com
@carlaeharder

Deborah Hartigan Viestenz
Dallas, TX
deborah@dhvartworks.com
dhvartworks.com
@dhv_artworks

Richard Heiens
Greenacres, FL
docheiens@gmail.com
dochartist.com
@dochartist

Tonda Howard
Dallas, TX
tondahoward59@gmail.com
tondahowardart.com
@tonda_howard_art

Kelly Steller Hrad
Plano, TX
kelly@kellystellerhrad.com
KellyStellerHrad.com
@kellystellerhrad

Tina Hunt
Houston, TX
tinahunt1@outlook.com
tinahuntart.com
@artbytinahunt

Odilia Iaccarino
Plano, TX
odiliai@yahoo.com
odiliaiaccarinoart.com
@odiliaiaccarinoart

Dana Ingesson
Tidaholm, Sweden
dana-ingesson@hotmail.com
danaingesson.se
@dana_ingesson

Jiwon Jang
Gyeonggi-do, South Korea
jam0115w@naver.com
@jiwonjangart

Ulfert Janssen
Heimisbach, Switzerland
ulfertjanssen@gmail.com
ulfertjanssen.com
@ulfert.janssen

Jennifer Keeney-Bleeg
Bristol, United Kingdom
jennifer@jkbleeg.com
www.jkbleeg.com
@jkbleeg

Isabelle Lopez Kotara
San Antonio, TX
imlopez458@yahoo.com
isabellelopezkotaraart.com
@isabellelopezkotara_art

Andrea Lamarsaude
Dallas, TX
alamarsaude@gmail.com
andrealamarsaude.com
@andrealamarsaude

Patricia Langevin
Calgary, Alberta, Canada
langevin.patricia@gmail.com
patricialangevin.com
@patricialangevinart

Peggy Lee
La Habra, CA
peggy3art8@gmail.com
peggyhlart.com
@haeggy5

Michelle Marra
Delray Beach, FL
michellemarra@comcast.net
michellemarrastudio.com
@michellemarrastudio

Jinnie May
Randolph, NJ
jinnielou@aol.com
jinniemay.com
@jinnie_may_art

Beth McCoy
Berkeley, CA
lenabethe@gmail.com
Lenabethe.com
@lenabethe

C.S. McIntire
Walnut Creek, CA
craigmcintire@hotmail.com
csmcintire.com
@c.s.mcintire

Valerie McMullen
Phoenix, AZ
vmcmullen14@gmail.com
valeriemcmullen.com
@valeriemcmullenart

Fran McNamara
Sedona, AZ
frannymack1@gmail.com
franmcnamara.com
@franmcnamara

Kevin Megison
Anna, TX
kevinmegison@att.net
kevinmegisonart.com
@kevinmegisonart

Christi Meril
Dallas, TX
christimerilart@gmail.com
christimerilart.com
@christimerilart

Tatiana Moya
Santiago, Chile
tatianamoyao@gmail.com
@tatiana_moya_o

Belinda Nadwie
Galston, Australia
Julie@belindanadwie.com
belindanadwie.com
@belindanadwieart

Katherine Noone
New York, NY
katienoone223@gmail.com
@pink_tea_roses_art

Siobain O'Brien
Kilfenora, Ireland
siobainobrienart@gmail.com
siobainobrienart.com
@siobainobrien.art

Brenna Lee Olsen
Wayzata, MN
brennaleeolsenart@icloud.com
@brennaleeolsen

Linda O'Neill
Lafayette, CO
linda@abbycreekstudios.com
abbycreekstudios.com
@abbycreekstudios

Daniela Pasqualini
Coppell, TX
daniela.pasqualini@gmail.com
danielapasqualini.com
@art_by_dany

Sumali Piyatissa
Colombo, Sri Lanka
Sumali.piyatissa1@gmail.com
bukiarts.com
@bukicreations

Margaret Rehwinkel
Dallas, TX
shoe1955@aol.com
@margaretschumacherrehwinkel

Doreen Renner
Ontario, Canada
doreenrenner@rogers.com
doreenrenner.com
@doreen_renner

Carole-Yvonne Richard
Québec, Canada
Carole-Yvonne@CyRichard.com
CyRichard.com
@cyrichard

Catherine Richardson
Ontario, Canada
info@catherinerichardson.art
catherinerichardson.art
@catrichardsonabstract

Johanna Riddle
New Smyrna Beach, FL
johannariddle@gmail.com
johannariddle.com
@johannariddleart

Bette Ridgeway
Santa Fe, NM
ridgeway@artworkinternational.com
betteridgeway.com
@ridgewaystudio

Machiel Roest
Paris, France
machiel@machielr.eu
machielr.eu
@macphi

Leslie Rolnick
Woodstock, NY
leslierolnick@gmail.com
@leslierolnick52

Anastacia Sadeh
Dallas, TX
sadehstudioarts@gmail.com
anastaciasadeh.com
@sadehstudioarts

Karen H. Salup
Delray Beach, FL
monet12@bellsouth.net
karenhs.com
@ksalup

Peyton Sauer
Lubbock, TX
peyton.sauer@gmail.com
@peytonleighart

Carita Schmidt
Berlin, Germany
caritaschmidt@gmail.com
caritaschmidt.com
@caritaschmidt_painter

Neena Singh
New Delhi, Delhi
neena.art.singh@gmail.com
neenasingh.com
@neenasinghart

Catherine Eaton Skinner
Santa Fe, NM
ceskinner@artworkinternational.com
ceskinner.com
@ceskinner

Kerstin Sokoll
Karlsruhe, Germany
info@kerstin-sokoll.de
kerstin-sokoll.de
@arts_by_sokoll

Patricia Spoon
North Chesterfield, VA
spoonpatricia2@gmail.com
@Patriciaspoonartworks

Marine Strage
Belvedere-Tiburon, CA
marinestrage@gmail.com
marinestrage.com
@marinestrage

Barbara Stratmann
Neuss, Germany
barbara_stratmann@gmx.de
barbarastratmann.art
@barbarastratmann.art

Hanna Supetran
Taguig, Philippines
hanna@hannaintuitiveartist.com
hannasupetranartgallery.com
@h_supetran

Shereen Tabet
London, United Kingdom
shereentabetart@yahoo.com
shereentabet.com
@tangereenart

Roberta Tetzner
South Oxfordshire, UK
roberta@tetzner.com
robertatetzner.com
@robertatetzner

Sarah Todd
Dallas, TX
sarah@sarahtoddart.com
sarahtoddart.com
@sarahtoddart

Edith Torres
Plano, TX
edith@ebecolor.com
edithtorresfineart
@edith Torres Fine Art

James Trevelyan
Edmonton, Alberta, Canada
j.trevelyan@shaw.ca
jtrevelyan.com
@j.trevelyan2018

Chris Turner
Goodrich, TX
chris@christurnerartist.com
christurnerartist.com
@christurnerartist

Jasmina van Doorn
Luxembourg, Germany
jasmina.vandoorn@gmail.com
@jasmina_artandmore

Ross von Rosenberg
Dallas, TX
rossvon7design@yahoo.com
rossvon7design.com
@rossvon7

Adrienne Walker
Boynton Beach, FL
adriennew4199@gmail.com
adriennearts.com
@adriennewalkerart.com

Sandy Welch
West Hartford, CT
welcho@comcast.net
sandywelch.com
@sandywelchart

Krista Werdelin
Naerum, Denmark
krista@werdelin.dk
kristawerdelin.com
@kristawerdelin

Jet Willems
Zwaag Noord, Holland
jet.willems@chello.nl
jetwillemsart.com
@jetwillemsart

Terese Young
Atlanta, GA
teresemyoung@icloud.com
teresemyoung.com
@teresempaintings